The Short Oxford History of Germany

Imperial Germany 1871–1918

D1565566

The Short Oxford History of Germany

Imperial Germany 1871–1918

Edited by James Retallack

OXFORD
UNIVERSITY PRESS

OXFORD

UNIVERSITY PRESS

Great Clarendon Street, Oxford OX2 6DP

Oxford University Press is a department of the University of Oxford.
It furthers the University's objective of excellence in research, scholarship,
and education by publishing worldwide in

Oxford New York

Auckland Cape Town Dar es Salaam Hong Kong Karachi
Kuala Lumpur Madrid Melbourne Mexico City Nairobi
New Delhi Shanghai Taipei Toronto

With offices in

Argentina Austria Brazil Chile Czech Republic France Greece
Guatemala Hungary Italy Japan Poland Portugal Singapore
South Korea Switzerland Thailand Turkey Ukraine Vietnam

Oxford is a registered trade mark of Oxford University Press
in the UK and in certain other countries

Published in the United States
by Oxford University Press Inc., New York

British Library Cataloguing in Publication Data

Data available

Library of Congress Cataloging in Publication Data

Imperial Germany, 1871–1918 / edited by James Retallack.
      p. cm.—(Short Oxford history of Germany)
    Includes index.
    ISBN 978–0–19–920487–8—ISBN 978–0–19–920488–5   1. Germany—History—1871–1918.
I. Retallack, James N.
    DD220.I645 2008
    943.08'4—dc22

2008000936

Typeset by Laserwords Private Limited, Chennai, India
Printed in Great Britain on acid-free paper by Biddles Ltd, King's Lynn, Norfolk

ISBN 978–0–19–920487–8 (Pbk)   978–0–19–920488–5 (Hbk)

10 9 8 7 6 5 4 3 2 1

The Short Oxford History of Germany

The *Short Oxford History of Germany* series provides a concise, readable, and authoritative point of entry for the history of Germany, from the dawn of the nineteenth century to the present day. The series is divided into five volumes, each one dealing with a distinct phase in the country's history. The first two volumes take the reader from the dying days of the Holy Roman Empire, through unification under Prussian leadership in 1871, to the collapse of the Wilhelmine Reich at the end of the First World War. The subsequent three volumes then focus on the Weimar period from 1919 to 1933; the calamitous years of the Third Reich and the Second World War; and Germany since 1945, first as two separate states on the front line of the Cold War and later as a reunified country at the heart of Europe.

NOW AVAILABLE:

Germany, 1800–1870

Nazi Germany, 1933–1945

IN PREPARATION:

Weimar Germany, 1919–1933

Germany since 1945

Contents

Looking forward   264

James Retallack

List of maps

(Maps 2 and 3 are © James Retallack / German Historical Institute,
Washington, DC, 2007.)

List of contributors

CELIA APPLEGATE is Professor of History at the University of Rochester. She is the author of *Bach in Berlin: Nation and Culture in Mendelssohn's Revival of the St Matthew Passion* (Ithaca, NY, and London, 2005), and *A Nation of Provincials: The German Idea of Heimat* (Berkeley, 1990). She is co-editor of *Music and German National Identity* (Chicago, 2002) with Pamela Potter. She currently serves as vice-president of the German Studies Association.

ROGER CHICKERING is Professor of History in the BMW Center for German and European Studies at Georgetown University. His publications include *Imperial Germany and a World without War: The Peace Movement and German Society, 1892–1914* (Princeton, 1975); *We Men Who Feel Most German: A Cultural Study of the Pan-German League, 1886–1914* (London, 1984); *Karl Lamprecht: A German Academic Life (1856–1915)* (Atlantic Highlands, NJ, 1993); *Imperial Germany and the Great War, 1914–1918* (Cambridge, 1998, 2nd edn 2004), and *The Great War and Urban Life in Germany: Freiburg, 1914–1918* (Cambridge, 2007). He is currently undertaking a project on the mobilization of agriculture in modern German history.

CHRISTOPHER CLARK is Reader in Modern European History at St Catharine's College, University of Cambridge. His most recent publication is *Iron Kingdom: The Rise and Downfall of Prussia 1600–1947* (Cambridge, MA, 2006). He is also the author of *Kaiser Wilhelm II* (Harlow and New York, 2000); *Politics of Conversion: Missionary Protestantism and the Jews in Prussia 1728–1941* (Oxford and New York, 1995); and co-editor of *Culture Wars: Catholic–Secular Conflict in Nineteenth-Century Europe* (Cambridge, 2003) with Wolfram Kaiser. His current writing project has the working title *The Age of Circulation: Europe after 1848*.

SEBASTIAN CONRAD is Professor of Modern History at the European University Institute, Florence. His publications include *Globalisierung und Nation im Deutschen Kaiserreich* (Munich, 2006) and several edited works, among them *Competing Visions of World Order: Global Moments and Movements, 1880s–1930s* (New

York, 2007) with Dominic Sachsenmaier; *Globalgeschichte. Theorien, Ansätze, Themen* (Frankfurt a.M., 2007) with Andreas Eckert and Ulrike Freitag; 'Beyond Hegemony? Europe and the Politics of Non-Western Elites, 1900–1930', thematic issue of the *Journal of Modern European History* 4 (2) (2006); and *Das Kaiserreich transnational. Deutschland in der Welt, 1871–1914* (Göttingen, 2006) with Jürgen Osterhammel.

EDWARD ROSS DICKINSON is Associate Professor of History at the University of California at Davis. He received his PhD from the University of California, Berkeley, in 1991, after which he taught for nine years at Victoria University in Wellington, New Zealand. He has published on German child welfare policy, sex reform and Christian moral reform in Germany, the German women's movements, social reform and eugenics, the history of sexuality in modern Germany, and the policing of sex crimes in Germany. He is currently working on a project on the Alps.

BRETT FAIRBAIRN is Professor and Head of the Department of History and Fellow of the Centre for the Study of Co-operatives at the University of Saskatchewan. He conducts research and teaches in the fields of the history of democracy and social movements in Germany, North America, and worldwide, as well as the interdisciplinary study of co-operatives and social economy. His publications in the area of German history include *Democracy in the Undemocratic State: The German Reichstag Elections of 1898 and 1903* (Toronto, 1997) and also articles and essays on German politics and social movements.

MARK HEWITSON is a Senior Lecturer in German Politics and History at University College London. His publications include *National Identity and Political Thought in Germany: Wilhelmine Depictions of the French Third Republic, 1890–1914* (Oxford, 2000) and *Germany and the Causes of the First World War* (Oxford, 2004). He has written articles on the construction of national identities and on aspects of German political, economic, social, military, and diplomatic history. He is currently working on a study of the politics of nationalism in Germany in the period from the 1840s to the 1930s.

THOMAS KÜHNE is Professor of History and Strassler Family Chair in the Study of Holocaust History at Clark University, Worcester, Massachusetts. His book *Dreiklassenwahlrecht und Wahlkultur in Preussen 1867–1914* (Düsseldorf, 1994) won the German Bundestag Prize. Since changing his focus to twentieth-century gender and military history, his recent work deals with the mythical ideal of comradeship among German soldiers, including *Kameradschaft. Die Soldaten des nationalsozialistischen Krieges und das 20. Jahrhundert* (Göttingen, 2006). His edited books include *Männergeschichte—Geschlechtergeschichte* (Frankfurt a.M. and New York, 1996) and *Massenhaftes Töten. Kriege and Genozide im 20. Jahrhundert* (Essen, 2004) with Peter Gleichmann.

KATHARINE ANNE LERMAN is Senior Lecturer in Modern European History at London Metropolitan University. She is the author of *The Chancellor as Courtier: Bernhard von Bülow and the Governance of Germany, 1900–1909* (Cambridge, 1990) and *Bismarck* (Harlow, 2004). She has written widely on Imperial Germany's political history and political culture. Most recently she has researched the ceremonial function of royal hunts and shooting parties in the German Empire. She is currently working on a study of women in the Wilhelmine ruling elite.

JAMES RETALLACK is Professor of History and German Studies at the University of Toronto. He is the author of *The German Right, 1860–1920* (Toronto, 2006); *Germany in the Age of Kaiser Wilhelm II* (Basingstoke and New York, 1996); and *Notables of the Right* (Boston and London, 1988). He has co-edited *Localism, Landscape, and the Ambiguities of Place* (Toronto, 2007) with David Blackbourn and *Wilhelminism and Its Legacies* (Oxford and New York, 2003) with Geoff Eley. He has also edited a volume of online documents and images on Bismarckian Germany for the German Historical Institute, Washington, DC. He is nearing completion of a book on electoral culture and the authoritarian state in Saxony and Germany from 1860 to 1918.

ANGELIKA SCHASER is Professor of Modern History at the University in Hamburg. Her recent publications include studies on minorities, on collective memories, on nation and gender in nineteenth- and twentieth-century German history, and on self-narratives. She is the author of *Josephinische Reformen und sozialer Wandel in Siebenbürgen. Die Bedeutung des Konzivilitätsreskriptes für Hermannstadt* (Stuttgart, 1989); *Helene Lange und Gertrud Bäumer. Eine politische Lebensgemeinschaft* (Vienna, 2000); and *Frauenbewegung in Deutschland 1848–1933* (Darmstadt, 2006). She is currently working on a study of religious conversions in the nineteenth century.

JEFFREY VERHEY teaches at Humbolt University Berlin. He studied history at the University of California, Santa Barbara, the University of Göttingen, and the University of California, Berkeley. He has taught at the University of California, Berkeley, the University of California, Davis, and the Free University Berlin. He is the author of *The Spirit of 1914: Militarism, Myth, and Mobilization in Germany* (Cambridge, 2000). He contributed to volume 2 of Jay Winter and John-Louis Robert (eds), *Capital Cities at War: Paris, London, Berlin, 1914–1919* (Cambridge, 2007) and is currently working on propaganda, public opinion, and democracy in Germany, 1914–1933.

Introduction

James Retallack

Why has a fascination with Germany under Otto von Bismarck and Kaiser Wilhelm II persisted to this day, even though a more recent and darker period of German history—the Third Reich—competes for attention? The following chapters provide their own answers to this question and suggest starting points for further study. They consider the German Empire (*das Deutsche Reich*) of 1871–1918, which emerged from the diverse collection of kingdoms, grand duchies, principalities, and free cities in central Europe. This new empire was a semi-parliamentary constitutional monarchy of about 41 million inhabitants (growing to over 65 million in 1914). It was founded in January 1871 not only on the basis of Bismarck's 'blood and iron' policy in the 1860s but also with the support of liberal nationalists. Under Bismarck and Wilhelm II, Germany became the dynamo of Europe. Its economic and military power were pre-eminent; German science and technology, education, and municipal administration were the envy of the world; and its avant-garde artists reflected the ferment in European culture. But Germany also played a decisive role in tipping Europe's fragile balance of power over the brink and into the cataclysm of the First World War, eventually leading to the empire's collapse in military defeat and revolution in November 1918.

The chapters of this book offer thematic discussions of this tumultuous half-century of German development and consider competing scholarly interpretations of its significance. This introduction sets the stage for those discussions. It does so, first, by questioning the accepted chronological framing of the Bismarckian (1871–90) and Wilhelmine (1890–1918) eras. How can we best assess Imperial Germany's place in the larger sweep of German history: by emphasizing continuity or rupture? Second, what happens when we situate Imperial Germany outside the usual framework of the unitary nation state? One way to appreciate the diverse experiences of Germans living in the empire is to recalibrate our perspective to the subnational and transnational levels. This allows historians to explore local and regional peculiarities, on the one hand, and international and global influences, on the other. Third, historians have offered strongly divergent views about Imperial Germany's 'authoritarian' and 'modern' features and how best to study them. But which approaches and conclusions have stood the test of time? Which have brought the German Empire into sharper focus and which offer more ambivalent judgements? A last section introduces key themes that run like a red thread through the volume, suggesting why Imperial Germany is still so relevant and accessible to students in the twenty-first century.

Continuity and rupture

University students today belong to a generation born after the Berlin Wall was breached on 9 November 1989. Their teachers were socialized and, in many cases, trained as historians when the idea of a single German nation state still seemed far-fetched. This difference of outlook provides a welcome opportunity to rethink the ruptures of German history that *seem* self-evident—1815, 1848, 1871, 1918, 1933, 1945, 1989–90. With the demise of East Germany and formal unification of the two German states on 3 October 1990, the first unification of 1871 leapt again to the forefront of historical thinking about the significance of a large, unified, powerful nation state in the heart of Europe. In 1989–90 this nation state emerged with remarkable suddenness. But when we consider the prehistory of German unification in 1871, we see that stressing discontinuity too vehemently has its pitfalls.

If we work backward in time, we discover that the empire proclaimed in the Versailles Hall of Mirrors on 18 January 1871 adopted important institutions—a national parliament, for example, and a constitution—that had been devised four years previously at the birth of the North German Confederation. (The German Empire's institutional configuration is outlined in more detail in Chapter 1.)

The 'novelties' of 1867–71, however, need to be considered against a wider historical canvas. On that canvas we must find room for the Wars of Unification fought against Denmark in 1864, against Austria and her German allies in 1866, and against France in 1870–71. We also need to include Bismarck's constitutional conflict with the Prussian state parliament (Landtag) after 1862; attempts by the middle-sized German states in the 1850s and early 1860s to chart a 'third path' to nationhood between the great powers of Prussia and Austria; the quickening tempo of political life during and after the revolutionary upheavals of 1848–49; Napoleon I's reorganization of central European states in 1803–14; and the demographic and technological changes that fuelled Germany's industrial revolution, stretching back into the eighteenth century and beyond. These considerations remind us that Germans, at the outset of their national history in 1871, still had one foot in a distant, pre-modern world.

Sensitizing ourselves to continuities that span 1871 makes us sceptical of any neat separation between the Bismarckian and Wilhelmine eras. Associating epochs with their leading statesmen allows historians to explore the role of personality in history; it can also emphasize how different the German Empire looked in 1871 and 1918. But stressing the turning point of Bismarck's departure from office in 1890 also has its drawbacks. It suggests, for example, that Germany in the 1870s and 1880s was mired in tradition and backwardness: it was neither 'on the move' nor 'up to date'. By contrast—the argument continues—Kaiser Wilhelm II's determination to make his mark on the world after 1890 and his moniker 'Wilhelm the Sudden' seemed to mirror the 'new' Germany. A dynamic, prosperous society, now largely concentrated in towns and cities, had already undergone the transformation to modern industrial capitalism and a modern class structure.

These contrasting views of the early and late empire are plausible, but they raise a number of objections, three of which deserve mention. First, alternative ways of slicing up the imperial epoch have been proposed. Some scholars have suggested that Bismarck adopted a conservative course only in 1878–79; before then, his policies had been remarkably innovative and even progressive. Others have argued that the 'Great Depression' of 1873–96, spanning the Bismarckian and Wilhelmine eras, imposes its own unifying pattern on Imperial German history: during these middle years, socio-economic tension precipitated lower-middle-class resentments against the Jews and gave rise to a 'political mass market'.[1] And once the First World War erupted in 1914, peacetime Germany seemed indescribably distant, as Jeffrey Verhey explains in Chapter 11. Another reason not to overdraw the 'before' and 'after' argument is that many seeds of German modernity which flourished in the era of Wilhelm II were planted before 1890: one thinks of Bismarck's social insurance legislation, Germany's bid for colonies, and universal manhood suffrage for national elections. Conversely, the modernity we associate with Wilhelmine Germany had its darker sides. These include the diffusion of militarist and nationalist values in German society; the yearning to be a 'world power', if necessary through reckless foreign adventures; the slackening of efforts to implement parliamentary democracy; and the belief that German culture could be preserved only through a war of titanic proportions. Finally, it is impossible to put contemporary Germans on the psychoanalyst's couch; how, then, can we appraise their reactions to the accelerating pace of modern life—one of the hallmarks of modernity? Germans born after 1871 came to adulthood in the Wilhelmine era; but were they really more prone to 'nerves' and other modern disorders, as one scholar has argued?[2] Was the mixture of optimism and *Angst* in German society after 1900 very different from the hopes and fears for Germany's future expressed in the 1870s?

To address such questions we need to keep Bismarckian and Wilhelmine Germany within a single interpretative frame. In that frame we need to place Germans who felt their nation was vulnerable, their society fragmented, their culture stifling; but we also need to include Germans who were proud to live in a strong and self-confident nation, who enjoyed individual and civil liberties in a tolerant, pluralist society, and who demonstrated their zest for innovation and appreciation for genius. Hence we must ask what Germans meant when they said they stood 'on the threshold of a new age' of German history[3]—an outlook voiced often in the Bismarckian era. As Edward Ross Dickinson suggests in Chapter 7, we should look to Wilhelmine rather than Bismarckian Germany to appreciate the significance of 'reform' as the watchword of a dynamic, optimistic, future-oriented Germany.

But if we paint the pre-1890 period as one of conventionality and mediocrity, we will never find a place for the reforming giants of that era—for the composer Richard Wagner, for the philosopher Friedrich Nietzsche, for Bismarck himself.

The empire's other bookend, 1918, also prompts reflection about the periodization of modern German history. It is difficult to corral the divergent interpretations according to which the German Revolution of 9 November 1918 constituted the death of the empire, the birth of the Weimar Republic—or no real break at all. The first point to stress is that a few days of revolutionary action in 1918 did not bring about the collapse of Imperial Germany: that required four years of unprecedented slaughter and deprivation during the First World War. The war has rightly been described as '*the* great seminal catastrophe of the twentieth century'.[4] This suggests, incidentally, why counterfactual arguments about what Imperial Germany might have looked like in the 1920s without the experience of 'total war' offer so few insights. Yet from continuities stretching beyond 1914–18 we can draw divergent conclusions. To cite one intriguing line of argument, historians have reconsidered the 'German way of war', which unleashed genocide against the Herero and Nama peoples in Africa in 1904–7 and, after 1 August 1914, perpetrated atrocities in Belgium, France, and Russia. This evidence has rekindled debate about Europe's 'Thirty Years War' in the twentieth century and the role of racialist thinking in an alleged German tendency to seek 'absolute destruction' of the enemy.[5] However, a more convincing conclusion is that the German army's misdeeds before November 1918 bear little resemblance to—and thus fail to explain—the Wehrmacht's complicity in the extermination of European Jews during the Second World War.

As this example suggests, the trajectory of German history towards some defining 'endpoint' has consistently drawn historians' attention back to Imperial Germany to uncover the roots of the Third Reich's crimes—or the Federal Republic's success. Some scholars believe that national unification in 1990 illuminates the 'real' significance of 1871. For others the appropriate endpoint is 1941, when the invasion of the Soviet Union (Operation Barbarossa) and the construction of the first death camps in Poland established historical markers against which Germany's warlike and 'eliminationist'[6] tendencies can be measured. But it is another terminus that has made Imperial Germany so contentious over the past half-century. This is the endpoint of 1933, signifying Hitler's appointment as chancellor and the beginning of the Nazi regime. Because Nazism represents the single most compelling problem of German history, 1933 is paradigmatic: it 'ended' any possibility that Germans could implement liberal democracy, resist the lure of Hitler, and escape the darkest stain on their history.

The imperial era figures centrally in every variant of this story. Why? Because Germany's course towards disaster was allegedly set between the middle of the nineteenth century and 1918. This interpretation constitutes the core of the thesis that German history was deflected from the 'normal' course towards modernity followed by other Western nations and took its own 'special path', or *Sonderweg*. How did this happen? According to the *Sonderweg* thesis, the failure of liberal democracy to take root in Germany was caused by the lack of a bourgeois revolution, as had occurred in England and France; by the survival of pre-industrial elites who continued to dominate key positions of power; by the friend–foe polarities conjured up by Bismarck to rally in-groups and target 'enemies of the empire'; and by myriad other manipulative strategies to preserve monarchical and executive power. Many chapters of this book refer to the *Sonderweg* thesis and to the substantial challenges it has faced since the 1980s. For now it is important to note that both the proponents of the *Sonderweg* and its critics agree that continuities and national comparisons are valid: they disagree mainly about *which* continuities and *which* comparisons are important. Thus discussion of the *Sonderweg* is not inadmissible; only the demand that it be accepted or rejected as an all-or-nothing proposition should be resisted.

'Playing with scales'

What happens when we refuse to accept that the best way to study the history of people living in a given territory is within the frame of the nation state? One answer is to place a national history within a constellation of histories conceived on a different scale, and then engage in the 'play of scales' (*jeu d'échelles*) that the French historian Jacques Revel once advocated.[7] In Chapter 10, Sebastian Conrad considers Germany's place in Europe and the world. Other chapters also assess the repercussions of transnational entanglements. For example: could a 'Bismarckian' style of diplomacy have channelled and accommodated global pressures after 1890? Was the search to define 'German' art in a world of nations, examined by Celia Applegate in Chapter 5, likely to foster a distinctive national culture? But it is also possible to place Germany in a smaller frame and explore its *sub*national regions and localities. Consider the themes that typically interest the historian of politics: they look quite different when we view them from the perspective of the rural county seat, the small-town mayor's office, the council chambers of a middle-sized city, or the Bavarian state ministry. This example is drawn from the political realm, but readers willing to make similar spatial leaps will find other examples in every chapter of this book. Our authors do not privilege the local and the regional at the expense of national and global contexts: this is certainly not the way to navigate what has been called the 'spatial turn' (an approach that explores 'space', 'place', and 'territoriality' in history by taking geography seriously). Instead, playing with scales is akin to looking through a kaleidoscope: each slight twist reorients our understanding of German histories in subtle ways, rearranging shards of historical evidence and casting them in a new light. This change of perspective is especially useful when we consider questions of locality, identity, and mobility.

In the German Empire, what made a person refer to a particular place as home? 'Home' might simply be one's place of birth. But a *sense* of 'home' might result from a language shared with neighbours, or attachment to a familiar landscape, or feeling secure within the kind of confessional milieux described by Christopher Clark in Chapter 4. Alternatively, it might be captured in a piece of music, or a painting, or the weekly meeting of 'regulars' at the *Stammtisch* of the local pub. All of these stimuli could be a marker of identity; but all were coded in more than one way. Where you were born had a different meaning if you had migrated to a new city, province, or federal state. Representing the 'national interest' in parliament became more difficult when voters demanded attention to local issues, as Thomas Kühne explains in

Chapter 8, or when class, confessional, or ethnic tensions mobilized new solidarities. It makes little sense, therefore, to assume the primacy of national allegiance or to impose national patterns on the everyday experiences of Germans in extraordinarily diverse situations. When playing with scales or giving the kaleidoscope a twist, the point is not to suggest that one measure or pattern reflects a truer image than another, but rather that each one refracts a familiar picture of Imperial Germany in fresh and interesting ways.

If all this twisting and turning and leaping tempts readers to leave the nation behind, they do so at their peril. Our authors offer many signposts that point back to the nation and its role in German history. During the imperial era, nationalism grew more significant as an idiom of public activity and as an issue on which major political conflicts and controversies turned. State ministers, party leaders, members of voluntary associations, reform activists, and many others tested different ways to finesse the dilemma of a divergence between the interests of the authoritarian state and what *they* defined as the national interest. Thus nationalism became more contested over time, as did the alleged benefits of ethnic homogeneity or social cohesion on a national scale. Many of the following chapters ask whether it is still helpful to speak of a national economy, a national electorate, or a national culture at all. They thereby underscore the difficulty of finding 'German' uniformity within local and regional diversity.

Contesting the past

The authors of this volume are well placed to synthesize existing scholarship on Imperial Germany, take stock of new findings, and identify open questions for future research. They represent diverse historiographical traditions in Canada, the United States, Great Britain, and Germany. They are a relatively young group, and they are all engaged in teaching undergraduates. They are also close to the archives, actively involved in pioneering research in their chosen field. Because they are alive to the complexity of Imperial Germany and the divergent means historians use to explain that complexity, they see no need to try to manufacture an artificial consensus about the German Empire. Collectively they opt for two kinds of openness: towards historical contingency, in the sense that contemporary Germans could not know the future that awaited them; and towards interpretative plurality, in the recognition that competing methods, theories, and schools of historical explanation complement each other—at least in the long run.

Since the 1980s many approaches that once fired the imaginations (and poisoned the pens) of historians have fallen from favour, while others have come to the fore. But if theoretical and methodological premises are constantly changing, the task of locating the German Empire in the longer course of modern German history has certainly not been swept off the table. According to some scholars, the *Sonderweg* controversy is now dead, or seriously deflated. According to others the debate about Imperial Germany's multivalent modernities should be allowed to die of its own lethargy. Still others believe historians' most pressing task is to answer the question 'Why did Germany go to war in 1914?' Each opinion can be overstated, and each elicits varying (and fluctuating) support among scholars on either side of the Atlantic. Every nation's history is unique; but historians of Germany are not likely to abandon the search for longterm clues to why only Germany embraced Nazism in 1933. According to one recent assessment,[8] the German Empire has never looked more modern to historians than it does today, but the interpretative pendulum may now have swung too far. And if relatively few scholars still regard the causes of the First World War as the most interesting or important aspect of Imperial German history, it should not be forgotten that Germany's decision for war in 1914 was the issue that first opened up the field for sustained scrutiny in the early 1960s. At that time the Hamburg historian Fritz Fischer proposed that an aggressive German policy in 1914 and the quest for vast territorial annexations resembled Hitler's war aims after 1939.[9] The Fischer controversy then dovetailed in the 1970s with an increasingly sophisticated and forceful elaboration of the *Sonderweg* concept.

The idea of Germany's 'special path' was integral to a pioneering work of synthesis on the German Empire published in 1973 by the Bielefeld historian Hans-Ulrich Wehler.[10] But by 1980 it had been challenged by two British historians, David Blackbourn and Geoff Eley, whose book *The Peculiarities of German History* suggested that Wehler had used inappropriate comparative yardsticks to measure Germany's 'misdevelopment'.[11] They criticized Wehler's still-life portrait of a drab, brutish empire dominated by 'pre-modern' elites. They also refused to accept the prevailing emphasis on what *didn't* happen in German history—as with Wehler's theses about the 'backwardness' of the political system, the empire's 'imperviousness' to reform, and the 'deficit' of bourgeois influence. Instead Blackbourn and Eley argued that Imperial German society was far more dynamic, progressive, and beholden to bourgeois interests and values than Wehler's account allowed. This challenge provided one impetus for collaborative research projects on the German middle classes (*Bürgertum*) in the 1980s.[12] Drawing on other national historiographies was another way to advance the field. Gradually local and regional studies—though never lacking in the German historical tradition—grew in number and sophistication, as did studies of gender, masculinity, religion, antisemitism, colonialism, transnationalism, and much more. It is not easy to chart these scholarly innovations on a timeline, but the trend has been towards a plurality of methods. Abandoning the quest for a meta-narrative and surrendering the assumed priority of a national paradigm have been helpful steps forward. Even as research on the German bourgeoisie reached its peak in the 1980s it was being superseded by the 'new cultural history', gender studies, the 'linguistic turn', 'virtual history', the 'spatial turn', the 'visual turn'—the process continues.

Some historians have reacted to methodological pluralism by wringing their hands and decrying the fragmentation of the discipline: 'What does it all mean?', they ask. They also worry that clear dividing lines can no longer be drawn between orthodox and revisionist interpretations, and that grand synthetic works may be passé. A more positive assessment is widely shared among historians who believe that research in their field, as in every other sphere of scientific inquiry, is always work in progress. Fitting comfortably into this mould, the authors represented in this volume assess the historiographical 'state of the art' about the contradictions and tensions found in Imperial Germany. They provide firm statements—original but not quirky—about where consensus among historians can be found and where it cannot. In doing so they celebrate the fact that familiar problems, when addressed from new vantage points, continue to make this period of German history so interesting.

Key themes

Despite the variety of topics discussed in the following chapters, four central themes stand out. Identifying these themes at the outset draws an interpretative arc from the beginning of the book to its end and illustrates how the individual chapters speak to each other.

The vignettes that open each chapter illustrate the pervasiveness and far-reaching ramifications of *social and economic change* in Imperial Germany. They also illuminate the interpenetration of everyday life and high politics. We often see that the socio-economic 'predicament' of ordinary Germans shaped their attitudes towards cultural and political change. Germany's socio-economic development is the focus of Brett Fairbairn's analysis in Chapter 3, which provides a transition from Katharine Anne Lerman's and Mark Hewitson's overviews of Bismarckian and Wilhelmine Germany to the more thematic chapters that follow. But these first three chapters are no less interpretative than the others. They highlight the historical significance of social transformations resulting from population growth and increased mobility, Germany's transition to an industrial capitalist economy, and the centrality of work to the everyday lives of the overwhelming majority of Germans. As traditional social bonds were loosened or dissolved, Germans sought to resurrect older solidarities or create new ones. Often the operation of unfamiliar market forces frustrated such attempts. Like the advance of industrial capitalism itself, processes of expansion, innovation, and penetration increasingly locked Germans into networks of social activity that made them less autonomous as individuals, though they could prove empowering as well (this ambiguity is especially evident in Angelika Schaser's chapter on gender). The advance of science and technology, particularly in transportation and communication, brought both problems and benefits that were distributed unevenly. By the midpoint of the Wilhelmine period, globalization had introduced transnational flows of people and products that were being felt by all Germans in their daily lives, regardless of whether they cared about colonies or 'world policy' (*Weltpolitik*).

The German middle class and the state both loom large in these chapters. Of course, to speak of either the bourgeoisie or the German state in the singular is to begin on the wrong foot. Imperial Germany's federal structure demands that we differentiate between the 'imperial' (Reich) government in Berlin and the governments of the two dozen states—Prussia, Bavaria, Saxony, and others—that made up the empire. It is also prudent to speak of the middle ranks or middle strata of German society, even though the foreign terms that historians often use to describe these groupings (bourgeoisie, *Bürgertum*) belie this plurality. The German middle classes were finely layered, and that layering was always in flux. Yet considered as a group, bourgeois Germans were disproportionately influential in the economic and cultural life of the nation and in its administration at the local and regional levels (for example, playing a dominant role in municipal councils). Indeed, in comparison to members of the middle classes in other Western nations, those in Germany were conspicuously 'close' to the state or attuned to state interests. They were often employed by the state, as in the case of soldiers, civil servants, and school-teachers; or they relied on its preferment—for example, when industrialists sought state contracts, professors sought university chairs, or commercial councillors sought titles and decorations. The state penetrated into the lives of middle-class Germans to a degree that has rightly captured historians' attention. Nevertheless, this is not to argue that such groups and individuals were lackeys of the state. Middle-class Germans often chose to forego official distinctions and patronage, coveting their independence and autonomy. They were also able to distinguish more clearly than historians sometimes imagine between elements of state authority they could endorse and those they could not. Thus Germans could embrace the monarchical principle but excoriate Wilhelm II for his personal and political blunders; they could take pride in an efficient Prussian bureaucracy but feel outrage at the haughty demeanour of a post-office clerk; they could respect and perhaps even revere the army as the guardian of the nation but feel acute embarrassment when military arrogance got out of hand. In each instance, were Germans displaying their affection for the state, trying to rein it in, or doing both at the same time? Elements of each view can be found in the chapters that follow.

Conflict—imagined and real—was ubiquitous in Imperial Germany. Less clear is whether the passing of the years made conflict more onerous for contemporaries or significant for historians. Compared with the revolutionary and military events of 1848–49 and 1864–71, the 1870s and 1880s might appear as an age of equipoise, when the first duty of every citizen was to remain calm. One of Bismarck's biographers labelled these decades periods of 'consolidation' and 'fortification'—not terribly exciting interpretative keys either.[13] But looking beneath the surface calm of Bismarckian Germany reveals a quite different picture, shot through with contradictions, conflicts, and crises. Contradictions resulted from attempts both to entrench and to extend the international and constitutional agreements achieved at the time of unification. Conflict was inevitable when the effects of rapid economic, social, cultural, and political change became self-reinforcing and as a younger generation of Germans sought new challenges to match the great deeds of their fathers. Crises arose whenever Bismarck felt his authority to be in jeopardy. Then, after 1890, the anxiety that other nations were denying Germany its 'place in the sun' became more pervasive. The belief that social conflict was growing and that Germany's national mission had been left unfinished in 1871 made Germans strive even more earnestly for togetherness at home and expansion abroad. Military motifs about 'embattled' Germany and its struggle for existence in a hostile world fired the imagination of radical nationalists, as Roger Chickering explains in Chapter 9; but they also fuelled confessional conflict, class conflict, party conflict, and the 'war between the sexes'. How do we assess the significance of all this turmoil?

Again we must not ignore the role of Germany's middle classes in determining whether conflict was successfully accommodated. Paradoxically, the bourgeoisie contributed both to the pluralization and polarization of contending classes and ideologies. Sometimes middle-class Germans appear to be complacent and conformist, seeking to avoid conflict at every turn; sometimes their anxiety and arrogance come to the fore as bourgeois canons and boundaries are challenged and become more porous. Yet it is impossible to overlook the bourgeoisie's faith in progress, its enthusiasm for experimentation, its ability to poke fun at itself. These contending propositions are actually two sides of the same coin, allowing us to see middle-class Germans as reluctant modernizers. They embraced change to accommodate conflict, but at the same time they sought to monitor, control, and channel it. Acknowledging this dual strategy to deal with conflicts generated by a highly dynamic society is ultimately more helpful than rehearsing the older view that Germany diverged from other nations because its bourgeoisie was economically strong but politically weak. One of Blackbourn's and Eley's most important arguments was that even a modern, dynamic, self-confident bourgeoisie may feel that its interests and values are accommodated under an authoritarian system of government that falls short of some normative liberal democratic ideal.

Imperial Germany has often been described as Janus-faced. The idea that Germany faced both forward and backward is suggestive of the tensions permeating imperial society, but recently it has tended to lead historians into the trap of blinkered, binary thinking. One symptom of this problem is that students and scholars are often asked to choose whether the German Empire was *authoritarian or modern*. Another symptom is the persistent notion of a sharp dividing line around 1890, where everything 'before' is seen as unmodern and everything 'after' hypermodern. These either–or choices and discontinuities are untenable. Nevertheless, attentive readers will find elements of this authoritarian/modern dualism throughout this book: every author considers these descriptors and explores the interpretative sparks that fly between them. These sparks correspond to actual conflicts that arose in Imperial Germany when the hammer of change struck the anvil of tradition. This metaphor, too, can be stretched too far; yet it directs our attention towards reforming conservatives and conserving liberals who, like the 'white revolutionary' Bismarck,[14] forged a transitional, protean form of German authoritarianism in the unification era and then sought to remould it into new and more durable forms in subsequent decades. Insofar as a preference for stasis and motives for reform could be reconciled—and often they could not be—it became more likely that Imperial Germany's authoritarian political system could survive in the modern age.

This is not the only way to assess the durability of the empire's founding political configuration or the longterm consequences of 'skirted decisions' in 1871.[15] Some of our authors acknowledge the empire's modernity as a central issue but mainly to say that it is not as central as historians once believed. Others break down authoritarian structures, roles, and habits of mind into their component parts and explore their implications—for example, as reflective of strong yearnings for a unified national community. Above all, these chapters demonstrate why neither German authoritarianism nor German modernity can be frozen in time. They evolved constantly and reciprocally. Modern technologies, the expanding role of the state, and evolving social relationships forced traditionalists to work out new strategies to defend the principle of authority. Conversely, the weight of tradition, the preference for gradual change, and the persistence of familiar identities, belief structures, and class distinctions forced modernizers to reassess and recalibrate their forward progress. Another useful way to think about this reciprocal relationship is to abandon the search for victims of either modernization or the authoritarian state; instead these chapters focus on the agency of Germans who took practical steps to determine their own future. By considering each group's aspirations, readers will discover how flesh-and-blood Germans breathed life into a dynamic, flexible, even consensual form of authoritarianism—one that differs substantially from the fascist and totalitarian models with which it is so often confused.

More than once this introduction has cited portents of a calamitous future awaiting Germans after 1918. If this appears to read history backwards, the historian John Breuilly has offered useful counsel: 'There is nothing wrong in principle with hindsight; indeed it is difficult to see how the historian could or should dispense with it. The major advantage the historian has over those he or she studies is knowing what came afterwards and it is not an advantage to be lightly thrown away.'[16] However—Breuilly continued—what must be resisted is the tendency to regard the actual outcome as the only *possible* outcome at any given point in time. The history of Imperial Germany is a book whose final chapter, because it was unknown, fostered both unease and excitement among contemporaries. Germans shortly before the war had every right to be astounded by how much had changed since their parents or grandparents had experienced unification in 1871, and how rapidly. They sensed that the future was becoming less predictable with each passing day. Yet even though historians now emphasize the diversity, dynamism, and paradoxes of German development in the imperial era, they have not lost sight of what did *not* change quickly or fundamentally between 1871 and 1918. Would the authoritarian or the modern features of the German Empire become more pronounced in the future? In the early twentieth century this question remained tantalizingly open.

[1] Hans Rosenberg, 'Political and Social Consequences of the Great Depression of 1873–1896 in Central Europe' (orig. 1943), in James J. Sheehan (ed.), *Imperial Germany* (New York and London, 1976), 39–60.

[2] Joachim Radkau, *Das Zeitalter der Nervosität. Deutschland zwischen Bismarck und Hitler* (Munich, 1998).

[3] As one liberal newspaper editor wrote shortly after the Austro-Prussian War: 'Never in my life did I breathe fresher, more invigorating air than that which blew across the north of Germany in the late fall of 1866. . . . We stood on the threshold of a new age, of a time "which still promised wonders".' Julius von Eckardt, *Lebenserinnerungen*, 2 vols. (Leipzig, 1910), i. 56–7.

[4] George F. Kennan, *The Decline of Bismarck's European Order: Franco-Russian Relations, 1875–1890* (Princeton, 1979), 3, emphasis in the original.

[5] Isabel V. Hull, *Absolute Destruction: Military Culture and the Practices of War in Imperial Germany* (Ithaca, NY, 2005); cf. works cited in 'Further reading' for Ch. 10.

[6] This refers to the central thesis of Daniel Jonah Goldhagen, *Hitler's Willing Executioners: Ordinary Germans and the Holocaust* (New York, 1996).

[7] See David Blackbourn, *A Sense of Place. New Directions in German History*, The 1998 Annual Lecture of the German Historical Institute, London (London, 1999).

[8] Sven Oliver Müller and Cornelius Torp, 'Einleitung', in Müller and Torp (eds), *Das Deutsche Kaiserreich in der Kontroverse. Probleme und Perspektiven* (forthcoming, 2008).

[9] Fritz Fischer, *Germany's Aims in the First World War* (orig. German edn 1961) (New York, 1967).

[10] Hans-Ulrich Wehler, *The German Empire 1871–1918* (orig. German edn 1973), trans. Kim Traynor (Leamington Spa, 1985).

[11] David Blackbourn and Geoff Eley, *The Peculiarities of German History: Bourgeois Society and Politics in Nineteenth-Century Germany* (orig. German edn 1980) (Oxford and New York, 1984).

[12] See the useful résumé in Jonathan Sperber, 'Bürger, Bürgertum, Bürgerlichkeit, Bürgerliche Gesellschaft: Studies of the German (Upper) Middle Class and Its Socio-cultural World', *Journal of Modern History*, 69 (1997), 271–97.

[13] Otto Pflanze, *Bismarck and the Development of Germany*, 3 vols, vol. 2, *The Period of Consolidation, 1871–1880*, and vol. 3, *The Period of Fortification, 1880–1898* (Princeton, 1990).

[14] Lothar Gall, *Bismarck: The White Revolutionary* (orig. German edn 1980), trans. J. A. Underwood, 2 vols. (London, 1986).

[15] Wolfgang J. Mommsen, 'The German Empire as a system of skirted decisions' (orig. German 1978), in Mommsen, *Imperial Germany 1867–1918: Politics, Culture, and Society in an Authoritarian State*, trans. Richard Deveson (London, 1995), 1–19.

[16] John Breuilly, 'Introduction', in Breuilly (ed.), *Nineteenth-Century Germany: Politics, Culture and Society 1780–1918* (London, 2001), 4.

Bismarckian Germany

Katharine Anne Lerman

In the spring of 1870 a south German aristocrat, Prince Chlodwig zu Hohenlohe-Schillingsfürst, was visiting Berlin. Born of a Protestant mother, brought up a Catholic, and married to a Russian princess, Hohenlohe was liberal in his political views and, unusually for a man of his background, he had come to support the idea of a united Germany under Prussian leadership. Some twenty-four years later he would become the first chancellor of the German Empire who did not come from Prussia. But at the time of his visit in April 1870 the German Empire did not exist, and the only representative political institution linking the recently created North German Confederation with the German states south of the River Main was a customs parliament. Moreover, just six weeks before his visit, Hohenlohe had been forced to resign as chief minister of Bavaria because of his political views. Having spent three years working to improve relations between Prussia and the south German states after they had fought on opposing sides in the Austro-Prussian War of 1866, Hohenlohe had finally accepted in March 1870 that his policies were out of tune with a Bavarian electorate that was increasingly clerical and anti-Prussian.

Hohenlohe's mood during his stay in the Prussian capital was gloomy. The future of Germany seemed even less certain than his own political prospects: he told a Prussian diplomat that he 'should doubtless not live to see the formation of an acknowledged German State'.[1] He had serious misgivings about internal developments in the Kingdom of Prussia and the nature of the North German Confederation, established after the war of 1866. There were also rumours circulating in Berlin that Otto von Bismarck, the minister president of Prussia and chancellor of the North German Confederation, was planning to persuade Wilhelm I, the Prussian king, to assume the old imperial title of German Kaiser (emperor) and thereby force the kings of Bavaria and Württemberg in the south to recognize Prussian hegemony.[2] On 25 April 1870, Hohenlohe attended the inaugural meeting of a small number of south German national liberal parliamentarians who called themselves the Main Bridge group. As they sat around a large table and drank beer, Hohenlohe heard little to encourage optimism. When one of the deputies suggested that they should drum up support for the national cause by holding a political banquet (as had been done before the revolutions of 1848), another replied waggishly that all the food eaten over the years in the name of German unity could have filled the River Main.[3]

Only on 9 May, when he witnessed the grand parade of the Berlin garrison on the Kreuzberg, did Hohenlohe adopt a more positive outlook. 'The whole garrison of Berlin had turned out. A great show of princes, generals and so forth', he wrote in his journal. 'I mingled with the crowd and was struck with the interest manifested by the lowest of people in things military. No trace of the former animosity against the military which used to be noticeable among the lower classes. The commonest working man looked on the troops with the feeling that he belonged or had belonged to them.'[4] Hohenlohe's remarks attest to the popularity and prestige of the Prussian army after the Austro-Prussian War, an army which had been reformed and expanded in the 1860s in the face of bitter opposition from the Prussian parliament. Its role in forging the North German Confederation already suggested its new status. But in May 1870 Hohenlohe could scarcely have anticipated how those same troops on parade in Berlin would soon help to turn his dream of a united Germany into a reality. In July 1870 the Franco-Prussian War broke out as a consequence of Prussian provocation and French diplomatic blunders. On 1–2 September the Prussian army, together with its south German allies, smashed the forces of the French Second Empire at Sedan. Within weeks agreement was reached to found a new German Empire (Reich), which was proclaimed from the Hall of Mirrors at the palace of Versailles outside Paris on 18 January 1871, even before the formal conclusion of the Franco-Prussian War. The army had finally overcome the obstacles to political unification and silenced the pessimistic prognostications of national liberal parliamentarians.

Henceforth it could claim to be both the guardian and guarantor of German national unity, but its pre-eminent position within the emerging new empire would also cast a long shadow over Germany's political development.

The new empire

Bismarckian Germany was born on the battlefield. There were doubtless many forces in the nineteenth century that favoured the emergence of a united German state under Prussian leadership. But it was never self-evident that in less than a decade, between 1864 and 1871, the Kingdom of Prussia would fight three successful wars against Denmark, Austria, and France. Nor, as Hohenlohe's experience confirms, was it possible for anyone to predict with certainty before the Franco-Prussian War what the future shape and institutional structure of a united Germany might be. In the heady atmosphere of heightened nationalism generated by war against the old enemy France, the south German states instinctively gravitated to Prussia for reasons of self-preservation as well as military obligation. They eventually acceded to the political union in return for very few amendments to the constitution of the former North German Confederation. Just as in 1866 Bismarck himself had remarked, 'If there is to be revolution, we would prefer to make it than to suffer it',[5] so in 1871 the rulers of Bavaria and Württemberg reluctantly accepted Prussian domination of a new federated empire of sovereign princes for fear that the Franco-German 'racial war' (*Völkerkrieg*) could unleash something far worse. Only the south German state of Baden, whose grand duke was married to the sister of the Prussian king, was enthusiastic about the union.

The foundation of the German Empire signified a revolution 'from above', facilitated by military conquest and agreed by princes. It appeared to present a definitive solution to the problem of political fragmentation which had bedevilled German-speaking Europe throughout the nineteenth century. Its violent birth overtook decades of debate and discussion among the educated middle classes in parliamentary assemblies, state bureaucracies, social salons, and the press about the future shape of a German national state. It ended whatever prospects might still have existed for the peaceful emergence of modern Germany through the slow, organic convergence of the economic and political interests of the German states. Indeed, almost overnight, what had long been recognized as a complex political problem was apparently rendered simple by the application of military might. Politics and diplomacy in German-speaking Europe were also changed beyond recognition. Less than a month after the proclamation from Versailles, the British Conservative statesman, Benjamin Disraeli, addressing the House of Commons, insightfully remarked that the world was witnessing what amounted to 'the German revolution, a greater political event than the French Revolution of last century'.[6]

The emergence of a united Germany under Prussian leadership in 1871 was neither a simple nor a definitive solution to the questions surrounding German identity, nationhood, and state formation in Europe. The fallout from the German 'revolution from above' would affect Europeans for decades to come, until the First World War and beyond. Moreover, the struggle to achieve a German nation state was scarcely over in 1871; rather, it can be argued that a distinctive German national identity was only just beginning to emerge with the foundation of the German Empire and that German nationalism was now entering a new, more aggressive phase. German political unity under Prussian leadership involved severing centuries-old ties with the Austrian Germans living in the Habsburg Empire; this political and cultural shift would prove particularly challenging to Catholics in the south who had traditionally looked to Austria for leadership on German issues. It also ensured that the Danes of northern Schleswig and over two million Polish subjects in Prussia's eastern provinces would be incorporated into a new political entity which now laid claim to being a German national state. The Prussian decision to annex two French provinces, Alsace and Lorraine, after the French defeat of 1870–71 signified the inclusion of another disaffected national minority within the new German Empire. How these minorities would be treated and what kind of relationship the empire would develop with the millions of Germans who lived outside its borders was not yet clear.

Nor were the political arrangements in the empire unambiguous. Whether the new entity was really a federation of sovereign states or a state owing allegiance to a single monarch, how power was to be divided between the theoretically sovereign princes and the new Kaiser, and how much weight was to be accorded to the views of the German people, represented in a German parliament (Reichstag) directly elected by universal male suffrage, all remained to be clarified. As with all battles, the struggle for unification involved winners and losers, those who supported the outcome and those who opposed it, men of conviction and fellow travellers. In the euphoria of 1871, inducements were offered, compromises were struck, and doubts suppressed or disregarded. Many liberals were seduced by the fruits of military victory, reconciling themselves to a less centralized and less liberal state than they had anticipated: they hoped that it would have the potential to develop over time into a constitutional nation state more to their liking. Prussian conservatives, for their part, lamented the concessions to liberalism and parliamentarianism and expressed their anxieties over the further 'dilution' of Prussia and Prussian values in a larger German entity. The new political arrangements could also scarcely mask the deep social, regional, and confessional divisions which the new German Empire inherited. Thus only time could reveal how permanent these arrangements would be and whether the solutions forged on the battlefield would attract popular support.

These unresolved questions were perhaps most apparent to the man widely acclaimed as the architect of German unification: the first imperial German chancellor, Otto von Bismarck. Bismarck achieved far more in 1871 than he had ever anticipated or believed possible, and he was to spend most of his remaining years in office fretting that his new political edifice could disintegrate, exposing him to the ridicule of the world. From 1862 Bismarck had steered the foreign policy of Prussia as its minister president and foreign minister, but his diplomacy only appears clear-sighted and resolute with the benefit of hindsight. Bismarck was always eager to expand the power of Prussia in Germany and instinctively knew what he wanted to avoid. But ultimately he only groped his way to a solution of the 'German problem', almost as a by-product of his quest to ensure Prussian strength and security in Europe. Moreover, having come to power in 1862 as an entrenched and pugnacious conservative who was determined to defend the powers of the Prussian monarchy against any liberal or democratic encroachments, Bismarck stunned his political opponents by his willingness to trump them with radical initiatives and his propensity to gamble his country's fortunes in the lottery of war. From 1871 Bismarck was the dominant figure in German political life, determining the political development of the empire for the first nineteen years of its existence until he was eventually dismissed from office—two weeks before his seventy-fifth birthday—by the young Kaiser Wilhelm II in 1890. But, despite his awe-inspiring stature as the 'founder of the Reich' (*Reichsgründer*) and his manifest determination to impress his personality on his new creation, it was also far from certain in 1871 whether Bismarck had the requisite political skills to build the broad coalition of domestic support necessary for the future political consolidation of the empire. Nor was it clear whether, in the aftermath of war, he could safeguard the international position of his new Reich, which was bound to have profound implications for the stability of the European state system.

Germany in Europe

Before 1871 the great powers had traditionally been able to make adjustments to the European balance of power at the expense of the German-speaking lands. This was no longer the case after the German Empire was founded. Moreover, that empire was second only to Britain in terms of its industrial development, and over the subsequent two decades it was to provide ample demonstration of its growing economic power. The foundation of Imperial Germany marked a caesura in European international relations. It not only changed the political map of Europe, it also had a major impact on all its neighbours. With hindsight its dramatic arrival on the scene can be seen as contributing fundamentally to the longterm origins of the First World War. In the first two decades of its existence, the German Empire enjoyed what is often described as a 'latent hegemony' in Europe or a 'semi-hegemonial' position. Bismarck was adamant about reassuring the other powers that Germany was not a threat to the peace of Europe and he generally cautioned restraint. After 1890 the men in charge of German foreign policy were not so willing to work within these self-imposed restrictions.

The European great powers did not intervene during the Franco-Prussian War to forestall the emergence of a united Germany. Indeed, compared to the alternative of a resurgent France, Prussia's consolidation of its influence over the south German states appeared to Britain and Russia to be a limited and acceptable aim in 1870. Russia ultimately rejected proposals for international mediation in the crisis, preferring to exploit the war to revise unilaterally the peace terms imposed after its defeat in the Crimean War in 1856. Britain, too, was not inclined to aid Napoleon III, especially after Bismarck publicized the French emperor's plans to occupy Belgium. The likely emergence of a second-rank German power, soon to be headed by a liberal crown prince who was married to the eldest daughter of Queen Victoria, was generally welcomed in London. The new state would surely be a useful counterweight to the Continental dominance of Paris and St Petersburg. Austria, which had so recently been defeated by Prussia in the war of 1866, might have been expected to take France's side in 1870. But even if its anti-Prussian chief minister, Friedrich von Beust, prayed for a French victory, there was no great animosity towards Prussia within the Habsburg Empire after the relatively lenient peace of 1866; and it was so beset with internal tensions and financial problems after reorganizing its monarchy in 1867 that it ultimately could not run the risk of supporting either side in 1870.

The great powers of Europe may have looked with relative equanimity on the German subjugation of France in 1870–71, but they undoubtedly underestimated Prussia's military strength during the Wars of Unification and awoke from their complacency to a startling new reality. The outcome of the Franco-Prussian War was in doubt only between 15 July 1870 and 2 September; thereafter the negotiations between Prussia and the south German states to found the empire presented the other powers with a fait accompli. The victory at Sedan helped to destroy any remaining illusions about the military power of the emerging new Germany. The professionalism and efficiency of the Prussian army manifestly eclipsed the military strength of any other Continental power. Moreover, the annexation of Alsace and Lorraine signalled that

France and Germany were unlikely to be reconciled and that the issue would be an open wound in European international relations. Bismarck cited political, strategic, and economic arguments in favour of the annexations but, in exceeding his stated goals, he undoubtedly heightened mistrust of his intentions. The German Empire not only incurred the lasting enmity of France; it also now appeared to seek aggrandizement at the expense of its neighbours and to threaten European stability and security.

The political unification of Germany also marked the culmination of a remarkable period of upheaval in Europe, when older forms of diplomacy were discarded and Bismarck harnessed new ideological and social forces to justify and legitimize his foreign policy. In 1866, for example, Bismarck was willing to use revolutionary nationalism to potentially destructive effect against the multinational Austrian Empire, seeking contacts with the leaders of its Hungarian, Czech, and other minorities with the aim of encouraging internal ferment. In 1871 he deliberately whipped up German nationalism as a means of uniting the people behind the war against their old enemy, France. All this further unsettled the established powers of Europe, making them wary of the implications of German unity and unable to predict its consequences. Bismarck and many German nationalists declared themselves satisfied with a 'lesser Germany' (*Kleindeutschland*), which did not include German-speakers in Austria; however, if taken to its logical conclusion, the idea that all ethnic Germans should live in one state or that the new Germany should have a claim on their national loyalty was likely to destabilize Continental Europe. This concern was not unfounded. The euphoria after 1871 lent credence to the arguments of German nationalists who saw the creation of the empire as the beginning rather than the end of a process and who urged that Germany should consolidate the 'partial unification' of 1871 by seeking further expansion.

Thus, however complacent the rest of Europe had been about the political unification of Germany, from 1871 onward the new empire faced a variety of external threats, not the least of which was Bismarck's recurring nightmare that the other European powers might come together in a hostile coalition to undo his work of unification. Bismarck was acutely aware of Germany's geopolitical and strategic vulnerability, exposed on virtually all sides by the lack of natural borders and with only limited access to the North Sea and the Baltic Sea. However much he assured the chancelleries of Europe that the new Germany was now a 'satiated' state with no further territorial ambitions and that it constituted no threat to the balance of power, Bismarck's reputation for diplomatic cunning created a persistent sense of unease in other European capitals in the 1870s and 1880s.

Bismarck's foreign policy

Bismarck alone determined almost every facet of German foreign policy during the first two decades of the empire's existence. Indeed, he was also the dominant figure in European diplomacy from 1871. He commanded enormous respect at home and abroad, as well as the awe and obedience of his subordinates in the German Foreign Office. But even he found that the requirements of German foreign policy challenged all his diplomatic ingenuity and skill during his remaining period in office. He initially underestimated the implications of Germany's latent hegemony in Europe, and he adjusted only slowly to the new reality. Moreover, while his diplomacy is generally seen as successful, especially in comparison to the blunders and hubris of his successors, by the late 1880s he was finding it increasingly difficult to stave off unwelcome international developments, some of which can be seen as the inevitable (albeit delayed) consequence of German unification.

That Bismarck was fully alert to the potential danger of a hostile coalition emerging to undo his work of unification became apparent in 1875 during the so-called War in Sight crisis. The chancellor himself precipitated this crisis between Germany and France, not least to intimidate France, which had revived surprisingly quickly after being defeated and burdened with a heavy indemnity in 1871. But the crisis resulted in Russian and British warnings to Berlin that Germany should not indulge in any further aggression against its western neighbour. The spectre of a possible coalition between France, Russia, and Britain to contain German expansionism now became a real danger for Bismarck—as real as his earlier fear of a coalition of the Catholic powers of Europe, centred on the Papacy, Austria, or France to reverse Prussian gains (though he calculated that France would be less likely to embark on such a course under a republican government than a monarchy). Likened by Tsar Alexander II to Napoleon I, 'who, at the end of each war sought a pretext to begin another one',[7] Bismarck knew he had nothing to gain in Europe by being seen as an aggressive disturber of the peace.

Such considerations encouraged Bismarck to conclude a series of alliances from the late 1870s to preserve and stabilize Germany's position in Europe. These alliances were designed to ensure that France rather than Germany would be isolated in Europe, that Germany would always be friends with three of the five major European powers, and that if possible all the great powers, with the exception of France, would look to Berlin for support. Bismarck set out his ideas on German foreign policy in June 1877 in a document known as the Kissingen Dictation. His stated aim was to achieve 'an overall political situation in which all the great powers except France have need of us and are as far as possible kept from forming coalitions against us by their relations with one another'.[8]

The lynchpin of this Bismarckian 'alliance system' was the Dual Alliance concluded with Austria in 1879 and expanded by Italian accession into the Triple Alliance in 1882. This treaty proved a landmark in European international relations, coming thirteen years after Prussia and Austria had fought to resolve their rivalry for influence over German-speaking Europe. It formed the cornerstone of both countries' foreign policy right up to their disastrous partnership in the First World War. Cultural and domestic interests linked the two powers, and Bismarck's intentions are generally seen as defensive in concluding what nevertheless constituted an offensive–defensive alliance. But Austria clearly saw the alliance primarily as a vehicle for German support against Russia, and there were also strategic considerations on the German side which cast some doubt on Bismarck's professed aims. Despite his frequent assertions of German disinterest in south-eastern Europe, for example, the Dual Alliance was by no means incompatible with an ambition to promote German hegemony there. Kaiser Wilhelm I strongly resisted signing a treaty which he anticipated would constitute a significant snub to Russia, but after six weeks of opposition he eventually submitted to the will of his chancellor.

Bismarck successfully preserved Russo-German friendship after the conclusion of the Dual Alliance with Austria in 1879. Despite mounting Austro-Russian tensions in the Balkans from the late 1870s, he secured both powers' formal accession to a Three Emperors Agreement in 1881, which ensured their benevolent neutrality in the event of another Franco-German war. The arrangement was renewed with difficulty in 1884 but collapsed under the strain of a protracted crisis over Bulgaria in 1885–87. By this time Bismarck was also concerned about an increasingly nationalist government in France in which the *revanchist* General Boulanger was appointed minister of war. To preserve Germany's ties with Russia—the 'wire to St Petersburg'—and to ensure that France continued to be isolated in Europe, Bismarck thus concluded a Secret Reinsurance Treaty with Russia in 1887, the existence of which only became publicly known some ten years later, after Bismarck had left office and it had long lapsed. The treaty had to remain secret, not least because it highlighted the duplicitous nature of his diplomacy. It promised German support for Russian interests in the Balkans and thereby contradicted the terms of the Dual Alliance which supported Austria. But, at the same time, Bismarck secured further support for Austrian interests from Britain and Italy by encouraging them to conclude a tripartite Mediterranean Agreement in order to maintain an effective balance in the region. This complicated balancing act is historically significant less because of its intricacy than because it helps us situate Bismarck in a larger historical context. Bismarck's great strength was to understand the multidimensional nature of European international relations and how Germany's bilateral diplomacy might have an impact on third parties. Always ready to improvise to achieve his desired aim, he developed a series of alliances centred on Berlin and frequently succeeded in manipulating the other powers of Europe to react in ways which furthered his purposes.

Although Bismarck had successfully engineered three victorious Prussian wars, after 1871 he recognized that German security largely depended on peace and stability in Europe. His diplomacy accommodated this shift. He deliberately posed as an impartial arbiter in international disputes, most memorably at the Congress of Berlin on the Near Eastern Question in 1878. Then, and during other crises, too, he correctly calculated that Germany had little to gain and everything to lose in a general European war. Above all, Bismarck feared Germany's involvement in a two-front war. Thus he consistently opposed provoking Russia. By the late 1880s some of his critics urged a 'preventive war' against what they perceived as a growing Russian threat. Bismarck always dismissed such a course as 'committing suicide for fear of death'.[9] Yet the chancellor was never converted to the idea of European peace as an ultimate ideal and he never ruled out the possibility of another war. Indeed, he calculated that in all probability Germany would have to go to war against France again sometime in the future. In the meantime he determined to keep France diplomatically isolated and to deflect French ambitions away from Alsace and Lorraine as far as possible, for example by encouraging the French to become involved in colonial ventures and imperialist rivalries with other powers.

Nor did Bismarck baulk at sowing dissension between the other European powers as a means of preserving Germany's position. The conflicts between the great powers on the periphery of Europe and overseas were certainly not engineered by Bismarck exclusively, and in some respects they gave Germany a breathing space after the Wars of Unification. But Bismarck understood how they could be turned to Germany's advantage. Paradoxically, in the mid-1880s Bismarck also embroiled Germany in her own bid for colonies, endorsing the acquisition of territories in Africa and the Pacific. He later regretted this move, which was largely determined by domestic considerations and was part of a broader strategy to bolster his personal position at a time when the Kaiser's health was failing and the succession of the liberal crown prince seemed imminent. Germany's new colonial empire not only exposed the Reich to international rivalries; it also proved more of an economic liability than an asset. After the turn of the century Berlin found itself obliged to send military expeditions to suppress colonial uprisings in the protectorates of German Southwest Africa and East Africa, which they did with great brutality. Above all, Germany's bid for colonies in the 1880s seemed to belie Bismarck's assurances that Germany was now a satiated Continental state and signalled its aspiration to be not just a European but also a world power.

Bismarck's diplomacy achieved its objectives while he remained in office, but ultimately its cost for the German Empire's future security in Europe was high. In initiating a series of formal alliances during peacetime, Bismarck contributed to a growing climate of mistrust and insecurity in Europe, in part because the content of the treaties was often suspected rather than known. Moreover, one method by which the chancellor bound the European powers to Berlin was by promising them territory at the expense of the increasingly fragile Turkish Empire, even while he promoted Germany's relations with the Ottoman regime in other ways. Bismarck lured Austria, Russia, Britain, Italy, and even, on occasion, France with the prospect of German support for their territorial ambitions in Europe and overseas. The logic behind his tortuous and often contradictory diplomacy appeared arcane to some of his subordinates, who never understood its wisdom, and their bafflement only grew as Bismarck's term of office neared its end in the late 1880s. In 1890, shortly after Bismarck's dismissal, his successors decided not to renew the Secret Reinsurance Treaty with Russia, believing it was incompatible with Germany's other commitments. Their action soon contributed to the formation of a Franco-Russian entente, cemented into a formal alliance in 1894. German diplomacy thereafter had to contend with a far less favourable international environment.

This is not to suggest that Bismarck's many diplomatic achievements were hollow, but rather that their historical ramifications and significance cannot properly be appraised if we are overawed by Bismarck's 'genius'. During Bismarck's chancellorship the new German Empire was elevated to a dominant position in European international relations. Germany was able to enjoy its latent hegemony, provided it exercised that hegemony with restraint. Bismarck was Europe's pre-eminent statesman whose abundant skills were satirized in the famous cartoon depicting the chancellor as a juggler able to keep five balls in the air simultaneously. At the same time the empire's economic dynamism in the decades after unification and the reputation of its army (essentially the Prussian army) further commanded international respect. Nevertheless, by the end of Bismarck's tenure in office the strains on his diplomacy were already in evidence, and it was becoming increasingly unlikely that his system of improvised checks and balances could endure.

Whether he could have prevented Russia from drifting into the arms of France after 1890, even if he had remained in office, is far from certain. It is also by no means clear how far his diplomacy could have channelled and accommodated the new global pressures the empire faced in the subsequent Wilhelmine era.

The task of national consolidation

The major task confronting the German Empire in the first decade of its existence was to achieve national consolidation. Political unification was not synonymous with national unity and the new Reich remained a federation. It comprised four kingdoms (Prussia, Bavaria, Württemberg, and Saxony), six grand duchies (notably Baden and Hesse), five duchies (for example, Anhalt and Braunschweig), seven principalities (such as Lippe and Schaumburg-Lippe), three free cities (Hamburg, Bremen, and Lübeck), as well as the 'imperial territory' (*Reichsland*) of Alsace-Lorraine. Since regional, ethnic, and confessional identities often underscored or superseded political, social, and ideological divisions, it became imperative to provide a focus for national loyalty. In this sense German nationalism, encouraged by the state, was to become a much more significant force after political unification than it had been in the decades leading up to the foundation of the empire. A useful means of integrating a diverse majority of Germans into the new polity, an appeal to the superior claims of the nation on every citizen's allegiance was also used to sometimes devastating effect both against national minorities living within the empire and against the so-called 'internal enemies of the Reich' (*Reichsfeinde*) who never endorsed the settlement of 1871.

The constitution of the new German Empire provided it with only two genuinely national political institutions. The federal states were represented in a Federal Council (*Bundesrat*), which was theoretically sovereign but in practice was easily dominated by the largest and most populous state, Prussia. The other national political institution was the Reichstag, which was directly elected by all men aged twenty-five years and over—a progressive suffrage for the time. The practice of voting every three years in national elections was to prove very important in forging a sense of German national identity as well as in encouraging the gradual emergence of a democratic civic culture. But despite significant budgetary and legislative powers, the influence of the Reichstag—and of party politicians more generally—over decision-making in the empire was severely limited. While the parliament genuinely represented the male half of the population and gained weight as a focus of national political life during the empire's existence, it was never effectively able to call Germany's rulers to account. Its scope was particularly limited with respect to foreign policy, and most domestic issues in the empire were regulated by the various federal state governments and parliaments rather than at a national level. Neither the Reich nor the Prussian constitution recognized a role for organized political parties, and the political parties in Imperial Germany never had to take responsibility for governing.

The Kaiser's potential as a national monarch was also circumscribed because he always also held the Prussian crown and was theoretically only 'first among equals' alongside his fellow sovereigns. He was granted specific powers and privileges in 1871, such as the right to conduct foreign policy, declare war, and conclude peace. His control of appointments and, above all, his personal control of the army made him a very powerful figure. But Kaiser Wilhelm I remained steeped in Prussian traditions throughout his life. Only his grandson, Wilhelm II, attempted after 1888 to elaborate and expand his role as an imperial monarch and national figurehead. There was also no provision for a national German government in 1871. The only man charged with responsibility for coordinating the affairs of the diverse empire was the imperial chancellor. Over time Bismarck developed a growing staff of subordinates to help him: their position was formalized in the late 1870s when a series of imperial offices were created, each headed by a state secretary. But all these men remained under the chancellor's authority, and the chancellor himself was appointed solely by the Kaiser. In Prussia, too, the king still ruled in a semi-autocratic way, appointing a government of higher civil servants and military men, not parliamentarians who represented the people. The role of the executive in Prussia and the Reich was to serve the Crown; it had no organic relationship with the legislature or the people.

BISMARCKIAN GERMANY | 33

The empire thus remained true to Germany's federal traditions, but the continuing vitality of the states and the Reich's political arrangements created a powerful obstacle to national consolidation. From 1866 Bismarck forged a tactical alliance with liberal nationalists. Throughout the 1870s the support of the National Liberal Party, the largest party in both the Reichstag and the Prussian parliament (Landtag), was essential in furthering the economic and legal unification of Germany. Yet the chancellor never identified with the National Liberal aim to create a more unitary, centralized, and liberal German state. On the contrary, he mainly sought to safeguard the position of the federal states, above all Prussia, and ensure their rights were protected. In the early years of the empire he proved more willing to adopt elastic and ambiguous terms in describing the power relationships in the new empire which could allow for evolution over time. But as the empire began to develop a momentum of its own, his interpretations lost their flexibility and his solutions to problems became more authoritarian and prescriptive. In 1878–79 Bismarck finally broke with many of his liberal allies, helping to split the National Liberal Party. Thereafter he sought to rule as far as possible 'above the parties' with shifting coalitions of support in the parliaments according to the issues. By the late 1880s Bismarck was unapologetic in his efforts to shore up what he regarded as the conservative pillars of the state against mounting pressures for change.

Although his methods often proved highly controversial and counterproductive, Bismarck's domestic policies were driven by his determination to consolidate the new national state. There is little doubt that when he supported universal male suffrage as the basis for elections to the Reichstag of the North German Confederation in 1867, he believed that it would result in a more compliant, conservative, and monarchist parliament than the plutocratic and liberal lower chamber he had been forced to contend with in Prussia in the 1860s. He clearly did not anticipate that a strong Catholic party would emerge in 1870–71—the German Centre Party, which rapidly sought to mobilize support from all those who resented their inclusion in a new Germany dominated by Protestant Prussia. Nor was he impressed in 1870–71 by the activities of the handful of popularly elected socialist deputies in the Reichstag. He was incensed when their leader, August Bebel, condemned the annexation of Alsace-Lorraine, opposed further credits for the Franco-Prussian war, and extolled the virtues of the revolutionary Paris Commune.

Bismarck launched campaigns against both the Centre Party and the socialists in the 1870s in an effort to choke off their popular support. But neither of these campaigns was successful and both ultimately encouraged the emergence of two parties with mass support in the empire. Furthermore, as he came to regret the Reichstag suffrage which gave Catholics and the working classes political representation, the chancellor began to look for ways to neutralize or undermine the influence of a parliament he could never control. He considered ways of bypassing the Reichstag constitutionally, for example by creating parallel or rival institutions, and he sought to influence the outcome of elections by precipitating domestic crises or manufacturing timely war scares to heighten the electorate's national consciousness. As the founder of the Reich, he never regarded its political and institutional arrangements as fixed and was quite prepared to threaten to revise them if he could not secure his own way. Throughout the first twenty years of the empire's existence, the political parties thus constantly had to labour under the threat of a possible *coup d'état* from above (*Staatsstreich*), an enforced change of the constitution backed up by military power. This might have involved revising the democratic Reichstag suffrage to ensure a more conservative chamber, or it might have entailed abolishing the parliament altogether and renegotiating the alliance of princes on which the empire was based. In the 1890s, too, Kaiser Wilhelm II's response to opposition from parliamentarians was not infrequently to threaten to send in the army to shoot the lot of them.

Bismarck's domestic policies

In the early 1870s, with enthusiastic liberal and popular anticlerical support, Bismarck and the Prussian government waged the *Kulturkampf*—which can be translated as the 'struggle for civilization' or the 'cultural struggle'—against political Catholicism. One of the campaign's main aims was to reconstruct (or restore to what it had been in 1840) the relationship between church and state in Prussia. State control was established over education and the appointment of the clergy; compulsory civil marriage was introduced; and the Jesuit Order, seen as an alien presence that served a hostile power, was expelled from Germany. But many excesses were committed during the struggle. Priests were imprisoned, parishes were left without clergymen, and church property was confiscated. Bismarck's commitment to the *Kulturkampf* was first and foremost an act of political calculation. He saw the Centre Party and the Roman Catholic Church as subversive forces within the new nation state that he wished to consolidate. In his view they were sustained by Germany's foreign enemies, they stirred up the hostility of Prussia's Polish population, and they even incited otherwise loyal Catholics to murder him (as was attempted by a twenty-one-year-old cooper's apprentice, Eduard Kullmann, in 1874).

The Centre Party mobilized its supporters against what it saw from the outset as an anti-Catholic onslaught; it became a far more formidable and cohesive political force as a result. Catholics (who made up about one-third of the German population), disgruntled particularists (whose first loyalty was to their state), Poles, Guelphs (from the former state of Hanover, which Prussia had annexed in 1866), federalists, and democrats all rallied to its banner. Many devout Protestants were also alienated by the attack on confessional peace. If Bismarck's primary aim was to suppress in its infancy a movement which he saw as a major threat to the work of national construction, he failed miserably. Far from facilitating national unity and strengthening the state, the *Kulturkampf* was deeply divisive. Bismarck was too astute politically not to recognize its effects and seek to undo the damage. From the late 1870s he found some basis for cooperation with conservative Centre Party politicians on economic issues; and in sanctioning the slow dismantling of the *Kulturkampf* legislation from the mid-1880s onwards he undoubtedly hoped that, with the removal of the most blatant grievances, the Centre Party might eventually wither and disappear. But German Catholics never forgot or forgave the chancellor for the *Kulturkampf*: the Centre Party remained hostile to the government on a wide range of issues, even if its stance softened after 1890. The struggle left deep and lasting scars on German society, and the Centre Party continued to be a powerful force in German politics until Hitler's accession to power in 1933.

In the late 1870s Bismarck shifted his attention away from political Catholicism and launched an assault on the nascent German socialist movement. Like German Catholics, Social Democrats were branded and persecuted as 'internal enemies', this time because they preached international class solidarity rather than national loyalty and sought to 'infect' the working class masses who otherwise—Bismarck believed—had monarchist sympathies. After two assassination attempts on Kaiser Wilhelm I in 1878 (though there was no evidence of socialist involvement in them), Bismarck supported the introduction of an Anti-Socialist Law that would effectively proscribe their organization and prevent socialists from campaigning effectively. This was an 'exceptional' law because it singled out members of one political party for persecution.

In declaring war on Social Democracy, the chancellor was also intent on undermining democratic liberalism, for left-wing liberals could never agree to such an illiberal law. Thus he used the issue of the Anti-Socialist Law in 1878 to force new Reichstag elections, which resulted in liberal losses and the eventual passage of the law by a majority of National Liberals and conservatives. Bismarck then further exploited the growing clamour for economic protectionism in 1878–79 to divide his erstwhile allies in the National Liberal Party and free himself from his years of dependence on a liberal parliamentary majority. But just as the anti-socialist legislation, which remained in force until September 1890, could not retard the growth of Social Democracy, so Bismarck could not seriously contemplate governing on any lasting basis with shifting parliamentary coalitions that excluded the majority of those most supportive of the idea of a national state. Ultimately the support of National Liberals was essential to his project: outside Prussia, they represented the only enthusiastic adherents of the imperial idea.

Bismarck launched further initiatives which he believed would promote national and social cohesion. Not all of these were successful, however. In the Reichstag elections of 1881 and 1884 the oppositional parties (including a vigorous, new, left-liberal Radical Party) were victorious, and thereafter they could effectively block many of the government's proposals. Bismarck's efforts, for example, to place the empire on a more secure financial footing were largely a failure: the Reich remained dependent on income from customs and tariffs as well as on contributions from the federal states. Throughout most of the empire's existence, the states alone had the power to raise direct taxation; over 90 per cent of the imperial budget was spent on the army (which occupied a unique position as 'a state within a state' and was answerable only to the Kaiser). Although raising tariffs on agricultural and industrial products was one way of increasing the Reich's revenue in the 1880s, in the longer term the empire became a victim of its own success, confronting a mounting deficit that could not be resolved without fundamentally changing the constitution.

One of the most innovative domestic developments in Bismarckian Germany was the introduction of social insurance legislation in the 1880s. A series of laws provided German workers with sickness, accident, and invalidity insurance as well as old age pensions. Imperial Germany became a model for other countries to follow, because these measures provided real benefits for Germany's rapidly growing working-class population. This programme of reform was supported by Bismarck because he believed it would give the lower classes a stake in the state and help to woo them away from socialism. But it proved no more successful than Bismarck's anti-socialist legislation in undercutting the appeal of the Social Democratic message to the working class. The social welfare legislation increased the power of the state, which generally became more authoritarian and interventionist in the 1880s once it no longer felt itself to be in thrall to its liberal allies. But, for a variety of reasons, Prussia and the Reich proved conspicuously unable to ameliorate many of the serious economic and social problems that confronted the urban and rural poor as Germany developed rapidly into a more urban and industrialized society in the decades after unification.

Finally, in the last years of his chancellorship, Bismarck launched campaigns against Germany's national minorities in his effort to consolidate and fortify the empire. Germanization policies were aimed above all against the Poles in Prussia's eastern provinces—a substantial minority whom Bismarck had always seen as a major threat to Prussian security. These policies were supported by the

National Liberals, who endorsed a concept of German nationality based on language and ethnicity. The measures introduced by the Prussian government involved enforcing the German language in schools, imposing German customs on the Polish population, and implementing a land purchase programme to settle Germans on land previously owned by Poles. However, as with the *Kulturkampf*, these harsh and illiberal measures were ultimately counterproductive in their effects. They mobilized the opposition of the Prussian Poles and politicized formerly loyal subjects of the monarchy. Similarly coercive policies were considered against the French-speaking population of Alsace-Lorraine in 1887 and pursued against the Danes in northern Schleswig from 1888.

The end of the Bismarckian era

Such measures undoubtedly reflected a growing climate of racism, xenophobia, and intolerance in the 1880s, fuelled in part by economic insecurities associated with the rapid transition of Germany from an agrarian to an industrial society. After the optimism and triumphalism of the empire's 'founding years', there was a perceptible shift by the 1880s to a more pessimistic and conservative era. The adoption of protectionist economic policies was a response to the slowdown of economic growth after the post-unification boom (contemporaries referred to the period from 1873 to the mid-1890s as the 'Great Depression') and to growing competition within an increasingly global market. But it was also symptomatic of a deeper political and cultural malaise. Just as the international outlook appeared bleaker than it had been in the dynamic years after unification, by 1890 even a political observer who was sympathetic to the chancellor could complain that 'a terrible miasma' was affecting all aspects of domestic policy.[10]

The ageing *Reichsgründer* who, in office, had always been a divisive rather than a unifying figure, was also increasingly perceived by a younger political generation as out of touch and an impediment to change. Liberal hopes that the accession of Crown Prince Friedrich Wilhelm might reinvigorate German political life and remove the obstacles to reform were soon dashed. Not only did the old Kaiser Wilhelm I prove far more resilient than any-one anticipated, but his son became fatally ill with cancer of the throat. Friedrich Wilhelm finally succeeded to the throne as Kaiser Friedrich III (a title which emphasized his Prussian heritage) in March 1888. He reigned, however, for a mere three months, during which time he was even more dependent on the chancellor he detested than his father had ever been.

In the end it was to be Friedrich's son, Wilhelm, who proved to be Bismarck's nemesis. When he succeeded to the throne in June 1888 at the age of twenty-nine, Wilhelm inevitably could not share the perspectives of the 'iron chancellor' who had already held high political office for almost twenty-six years. Kaiser Wilhelm II wanted to rule personally and, despite the contradictions in his personality, he sought to embody a Germany that was modern, confident, and outward-looking. He soon clashed with Bismarck, who refused to relinquish power gracefully. If the ensuing political crisis was protracted, its outcome was never in doubt. In Berlin the young and the ambitious were inevitably drawn to the 'new sun' and had high expectations of basking in its glory. By March 1890 the young Kaiser felt sufficiently emboldened to insist on the old chancellor's resignation after a final rupture between the two men. The Bismarckian era thus gave way to the Wilhelmine age. The test of the latter was to be how far the empire could prosper and live in peace with its neighbours in the absence of its creator.

---

[1] Friedrich Curtius (ed.), *Memoirs of Prince Chlodwig of Hohenlohe Schillingsfuerst*, trans. George W. Chrystal, 2 vols (London, 1906), ii. 11, journal entry of 11 May 1870.

[2] Ibid. 6, 8, entries of 23 and 27 April 1870.   [3] Ibid. 7, entry of 27 April 1870.

[4] Ibid. 11, entry of 11 May 1870.

[5] Otto von Bismarck, *Die gesammelten Werke* (Friedrichsruher Ausgabe), 19 vols in 15 (Berlin, 1924–35), vi. 120, Bismarck to Manteuffel, 11 August 1866.

[6] Speech of 9 February 1871, cited in Lothar Gall, *Bismarck: The White Revolutionary*, trans. J. A. Underwood, 2 vols (London, 1986), ii. 40.

[7] Cited in Ulrich Lappenküper, *Die Mission Radowitz. Untersuchungen zur Russlandpolitik Otto von Bismarcks (1871–1875)* (Göttingen, 1990), 506.

[8] Johannes Lepsius, Albrecht Mendelssohn-Bartholdy, and Friedrich Thimme (eds), *Die Grosse Politik der Europäischen Kabinette 1871–1914*, 40 vols in 54 (Berlin, 1922–27), ii. 153–4, 15 June 1877.

[9] Bismarck, *Die gesammelten Werke*, xi. 431, speech of 9 February 1876.

[10] Rudolf Vierhaus (ed.), *Das Tagebuch der Baronin Spitzemberg. Aufzeichnungen aus der Hofgesellschaft des Hohenzollernreiches* (Göttingen, 1960), 271–2, 10 March 1890 (*sic*). The correct dating of this diary entry appears to be 20 March 1890.

Wilhelmine Germany

Mark Hewitson

Royal Highness, a 360-page novel by Thomas Mann about artistic detachment and princedom, also functioned as a gentle satire of life in Germany at the turn of the century. The work is set in an unnamed German state of 80,000 square kilometres and one million inhabitants, modelled on the Grand Duchy of Baden. The plot turns on the love affair between the younger prince, Klaus Heinrich, who is returning to his family birthplace, and Imma Spoelmann, the daughter of an American millionaire.[1] Mann's novel provides an intriguing portrait of a local, state-bound, inward-looking society, and of the archaic oddities of the etiquette-ridden, ineffective, parochial 'high politics' of the royal court and government. It stands in marked opposition to his brother Heinrich's satire of Wilhelmine Germany in *The Loyal Subject*, published in 1918 as part of a trilogy on the German Empire. Heinrich portrays a world in which local politics has been undermined by nationalism and where the modern, powerful, industrial imperialism of the 'Kaiser' has replaced traditional liberalism. By contrast, Thomas depicts a quaint and apolitical setting—one he had already used in his first novel *Buddenbrooks* (1901) and which he explored further in *Reflections of an Unpolitical Man* (1918) and 'Lübeck as a Spiritual Way of Life' (1926).

The substance of the brothers' disagreement about the nature of Wilhelmine Germany continues to divide historians in the wake of the *Sonderweg* debate, which reached its high point in the 1980s. Revisionist historians, challenging the notion of a 'special path' (*Sonderweg*) for Germany, have tended to stress the modernity of Wilhelmine society, culture, and even politics. The year 1890 is seen as an important watershed, not because Kaiser Wilhelm II succeeded in establishing a 'personal regime' but because the modernizing effects of industrialization, urbanization, social transformation, and democratization were felt more fully after Bismarck's dismissal. During the Wilhelmine era the problems and potential of industrial production, migration to cities, and changing means of communication became impossible to ignore. Politics changed with the advent of extra-parliamentary leagues and new forms of party organization, pioneered above all by the German Social Democratic Party (SPD) and the Catholic Centre Party. As the idea of a single lesser-German (*kleindeutsch*) nation state came to seem more and more natural to those reaching adulthood after 1871, the balance between the Reich ministries in Berlin and the federal states also evolved, with implications for the polity as a whole. What is more, the impact of national unification could be felt in the realm of foreign policy: the government, press, and public opinion were more inclined to debate the imperatives of national interest and power politics at a time when the old European state system was threatening to collapse. Yet what would replace the traditional precepts of German diplomacy? What system of government would be adopted at home and with what degree of legitimacy? Which parties or coalitions would become dominant and with what consequences? What would be the effects of accelerating economic and social change, and which policies could be framed to mitigate or harness those effects? These were the questions facing contemporaries, and they continue to confront historians.

Social traditions and conflicts in a nervous age

Arguably the most pressing of all these questions concerned the transformation of Germany's economy. The timing and impact of this transformation were—and remain—contentious. Contemporary commentators, including conservative ones, were certain that the Wilhelmine era was characterized by constant change and upheaval. Max Weber and Georg Simmel, two scholars who founded the new academic discipline of sociology in this era, were both convinced that fundamental changes had occurred within modern capitalist economies, and that these changes had profound political, social, cultural, and psychological ramifications. Notwithstanding their different approaches and outlooks, both sociologists were acutely sensitive to the immediacy and force of alienation. They were also aware of the threat that the incursions of modern capitalism and the broader socio-economic transformation it fueled posed to the integrity of individuals, their values, and the legitimacy of politics and systems of government.

With the crystallization of new classes and the emergence of new social conflicts, the rift between the working classes and the rest of society was reinforced by myths of urban squalor and criminality, even of imminent proletarian revolution. This rift had led to the anti-socialist legislation in 1878, it underpinned most of the government's social policies from the 1880s onwards, and it gave rise to a series of anti-socialist alliances among the middle and right-wing parties after 1890. Yet it is easy to exaggerate the destabilizing effects of such changes. The fault-lines produced by class conflict were bisected and complicated by older divisions based on religion, ethnicity, and region. In contrast to much of the historical scholarship of the 1960s and 1970s, historians now argue that the fear of socialism among middle-class Germans did not lead to a defensive coalition (*Sammlung*) of industrialists and agrarians, did not produce a successful diversionary foreign policy of 'social imperialism', and did not 'feudalize' the bourgeoisie (*Bürgertum*) by compelling it to imitate the landowning nobility. Rather, broad sections of the bourgeoisie became increasingly wealthy, confident, urbane, educated, and likely to marry within their own class. As they did so they also became more politically active in their localities and in political parties and leagues. In many respects, the bourgeoisie's striving for honours, their self-discipline, their eagerness to serve in the reserve officer corps, their codes of honour, their insistence on social distinctions, and their frequently authoritarian managerial style were all indicative of their independence and support for the state on their own terms—not, that is, a sign of their subordination to another class. In this way the German bourgeoisie achieved a significant measure of internal cohesion.

The framework of most Wilhelmine Germans' daily lives remained similar to that of their parents and grandparents. The shift from a rural and agricultural society to an urban and industrial one proceeded slowly. Agriculture employed almost 1.4 million more people in 1907 than it had in 1871, continuing the trend of the previous forty years. Relatively, the industrial sector was growing more quickly; yet the majority of Germans continued to work alone or in factories and workshops employing fewer than fifty people. Even though the guilds had lost many of their earlier privileges, Germany retained a bewildering variety of artisanal enterprises. Moreover, family businesses had by no means died out, and neither had a culture of domesticity and sentimentality based on the family. The family was the basic unit of authority, welfare, and income. Indeed, in 1900, the family was as central to both civil society and the private sphere as it had been a century earlier. Familiar structures of belief and identity persisted in two other areas: within each of Germany's confessional communities and in its localities. In both instances such continuity reinforced contemporaries' sense of stability. Local government was still entrusted with many powers and competencies: it changed much less markedly than higher tiers of administration and politics in the second half of the nineteenth century. Churches meanwhile remained prominent in shaping people's belief and informing their attitudes and allegiances: a high level of religious observance characterized many regions, despite secularization. When we consider the cumulative effect of these relatively stable social ties and markers of identity, we should not be surprised to find that many Germans wanted to preserve them as a means to insulate themselves from the turmoil and transience of the big cities, avant-garde artistic movements, and sensationalist journalism. 'Politics' in a more narrow sense—because it, too, remained open to traditional and local influences—was shaped by similar elements of order and continuity.

Domestic politics

Max Weber put forward the case—which was subsequently adopted by many historians—that there existed a disjunction between politics and economics in Imperial Germany: the bourgeoisie was economically strong but politically weak. However, Weber's claim

fails to explain either the evolution of Wilhelmine politics or the
rise and fall of the imperial state. The Reich, of course, was a
haphazard construction. At times it failed to function effectively.
In particular, the role of the Kaiser was a continuing source of
confusion and consternation after the accession of Wilhelm II
and Bismarck's dismissal. Wilhelm explicitly wished to 'shoulder'
more of the chancellor's functions himself.[2] But the Kaiser was
not the only source of confusion or impediment to reform. The
relationship between Prussia and the Reich remained uncertain
and contentious; the party system was fragmented and prone to
blockages; and extra-parliamentary nationalist organizations such
as the Pan-German and Navy Leagues seemed by 1911 to be beyond
government influence or control. To this list we can add the spectre
of a revolution from the left or a *coup d'état* (*Staatsstreich*) from
the right: the latter was considered by Prussian Minister President
Botho zu Eulenburg in 1894 and by the coterie around Crown
Prince Wilhelm in 1913. The threat from both the far Right and the
far Left persisted until 1918.

The vast majority of Germans did not think like Eulenburg or
the crown prince, however. 'Those crazies who are still talking
about the necessity of a *Staatsstreich* today don't need to be taken
seriously', noted the moderate conservative historian and journalist
Hans Delbrück in 1907.[3] For most contemporaries, the legitimacy
of the German Empire was already beyond question by 1890, not
least because the regime seemed to rest on historical foundations:
even its name—the Kaiserreich—harked back to the Holy Roman
Empire of the German Nation. The apparent historical continuity
of the German Empire was underwritten by the federal principle,
with most Germans agreeing that the continued existence of strong
individual states was essential to the functioning of the empire.
Federal states such as the kingdoms of Bavaria and Saxony, together
with German municipalities, accounted for 65 per cent of public
expenditure in 1913. They carried out most of the functions of the
'state'. Those functions included the collection of direct taxes, the
provision of schools and universities, the granting of subsidies to
the churches, the administration of poor relief, the maintenance
and regulation of the judiciary and the police, and the establishment
of rules governing politics, legislation, and government. They also
operated large state-run enterprises such as railways and mines. For

their part, the municipalities shared responsibility for poor relief and education, but they also looked after urban planning, public hygiene, hospitals, water, gas and electricity supply, and local roads and transport. Throughout the Wilhelmine era, traditional authorities at these local and federal tiers of government provided much of the infrastructure of public life and ensured a considerable degree of political continuity.

At the highest level of government, the existence of a German nation state seemed to guarantee such continuity. The nation was legitimate and sacred, so that the citizen would give his life for it, declared Hans Delbrück in 1913, betraying the extent to which the 'national mission' had become a personal vocation for many educated Germans. The political institutions of the empire had quickly acquired a national aura which, by the 1890s at the latest, seemed to be self-evident to all parties. Thus, it proved impossible to isolate Catholics and Social Democrats any longer as 'enemies of the Reich', as they had been when the foundations of the German Empire appeared less secure in the 1870s and 1880s. All political parties after 1890 competed to demonstrate their national credentials. Thus, left liberals were ready to participate between 1907 and 1909 in the Bülow Bloc, which was predicated on a defence of Germany's colonies (the Bloc was formed after the Centre Party had criticized the corruption of the Reich's colonial administration). The government's decision to distance itself from the powerful Centre Party was anomalous and soon regretted, however, because by 1907 the Centre's leaders had already spent 'a decade of efforts aimed at allaying passions and overcoming the confessional division by emphasizing national unity'.[4] Even in the Social Democratic Party, imperialists, revisionists, and some centrists—including the party leader August Bebel—repeatedly affirmed their 'patriotism'. Most political debate between 1890 and 1914 therefore focused on the improvement of material conditions rather than on any full-scale attempt to overturn the regime. To a large extent, Imperial Germany's political system was protected and preserved because it was closely associated with a popular fatherland.

Increasingly, the political institutions of the Reich gained legitimacy on their own account as organs of a 'constitutional' system of government. The system functioned adequately until 1918. It had many shortcomings, of course. Leo von Caprivi, the first chancellor of the Wilhelmine era and an advocate of more liberal trade policies, was forced to resign in 1894 after a stand-off with the advocates of a more reactionary and protectionist course. Chlodwig zu Hohenlohe-Schillingsfürst, the second chancellor, was seventy-five years old when he assumed office: he served, by his own admission, as a 'straw man' from 1897 onwards.[5] Bernhard von Bülow, his successor, frequently acted like a courtier rather than a responsible minister, and Theobald von Bethmann Hollweg, chancellor from 1909 to 1917, often complained that he was hamstrung by Germany's political parties, threatened from the right by mass-membership extra-parliamentary organizations such as the Navy League and the Army League, as well as from the left by the SPD, which had become the single largest party in 1912 with 110 Reichstag seats (of a total of 397) and thirty-five per cent of the popular vote. Notwithstanding such destabilizing factors, however, there was considerable continuity in the Reich's highest political offices. Caprivi's chancellorship lasted four years, Hohenlohe's six, Bülow's nine, and Bethmann's eight. Arthur von Posadowsky-Wehner served ten years as state secretary of the interior (1897–1907), and Alfred von Tirpitz no fewer than nineteen years as state secretary of the navy (1897–1916).

Party support remained constant enough to allow the Reich government to function without an immediate fear of deadlock—at least most of the time. The 'state-supporting parties' maintained a relatively steady share of seats in the Reichstag, despite a gradually shrinking share of the popular vote: the Conservatives oscillated between 13.5 and 18 per cent of seats during the period 1890–1907, the Imperial and Free Conservative Party between 5 and 7 per cent (1890–1907), the National Liberals between 11 and 13 per cent (1890–1912), and the Centre Party between 23 and 27 per cent (1890–1912). These parties were thus able to provide majorities in the period between 1890 and 1906, when they formed the backbone of support for the government in the Reichstag. Although the Conservatives flirted with a 'national opposition' to Bethmann Hollweg after disagreements over a reform of the Reich's finances and over foreign policy, they—like all parties except the SPD—continued to vote for a range of government bills between 1909 and 1914. In June 1913, the Social Democrats supported the administration, almost without precedent, in voting for the introduction of a capital gains tax: this opened up the prospect of future cooperation on the model of Baden's 'Grand Bloc'. In these circumstances, despite serious crises, it is misleading to talk of political 'stalemate' in the final peacetime years of the Wilhelmine era.

The legislative and administrative record of the various tiers of government in Germany compare favourably with those of other states. Tariffs and taxes increased during the Wilhelmine era in order to fund higher spending on the military, administration, and social insurance; yet the overall tax burden remained low. In 1891, Prussian Finance Minister Johannes Miquel introduced a progressive income tax in Prussia—'the clearest and most coherent regime' in Europe, according to the *Frankfurter Zeitung*. This tax exempted earnings of less than 900 Marks per year and rose incrementally for higher incomes, with a top rate of 4 per cent—low by comparison with the post-war era—for an annual income of more than 100,000 Marks.[6] Further reforms soon followed. At the level of the Reich, reliance on indirect taxes produced a shortfall of revenue that became increasingly acute after 1900: construction of the navy was the single greatest strain after that point. The principal reform here came in 1909 with a new tax on stocks and increased taxes on consumer goods. In 1913 a capital gains tax was introduced, as was a one-time-only 'defence contribution' of 996 million Marks. Although carrying much larger debts than in the Bismarckian era, the fiscal regimes of the Reich, the federal states, and the municipalities—like the German economy as a whole—were sufficiently viable, flexible, and progressive to find strong political support at home and admiration from abroad.

The same could be said of German social policies. The sociologist Albert Schäffle wrote that by the 1890s the term *Sozialpolitik* was one of the most used—and abused—words in the German language. 'Social policy' still included the provision of poor relief by municipalities, but since unification it had been extended to include modern necessities such as urban planning, education, social insurance, and large-scale bureaucracies. In most of these areas, the Wilhelmine system seems to have coped. Schools and universities introduced 'modern' curricula and the number of students continued to rise. Many of Germany's cities, including

Berlin, were seen to be models of planning, providing essential services: underground sewers, waterworks, a communal gas supply, electricity generating stations, and electric trams. Between 1871 and 1911, municipalities helped to quadruple the number of hospital beds. From the 1890s onwards, they began to employ doctors as health inspectors, with ever-tighter enforcement of regulations after the turn of the century. At the same time they set up employment bureaux and unemployment insurance schemes. Such advances were supplemented by the empire's own old-age pensions and accident and sickness insurance schemes, which were expanded in 1900 (in the case of accident insurance) and 1903 (sickness insurance) to cover 15 million and 28 million workers, respectively. They were accompanied by legislation prohibiting child labour in factories (1891), night shifts for women and youths (1891), work on Sunday (1891), and child labour on building sites (1903). Other protective measures included employment tribunals for trade as well as factories (1904), an eight-and-a-half hour workday for miners (1905), and an insurance scheme for widows and orphans, established in 1911.

Social policy was underpinned by the protection of civil liberties. Censorship still existed: for example, theatre scripts had to be submitted to the police before they were performed. But few books or plays were banned outright. Indeed, in 1899, when the Conservative and Centre parties added clauses to a government bill on prostitution, which penalized authors of literature that 'grossly injured feelings of decency', liberals successfully rallied against the Lex Heinze in defence of the 'freedom of culture'. *Lèse majesté*—the crime of insulting the Kaiser—was occasionally invoked, leading, for instance, to the three-month incarceration of the left-liberal academic Ludwig Quidde in 1896 for (implicitly) comparing Wilhelm II to the notorious Roman emperor Caligula; but the law was restricted to cases of clear intent in 1908 at the insistence of left liberals. After the Anti-Socialist Law was allowed to lapse in 1890, subsequent attempts were made by the Prussian and Reich governments, spurred on by Wilhelm II, to enact repressive legislation: the Anti-Revolution Bill of 1895 and the Hard Labour Bill of 1899 are good examples. But these measures, too, were thwarted by liberals and the Centre Party. Despite the efforts of reactionaries to increase repression in the 1890s, civil liberties were actually extended. A new Reich Association Law in 1908 unified the existing patchwork of state legislation.

It is true that obstacles to democratization remained. The liberal and Social Democratic campaign to reform the three-class suffrage for elections to the Prussian Landtag failed in 1910. Indeed, in Saxony, liberals and conservatives who feared the growing vote of the SPD in their own Landtag replaced its existing universal manhood suffrage with an indirect three-class suffrage in 1896, which in turn was replaced by a system of plural voting in 1909. In southern Germany, however, where Social Democracy consti- tuted less of an electoral threat, the movement was in the other direction, towards more democratic laws and practices. In the Kingdom of Württemberg, the state-supporting left-liberal Peo- ple's Party oversaw sweeping constitutional changes in 1906: these scrapped remaining 'corporate' voting rights in favour of univer- sal manhood suffrage—and even proportional representation in some constituencies—and reformed the upper house and local councils. In the Grand Duchy of Baden, the introduction of direct, equal, and secret voting in 1904 led to the formation of a 'Grand Bloc' of National Liberals, left liberals, and Social Democrats, which was designed to prevent a Centre Party majority. In Bavaria the introduction of direct voting and the drawing of fairer con- stituency boundaries in 1906 produced consistent Centre Party majorities and the imposition of a Centre Party government in 1912. At the level of the Reich, universal manhood suffrage, which was still rare in Europe, remained in place, even though the gov- ernment refused to redraw constituency boundaries. When the Reichstag in 1911 debated a new political structure for the imper- ial territory (*Reichsland*) of Alsace-Lorraine—until then it was a military protectorate—the parties (including the SPD) opted for a constitutional system that included a direct, secret vote based on universal manhood suffrage. In other words, although less democratic models were available, a majority of Reichstag deputies decided to introduce a system very similar to the one in place at the imperial level since 1871.

Contemporaries were aware of—and complained about—the empire's shortcomings. The constitution of 1871 did not satisfac- torily regulate or control the actions of the Kaiser, and it did not keep the army fully in check. The *Daily Telegraph* Affair erupted in 1908 after Wilhelm II had claimed in an interview that most Germans were anti-British. All parties except the Free Conservatives criticized the actions of the Kaiser in the Reichstag. Five years later, in 1913, the ill-defined relationship between the military and other organs of state was revealed during the Zabern Affair, when the army backed the decision of a young lieutenant to imprison the inhabitants of an Alsatian garrison town. A Reichstag vote of censure was launched against Chancellor Bethmann Hollweg, who refused to criticize the army; but no legislation was enacted to back up such censure. These failures to rein in monarchical and military autonomy did not mean that either the army or the Kaiser could act with impunity. The Reichstag continued to exercise its right to approve military budgets and to discuss military affairs and court scandals. Nevertheless, both the Kaiser and the military establishment continued to exert influence in another realm of governance where German failures were particularly salient to contemporaries: the conduct of foreign policy.

World empires and European politics

The chancellor and the Foreign Office, despite the interference of the monarch and the army, remained in overall control of the empire's foreign affairs. Thus Wilhelm II, even at his most impetuous—such as when he issued a 'blank cheque' to Austria-Hungary on 5 July 1914—admitted that 'he could give no definite answer before having taken counsel with the Imperial Chancellor'.[7] The monarch's uncharacteristic hesitancy in this instance was not merely the result of his weakened position after the *Daily Telegraph* Affair; Wilhelm was also acknowledging that after numerous voltes-face in the realm of foreign policy he needed the backing of the chancellor and the Foreign Office. Such constraint, in turn, limited the influence of the military, which relied on direct access to the monarch to influence policy-making. Correspondingly, cries of frustration from war ministers and Chiefs of the General Staff were common during the Wilhelmine years, as the generals often had to defer to the more peaceful political imperatives of civilians in the Foreign Office and chancellery. Even in the heat of the July crisis, the bellicose war minister Erich von Falkenhayn refused to oppose Chancellor Bethmann Hollweg: as Falkenhayn put it, 'it is his [Bethmann's] task to determine policy, and he is not to be disturbed in this by military advisors'.[8] Despite the precariousness of their position, Germany's civilian government leaders continued to make foreign policy.

In addition to interference from the army and the Kaiser, statesmen faced two major sets of difficulties: first, the increasing involvement of parties, press, and public opinion in foreign affairs; and second, uncertainty about Germany's role in a changing system of international relations. The apparent oscillations of German diplomacy were largely a consequence of such circumstances. The growing power of the empire and clashes between Austria-Hungary, Germany, and Russia in the Balkans militated against the older Bismarckian policy of maintaining alliances with both Vienna and St Petersburg. Germany's increasingly dominant position on the Continent, its unwillingness to cede Alsace-Lorraine, and the pursuit of German and Austrian ambitions in southeast Europe all provoked anxiety and anger in Paris, St Petersburg, and London. These fears were heightened by Germany's rush to acquire colonies and a strong navy, as policy-makers strove to attain the world empire and world-power status that seemed necessary to them in an age marked not only by British and French imperialism but also by Russian, American, and Japanese expansion.[9]

The contradictory pressures exerted by political parties and public opinion added to the confusion of policy-making. Different protagonists sought the backing of powerful constituencies and were swayed by popular fears of encirclement, world empires, and war. Thus State Secretary for Foreign Affairs Alfred von Kiderlen-Wächter invited Heinrich Class, the leader of the Pan-German League, to discussions of government policy during the Second Moroccan Crisis of 1911, only to see his attempt to enlist 'nationalist' support backfire when Class and other members of the far Right criticized Germany's acceptance of French 'compensation' in the Congo. By contrast, the majority of political parties and many sections of popular opinion acted as a brake on policy-makers, thwarting their efforts to pursue an aggressive policy of brinkmanship on the European mainland. Although prepared to go to war at the beginning of the First Moroccan Crisis in 1905, Chancellor

Bülow realized by 1906 that neither the German public nor parliament wanted to have anything to do with a war over Morocco. Similarly, after the Second Moroccan Crisis, Bethmann was certain that war for a piece of the Sus or Congo would have been a 'crime' in the eyes of the public. Leaving aside radical nationalists and others on the far Right, it appeared to most parliamentarians, newspaper editors, and the groups they spoke for, that German power politics and expansionism—both widely perceived to be essential components of diplomacy—had to be pursued in such a way as to avoid all but the most 'necessary' or 'defensive' wars. 'Much is now said of the possibility of war', noted one contributor to a Catholic journal at the height of militarist agitation in August 1913, 'but the great majority has no intention of fighting except in self-defence.'[10] The far Right nevertheless continued to call for expansion and war. Thus, political parties and the public were more agitated and more divided by the major questions of foreign policy during the decade or so before the First World War than they had been during the Bismarckian era, creating confusion at home and abroad.

Germany's 'world policy' (*Weltpolitik*) and battleship building after 1896 focused the public's attention—and that of other great powers—on the consequences of official recklessness and aggression. The focus of the clashes was still Continental Europe, since Germany's main military lever remained the army, which was believed by civilian policy-makers to be strong enough successfully to wage a two-front war against France and Russia. 'We did not plunge into world politics, we grew, so to speak, into our task in that sphere, and we did not exchange the old European policy of Prussia and Germany for the new world policy,' wrote Bülow, the architect of *Weltpolitik*, just before the outbreak of the First World War: 'our strength today is rooted, as it has been since time immemorial, in the ancient soil of Europe.'[11] Accordingly, Bülow and Admiral Tirpitz devised the notion of a 'danger zone', envisaging the careful construction of an imperial navy that would eventually be powerful enough to deter Britain from entering a war against Germany. This notion was underpinned by the so-called 'hostage theory', which advocated an attack against France as a means of influencing British policy and as compensation for the possible confiscation of German colonies and shipping by Britain in the event of an Anglo-German war. After 1909, Bethmann overturned his predecessors' policy, seeking an Anglo-German détente. But the kernel of his strategy remained the use of military force on the European mainland. 'Germany can only pursue a strong policy in the sense of world policy if it remains strong on the Continent,' the chancellor told Reichstag deputies in November 1911.[12] Throughout the Wilhelmine period German statesmen toyed with the idea of alliances and rapprochements with Russia, Britain, and France—this was true even during the July crisis itself. They also continued to hope that the plausible *threat* of a Continental war against the Entente powers would suffice to force territorial concessions from their opponents, win prestige, and otherwise achieve Germany's goals. But in the end their policies were always based on a willingness to accept a Continental war and the belief that the odds of winning it stood in Germany's favour. This policy of brinkmanship became more pronounced after 1900, when the idea of France's 'decline' became widely accepted and when Russia's military and domestic weaknesses—verging on collapse—were revealed by defeat in the Russo-Japanese war of 1904–5 and the outbreak of revolution in 1905.

As Germany attempted to stake a claim in Morocco in 1905, Chancellor Bülow initially seems to have countenanced the risk of war. Friedrich von Holstein, the chancellor's closest foreign-policy advisor, told a fellow diplomat privately that it was vital not to shrink back even from 'the ultimate step'. Three years later, after Holstein's removal from office, Bülow again risked war during the Bosnian annexation crisis in 1908. The chancellor was convinced that Germany had to stand at Austria's side, 'even at the risk of war'. Bülow's successor, Bethmann Hollweg, was equally certain that this was the way to conduct foreign policy in 1911, when a gunboat was sent to Agadir to reassert Germany's right to exert influence in Morocco. On this occasion the chancellor got his foreign secretary drunk in order to find out what his ultimate aim was. When he discovered that Kiderlen wanted war, he agreed that a conflict might be necessary. Throughout the decade before 1914—even during the Balkan wars when Bethmann strove for peace—German statesmen admitted that they were prepared to pursue a policy of 'utmost risk'.

Most parties and much of the public had consistently opposed such a risk.[13] By July 1914, however, such attitudes had changed.

Russia had become the principal enemy of the Reich, as demonstrated by the war scare in the spring of 1914. Russia was also the bugbear of the German Left—the archetype of an 'autocratic' and 'barbaric' regime. As Russia had rearmed after 1905 and had rattled sabres with Austria-Hungary and Germany in the Balkans, centre-left public opinion became more wary of St Petersburg's intentions. Most right-wing publications were sympathetic to Russia's dynastic heritage, its undemocratic political system, and its influential nobility; yet they too accepted the possibility of war. Bethmann Hollweg and the Foreign Office therefore knew that, if necessary, they could use the menace of a barbaric, unpredictable Russia to orchestrate a war that would appear to be 'defensive'.[14] Bethmann did not desire war in July 1914. Rather, he aimed at a successful act of brinkmanship. Unlike earlier crises, however, this time the chancellor knew that he would not be prevented from taking the 'ultimate step'.

At critical stages of the July crisis, Bethmann demonstrated the *offensive* nature of his strategy in a number of ways: by issuing a 'blank cheque' to Austria on 5 July; by formulating a deliberately harsh ultimatum to Serbia on 23 July; by attempting to localize the conflict so that it remained one between Serbia and Austria alone, thereby ensuring an Austrian victory; and by following only a conditional, eleventh-hour policy of conciliation between 29 and 31 July. Faced with delays in the Austrian capital Vienna, Germany pushed its ally into a quick, decisive, and aggressive action against Serbia, which, it hoped, would be accepted by the Entente as a fait accompli. German policy-makers differed from most of their counterparts in other countries by their willingness to contemplate a war in Europe's centre rather than on its periphery, in the Near East, or overseas. This policy was supported by most Reichstag parliamentarians and journalists in July 1914 because it unfolded against a background of longstanding enthusiasm for armaments, *Realpolitik*, and diplomatic attempts to break out of what German statesmen and radical nationalists called Germany's 'encirclement'. Thus Germany's bid for a quick, relatively cheap diplomatic success was portrayed to those at home as a war of national defence, though it was nothing of the sort. Then, as soon as the conflict had begun, another question became paramount: to what extent would public support—already fragile and conditional—survive the horror of industrial slaughter on two fronts?

The First World War

The solidarity and patriotism of the 'August days', after Germany's declaration of war on Russia on 1 August 1914, took most observers by surprise, obscuring the divisions and disagreements of the pre-war era. 'I have experienced such a physical and moral condition of luminosity and euphoria two or three times since, but never with that sharpness and intensity', recalled the writer Carl Zuckmayer.[15] However, the conflict became a war of attrition, dragging on for four years and straining Germany's resources and testing the steadfastness of its citizenry. By 1918, over 2 million German soldiers had been killed and over 4.1 million wounded. The psychological rupture that the experience of trench warfare injected into the lives of most conscripts was matched by a growing political rift between the fighting front, where soldiers felt abandoned and misunderstood, and the home front, which was believed by many soldiers to be characterized by indifference, profiteering, revolution, or treason. In fact, life became harder at every turn for the vast majority of the population. Severe malnutrition, which was common from the 'turnip winter' of 1916–17 onwards, was probably responsible for 750,000 deaths. Real wages fell, especially those of white-collar workers and functionaries, many of whom also lost savings. Rumours of war atrocities, enemy advances, criminality, female immorality, and economic and political corruption added to contemporaries' feelings of personal loss and social crisis. The efforts of the state to keep such feelings in check—through censorship, rationing, and increased social welfare—frequently backfired. Many government measures to secure manpower and material gave the impression of collusion between the authorities, big business, and organized labour. State intervention increased massively, but so did state indebtedness.

The political effects of psychological trauma and socio-economic change were visible by 1916, after the German failure at the Battle of Verdun. A growing number of voices began to call for a negotiated peace, rather than the complete victory and large-scale annexations favoured by the Right, the military, and some sections of big business and the government. From October 1916 onwards, left liberals and Social Democrats were able to put forward their views in the Reichstag and—within limits—in the press. From the summer of 1917 onwards, they were joined by most deputies in the Centre Party who, like Matthias Erzberger—a former annexationist—had been persuaded to change position on the war after hearing news about how badly the war was going for Austria-Hungary. By July 1917, these parties, which commanded a majority in the Reichstag, had passed a Peace Resolution, despite the opposition of Bethmann and the Army Supreme Command: 'The Reichstag strives for a peace of understanding and the permanent reconciliation of the peoples. Such a peace is inconsistent with forced acquisitions of territory and political, economic, or financial oppression.'[16] The Right, in response, became more radical, founding the German Fatherland Party in September 1917. A similar tendency could be observed in the sphere of domestic affairs. But here the parties of the centre and the Left enjoyed the support of Bethmann, who persuaded a reluctant Kaiser in the Easter Message of 1917 to offer reform of the Prussian three-class suffrage and initiate constitutional reform after the war had ended.

As the costs of war and its human misery mounted, hope slowly faded for a breakthrough at sea—the Battle of Jutland in 1916 did not undermine Britain's command of the seas—or on land, with the failure of Erich Ludendorff's offensive on the Western Front in the spring of 1918. Political positions became both more entrenched and more extreme. What is remarkable, however, is the durability of the empire's social and political fabric in such circumstances. Army rule was more or less accepted for the duration of the conflict, but mainly because the imposition of a genuine military dictatorship seemed unlikely. Even under the 'state of siege', the government retained the right to fashion legislation via the Federal Council. Regular sessions of the Reichstag had been temporarily suspended, but that body reconvened at six-month intervals to discuss the budget; it also established a structure of standing committees to oversee the business of government from 1916 onwards. That the Reichstag enjoyed popular legitimacy was demonstrated in December 1916 when the army chose to put the Auxiliary Service Law—perhaps the most important piece of wartime legislation—before the lower house rather than introduce measures by decree.

In the meantime, Chancellor Bethmann Hollweg's predicament had become more precarious. Now he had to mediate between the parties and the Reichstag, on the one hand, and both Wilhelm II and the military, on the other. Yet he still had direct access to the monarch and was able to balance the various organs of state, as he had done in peacetime. Bethmann was forced to resign in July 1917 because he lost support on both sides: in this case, the majority of the Reichstag, the Army Supreme Command, and a wavering Kaiser. His successor, the Prussian bureaucrat Georg Michaelis, was ousted by the reformist majority of the Reichstag in November 1917; he was followed by the Centre Party politician Georg von Hertling, who was guaranteed stronger party backing but did not prevail either. The Centre Party, the National Liberals, and the Conservatives supported the new chancellor, Prince Max von Baden, and his effort to preserve constitutional monarchy after the Supreme Command informed the Kaiser at the end of September 1918 that the war was lost and advised him to sue for peace. Thus the old system was replaced by a parliamentary regime on 3 October. Even at this point, though, the German Empire survived until 9 November, when, after a month of mutinies and revolution, the birth of the German Republic was declared. The word 'Reich' continued to be used in the constitution and public law throughout the Weimar era. If Germany had won the war or had negotiated a peace settlement before October 1918, it is unlikely that the German Empire would have collapsed; and if the empire had survived, it is debatable whether Germany's constitutional monarchy would have been superseded by government fully responsible to parliament.

Imperial Germany's place in history

Few great-power regimes survived defeat in the First World War unscathed; some, including Italy's parliamentary monarchy, ultimately failed to survive victory. The conflict had tested the mettle of the German nation, but not in the ways that many patriotic Germans had envisaged: rather than a titanic clash whose outcome was decided by national will or racial destiny, the conflict had been a test of the Reich's institutions and of its citizens' loyalties. In both respects, it can be said that Imperial Germany dealt surprisingly well with the strains imposed by war: it avoided mass mutinies, such as those experienced by France in 1917, revolution, as in Russia in the same year, and full-scale collapse, as in Turkey, Bulgaria, and Austria-Hungary in 1918. The German army certainly witnessed increasing rates of desertion as the war reached its end, but it remained intact: discipline was maintained and demobilization took place in a relatively orderly way. Accordingly, many Germans could continue to believe that the army was undefeated on the field of battle. Only the decision to put the Imperial Navy to sea provoked widespread mutinies and political collapse. Even then, in October and early November 1918, many institutions continued to function, giving substance to Max Weber's prediction that revolutions would not affect the bureaucratic foundations of the modern state.[17]

The German Empire had in some ways become a typical modern state in Weber's sense of the term. It had created or extended large and efficient bureaucracies to carry out such necessary functions as the regulation of an increasingly complex capitalist economy; the provision of social policies to give individuals a degree of security as the economy was transformed; access to education and cultural achievement; monopolization of the means of violence at home; and consolidation of a military machine powerful enough to defend and realize the interests of the state abroad. Above all, in the twenty years since unification, Germany had been able to establish itself—in contradistinction to the Italian monarchy—as a more or less unquestioned nation state. By the time of Wilhelm II's reign, even the Pan-Germans did not believe that large German-speaking populations beyond the Empire's borders fundamentally undermined the legitimacy of the new nation state. It may be true that many observers—conservatives and liberals alike—believed the German Empire had failed to gain the world empire and domination of other spheres of interest required of a modern 'world state'. But except for a faction of left-wing socialists, very few Germans seriously contemplated challenging the existing regime.

In Weber's opinion, Germany's diplomatic failures were compounded by its inability to establish a legitimate and functional set of political institutions that took account of the processes of democratization underway since 1867. Mistakes in foreign policy were 'a fault of the system, not of the person', argued the sociologist in 1908.[18] Few of Weber's contemporaries, however—even if they shared his frustration—knew what to put in place of the constitutional monarchy, especially given the perceived shortcomings of parliamentary government in France, Italy, and elsewhere. Germany's constitutional regime seemed to protect the neutrality of the state and to guard against corruption and inefficiency. More importantly, most Germans believed that the constitutional status quo would preserve and foster Germany's federal states and its municipalities, where most 'modern' functions of the 'state' were carried out. This marriage of the constitutional and federal principles—along with the principle of nationality—gave Germans the impression of historical continuity, and it provided a kind of governmentality that was, they felt, appropriately multitiered and accountable. Of course, frictions persisted among the different levels and agencies of the 'state'. But they were not serious enough before 1918 to endanger the functioning of the system as a whole.

The dualism inherent in the contrast between Thomas Mann's parochial society and Heinrich Mann's powerful nation state worked to the German Empire's advantage. Although most Germans followed events in the capital and abroad, backed a national party or read a national newspaper, and identified with the nation state, the majority continued to live in small towns and in the countryside, and there they found distinct identities, competent governments, and modernizing administrations. When their smaller homeland (*Heimat*) seemed anachronistic—too weak, petty, or oligarchic—Germans could appeal to the power of the nation and the authority of the Reich government. Conversely, if the central government appeared overly authoritarian—too distant, ineffective, or unaccountable—German citizens could console themselves with the long-established traditions of local government and municipal improvement. More often than not, locality and nation state complemented each other during the Wilhelmine era. In this respect, both Thomas and Heinrich Mann offered satirical portrayals of Wilhelmine Germany that were ultimately misleading.

[1] T. J. Reed, *Thomas Mann: The Uses of Tradition*, 2nd edn (Oxford, 1996), 96. Thomas Mann's *Königliche Hoheit* was originally published in 1907. The opening chapters of Heinrich Mann's *Der Untertan* were serialized in the satirical journal *Simplicissimus* shortly before war broke out in 1914; the novel was then published in full in November 1918.

[2] Comment by Wilhelm II in December 1887, cited in Lothar Gall, *Bismarck: The White Revolutionary*, trans. J. A. Underwood, 2 vols (London, 1986), ii. 196.

[3] Cited in Margaret Lavinia Anderson, *Practicing Democracy: Elections and Political Culture in Imperial Germany* (Princeton, 2000), 424.

[4] Georg von Hertling, 20 December 1906, cited in Helmut Walser Smith, *German Nationalism and Religious Conflict: Culture, Ideology, Politics, 1870–1914* (Princeton, 1995), 142.

[5] Chlodwig zu Hohenlohe-Schillingsfürst, *Denkwürdigkeiten* (Stuttgart, 1931), 344.

[6] *Frankfurter Zeitung*, 16 March 1909.

[7] Szögyény-Marich to Berchtold, 5 July 1914, cited in Samuel R. Williamson and Russel Van Wyk (eds), *July 1914: Soldiers, Statesmen, and the Coming of the Great War* (Boston, 2003), 93.

[8] Falkenhayn diary, 29 July 1914, cited in Holger Afflerbach, *Falkenhayn. Politisches Denken und Handeln im Kaiserreich* (Munich, 1994), 157.

[9] Otto Hintze, 'Die Hohenzollern und ihr Werk', cited in Michael Fröhlich, *Imperialismus. Deutsche Kolonial- und Weltpolitik 1880 bis 1914* (Munich, 1994), 76.

[10] Eber Malcolm Carroll, *Germany and the Great Powers, 1866–1914* (New York, 1938), 758.

[11] Bernhard von Bülow, *Imperial Germany*, 6th edn (London, 1914), 10.

[12] Cited in Fritz Fischer, *War of Illusions: German Policies from 1911 to 1914* (London, 1975), 90.

[13] *Frankfurter Zeitung*, 29 March 1909. For the preceding citations see Konrad H. Jaravsch, *The Enigmatic Chancellor* (New Haven, 1973), 62, and Annika Mombauer, *Helmuth von Moltke and the Origins of the First World War* (Cambridge, 2001), 148.

[14] Bethmann to Tschirschky, 28 July 1914, in Imanuel Geiss (ed.), *July 1914* (London, 1967), 259.

[15] Cited in Eric Leed, *No Man's Land: Combat and Identity in World War I* (Cambridge, 1979), 39.

[16] Cited in Roger Chickering, *Imperial Germany and the Great War, 1914–1918* (Cambridge, 1998), 164.

[17] Max Weber, *Wirtschaft und Gesellschaft*, 5th rev. edn (Tübingen, 1976), 570–1.

[18] Max Weber to Friedrich Naumann, 12 November 1908, in Horst Baier *et al.* (eds), *Max Weber. Gesamtausgabe* (Tübingen, 1990), v. 695.

Economic and social developments

Brett Fairbairn

The year was about 1900; the setting, a North German city, perhaps Hamburg. The life of a young German woman illustrated the daily 'struggle for existence'—the title of her anonymous autobiography.[1] At first the 18-year-old worked in a factory folding letter paper, six o'clock in the morning to six o'clock in the evening less a one-hour lunch break, for 6 Marks a week. The low wages and a run-in with the foreman (he didn't like her telling jokes to co-workers) led her to a cardboard box factory—8 Marks a week—but she was too frail for the work and was sent away. She tried working as a governess, then in two suspenders factories, and found herself fired and unemployed because the factory owner overheard her sing a crude verse to her co-workers. 'There began now a very tough period for me', she recalled. 'Everywhere I looked for work everything was always taken, so that I was really getting desperate.' At last an acquaintance found her a job at a glassworks, 9 Marks a week, though it was brutal twelve-hour shift-work, alternating days and nights, working with red-hot bottles—work 'of a kind that should have been done by men'. The workers slaked their thirst by paying some of their wives to bring buckets of beer from a brewery. She said the work was 'rather in disrepute with the other factory girls. The work was very dirty too; and we looked like Negroes when we went home. . . . We were very ashamed to walk down the street like this, but we couldn't wash up at the factory.' 'Also,' she added, 'I felt like a convict because at the glassworks everyone had a control number at the entrance and exit.'

This young woman's life continued to follow a path shaped by her search for higher wages and reputable work, by economic insecurity, and by run-ins with petty authorities. She pushed the boundaries of gender and propriety, but only to a point. She lost her next job, in a shoe factory, when she rebuffed the sexual pressures of a functionary. After working in a candy factory and a hat factory, she ended up in a cigar factory where her co-workers, all men, smoked constantly on the job. She tried to handle the thick smoke by taking up smoking herself, until she became physically ill. Abandoning factory work, she settled into a job as a barmaid. This was a profession (she claimed) where women could earn a better income by parlaying to their own advantage the sexual advances of customers.

Here in one autobiographical passage are key elements of the new industrial world of Imperial Germany, where lives were made and remade by the dictates of markets, where the 'struggle for existence' strained social mores and expectations, and where a kind of freedom—to seek employment and to define oneself—went together in complex fashion with hierarchies and relations of power.

Class society

Germany was created as a nation state in the midst of an industrial take-off and population boom—a spectacular conjunction that helped inscribe the social and economic changes facing Germans into a national narrative. The German 'double revolution' has been viewed by historians as a source of a distinctively crisis-ridden German modernity.[2]

While there are many ways to understand the tensions of Imperial Germany, 'class' is a good place to begin. Underlying the phenomenon of class was a re-ordering of economic, social, political, and cultural institutions. Technological innovations such as factories and steam engines made powerful impressions on the contemporary imagination and became symbols of the industrial age; but behind them lay a more basic and longer term social innovation: the spreading influence of the market as a dominant social institution. The market re-ordered the lives of citizens and the structures of communities, undermining incompatible social institutions, forcing the transformation of others, and creating new ones. Inequality and hierarchy were not new. What was new was the degree to which they were removed from the spatial, moral, and social context of traditional communities and defined instead in relation to the market.

The labour of our anonymous female worker was a market commodity; she had to figure out how to sell it in a changing economy, and how to live on what she got for it. Earlier in the nineteenth century, working people had been primarily self-employed, generally in agriculture and trades. Wage labour existed, but according to one estimate, it involved only 20 per cent of the German workforce in 1846. Terms of employment were limited by custom and guilds until the last barriers to freedom of occupation were eliminated in the 1860s. As industrialization took off, wage labour on open employment markets was the norm. The vulnerability of labourers was particularly great because the labour market, initially, was a buyer's market. Population was growing and most labour involved little skill. Labourers were in many respects interchangeable, as the young woman's story indicates: one's gender or previous experience did not count for much. Employees could be laid off when not needed—or when the employer disliked their conduct. Nor should it be assumed that labour markets were fair. The young woman's wages were in most cases no better than half what a male labourer earned at the time. Employers and markets were comparatively free of externally imposed rules, but they were certainly limited by prejudices and inequities rooted in widely shared patterns of thought.

As in most countries, industrialization in Germany actually increased inequalities of wealth and income. In 1911 the top 10 per cent of the Prussian population owned 63 per cent of total personal assets. But poverty was not only relative. In the 1870s German workers struggled at meagre income levels that made it difficult to cover basic needs: when illness or unemployment struck, calamity followed. Official unemployment was low—generally in the range of 1 to 3 per cent—but this statistic does not capture many workers' experiences of insecure, short-term employment, as illustrated in our young woman's precarious career path. Basic historical evidence about the diet, housing, and health of German workers provides insight into the circumstances of industrial class society.

Working-class families spent 52 per cent of their income on food and an additional 33 per cent on necessities such as housing, heating, light, and clothing. The remainder covered all expenses for church, school, social and intellectual life, insurance, health, transportation, debt, and savings.[3] Examples from the late 1880s suggest that something like 22–8 per cent of a working-class family budget was spent on bread, though consumption of meat increased as living standards improved. The quality of housing for urban workers was another key issue. In 1910, working-class apartments in towns over 5,000 people typically had only one or two rooms within which a family of 7 or 8 people might be accommodated. Conditions were worst in Berlin, where the city's swelling population (quadrupling from 1871 to 1914 to 3.7 million) was housed in 'rental barracks' (*Mietskasernen*) that were legendary for squalor, crowding, and unsanitary and unsafe conditions. As late as 1912, 30 per cent of the Berlin population lived 5 or 6 people to a room. Often, already overcrowded families took in boarders to share their rooms or beds, out of desperate need for added income. Workers paid dearly for a short supply of substandard housing: while national figures are hard to come by, local studies indicate that rents for the cheapest apartments in industrial centres increased the most—by as much as 63 per cent in 1870–85. Under the pressures of poverty, migration, subletting, and crowding, conventional marriage relations and sexual behaviour were not always observed; nevertheless, families remained the basic units of working-class existence even under new and stressful conditions. 'Viewed in historical context', one scholar has argued, 'the proletarian family was remarkably resilient. In fact, what the middle class viewed as family breakdown and rampant immorality are probably better understood as signs of continuity.'[4]

Working-class families coped as best they could, but illnesses induced by environmental and social conditions were common. One example was tuberculosis, a disease correlated with poverty and overcrowding. Tuberculosis may have been responsible for half of all deaths among 15- to 40-year-olds in 1880. While Robert Koch identified the tuberculosis bacterium in 1882, a discovery for which he won a Nobel Prize, it was decades before effective medical treatments were in widespread use. In the meantime, living conditions and hygiene remained leading determinants of health or disease. Poverty and inequality were expressed in high rates of infant mortality: in the 1870s, 21 per cent of children died between birth and age 1. The infant death rate was highest in cities and especially for children of unwed mothers. Some urban industrial districts had infant mortality rates of nearly 40 per cent as late as 1911. Generally, however, death rates began to decline in the 1890s as wages and standards of living improved. Cities gradually became healthier places, catching up to rural areas in indexes like death rates by the last decade before the First World War.

From all this evidence we can fairly conclude that the lives of ordinary Germans, especially in cities, were grim and insecure. Workers responded by persevering, by seeking better employment, or by looking for extra income from subletting a room, fetching pails of beer, putting children to work, or whatever legal (and sometimes illegal) activities came to mind. They also created networks of mutual aid with neighbours and co-workers. In so doing they laid the foundations for a new kind of politics and for distinctive working-class forms of organization. After 1869 the Social Democratic movement was one way that the conditions of workers were brought to public attention. The SPD's candidates and newspapers appealed to and mobilized working-class support. The first formal trade unions were also created in the late 1860s, as soon as laws of association were liberalized in ways that permitted them. Their efforts to organize workers and to improve wages and working conditions were resisted, often violently, by employers and the police. They grew in numbers and formed two broad federations: the Hirsch-Duncker trade unions affiliated to left liberalism and the Free Trade Unions associated with the Social Democrats. The growth of Social Democracy spurred Chancellor Bismarck's Anti-Socialist Law, which drove the party organization underground from 1878 to 1890, though still permitting Social Democratic candidates in elections. The party continued to build a following and adopted the verbal radicalism of Marxist ideology. At the same time Bismarck developed social insurance legislation, which took shape in the early 1880s, to reduce the most pressing grievances of workers. Nor was it only the workers and the state who were organizing to address the social question. Reform-minded civic and municipal leaders, many of them from the middle rather than the working classes, founded a wide variety of institutions and services, notably non-profit housing associations that achieved special prominence in Berlin.

After 1895 the German economy turned the corner on more than two decades of deflation and uneven growth—at one time scholars referred to 1873–96 as the 'Great Depression' of the nineteenth century—and entered a prolonged period of rising prices and even more rapidly rising wages.[5] Recessions became less frequent and the demand for labour remained high. Emigration from Germany slowed dramatically, and Germany began importing migrant labour from neighbouring countries, especially Poles to work on eastern agricultural estates. By 1913 an employed worker received 80 per cent more income, in real terms, than he or she would have received for the same work in 1871. Working-class Germans also had more leisure time. The 72-hour work-week typical in 1873 shrank to 57 hours or less. And workers also benefited from the collective-security mechanisms developed in the previous decades: trade unions, collective bargaining, state-sponsored social welfare programmes, cooperative and non-profit housing and other enterprises, and municipal services.

The Social Democratic union movement, known as the Free Trade Unions, surpassed one million members in 1904 and reached a plateau of 2.6 million in the last years before the war. After 1894, they were joined by a much smaller Christian Trade Union movement organized by Catholics so that workers could represent their interests without having to join socialist organizations. As unions grew stronger, strikes grew in number, from a low of 73 in 1892 to a peak of 3,480 in 1906. The Hamburg dock strike of 1896–97 marked a significant escalation in the size and bitterness of contests between workers and employers. In 1896, for the first time, more than 100,000 workers across Germany were on strike in a single year. A smaller wave of strikes followed in 1910–13. Employers also used lockouts more frequently to force agreements by their employees, affecting as many as 227,000 workers in 1910. These numbers were not high compared to other industrialized countries. A key point is that negotiated settlements became the norm. Unionism had entered a new, highly organized phase in the 1890s, as groups of different kinds of employees, skilled and unskilled, in the same branches of industry joined together into consolidated 'industrial' unions. This development helped force employers to band together; in the early twentieth century they formed sectoral associations to represent their interests both in government circles and during bargaining with labour representatives. Implicitly employers were recognizing the right of workers to bargain collectively.[6] Employers also began to introduce workers' councils within their firms to advise on issues of importance to employees. Collective bargaining and workers' councils may have contributed to the growth of German business by creating trust and reducing uncertainty.

Workers supported unions out of material interest and a sense of common purpose, but in the process workers were also politicized. Meetings, speeches, associations, elections, and the printed word were all aspects of this intensifying working-class political culture. By the end of the nineteenth century, illiteracy had declined drastically and cheap books and newspapers were numerous. Working-class people read in their spare time, mostly for entertainment, but one of the most popular non-fiction books they read was SPD leader August Bebel's *Woman and Socialism*. From the Social Democratic press workers acquired a general set of political convictions rather than detailed Marxist analysis, but when given the opportunity to vote they declared in overwhelming numbers their identification with Social Democracy. The party's increase in popular support exceeded the growth in unionism as such. The SPD already won the largest share (20 per cent) of the popular vote in the 1890 Reichstag elections, but its vote totals—drawn largely from Protestant urban areas—continued to rise. In 1903 the party broke a symbolic barrier with 3 million votes (32 per cent), more than any German party had ever received. After a slight decline in 1907, the party broke its own record in 1912, winning 35 per cent of the popular vote and taking 110 seats in the 397-member Reichstag.

The first two pillars of the workers' movement—the party and the trade unions—were joined in the 1890s and early 1900s by a third: consumer cooperatives. Worker-owned grocery stores had existed since the 1840s as scattered individual enterprises, but now they expanded and multiplied in association with the wider Social Democratic movement.[7] Large urban cooperatives operated factories, built housing complexes, and organized women's guilds. The party, the trade unions, and the consumer cooperatives were in each case the largest or second-largest such movements in the world—only their British counterparts were in the same league. Working-class cultural and recreational clubs also multiplied in the last decade before the war, filling out a panoply of worker-run organizations dealing with almost every aspect of life. Through this dense network of organizations, workers enhanced their security and quality of life, created working-class ownership and leadership, and built a cohesive subculture in urban areas of the empire.

The organization of the Social Democratic movement was only the most obvious example of how class was constructed and became a defining feature of socio-political organization in Imperial Germany—an illustration of 'the slow formation of class lines, the "pillarization" of the Kaiserreich, and the emergence of larger political and ideological blocs'.[8] A new kind of industrial society based on organized interests took shape between the 1870s and 1914. One historian exaggerated only a little when he wrote of 'the change from the individualism of the middle class—liberal age to the group solidarity of the age of the masses'.[9] Classes in Imperial Germany took shape as communities of discourse and ideology, centred around common status and interests. Each class had its own characteristic forms of association, its own newspapers, its own political organs; and each was reproduced primarily from within. The distinct modes of organization of each class help to explain the low degree of social mobility between classes, which otherwise one would be surprised to find in a society undergoing such thorough and rapid change.

A brief survey of Germany's principal classes reveals how stratification occurred within a dynamic industrial society. The aristocracy included nobles who made their careers through public or military office as well as the numerous rural, provincial *Junkers*. Aristocrats provided the backbone of the German Conservative and Free Conservative parties, both of which supported the monarchy, Protestant religion, economic elites, and the prerogatives of the army. The educated and commercial middle classes expressed their interests and aspirations in many different ways: through associational and cultural life, philanthropy, civic leadership, and a wide array of newspapers and political parties stretching from oppositional left liberalism to patriotic National Liberalism. Peasants formed leagues and parties to represent their economic and political interests. The *Mittelstand* (lower middle class) of small artisans and shopkeepers also felt threatened by industrialization and big business. It, too, began to reorganize politically in the 1890s, with Conservative patronage from above. In all of these examples, people of roughly similar socio-economic status acted in horizontal communities of interest: classes. Each class saw the 'national interest' through the lens of its own general values and experiences, and was convinced that its own welfare was essential to Germany's future.

But it would be a mistake to view classes as tightly knit: German society was not only 'stratified', but also 'pillarized'. People identified with regions, economic sectors, cultures, genders, and confessions in ways that complicated or defied class cleavages. All in all, the late nineteenth century struck contemporaries as an era dominated by new divisions of the nation based on interests of many kinds. Historians have generally agreed with them.

From agrarian to industrial state

Arguably the most important aspect of Germany's transformation was that it went from being a predominantly rural and agrarian society to being a mainly urban and industrial one. In 1882 people employed in agriculture, together with their dependents, were still the largest segment of the population, representing 42 per cent of the total compared to 35 per cent in industry and 19 per cent in commerce, the service sector, and the professions. By 1895 industry was the largest category, and by 1907 it had reached 42 per cent—exactly where agriculture had been twenty-five years earlier. Only about one in four Germans still depended on agriculture as a livelihood in the early twentieth century. Contemporaries were well aware of these changes, and they debated, in some cases with alarm, whether Germany should be an agrarian or an industrial state: an *Agrarstaat* or an *Industriestaat*.[10] Agriculture was associated with tradition, with ostensibly harmonious and healthy communities, and with loyalty to monarchy and Christian religion. Industrial cities seemed to be centres of change, danger, disease, and opportunity as well as being, increasingly, bastions of Social Democracy. The debate between industry and agriculture was therefore also a debate about cultural values and the positive or negative character of social change, not only about economic interests. But while the overall transformation was both unstoppable and undeniable, it is easy to exaggerate its uniformity and speed. Imperial Germany was a place where new and old coexisted; where town and country, Protestant and Catholic, and different regions were all changing in different ways and at different paces. One aspect of this unevenness was that tens of millions of Germans continued to live in rural towns and villages. In 1910 about one in five Germans lived in large cities of 100,000 or more inhabitants, but twice as many still lived in small communities of fewer than 2,000.

Economic historians define industrialization as the relative decline of agriculture in the overall economy. But this does not mean that agriculture declined absolutely—indeed, the agricultural workforce *grew* after the 1870s, particularly as more women were counted on family farms and elsewhere. Nor was agriculture technologically stagnant. The same processes of market-driven transformation that remade the urban landscape also remade the rural one. Increased food production helped make it possible for Germany's total population to increase from 41 million in 1871 to 65 million in 1910—with no Malthusian subsistence crisis or massive food imports. Agricultural growth made urban growth possible. Rather than seeing industry and agriculture in opposition, perhaps it is better to characterize the shift as one from an '*Agrarstaat* with a powerful industry to an *Industriestaat* with a strong agrarian base'.[11]

The institutional basis for the transformation of agriculture in Imperial Germany had been laid decades earlier with reforms and conventions that established how land, labour, and products could be bought and sold. The result was an increasingly 'capitalist' kind of agriculture: one in which factors of production were organized using new methods and technologies in an attempt to gain the greatest possible returns from markets. In earlier periods improved output had come from increased application of inputs—cultivating more land or applying more labour—but by the later nineteenth century it was productivity improvements that were driving a steady expansion of agricultural production, about 2 per cent a year from 1850 to 1913. The changes included new crops such as potatoes and sugar beets (by 1913 potatoes took up about one-seventh of agricultural land), new rotations (gradually eliminating the old three-field rotational system, in which one-third of land lay fallow every year), application of artificial fertilizers produced by the chemical industry, and mechanization. An additional factor may have been longer hours of unpaid labour by peasant family members.

Nor did changes come only from the production side of agriculture; in the imperial era German agriculturalists learned that they were critically dependent on increasingly interconnected global markets. From the 1860s onward, railroads and steamships brought new competition from grain produced in North and South America and Australia. German producers lost what had been their largest foreign market for grain: England. These shocks were part of a wave of economic globalization. What followed was a decades-long reorientation in which producers followed three main adjustment strategies: they focused increasingly on domestic markets, they shifted from grain to other crops or to dairying or livestock, and they pressed the state to use tariffs, subsidies, and other mechanisms to protect their markets from foreign competition. Different regions, sectors, and groups of producers used these strategies in varying degrees and combinations.

The large estate owners of eastern Prussia—the aristocratic *Junkers*—were one group that adapted to hard-headed capitalist agricultural practices. Low grain prices brought financial problems for many estates, but the *Junkers* were able to compensate for economic weakness by drawing on another resource: political power. The Prussian aristocracy was uniquely influential in court, government administration, and the army. In addition, aristocratic agrarian leaders joined with others to form the Agrarian League in 1893. This was an important mass-membership political organization that could claim to speak on behalf of agriculture as a whole and that was able to put considerable pressure on political parties. Responding to agrarian interests, but also desiring tariff revenues for the empire, Bismarck instituted protective tariffs in 1879 that were increased in subsequent years. Effectively the tariffs propped up prices for wheat and rye on the German market. Production greatly exceeded demand, so the government also subsidized grain exports, beginning in 1894. Another key crop grown on large estates was sugar beets which, like grain, enjoyed heavy subsidies. By 1907 Germany became the world's largest producer of sugar with 22 per cent of the global market. Agrarian organizations portrayed tariffs, subsidies, and other government interventions as good for agriculture and good for rural Germany as a whole. Although this may have been the case, particularly in the 1880s, detailed analysis shows that the big estate owners benefited disproportionately from protectionism in the 1890s.[12]

This is not to say that small farmers did badly; they adjusted to the new economy and nearby urban markets without much need for protection. Prosperous areas of small to middling farms were found in northern, western, and southern Germany. Grains, root crops, fruits, and wine were important in many of these areas, but the big story was livestock. Dairy cattle and pigs increased greatly in importance and offered ways for small farms to produce more intensively and more profitably. These products were not protected by tariffs and did not need to be. Health regulations prohibited foreign farmers from selling pigs into Germany: a non-tariff barrier to trade. Small farms did not disappear. From 1882 to 1907 they increased in number and in the total area they farmed; it was the large farms that declined.[13] Like urban workers, small farmers combined their strength in the marketplace. They built networks of cooperatives for credit, input purchase, marketing, and processing. By the early twentieth century Germany had the largest agricultural cooperative movement in the world. The development of agricultural cooperatives was a logical response by a highly decentralized sector of the economy—more than 5.5 million farm enterprises—to the growing concentration of industry. Agriculturalists, one contemporary observer wrote, were 'exposed to the danger of helpless exploitation by the great economic powers unless they achieved solid economic combinations of their own'.[14] This assessment hit the mark. Agriculture adapted and fitted within the industrial economy.

Big business, technology, and the state

The lives of people in all German localities reflected vast and often global transformative processes. From 1871 to 1914 Germany became the world's second strongest industrial power, rivalling Britain. Germany's economic growth occurred within the transnational context of a competitive and increasingly international system, where capital flowed across borders, and countries became dependent on trade to an extent unmatched until generations later. At first, Germany's success was based on keeping production costs and wages low, importing technology, investing in research and training, and streaming financial capital into strategic, technological growth sectors. Big business, big banks, and the state played important roles in this textbook example of industrialization. In the Bismarckian era the label 'Made in Germany' was taken as a sign of cheap merchandise produced by low-quality labour, and Britain complained about what would now be called economic 'dumping'. But as Germany's economy grew and changed, it became a leader in new sectors. It began to export highly manufactured articles, supplied nearby industrializing markets in central and eastern Europe, and became a supplier of foreign investment to others.

In the period 1895–1911 output grew steadily, averaging over 5 per cent growth per year in the industrial sector. Industrialization meant overall growth, but also change and dislocation. The rise of employment in new industries—above all, in construction and metal processing—went together with the decline or stagnation of others, notably textiles, clothing, and leather trades. After railways had led the way in the early industrial take-off, it was new industries such as steel, machine tools, electrical industries, and chemicals that led in the 'second industrial revolution' in the late nineteenth century. Rapidly growing industrial empires included familiar names such as Siemens and AEG (Germany's General Electric Company) in the field of electrical engineering and BASF, Bayer, and Agfa in chemicals. They joined older firms such as the leaders in the steel industry, Krupp and Thyssen. The

Hamburg–America Line (HAPAG) and Norddeutscher Lloyd led the shipping companies.

Capital fed the expansion of these huge firms. From 1871 to 1913 capital investment in industry grew from just under 10 billion Marks to over 85 billion. Banks facilitated this process. Germany had powerful 'universal' or mixed banks that were permitted to buy and sell on stock markets in addition to collecting savings and making loans. Banks invested in firms to which they were extending credit: indeed, bank representatives voted in their shareholders' meetings and sat on their boards of directors. Banks developed long-term interdependencies with the firms they supported and helped funnel large amounts of capital into the expansion of leading firms. Different banks were prominent in different industrial sectors and geographic regions, but the growth of the Deutsche Bank (connected to Siemens, AEG, and Norddeutscher Lloyd) was particularly impressive. In 1913 five big Berlin banks controlled about 7 billion Marks of capital, and the three largest enterprises in Germany were banks. In no other country in the world did a few banks play such a large role. Contemporary Germans debated whether this concentration of financial power was good or bad. The Marxist Rudolf Hilferding wrote a book on the subject in 1909, and the Darmstädter Bank's director, Jacob Riesser, answered with a defence of the banks.[15] Historians have continued the debate. On balance, Germany's big banks probably accelerated economic growth by injecting capital into high-risk, high-growth sectors like coal, steel, transportation, utilities, and heavy engineering. At certain times, they also intervened in restructuring German businesses and facilitated the emergence of massive industrial organizations. This happened during the economic downturn of the 1870s, when the Disconto-Gesellschaft forced western German steel producers to form a cartel to reduce competition among themselves. It happened again in the 1890s, when the Deutsche Bank helped reorganize the electrical engineering sector, leading to the consolidation of the giant companies AEG and Siemens.[16]

Besides capital, two other key ingredients in German industrial growth were technology and skilled labour. Germany initially experienced the advantages and disadvantages of a second-wave industrial economy, borrowing technology from Britain and using mechanisms like state ownership and big banks to push key developments. But Germany soon caught up in terms of know-how and became a technological and scientific leader. Industrial investments in research and development, university-based science, and (particularly in the 1870s) new technical institutes (*Technische Hochschulen*), which were largely funded by industry—these all contributed. Meanwhile, Germany developed a distinctive system of training and apprenticeship, building on artisanal traditions and relationships but recreating these within modern firms and trades. The result was a well-trained, skilled workforce, but arguably also one characterized by distinctive class and workplace relationships. With less antagonism between unions and employers in skilled trades, Germany resembled Japan more than it did Britain or the United States.

It is more than a little perplexing that this distinctive combination of large enterprises, concentrated investment, vertical and horizontal consolidation, and the systematic fostering of new technology, research, and skills has been taken by many historians as a sign of German 'backwardness'.[17] According to this camp, the interlocking corporatism of big institutions constituted a highly coordinated, corporatist, 'organized capitalism' that differed fundamentally from more freewheeling, entrepreneurial kinds of capitalism such as Britain's early industrial capitalism.[18] If liberal-individualistic capitalism is considered modern, then Imperial Germany's economy was, according to this school, less modern: it appears conservative, collectivist, patronizing, and risk-averse. It is certainly true that processes of concentration and cartelization shaped German industry. Associations of large firms dominated in mining, paper, iron, and cement, and were influential in other branches. Bureaucracy, new professional hierarchies, and associated mentalities permeated the corporate world. Salaried white-collar managers predominated, rather than self-made entrepreneurs. The result was the creation of a new middle class of perhaps two million people by 1907. But were corporations, cartels, bureaucracies, and the new middle class really 'backward'? That seems a stretch. Indeed, in many of these respects, Germany seems to resemble later, twentieth-century industrial economies, more ahead of its time than backward.

The state also played a fundamental role in Germany's economic transformation. Primarily this was by supporting the market and corporate industry. The state supported the relatively free operation of market forces and ensured a socio-political climate where corporate leaders and investors could plan confidently for the future. The state unified markets and used its legislative power to safeguard private property and corporate wealth. Prior to unification in 1871 the state (especially Prussia) had defined the laws governing property, labour, contracts, corporations, and finance; it had removed trade restrictions of various kinds; it had subsidized the development of infrastructure, especially railroads; and it had invested in technology (for example, in armaments). These roles continued and were extended. The unification era brought a unified, gold-backed currency, the Reichsbank was founded as an anchor for the national financial system, and new imperial laws culminated eventually in the new Civil Code (*Bürgerliches Gesetzbuch*), which was passed in 1896 and took effect in 1900. Prussian railways were nationalized in 1878, the government subsidized canal construction, and the state also contributed to training and research institutions that supported many new industries.

Perhaps the most precocious innovation was Bismarck's initiatives in social policy, which laid a formal basis for what in the twentieth century became known as the welfare state. Bismarck's concern to limit the growth of socialism in the 1870s involved both outlawing socialist political activities and developing what we today call a 'social safety net' that would reduce workers' most severe social and economic problems. An 1883 law provided medical insurance for working-class employees through a decentralized system of health insurance cooperatives that were semi-autonomous from the state. By 1889 5.5 million workers were covered. Employers paid two-thirds of the contributions on behalf of their employees, who received free medical care and weekly payments while ill. In 1884 came an accident insurance law, this time with the employers paying 100 per cent of the cost; 13 million Germans were covered by the end of the decade. In 1889 old-age and disability pensions arrived. Workers and employers shared the funding equally, with a top-up by the state. By 1899 pensions were paid at age 70, and anyone who was too infirm to work could request disability pensions. Employers complained about the high costs of all these programmes, while Social Democrats and trade unionists pushed for improved benefits. The big gap for workers was the lack of unemployment insurance; jobless workers could look for support only from local authorities.

We should not forget the local state. Governments in towns and cities—mostly led by local elites elected on the basis of narrow suffrages—developed services for water, sanitation, policing, fire protection, and transportation. Municipal planning and services directly addressed many of the most pressing issues of urban life. Public savings banks (*Sparkassen*) belonging to municipal governments were the largest deposit institutions for the general population, holding 23 billion Marks in 1913. In that year local government activities represented 6 per cent of Germany's economy, a larger share than that of the Reich government. German cities offered modern services unsurpassed anywhere in the world.

Complex identities

Transportation and communications revolutions shaped the new empire and connected it to the wider world. Railroads, steamships, and canals carried the material goods that were the lifeblood of the new economy, while postal service, telegraphs, and mass-distribution newspapers carried the information that was its mind. But a paradox of modern communication is that, while it links together disparate regions and identities, it also creates new awareness of disparities. It does not only homogenize things. Ideas blend and mix and become hybrid, but in different ways in different places. We can see this process economically in the survival of small and medium enterprises and the persistence (even growth) of regional specialization. The cultural equivalent is the persistence of regional, ethnic, and sectarian identities. Since neither a uniform industrial economy nor a uniform German culture existed, there is good reason to ask whether we can characterize 'Germany' as just one thing.

Despite the growth of big business, the old *Mittelstand* of tradespeople and artisans survived in changing forms. Like agriculture, small business persisted, perhaps even tenaciously, alongside the leading enterprises. The *Mittelstand* has often been seen as a somewhat reactionary and anti-modern part of society, and *Mittelstand* interest groups did tend to support Conservative and nationalist policies.[19] But small businesses were a huge part of the German economy. A process of concentration was occurring in which the smallest enterprises—those with five or fewer employees—shrank from providing 60 per cent of employment in 1882 to 31 per cent in 1907; but at the other end of the scale, very large enterprises with more than 1,000 employees still made up only 5 per cent of the workforce in 1907. Most Germans (like our anonymous factory worker) worked in small to middling enterprises. A government study in 1914 concluded that, in shopkeeping, the number of small enterprises was actually increasing.[20] Small tradespeople and shopkeepers did feel pressed to adapt, but after the mid-1890s they were doing so through new organizations such as reconstituted trade guilds and cooperatives.

Regional specializations increased as industrialization took off. Distinct regional economies were found, for example, in Thuringia, where smallholders in the hills combined agriculture with forestry, and in the Kingdom of Saxony, an area of long-established crafts and small artisanal manufacturing enterprises. Areas dependent on extensive grain production, such as the Prussian east, began to decline and sent migrants to the cities, and textile centres suffered as well. Meanwhile, the Ruhr valley (in the provinces of Rhineland and Westphalia) emerged by 1880 as a distinct and powerful industrial district, eventually becoming Germany's most important industrial region. Saxony renewed its growth with new industries such as the big chemical industry centred around Halle-Merseburg and Leipzig; and Silesia, too, developed as a centre of mining and manufacturing. Late in the nineteenth century a west–east axis of new or resurgent industrial centres stretched from Lorraine through the Ruhr and central Germany, to Saxony and Silesia. Meanwhile Hamburg and Berlin expanded as commercial and manufacturing centres in the north and northeast. But even the areas that grew did not all do so in the same way. In important regions of Germany, the dominant industrial form was not big corporate businesses but rather flexible networks of small to medium enterprises. These networks were modern, competitive, and produced high-quality goods such as metalware in Remscheid and Solingen, optical equipment in Württemberg, and specialized machinery on the left bank of the Rhine and in Saxony. These 'vibrant districts of small- and medium-sized enterprises' constituted a second industrial economy parallel to the highly concentrated world of the big businesses.[21]

The class and regional variations created by industrialism overlay and did not eliminate ethnic, religious, and dynastic loyalties of Germans. As Chancellor Bernhard von Bülow later wrote, 'the German remained a particularist even after 1871: . . . different, more modern, but he is one still'.[22] Signs of regional and local identities (such as separate political parties and monuments to local rulers) did not vanish even though national ones (such as monuments to Bismarck and the Kaiser) multiplied. 'Middle states' such as Hanover, Saxony, and Württemberg defined themselves in new ways using modern institutions.[23] Ethnic and religious patterns also worked against a uniform national culture. Poles, Sorbs, and Lithuanians in the east; Danes in the north; Alsatians in the west—all these groups fought politically for local rights and autonomy. Catholics (mostly in the west and south, apart from the Poles in the east) tended to resist the centralizing tendencies of the Protestant-dominated nationalist state and expressed this in their support for the Catholic Centre Party. The social realities of ethnicity, community, and locality posed significant challenges to national integration—in reality, but especially in the minds of German nationalists. The Polish situation in the east was a particular preoccupation of such nationalists and of the Prussian government. They cooperated in cultural, economic, and resettlement campaigns aimed at promoting 'Germanization'.

All such identities had to be actively constructed. Germans who wished to mobilize nationwide classes or ideological groupings had to work to bridge regions and cultures, while those who appealed to region, ethnicity, or confession had to cross potential class divides. Social Democrats, of course, aimed to mobilize people along class lines. They struggled to make inroads in Catholic areas, but in Protestant ones they found unexpected success in drawing support from tradespeople, officials, and consumers, not just from unionized workers. The Catholic Centre had the opposite problem: as a party defined on the basis of confession it had to deal with divergent class interests of Catholic workers and peasants. It did so by organizing separate party affiliates for these groups and by fighting Social Democratic influence among workers. The Social Democratic Party and the Catholic Centre were the strongest parties, with the greatest mass support, because of how they dealt with the cleavages of German society. Other parties tried to compete with them. Left liberals had their own trade unions and cooperatives, and a short-lived National Social movement around the turn of the century tried to give liberal nationalism mass appeal. The Conservatives allied themselves with antisemitic agitators and the Agrarian League: these alliances gave them a social programme of sorts and consolidated their support among farmers and parts of the *Mittelstand* in their core, mostly rural and Protestant, regions. Nevertheless, like the liberals they fell well short of creating a mass or truly nationwide following. Perhaps the reason these parties perceived German political culture to be fragmented is because the political system was reflecting the realities of German society.

Conclusion

Imperial German society was a complex, shifting, and sometimes enigmatic matrix of classes, economic sectors, and localities, all further differentiated by divisions of age, gender, education, confession, and ethnicity. The degree of flux among these social and economic relationships can hardly be overemphasized. Industrialization had changed almost everything and eliminated nearly nothing. Did social and economic change reinforce or undermine German authoritarianism, strengthen the state or destabilize it? Surely it did both. While there were many focal points for anxiety, the near-relentless growth of the Social Democratic movement was a concern to many Germans in what has been called the 'nationalist camp'.[24] It is not easy to see such a camp unless one chooses to ignore all the other divisions. Nevertheless, it is striking that many middle-class and aristocratic Germans saw the evolution of their society as a source of anxiety, despite its economic power and its many modern facets and accomplishments. The traditional social order and loyalty to the state were being undermined, proclaimed the Conservatives. Selfless leaders dedicated to the common national interest had disappeared with the rise of self-interest politics, declared the liberals. Classes that had formed the bedrock of the social and political order were threatened by modern big business, said advocates of the peasantry and the *Mittelstand*. For all its power and progress, Imperial Germany, like other industrial societies, was not a comfortable place or a well-integrated whole. It accurately reflected the tensions and contradictions of a new age.

[1] Anon., *Im Kampf ums Dasein! Wahrheitsgetreue Lebenserinnerungen eines Mädchens aus dem Volke als Fabrikarbeiterin, Dienstmädchen und Kellnerin*, ed. Dr. G. Braun (Stuttgart, n.d. [*c.* 1908]), 67–109, excerpted as 'A Barmaid', in *The German Worker: Working-Class Autobiographies from the Age of Industrialization*, ed. and trans. Alfred Kelly (Berkeley, 1987), 252 ff. The following quotations are from the same source.

[2] Hans-Ulrich Wehler, *Deutsche Gesellschaftsgeschichte*, 4 vols to date, vol. 3, *Von der 'Deutschen Doppelrevolution' bis zum Beginn des Ersten Weltkrieges 1849–1914* (Munich, 1995).

[3] 1909 figures from Gerd Hohorst, Jürgen Kocka, and Gerhard A. Ritter, *Sozialgeschichtliches Arbeitsbuch II: Materialien zur Statistik des Kaiserreichs 1870–1914*, 2nd edn (Munich, 1978), 113 ff. Most of the following statistics are from the same source.

[4] Kelly, *German Worker*, 31.

[5] Hans Rosenberg, *Große Depression und Bismarckzeit. Wirtschaftsablauf, Gesellschaft und Politik in Mitteleuropa* (Berlin, 1967). Others object to the term 'depression' as inaccurate, except perhaps for agriculture, because industrial output continued to grow overall.

[6] Hartmut Kaelble and H. Volkmann, 'Konjunktur und Streik während des Übergangs zum organisierten Kapitalismus in Deutschland', *Zeitschrift für Wirtschafts- und Sozialwissenschaften*, 92 (1972), 513–44.

[7] Michael Prinz, *Brot und Dividende. Konsumvereine in Deutschland und England vor 1914* (Göttingen, 1996).

[8] Volker R. Berghahn, *Modern Germany: Society, Economy and Politics in the Twentieth Century*, 2nd edn (Cambridge, 1987), xvii.

[9] Karl Erich Born, 'Der soziale und wirtschaftliche Strukturwandel Deutschlands am Ende des 19. Jahrhunderts', in Hans-Ulrich Wehler (ed.), *Moderne Deutsche Sozialgeschichte* (Düsseldorf, 1981), 274.

[10] Kenneth D. Barkin, *The Controversy over German Industrialization, 1890–1902* (Chicago, 1970).

[11] Klaus Bade, cited in Berghahn, *Modern Germany*, 2.

[12] Toni Pierenkemper and Richard Tilly, *The German Economy during the Nineteenth Century* (New York, 2004), 84 ff.

[13] Hohorst *et al.*, *Sozialgeschichtliches Arbeitsbuch II*, 74.

[14] Max Grabein, *Wirtschaftliche und soziale Bedeutung der ländlichen Genossenschaften in Deutschland* (Tübingen, 1908), 1–2.

[15] Rudolf Hilferding, *Das Finanzkapital. Eine Studie über die jüngste Entwicklung des Kapitalismus* (orig. 1909) (Berlin, 1955); Jacob Riesser, *The German Great Banks and Their Concentration: In Connection with the Economic Development of Germany*, trans. Morris Jacobson (Washington, DC, 1910).

[16] Pierenkemper and Tilly, *German Economy*, 117 ff.

[17] Alexander Gerschenkron, *Economic Backwardness in Historical Perspective: A Book of Essays* (Cambridge, MA, 1962).

[18] Heinrich August Winkler (ed.), *Organisierter Kapitalismus. Voraussetzungen und Anfänge* (Göttingen, 1974).

[19] Heinrich August Winkler, 'Der rückversicherte Mittelstand. Die Interessenverbände von Handwerk und Kleinhandel im deutschen Kaiserreich', in Walter Rüegg and Otto Neuloh (eds), *Zur soziologischen Theorie und Analyse des 19. Jahrhunderts* (Göttingen, 1971), 163–79; David Blackbourn, 'The Mittelstand in German Politics, 1871–1914', *Social History*, 4 (1977), 409–33.

[20] Bundesarchiv Berlin, Finanzministerium Nr 6204, Untersuchungen über die Verhältnisse im Kleinhandel, 1914.

[21] Gary Herrigel, *Industrial Constructions: The Sources of German Industrial Power* (Cambridge, 1996).

[22] Prince [Bernhard] von Bülow, *Deutsche Politik* (Berlin, 1914), 57.

[23] Abigail Green, *Fatherlands: State-Building and Nationhood in Nineteenth-Century Germany* (Cambridge, 2001).

[24] Karl Rohe (ed.), *Elections, Parties, and Political Traditions: Social Foundations of German Parties and Party Systems, 1867–1987* (New York, 1990).

Religion and confessional conflict

Christopher Clark

In November 1883, the Protestant pastor in Affaltrach, a small confessionally mixed community in Württemberg, decided to celebrate the four hundredth anniversary of Martin Luther's birth by planting a linden tree in the village. The idea was in itself uncontroversial—in that year 'Luther-lindens' were planted all over Germany. The question of location was less straightforward. The pastor and members of his congregation opted to plant the tree on the courtyard beside the little church shared by the village's Catholic and Protestant congregations. The courtyard lay directly in front of the village's Catholic rectory. The Catholic priest, Father Geiger, made a formal protest to the district authorities, but the planting went ahead all the same. To add insult to injury his Protestant colleague, excited no doubt by the Lutheran celebrations unfolding across Germany, used the occasion to deliver an intemperate speech full of polemical denunciations of the Catholic Church.

Hardly had the young tree begun to spread its roots when it was attacked under the cover of darkness by a person or persons unknown. The trunk was sawn through so that only a stump was left. And thus it remained until June, when the feast of Corpus Christi was drawing near. In the warmer weather, new green shoots appeared around the rim of the stump, and one morning the priest woke to find that a sturdy wooden fence—built by an unknown (presumably Protestant) villager during the hours of darkness—had sprung up around the mutilated tree. The Catholic village council responded with a formal complaint demanding that the district authorities remove the fence and pull out the offending stump. The mood between the two congregations deteriorated and the Corpus Christi celebrations of that year were marked by tension and conflict between Protestant and Catholic villagers. In his annual parish report for 1884, the Protestant pastor looked back with a certain pride on these parochial quarrels: 'The Luther anniversary of last year awoke us to a keener awareness of the treasure of our Protestant faith, but it also sharpened our opposition to the Roman church. This is an undeniable improvement.'[1]

The conflict over the linden tree in sleepy Affaltrach is hardly the stuff of historical epic, but it encapsulates one of the most distinctive features of society in Imperial Germany. 'In no other era of German history have religious questions been approached with greater zeal than at this moment,' the Social Democrat Wilhelm Liebknecht told an audience of Dresden workers in February 1872. 'One feels that one has been transported back into the wildest years after the Reformation, so widespread is the quarrelling over religion.'[2] Liebknecht, a socialist and atheist with little sympathy for the religious stirrings of his time, was exaggerating, but he had a point. After the foundation of the German Empire in 1871, religion, always an important social force in German public life, acquired a new and heightened significance. Confessional conflicts became interwoven with other social, political, and economic forces at work in the new nation state. They polarized politics, cultural and associational networks, neighbourhood relations and national solidarities, kinship groups and business dealings. Religion became one of the structuring facts of German public life. There has always been intermittent tension between church and state in German-speaking Europe—as almost everywhere else on the Continent. What distinguished the culture wars of the late nineteenth century was their scope. They were a socially deep phenomenon, whose effects were felt not only in parliamentary committees but also in small towns and villages. They involved not only political parties, ministerial factions, and senior clergymen, but also journalists, vicars, parish priests, and the masses of the faithful. The culture wars transcended the divide between politics and everyday life.

It is only relatively recently that the history of religion has begun to attract serious interest from historians of the German Empire. Until the 1980s, it was something studied by people called 'church historians' who attended their own conferences, published their own journals, and inhabited their own faculties and institutions. Their 'profane' (*profanhistorisch*) mainstream colleagues in the history faculties took little interest in their doings. The most influential historical treatments of the imperial era proceeded from the assumption that religion was on the wane in a swiftly modernizing society. The traditional collective affiliations of confession were supposedly making way for the new secular identities of class and nation. Such religious commitments as persisted were survivals from an earlier era; religious conflicts were thus little more than rearguard actions that could neither halt nor deflect the onward march of history into a secular modernity.

Times have changed, and so has the writing of history. Beginning in the early 1980s, the 'cultural turn' in historical studies focused attention on those forms of collective subjectivity that mediate behaviour and bestow meaning on human experience. In West Germany, historians of democratic politics became increasingly interested in the role played by religion in stabilizing the constituencies of the major political parties. In the process, religion became one of the most vibrant growth areas in the historiography of Imperial Germany. Innovative studies illuminated the role played by religion in associational networks, voting behaviour, political mobilization, and the emergence of distinct socio-moral milieux.[3]

The dramatic expansion of interest in what was once a marginal and neglected subject matter has transformed our understanding of the history of modern Germany. However, it has also given rise to new and difficult questions. How deep was the divide between the confessional camps in the German Empire? Was religion a modernizing force? Did the mobilization of confessional commitments help or hinder processes of emancipation—of religious minorities, for example, or of women? Should the prominence of confessional questions and confessional conflicts in German society be seen as one strand in a unique German path to modernity (the *Sonderweg*)? Is 'secularization'—once a presiding rubric of historiography on the late nineteenth century—still a useful framing concept for the era? And if secularization did indeed take place, how can we reconcile that fact with the phenomena of religious revival and confessional conflict?

Conflict

Hardly had the German Empire been proclaimed, but a bitter conflict broke out between the Prussian government and the Catholic Church. By the end of 1878, more than 1,800 German Catholic priests had been incarcerated or exiled and over 16 million Marks worth of ecclesiastical property seized. In the first four months of 1875 alone, 241 priests, 136 Catholic newspaper editors, and 210 Catholic laymen were fined or imprisoned, 20 newspapers were confiscated, 74 Catholic houses were searched, 103 Catholic political activists were expelled or interned, and 55 Catholic associations or clubs were closed down. As late as 1881, one-quarter of all Prussian parishes remained without priests. This was Germany at the height of the *Kulturkampf*, a 'struggle of cultures' that would shape German politics and public life for generations.

Germany was not the only European state to see tension over confessional questions in this era. In the 1870s and 1880s, there was heightened conflict between Catholics and secular or anticlerical liberal movements across the European Continent. But the German case stands out. Nowhere else did the state proceed so systematically against Catholic institutions and personnel. Administrative reform and the law were the two main instruments of discrimination. In 1871, the Criminal Code was amended to enable the authorities to prosecute priests who used the pulpit 'for political ends'. In 1872, further state measures eliminated the influence of clergymen over the planning and implementation of school curricula and the supervision of schools. Members of religious orders were prohibited from teaching in the state school system and the Jesuits were expelled from the German Empire. Under the 'May Laws' of 1873, the training and appointment of clergy in Prussia were placed under state supervision. In 1874, the Prussian government introduced compulsory civil marriage, a step extended to the entire German Empire a year later. Additional legislation in 1875 abolished various allegedly suspect religious orders and choked off state subsidies to the church. As Catholic religious personnel were expelled, jailed, and forced into hiding, state-authorized 'agents' were sent in to take charge of vacated bishoprics.

Otto von Bismarck was the driving force behind this unprecedented campaign. Why did he undertake it? The answer lies partly in his emphatically Protestant and partisan understanding of the German national question. In the 1850s, during his posting in Frankfurt am Main as Prussia's representative to the German Confederation, Bismarck had come to believe that political Catholicism was the chief 'enemy of Prussia' in southern Germany. The spectacle of Catholic revivalist piety, with its demonstrative pilgrimages and public festivities, filled him with disgust, as did the increasingly Roman orientation of mid-century Catholicism.[4] At times, indeed, he doubted whether this 'hypocritical idolatrous papism, full of hate and cunning', was a religion at all, because its 'presumptuous dogma falsified God's revelation and nurtured idolatry as a basis for worldly domination'.[5] A number of larger themes were bundled together in Bismarck's appraisal: a fastidious Protestant contempt (accentuated by his Pietist spirituality) for the outward display so characteristic of the Catholic revival, a strain of half-submerged German idealism, and political apprehensions (shading into paranoia) about the Church's capacity to manipulate minds and mobilize the masses.

These antipathies were deepened by the conflicts that brought about the unification of Germany. German Catholics had traditionally looked to Austria for leadership in German affairs and they were unenthusiastic about the prospect of a Prussian-dominated 'lesser Germany' (*Kleindeutschland*) excluding the six million (mainly Catholic) Austrian Germans. Conversely, after 1871, doubts about the political reliability of the Catholics were reinforced by the fact that, of the three main ethnic minorities (Poles, Alsatians, and Danes) whose representatives formed opposition parties in the Reichstag, two were emphatically Catholic. Bismarck was utterly persuaded of the political 'disloyalty' of the 2.5 million Catholic Poles in the Prussian east, and he suspected that the Church and its networks were deeply implicated in the Polish nationalist movement. 'From the Russian border to the Adriatic Sea', he told a Prussian cabinet meeting in the autumn of 1871, 'we are confronted with the combined propaganda of Slavs, ultramontanes [papalist Catholics] and reactionaries, and it is necessary openly to defend our national interests and our language against such hostile activities.'[6]

These concerns resonated more destructively within the new nation state than they had before. The Bismarckian empire was not in any sense an 'organic' or historically evolved entity: it was the highly artificial product of four years of diplomacy and war. There was an unsettling sense that what had so swiftly been put together could also be undone—that the empire might never acquire the political or cultural cohesion to safeguard itself against fragmentation from within. These anxieties may seem absurd to us, but they felt real to many contemporaries. In this climate of uncertainty, it seemed plausible to view the Catholics as the most formidable domestic hindrance to a process of national consolidation that had still to be accomplished after the formal unification of 1871.

In lashing out against the Catholics, Bismarck knew that he could count on the enthusiastic support of the National Liberals and left liberals, whose powerful position in the new Reichstag and the Prussian House of Deputies made them indispensable political allies. In Germany, as in much of Europe, anti-Catholicism was one of the defining strands of late-nineteenth-century liberalism. Liberals deplored Catholicism as the absolute negation of their own world-view. They denounced the 'despotism' and 'slavery' of the doctrine of papal infallibility adopted by the Vatican Council in 1870, according to which the authority of the pope is unchallengeable when he speaks officially—*ex cathedra*—on matters of faith or morals. Liberal journalists depicted the Catholic faithful as a servile and manipulated herd. They drew a sharp contrast between the allegedly slavish and feminized character of the Catholic subculture and their own social universe centred on autonomous, manly tax-paying worthies with unbound consciences. A bestiary of anticlerical stereotypes emerged: the satires in liberal journals thronged with wily, thin Jesuits and lecherous, fat priests—amenable subjects because the cartoonist's pen could make such artful play with the solid black of their garb. By vilifying the parish priest in his role as father confessor or by impugning the sexual propriety of nuns, liberals underscored their faith in the sanctity of the patriarchal nuclear family. For liberals, the *Kulturkampf* was nothing less than a 'struggle of cultures': the term was coined by the liberal Protestant pathologist Rudolf Virchow in a speech of February 1872 to the Prussian Landtag.[7]

Bismarck's campaign against the Catholics was a failure. He had hoped that an anti-Catholic crusade would create a broad, Protestant liberal–conservative lobby that would help him to pass legislation consolidating the new empire. But the integrating effect of the campaign was more fleeting and fragile than he had anticipated. By the mid-1870s, left-wing liberals had begun to oppose the campaign on the grounds that it infringed fundamental rights. The increasing radicalism of anti-Church measures also prompted misgivings among many Protestants on the 'clerical' wing of German conservatism. The view gained ground that the real victim of the *Kulturkampf* was not the Catholic Church or Catholic politics as such, but religion itself.

Even if the support for Bismarck's policy had been more secure, it is highly doubtful that he could ever have succeeded in neu-tralizing Catholic dissent by any of the means available to a constitutional and law-abiding state. Bismarck and his partisans made the familiar mistake of overrating the power of the state and under-estimating the determination of their opponents. In many areas, Catholic clergy simply failed to acknowledge or abide by the new laws. The authorities, who had rushed these measures through parliament and had not thought very deeply about how to ensure compliance, responded with improvised sanctions ranging from fines of varying severity to terms of imprisonment and exile.[8] But these measures had little practical effect. The Church continued to ignore the new laws and the fines levied by government authorities continued to accumulate. When fines remained unpaid, the local authorities confiscated the property of bishops and offered it up at public auction. But this, too, was counterproductive, because loyal Catholics would rally to manage the auction in such a way as to ensure that the goods were sold at the lowest possible prices and returned to the expropriated clergyman. Imprisonment was equally futile. After even brief jail terms, priests returned as heroes to their parishes. The government attempted to resolve this prob-lem in May 1874 by introducing a new set of regulations known collectively as the Expulsion Law. This law provided for the exile of insurgent bishops and clergy to remote locations—a favourite was the Baltic island of Rügen. Several hundred priests were thus exiled between 1875 and 1879. But this measure created more problems than it solved. It proved impossible to police the expulsion orders and difficult to replace the displaced priests with politically reliable successors. The state's scheme to introduce its own nominees ('state agents') to replace exiled clergymen was an abject failure: these men were despised and avoided by the Catholic populace.

Perhaps the most conspicuous evidence of Bismarck's failure was simply the spectacular growth of the German Centre Party, the party of Catholics. Although Bismarck did succeed in isolating the Centre Party politically, at least for a time, he could do nothing to prevent it from increasing its share of the popular vote in national elections. Whereas only 23 per cent of Prussian Catholics had voted for the Centre in 1871, 45 per cent did so in 1874. Thanks in large part to the challenge of responding to the intimidation of their church by Bismarck's *Kulturkampf*, the Centre Party 'peaked early', efficiently colonizing its social milieu, mobilizing Catholics who had hitherto been politically inactive, expanding the frontiers of partisan politics. The most intense phase of the church–state struggle came to an end in 1878, when the accession of Pope Leo XIII opened the way to an improvement in relations. But the antagonisms stirred by the conflict were slow to disperse. This was in part because the legislative machinery of the *Kulturkampf* was only very gradually dismantled. In 1890, when Bismarck was forced to resign as chancellor, Catholics were still seeking the repeal of the Expatriation Law, the removal of restrictions on missionary activity, the scaling down of state controls on clerical appointments, and the readmission of the Jesuits to Germany. This long half-life of the anti-Catholic laws ensured that there was always sufficient combustible material available for politicians and journalists who were inclined to protest—or support—specific discriminatory measures.

By the late 1880s, in any case, the German culture war had acquired an impressive momentum, quite independent of initiatives from the political authorities. The associational landscape of the empire was dominated by two mass organizations representing confessional interests. The Protestant League was founded in 1886 to 'defend the spiritual property' of Protestantism and to 'break the power of Rome on German soil'.[9] It had acquired 100,000 members by 1895 and over half a million by 1914. The Protestant

League specialized in the coordination of anti-Catholic rallies and demonstrations. The tone was set by speeches peppered with 'gross denunciations and insults'. The league's Catholic counterpart, the People's Association for Catholic Germany, was founded in 1890 to provide adult education and cultural programmes. It counted over 800,000 members on the eve of the First World War. The tendency to form confessionally separate networks could also be observed in other mass organizations, including the ultra-nationalist Pan-German League (founded in 1891) and the Imperial League Against Social Democracy (1904). Such foundings contributed to intermittent phases of rhetorical escalation, in which champions of each camp broadcast their core values and defined each other in terms of the negation of those values. Protestant agitators thus denounced Catholics as culturally retrograde adherents of the pope and nationally unreliable ('Romelings without a fatherland'); Catholic publicists warned against the godless pagans who sought to expunge every trace of true Christianity from German society. Rhetorically skilled 'spiritual snipers'[10] in both camps used well-aimed shots to raise the emotional temperature of confessional relations throughout Germany.

A distinctive feature of German confessionalism was the fact that it extended beyond the domain of religious institutions and practices to the realm of everyday life. Recent research on German associational networks has shown how successfully the clergy and their lay auxiliaries confessionalized the contexts in which even non-religious activities—sport, reading, labour representation, and consumption, for example—were conducted. The concentration of social and cultural life within separate confessional frameworks fostered the consolidation of distinct 'milieux' characterized by relatively high levels of exclusivity and group cohesion. Even within the more intimate world of the village or the small rural town, confessional antagonisms remained virulent, as the fate of the Luther-linden in Affaltrach suggests. In many confessionally mixed towns, the two camps each had their own bakers, butchers, and doctors. Where both congregations shared the local church, there were intermittent conflicts over the frequency and timing of services and the maintenance and decoration of the church interior. Cemeteries offered up another bone of contention: in 1904 the Bishop of Metz issued an interdict against the cemetery in a nearby village because the body of a Protestant had been buried in it. He was forced to withdraw the interdict after a nationwide wave of protests. As these examples make clear, it was not only the Catholics who felt victimized. Although Catholics accounted for 36 per cent of the empire's population in 1900, in many areas of mixed confession it was the Protestants who felt threatened.

German political life, too, was divided along confessional lines. In national elections, the Centre Party routinely secured the ballots of around half of all Catholics eligible to vote. It also achieved remarkably high rates of voter loyalty: Centre Party voters were less likely than the supporters of any other major party to 'defect' to another party in a subsequent election. By contrast, the base of support for the liberal and conservative parties was predominantly Protestant, especially after the '*Kulturkampf* elections' of 1874. For all its claims to represent the German nation as a whole, the National Liberal Party was an overwhelmingly Protestant institution, especially after the confessional struggle of the 1870s. Of the 620 Christian Reichstag deputies fielded by the party between 1867 and 1917, only 51 were Catholic, and of these, the majority were men who had already established themselves within the party before 1870. In 1874, the Conservative Party's caucus in the Prussian House of Deputies did not include a single Catholic.

These tensions were also felt at the apex of the political system. Throughout the 1890s, the Centre Party continued to be seen by some of Germany's most senior political decision makers as a Trojan horse, with which ultramontane Catholicism intended to smuggle particularism into national cultural matters and infiltrate German foreign policy with narrowly 'Roman' viewpoints. There was particular concern that the Centre Party would undermine the strategically important alliance with Italy through its open partisanship for the Vatican, which was at this time locked in struggle with the Italian state. Friedrich von Holstein, a powerful counsellor in the Foreign Office and an influential advisor to Kaiser Wilhelm II, repeatedly warned that concessions to the Centre Party would cause the empire to disintegrate under the pressure of internal confessional tensions. The Kaiser's intimate friend and advisor Philipp zu Eulenburg was also given to fantasizing about ultramontane plots to relaunch the Counter-Reformation. The Kaiser himself was not immune to these partisan temptations: in a speech of May 1897 he triggered a minor political crisis by referring to the leaders of the Centre Party as 'fellows without a fatherland' (*vaterlandslose Gesellen*).[11]

Integration

At times, then, it seemed that the confessional struggle had split Germany into two distinct life-worlds (*Lebenswelten*). If the cleavage between the two confessions appeared so deeply entrenched, this was because it was not just a matter of religious difference. Underpinning it was the social geography of the German states. Catholics and Protestants were concentrated in specific regions of the empire (the Protestants, broadly speaking, in the north, north-east, and central regions, the Catholics on the Polish eastern periphery, the west, and the south-east). In the very extensive areas of mixed confession, such as the Rhineland, Bavarian Franconia, Württemberg, and Alsace, the two confessions had quite distinct occupational and cultural profiles. Catholics were on average poorer than Protestants; they were less likely to complete secondary school; and they were far less likely to attend university or to work in one of the 'liberal' professions. Even in rural areas of mixed confession, Catholics tended to farm smaller and less fertile plots of land. These structural differences lent an appearance of permanence and intractability to the confessional divide. They meant that confessional difference correlated—in many areas—with differences in mentality, attitude, wealth, and opportunity.

Nevertheless, when we speak of a Germany sundered into opposed 'milieux' or when we posit a return to the all-embracing 'confessionalization' of the post-Reformation era, there is a danger of pushing the argument too far. The conflict between Protestant/anti-clerical and Catholic/ultramontane forces was marked, as we have seen, by violent rhetorical exchanges. So all-pervasive was this process of discursive inflation that it came to constitute a kind of virtual reality. But the harsh binary oppositions of culture-war rhetoric belied a more complex reality of compromise, interdependence, and convergence. Even at the height of

Bismarck's assault on political Catholicism, the Prussian-German state maintained a working relationship with parts of the Catholic hierarchy. It was thanks to these contacts that Bismarck was able to inaugurate negotiations with the Vatican to put an end to the *Kulturkampf* in the late 1870s. During the following decade, Centre Party leaders and many politically active Catholics entered into a more positive relationship with the imperial state and embraced its great causes. Colonial policy was one important area of fruitful collaboration: the Centre Party supported colonialism as a means of hastening the Christianization and cultivation of the 'pagan' peoples of Africa. Here was a domain where Catholics could reconcile their commitment to universal Christian imperatives with support for a specifically national project. By the 1890s, conversely, the government had recognized that it would have to come to some kind of arrangement with the powerful Centre Party. It was not, of course, easy for the government to reconcile the need for Centre Party support with the sensitivity of the Protestant public to the slightest suggestion of a concession to Catholic interests. But it is clear nonetheless that the Centre Party gradually entered into a relationship of conditional collaboration with the administration. By 1907, indeed, following a flare-up of confessional tensions over colonial policy, the pressure for an accommodation with Germany's national and imperial goals was sufficient to open a rift within the Centre Party. Nationally minded Catholics within the party formed the German Union, whose purpose was to support patriotic projects and overcome the confessional divide that 'threaten[ed] to poison the life of our nation'.[12] In March 1906 the Catholic publisher Julius Bachem issued a controversial call to open the doors of the party to non-Catholics. Referring to the metaphorical bastion of Catholic self-defence, Bachem declared: 'We must leave the tower!'

There were other signs that the intensity of confessional antagonism was on the wane. Two recent studies of Catholic reading habits have shown that there was a tendency at the grass roots of popular Catholicism to move away from the insular culture of the 1870s towards a less church-centred and more nationally oriented spectrum of texts. Clergymen on both sides of the divide frequently lamented the growth of interconfessional fraternization, especially among younger people. There was also a steady, if inconspicuous, rise in the incidence of interconfessional marriages, despite the dire warnings of pastors and priests. In Prussia, the rate of mixed marriage doubled over the period 1840–1900, rising from 3.7 to 8.4 per cent; the percentage for the empire as a whole had reached 10.2 per cent by 1914. Perhaps unsurprisingly, such marriages were most common in the relatively secularized environment of the industrial cities: in 1896 mixed marriages accounted for 34 per cent of all unions in Frankfurt am Main and 36.5 per cent in Wiesbaden. But even in areas where confessional tensions had traditionally been quite pronounced, such as rural Alsace, there was a gradual rise, from 8.4 per cent in 1882 to 12.0 per cent in 1912. And there were conspicuous individual episodes of interconfessional rap-prochement. In Weitbruch, Alsace, local authorities representing both confessions attended first one church and then the other to celebrate the Kaiser's birthday. In 1904, in a celebrated gesture of ecumenical outreach, the Catholic priest in Weiterswiller invited the local Protestant pastor to join him in a confessionally mixed household at the bedside of a dying Catholic.

The Jews

Where did all this leave the Jews of the German states, who accounted for about 1 per cent of the population? After 1869, Jews were no longer subject to discriminatory legislation of any kind. The North German Confederation's Law of Religious Freedom (3 July 1869), which was subsequently incorporated into Reich law, explicitly abolished the link between citizenship rights and religious creed. The Jews were thus no longer a legally separate caste. But were they a 'confessional minority' comparable with other religious groups? Advocates of both legal emancipation and the social assimilation of Jews aimed to transform them from an ethnic entity into a German confessional group. The most important platform for the defence of Jewish civil rights after 1871 was the Central Association of German Citizens of Jewish Faith, founded in 1893. In the face of those who claimed to speak for a homogeneous German *Volk*, the activists of the Central Association insisted that citizenship was a purely legal category, defined and guaranteed by the principles enshrined in the constitution. Thus the association's members were not, according to their founding resolutions, 'German Jews' but 'Germans of Jewish faith'. According to the association's founding statutes, they had 'no more in common with the Jews of other countries than the Catholics and Protestants of Germany [had] with the Catholics and Protestants of other countries'.[13]

There were certainly parallels between the Jewish and Catholic experience. The term 'emancipation', widely used with reference to the Jews, had initially entered the German language in the context of the struggle of Catholics for legal equality in Britain. There were analogies, too, in Protestant perceptions of the two minorities. Protestant polemical attacks against Catholic observance focused on the allegation that it was purely formal, legal, and ritualistic, and that it lacked the true subjectivity associated with 'positive religion'; these themes also featured prominently in Protestant idealist critiques of Judaism. And like the Jews, the Catholics were accused of forming more than just a confession; to many Protestants they constituted something alien within the German body politic. The term 'state within a state' was used by Protestants to target Catholics (and Jesuits in particular) long before it passed into the lexicon of the antisemites. Finally, German Jews and German Catholics both suffered state discrimination after 1871, despite the absence of a legal sanction for such a policy. Both groups had difficulty gaining access to certain prestigious sections of the bureaucracy and to the upper ranks of the military.

German Jews were divided on how to define and safeguard their entitlements in the post-emancipation era. For politically progressive, assimilationist Jews, the key objective was to hold the state authorities to the letter of the law and protect *individual* Jews from discrimination on the grounds of their Jewishness. On this premise, the Central Association campaigned energetically for an end to unofficial discrimination against Jewish candidates for public service posts. Other Jewish groups, especially those of orthodox religious orientation, were more concerned with securing official recognition of the *corporate* claims of Judaism as a faith community. They pressed, for example, for exemptions from local regulations forbidding Sunday labour. They also sought the right to withdraw children from school during Jewish holidays. But while some Jews saw the quest for legal exemptions as a means to secure recognition for Judaism as a collective practice, others argued that such 'special treatment' would merely undermine the civil equality of the Jews and inhibit their quest for 'invisibility' as German citizens. This was an issue that drew a dividing line between the most and least assimilationist elements within the minority. During a debate on restrictions to Sunday labour in the city of Frankfurt, the Jewish councillor Berthold Geiger defended his opposition to exemptions for the Jews on the grounds that these amounted to a 'yellow badge in modern form'.[14]

In several important respects, of course, the Jews were quite unlike either of the two mainstream Christian groups. The 'Jewish Question', which produced a flood of pamphlets, books, news-paper articles, and political speeches from the 1870s onwards, had no direct parallel in the historical experience of the other minorities. No other minority faced a concerted campaign of vilification to compare with the assault mounted by the political antisemites against the German Jews. The presumption among antisemites and their fellow travellers—that 'Jewishness' retained an indissoluble core of ethnic otherness—and their paranoid preoccupation with the role of Jews within the economy were features that set the Jewish predicament apart. The smallness of the Jewish minority was another defining factor: unlike the Catholics, the Jews would never be able to muster the numbers to bring direct pressure to bear on the government; there could no Jewish Centre Party. Nor could there be a Jewish 'milieu' in the normally accepted sense: assimilated Jews tended instead to opt for a pragmatic accommodation with the culture of the (mainly Protestant) urban middle classes, while at the same time preserving elements of a German-Jewish subculture.[15] This was a strategy for which one historian has coined the term 'situative ethnicity'.[16]

How should we characterize the relationship between German antisemitism and the cultural landscape of the Christian confes-sions? Discussion of this relationship has been dominated by two quite different approaches. The first distinguishes sharply between a traditional anti-Judaism founded in religious arguments and beliefs, and the essentially modern phenomenon of racial anti-semitism that appeals to the materialist, biological arguments of racial pseudo-science. This approach emphasizes the anti-Christian animus in much modern, racial antisemitism. It draws upon such evidence as the famous comment by Wilhelm Marr, inventor of the term 'antisemitism', to the effect that Christianity was 'a disease of the consciousness', or Marr's demand that the 'Jewish question' be framed in 'non-confessional' terms. This approach, which could also be labelled the 'rupture thesis', also stresses the incompatibility of racist arguments with the various Christian doctrines of grace. According to this view, the rise of racial antisemitism was the consequence of a 'failure' of Christianity. Antisemitism either arose because people were not Christian enough, or it developed in the vacuum that secularization left behind, becoming a kind of ersatz religion that usurped the inherited functions of Christianity. The rupture thesis indirectly derived some of its plausibility from the presumption that secularization is a defining feature of modernity.

An alternative view—we can call it the continuity thesis—has always had its own scholarly exponents, but has enjoyed a revival in recent years. This view stresses the linkages between Christian judaeophobia and modern antisemitism. It argues that the latter should be seen not as a distinct phenomenon that arises only once secularization is well advanced, but as the further evolution and expression of an anti-Judaism that was always implicit in the Christian tradition. Some exponents of this view stress the presence of believing Christians among the ranks of the racial antisemites, whereas others point to the close proximity of religiously motivated arguments to those derived from racial pseudo-science. This view sits comfortably with the recent emphasis on the continuing importance of religion in the modern era.

These two viewpoints should be seen as complementary rather than contradictory. They coexist precisely because the phenomenon of antisemitism was diffuse enough to admit a range of interpretations. German antisemitism was not a clearly defined, internally consistent system of beliefs. Rather, it was a loose cluster of discourses drawn from a wide range of traditions that could be mixed in varying proportions. Principled, racist antisemitism, in which a pseudo-philosophical judaeophobia supplied the foundations and determined the horizons of a world-view, was the affair of a small minority on the fringes of German politics. The antisemitic political parties—single-issue lobby groups focussed above all on the 'Jewish Question'—were an electoral failure.

But expressions of virulent hostility to the Jews could be found throughout the mainstream of Christian public life. In his repellent pamphlet, *The Talmud Jew*, the sometime Catholic theologian August Rohling depicted the Jews as morally corrupt and bent upon securing the economic domination of Germany through the most unscrupulous means. His pamphlet was one of the bestsellers of late-nineteenth-century antisemitism: it was widely excerpted and serialized in the popular Catholic press.

The Protestant political agitator Adolf Stöcker is another case in point. Stöcker, a chaplain to the imperial court who founded the populist Christian Social Party in 1878, combined traditional Christian judaeophobe themes—the Jews as killers of Christ, for example—with denunciations of their economic influence as drivers of capitalist exploitation, usurious lending, and financial speculation. Stöcker was a controversial figure who aroused ambivalent views even among conservative Protestant contemporaries. During the early years of his agitation, he found many supporters within north-German Protestant circles. His appeal to clergymen and their congregations lay precisely in the fact that he claimed to view the 'Jewish Question' as a 'socio-ethical', rather than a racial, issue. This was thought to set him apart from the beer-hall rabble-rousing of the racial antisemites. But the truth is that Stöcker blended traditional, modern anti-capitalist and racist arguments in promiscuous fashion. 'We view the Jewish Question neither as a religious question, nor as a racial question, although in its roots it is both,' he told a mass meeting in 1887. 'Insofar as it appears in its external dimension as a socio-ethical question, we handle it thus.'[17] It is remarkable how ubiquitous this circular interweaving of religious, 'socio-ethical', economic, and ethnic themes was in the various discourses of German antisemitism. This loose ideological formation meant that Christian publicists could expound antisemitic views while at the same time claiming on theological grounds to reject the doctrine of race.

How were the confessional antagonisms of the imperial era refracted in German antisemitism? After all, if we include the Jews, Germany was a 'tri-confessional' land.[18] It thus makes no sense to think in terms of a bipolar relationship between a monolithic Jewish minority and a monolithic 'Christian' bloc. We must acknowledge that Protestants and Catholics engaged with the Jewish minority on their own terms, and also that the relationships between Christians and Jews were intimately affected by those within and between the Christian confessions. There is still disagreement among historians as to whether Protestantism and Catholicism generated distinct variants of antisemitism. Insofar as antisemites adhered to chauvinist ultranationalist views, they were more likely to be found (and feel at home) in the Protestant milieu. There was a growing tendency within late-nineteenth- and early twentieth-century Protestant discourse to detach the German Protestant tradition from broader universalist affiliations by stressing its specifically national or Germanic quality. Among the key texts mined by antisemitic orators were the judaeophobe pamphlets of Martin Luther and the defamatory treatise *Jewry Revealed* written by the eighteenth-century Protestant orientalist Johann Andreas Eisenmenger. Catholics, by contrast, were anchored in an international ecclesiastical structure and felt themselves to be among the 'losers' of the nation-building process. For these reasons, one historian has argued that German antisemitism—in its modern racist form—was an 'essentially Protestant phenomenon'.[19]

This argument is based on only a partial reading of the Catholic tradition. This becomes immediately apparent when one reads what was actually written in the late-nineteenth-century Catholic daily press. Here we find what appears to be the entire armoury of modern antisemitism, save for the doctrine of race itself: denunciations of the damaging economic influence of Jews and of their undue political prominence, their role in promoting a materialist culture founded on the negation of Christian values, conspiracy theories involving collaboration between Jews and Freemasons, wilful misreadings of the Talmud, even accusations of ritual murder. Yet, while there is no doubt that local Catholic newspapers and journals in most regions of Germany were contaminated by anti-Jewish prejudice, it is also the case that Catholic journals—and other Catholic writings, including especially the official pronouncements of the Centre Party—routinely condemned racial antisemitism. They did so in part because the new term 'antisemitism' was freighted with anti-Catholic connotations. But Catholics also denounced antisemitism because it conflicted with their own belief in the indivisibility of the grace bestowed upon humanity by God.

There is also evidence to suggest that the intensity of Catholic antisemitism varied over time and may in part have been a function of the tensions generated in the *Kulturkampf* era. Antisemitism was especially pronounced in the regional Catholic press during the 1870s, when the conflict between Catholics and their antagonists was at its height. But it swiftly subsided and had largely died away by the 1910s and 1920s, when German Catholics were less beleaguered, and therefore less combative and defensive. A comparative analysis of Catholic antisemitism in Württemberg, Bavaria, and Baden has shown that it was a far less prominent feature of Catholic publications in Württemberg, where there was no *Kulturkampf* to speak of, than it was in either of the other two states in the 1870s.[20] These observations highlight the need to move beyond a binary model of the relationship between Christians and Jews. When we penetrate to the regional and local level, we begin to discern the complex dynamics of a tri-confessional system.

Religion, secularization, modernization

Is there any mileage left in the notion that Imperial Germany was a secularizing society? Germany remained, in most formal senses, an overwhelmingly Christian country. The German churches, Catholic and Protestant, remained powerful and well-resourced institutions, thanks in part to the ecclesiastical levy added to income taxes in most federal states during the last decades of the nineteenth century. In some areas, the churches were able to extend their involvement in charitable activities and other means of alleviating social hardship, despite the gradual expansion of state-sponsored welfare. In 1906, no less than 95 per cent of Protestant and 91 percent of Catholic children in the German Empire were educated in schools of their own confession. It was legally possible for Germans to distance themselves from a religious institutional affiliation of any kind by declaring themselves 'without confession' (*konfessionslos*), although by 1900 only 0.2 per cent of the population had taken up this option. New or modified forms of piety could still stimulate mass allegiance, as the blossoming of Catholic devotional groups demonstrates. We have already seen that confessional identities permeated many of the popular political movements of the day.

And yet there is no doubt that secularization was also underway in the German Empire. After 1890, the emergence of Social Democracy as one of the elemental forces in German politics brought to the fore a party whose outlook was avowedly secular and atheist (notwithstanding the residual confessional attachments of some of the party's largely Protestant following). There were also signs of a dramatic decline in church attendance. Between 1862 and 1913, the proportion of Protestants taking communion in the city of Lübeck fell from 34 to 14 per cent. The figures for Prussia fell over the same period from 52 to 30 per cent. As Hugh McLeod has observed, the German experience combined strong religious institutions with weak religious participation (in contemporary Britain, theses poles were reversed). A distinction must be drawn, admittedly, between the two Christian confessions. Secularization was more marked among Protestants than among Catholics. In the confessionally mixed cities of Bochum and Münster in western Germany, Protestant rates of observance plunged between 1845 and 1930, following patterns that can be observed nationwide. By contrast, the corresponding figures show that Catholic observance was astonishingly resilient: by the 1920s, Catholic participation rates were twice as high as for Protestants. This asymmetry helps to explain the sense of paranoia experienced by many Protestants who believed that Germany was in the grip of an all-embracing process of re-Catholicization.

We might thus say that the imperial era was marked by the paradoxical intertwining of secularization and religious revival. The two processes did not merely coexist, however: they were dialectically interdependent; they conditioned each other. The secularizing measures of the *Kulturkampf* compelled Catholics to close ranks, thereby providing the fuel for a new generation of revival and expansion. The Centre Party, conversely, was conceived as a vehicle for defending and focusing Catholic interests, but was steadily drawn ever more deeply into the secular calculus of democratic politics. Paradoxically, as one historian of the Catholic parties in nineteenth- and twentieth-century Europe has observed, the organizations formed to bring religion into politics actually ended by taking it out. Secular liberal democracy was thus 'expanded and consolidated by its enemies'.[21]

As this line of argument suggests, the confessional conflicts and revivals of the imperial era in some ways facilitated the modernization of German society. It is worth emphasizing this point, because it has often been claimed that the marshalling of popular religious commitments characteristic of this era was an essentially regressive phenomenon. Catholic revival in particular is thought to have retarded processes of political modernization, first, by pledging committed Catholics to a struggle against 'modern civilization' and, second, by concentrating them in a sociologically, ideologically, and culturally backward 'ghetto'. This view cannot easily be reconciled with the transformations we have examined in this chapter. On both sides of the confessional divide, the mobilization of the faithful exhibited quintessentially modern features. German Protestantism participated in the great flowering of voluntary associational activity that transformed nineteenth-century German society. For Protestant women in particular, this activity developed a genuinely emancipatory momentum: it provided opportunities to become involved in the management of girl's schools, childcare facilities, teachers' associations, and a range of charitable and missionary activities. The relatively professionalized environment of the City Missions provided many middle-class Protestant women with an entry into what would later be known as 'social work' with children, the infirm, the poor, and the elderly. On the Catholic side, too, confessional allegiances were mobilized by quintessentially modern means: mass-circulation media, voluntary associations, mass meetings and demonstrations, the expansion of schooling among deprived social groups, and the increasingly prominent involvement of women in positions of responsibility as teachers, nurses, and administrators. Moreover, it is far from clear that Catholic mobilization hindered or delayed processes of political modernization. On the contrary, confessional conflict contributed to the broadening of political participation by providing Catholics (especially in rural areas) with a reason for entering the political arena as activists, deputies, or voters. As Margaret Lavinia Anderson has shown, Catholic women took part in street demonstrations, sit-down strikes, and election campaigns. In the 1880s, they were even invited to some Centre Party political meetings—this at a time when female attendance was still illegal (the Centre Party supported the Reich Association Law of 1908 that granted women the right to attend political meetings).[22] For all the anti-modernism of its rhetoric, then, the Catholic Church, its lay auxiliaries, and its political allies were deeply implicated in Germany's social and political transformation.

The *Kulturkampf* has often been seen as a chapter in a uniquely German story of interconfessional conflict whose roots lay in the Lutheran Reformation. But if we cast our eyes across Europe, we find that Germany's quarrels were part of a broader Continental struggle. In Belgium, Italy, France, and the Austro-Hungarian Empire, anti-clericals aligned themselves with the cause of the nation, which they imagined as an autonomous collectivity of unbound (male) consciences. They denounced their opponents as the stooges of a 'foreign' power structure bent on undermining the integrity and distinctiveness of the nation states. What was at stake in this struggle, they argued, was the very soul of the nation—its autonomy, its independence, its cultural, political, and economic modernity. It would thus be mistaken to see confessional struggles in Imperial Germany as way-stations on a path leading to the 'German catastrophe' of 1933. To be sure, traces of the confessional struggle can be discerned in the contours of Nazi Germany—not least in the relative impermeability of the Catholic electorate to the Nazi Party's appeal. But religious conflict in the Bismarckian and Wilhelmine eras also held other possible futures. After 1945, following what seemed to many to be the debacle of the liberal nation-building project, the Catholic parties in Germany, France, Belgium, Italy, and the Netherlands emerged as the champions of both subnational rights movements and of a close transnational union. In this—but not only this—sense, the Europe of today bears the imprint of the nineteenth century's culture wars.

[1] Details from Christel Köhle-Hezinger, *Evangelisch-Katholisch. Untersuchungen zu konfessionellem Vorurteil und Konflikt im 19. und 20. Jahrhundert vornehmlich am Beispiel Württembergs* (Tübingen, 1979), 376–8.

[2] Wilhelm Liebknecht, speech of 5 February 1872, cited in Olaf Blaschke and Frank-Michael Kuhlemann (eds), *Religion im Kaiserreich. Milieus—Mentalitäten—Krisen* (Gütersloh, 1996), 7.

[3] Key works include Margaret Lavinia Anderson, *Windthorst: A Political Biography* (New York, 1981); Anderson, *Practicing Democracy: Elections and Political Culture in Imperial Germany* (Princeton, 2000); Jonathan Sperber, *Popular Catholicism in Nineteenth-Century Germany* (Princeton, 1984); Sperber, *The Kaiser's Voters: Electors*

and *Elections in Imperial Germany* (Cambridge, 1997); Thomas Nipperdey, *Religion im Umbruch. Deutschland 1870–1918* (Munich, 1988); David Blackbourn, *Marpingen: Apparitions of the Virgin Mary in Nineteenth-Century Germany* (New York, 1993); Helmut Walser Smith, *German Nationalism and Religious Conflict: Culture, Ideology, Politics, 1870–1914* (Princeton, 1995).

⁴ The nineteenth-century champions of papal authority were known as 'ultramontanes' because, from the perspective of northern Europeans, Rome lies *ultra montes*, or beyond the Alps.

⁵ See Otto Pflanze, *Bismarck and the Development of Germany*, 3 vols (Princeton, 1990), i. 368, and ii. 188.

⁶ Bismarck's remarks of 1 November 1871 cited in Adelheid Constabel (ed.), *Die Vorgeschichte des Kulturkampfes* (Berlin, 1956), 136–41.

⁷ Pflanze, *Bismarck*, ii. 205.

⁸ See Ronald J. Ross, *The Failure of Bismarck's Kulturkampf: Catholicism and State Power in Imperial Germany, 1871–1887* (Washington, DC, 1996).

⁹ Cited in Smith, *German Nationalism*, 58.

¹⁰ See Martin Papenheim, ' "Roma o morte". Culture Wars in Italy', in Christopher Clark and Wolfram Kaiser (eds), *Culture Wars. Secular-Catholic Conflict in Nineteenth-Century Europe* (Cambridge, 2003), 202–25.

¹¹ Cited in Smith, *German Nationalism*, 120.

¹² Cited ibid. 144.

¹³ *Im Deutschen Reich*, 4 (1898), 1–6, here 6.

¹⁴ Cited in Mordechai Breuer, *Jüdische Orthodoxie im Deutschen Reich 1871–1918. Sozialgeschichte einer religiösen Minderheit* (Frankfurt a.M., 1986), 290.

¹⁵ See David Sorkin, *The Transformation of German Jewry, 1780–1840* (Oxford, 1987).

¹⁶ See Till van Rahden, *Juden und andere Breslauer. Die Beziehungen zwischen Juden, Protestanten und Katholiken in einer deutschen Großstadt von 1860 bis 1925* (Göttingen, 2000).

¹⁷ Adolf Stöcker, *Christlich-Sozial. Reden und Aufsätze* (Bielefeld and Leipzig, 1895), 211.

¹⁸ On modern Germany's 'tri-confessional' culture, see Kurt Nowak, *Geschichte des Christentums in Deutschland. Religion, Politik und Gesellschaft vom Ende der Aufklärung bis zur Mitte des 20. Jahrhunderts* (Munich, 1995).

¹⁹ Hermann Greive, *Geschichte des modernen Antisemitismus in Deutschland* (Darmstadt, 1983), 67.

²⁰ Siegfried Weichlein, 'Anti-Liberalism and antisemitism in Catholic Germany, 1871–1914', unpublished paper presented at the annual meeting of the German Studies Association, New Orleans, 2003. I am extremely grateful to the author for allowing me to cite his paper in this chapter.

²¹ Stathis N. Kalyvas, *The Rise of Christian Democracy in Europe* (Ithaca, NY, 1996), 262.

²² Anderson, *Practicing Democracy*, esp. 126–31.

Culture and the arts

Celia Applegate

In 1873, Friedrich Nietzsche, then twenty-nine and teaching philology at the University of Basel in Switzerland, began writing a series of *Untimely Meditations* on the current state of German culture. The first essay took as its target the theologian David Strauss, whose book, *The Old Faith and the New: A Confession* (1871), struck Nietzsche as the expression of all that was wrong with the so-called cultivated classes in German society. Published in the all-engulfing wake of German unification, *The Old Faith and the New* championed science as the new faith, rationally demonstrable in the evidence of historical progress. Nietzsche, long parted from the 'old faith' of his Lutheran forbearers, still regarded this glorification of the status quo as the embodiment of 'philistine culture' with its motto, 'all seeking is at an end'.[1]

What provoked Nietzsche most in Strauss's long and dull book was his impenetrable smugness. 'During recent years', declared Strauss, we 'have participated in the liveliest way in the great national war and the construction of the German state, and we feel ourselves profoundly uplifted by this turn, as glorious as it was unexpected, in the history of our much-tried nation.' He delighted in 'our knowledge of nature', the 'writings of our great poets', and 'the performances of the works of our great composers', and in all of this found 'a stimulus for the spirit and the heart, for the imagination and the sense of humour, that leaves nothing to be desired'. 'Thus we live', he concluded, and 'go our way rejoicing.'[2] Repelled by such complacency, Nietzsche saw instead 'the defeat, if not the extirpation, of the German spirit for the benefit of the "German Reich"'. Responding to Strauss's implication that German culture had been victorious on the battlefields of the war with France, Nietzsche doubted whether

'German culture' even existed. 'Culture', he declared, 'is above all the unity of artistic style, in every expression of the life of a people.' But the German could claim only 'a chaotic jumble of all styles',

and one seriously wonders how, with all his erudition, he can possibly fail to notice it, but, on the contrary, rejoices from the very heart at the 'culture' he at present possesses. For everything ought to instruct him: every glance he casts at his clothes, his room, his home, every walk he takes through the streets of his town, every visit he pays to a fashionable shop; in his social life he ought to be aware of the origin of his manners and deportment, in the world of our artistic institutions, of our concerts, theatres and museums, he ought to notice the grotesque juxtaposition and confusion of different styles.... But with this kind of 'culture', which is in fact only a phlegmatic lack of all feeling for culture, one cannot overcome enemies, least of all those who, like the French, actually possess a real and productive culture, regardless of what its value may be, and from whom we have hitherto copied everything, though usually with little skill.

'Up to now', Nietzsche concluded, 'there has been no original German culture.'[3]

Taken together, Strauss's paean and Nietzsche's tirade raise the issues that shaped the German pursuit of culture in Imperial Germany. Informing all considerations of culture and the arts was the issue of German identity, which intruded itself into every discussion about a building, a concert, or an exhibition, every production of a new opera or play. The compulsion to define what the composer Richard Wagner called the 'true meaning and peculiarity of that German essence' also bumped up against, as in Nietzsche's meditation, the rest of the world.[4] The purveyors and creators of art in the imperial period tried, at times awkwardly, to reconcile their desire for international cultural exchange, on the one hand, and for an authentically German art, on the other. Germany's difficult relationship with France was often the focus of this tension. One can speak equally of Francophobia and Francophilia as defining features of imperial German culture.

The search for 'Germanness' in a world of nations exposed further tensions that found expression in the arts and cultural institutions of these years. First among these were religious tensions. Nineteenth-century Germans were profoundly divid-ed on the question of religion's place in their rapidly changing society. These divisions came out explicitly in the *Kulturkampf* ('cultural struggle') against Catholicism waged by German liberals and the Bismarckian state. But they also came out implicit-ly in many efforts to represent the sacred in visual, dramatic, and musical forms. Second, the question of religion reflected an even more general questioning of the hold the past had on the present. Nietzsche's second 'untimely meditation' on 'The Uses and Disadvantages of History for Life' extended his lament about Germany's lack of cultural vitality by suggesting that an excess of historical consciousness had inhibited Germans' abil-ity to live and create. Critics other than Nietzsche worried that too many artistic works relied on historical precedents to the point of lifeless conventionality. Moreover, many artists and con-sumers of art found, on the contrary, that the past was the only sure guide in society's march forward. Nevertheless, between the categories we still use in studying art—the establishment and the avant-garde, the traditional and the modern—the differences were not always dramatic. Ambivalence about both tradition and modernity formed a subtext of much cultural activity and artistic creation.

Third and finally, the relationship of culture and the arts to political and social life raised a series of questions for Germans. Who were the cultural leaders in society—artists or scholars or critics or even a new category of commercial producers and sponsors? Who could or should participate in cultural life? Did culture and the arts have a role to play in the collective life of the nation? And if they did, was it celebratory and affirming or critical and interrogative? As artistic movements alternated and collided in the increasingly rapid pace of cultural activity after 1870, these questions elicited no clear answers. Nor could even the most optimistic of cultural observers have found in these decades a 'unity of artistic style, in every expression of the life' of the German people. But amidst the 'chaotic jumble of styles' that Nietzsche derided as the pedants' modernity, Imperial Germany sustained a cultural life that created as many glimpses of the future as homages to the past.

Institutions of the cultural world

The founding of the German Empire in 1871 had no immediate effect on the ways that cultural and artistic institutions operated or that Germans participated in cultural life. Cultural policy remained decentralized and in the hands of individual states and municipalities and constituted a vigorous survival of particularism in German Europe. Particularism and decentralization did not necessarily produce backwardness and provincialism in cultural affairs, although critics were always quick to find both. One English observer of Germany in the 1870s wrote that 'Kleinstädterei [sic], or the niggling government of petty princes', with its 'consequent narrow views and interests, place-hunting, and stagnation of culture', was 'the bane of Germany'.[5] But its consequences after 1871 were less dire than that. For one thing, the persistence of a pattern of dispersed cultural organization generated local pride in the offerings of a state's or a city's cultural institutions. This in turn led to perpetual competition for the best conductors and the best orchestras, the best international art exhibitions and the best permanent art collections. A network of nearly 100 art unions and guilds in the many cities of Germany organized artists and their exhibitions: by 1914 it had developed extensive international links, particularly between the larger art centres like Munich, Berlin, Hamburg, or Düsseldorf and France and Great Britain. The rare national cultural associations that came into existence in these years, like the loosely organized General German Art Association, had to avoid connection with any one city or region if they were to be effective. Cultural activists, especially in the area of music, often had only limited interest in political borders, because the German culture that they sought to nurture had much to lose, as both historical tradition and continuing project, from too much attention to political borders. The General German Music Association, founded in 1861 in Weimar as the first national music society in Germany, sponsored annual music festivals which alternated among different German and German-speaking cities. It also established scholarship funds for which many more Germans than the residents of Bismarck's empire were eligible to compete. For instance, Arnold Schoenberg of Vienna was a recipient of an award from the association's Beethoven Foundation, established in 1872.

The stimulating effects of so many different localisms in competition with each other, along with a general expansion of commerce, wealth, and tax revenues, meant that more and more money was spent on artistic undertakings. Funds for projects ranging from grand new buildings to band music in the town park also came from a wider variety of sources, with an inexorable shift away from courts and aristocratic patrons to public coffers, at the state and civic level. Just as significant was the presence of private, non-state sources of funding even for public projects. Voluntary associations played a crucial role in music and the visual arts, helping local orchestras, conservatories, and art museums in their work, raising subscription funds for national monuments, and organizing amateur performance groups for public performances. Little of this was new. Art associations and choral societies had been around for decades. The opening up of court concerts and princely museums to a paying public had its beginnings in the eighteenth century. And the transformation of civic cultural institutions into joint ventures between taxpayers and wealthy local citizens had long characterized the cultural life of commercial cities like Hamburg and Frankfurt. Furthermore, churches now provided very little patronage of new art, which reflected changes in church independence going back to the decline of the Holy Roman Empire. In sum, the imperial period after 1871 saw the final consolidation of a complicated system of densely interrelated but dispersed cultural institutions.

The biggest changes came with the ever more complete integration of cultural activities into the commercial market, with mixed consequences for artistic autonomy. Works of art became products for sale in a marketplace of art galleries and auction houses, music publishers and concert series. Artists could potentially make enough money to remain independent of governments and wealthy patrons. Or they could, as many feared, become as co-opted by the market as they had been controlled by the courts. The expansion of the art trade was particularly notable by the end of the century, with more dealers offering artists more commercial opportunities

than did established institutions, as well as better promotional services beyond the purview of the old-fashioned art academy and its
salon exhibition. The range of commercial opportunities for artists
was considerable. Johannes Brahms, one of the first composers to
earn a comfortable living from his compositions' royalties alone,
composed a lucrative line of Hungarian dance music for amateur
pianists. In his early, impoverished years, Wagner wrote short articles and prepared piano reductions of opera scores for the Parisian
publisher Schlesinger. Hermine Preuschen, the 'Advertising Artist',
parlayed the notoriety of rejection by the Berlin Academy Exhibition in 1887 into an exhibition she arranged and publicized herself
with great success.[6] The Russian-born avant-garde artist Wassily Kandinsky, who likewise had a painting rejected for a juried
exhibition in 1911, formed a touring exhibition with several other
avant-garde artists under the intriguing and commercially effective
name of The Blue Rider (*Der Blaue Reiter*). Between ticket sales
and exhibition receipts, the market became an equal player in the
operations of cultural life, and by 1914 it was perhaps even the
dominant one, for traditional and avant-garde artists alike.

For their part, the directors of cultural institutions showed
increasing ingenuity in their search for commercial revenue and
private donations. The greatest innovator of all may have been
Richard Wagner, whose long march through the nineteenth century's moneyed institutions, in search of funding for his Festival
Theatre (*Festspielhaus*) at Bayreuth, took him from traditional royal patronage (King Ludwig II of Bavaria) to the more impersonal
patronage of the new German national government (an appeal
to Bismarck, who declined the honour) to an even more novel
scheme involving the founding of 'Wagner clubs' across Germany
and around the world to raise funds for Bayreuth.[7] Germany's
complex arrangements for the maintenance of culture and the arts
did make artistic innovation on a grand Wagnerian scale difficult.
But the very difficulties Wagner encountered in his epic quest
for money reveal the norms—and the limitations—of his time.
In the jaundiced view of George Bernard Shaw, the 'energetic
subscription-hunting ladies' of the Wagner clubs soon triumphed
over Wagner's own 'fabulous and visionary' experiment to 'keep
the seats out of the hands of the frivolous public and in the hands of
earnest disciples'. As 'an attempt to evade the ordinary social and

commercial conditions of theatrical enterprise', Shaw concluded that Bayreuth 'was a failure'.[8]

Amateurs and art culture

Shaw's juxtaposition of ordinary conditions and visionary projects hints at a fundamental division of European culture into two categories of unstable definition—the high and the low, the serious and the thoughtless, the avant-garde and everybody else. Shaw was not alone in viewing the cultural scene dichotomously. Many commentators defended the fortress of art from incursions of triviality and trash. More recently, musicologist Carl Dahlhaus suggested that the great dividing line in nineteenth-century culture lay between a strong and a weak concept of art, corresponding to two kinds of artists and audiences. The strong concept of art regarded it as a serious undertaking, demanding of the listener or viewer high levels of training and attention, along with a philosophical commitment to self-cultivation (*Bildung*) and artistic autonomy. Adhering to the strong concept of art, an advance guard of creative artists constituted an elite few who were able to move beyond the conventions of the time and conquer ever more demanding artistic heights. Adhering to the weak concept of art, by contrast, were those who regarded art as entertainment, diversion, and pleasure, who valued transparency of meaning and ease of consumption, and who expected little staying power from the objects of their artistic attention, given that repetition of such work would inevitably produce boredom.

But to illuminate the many ways that people actually participated in cultural life, we need to make a more extensive set of distinctions. Imperial Germany was marked by at least four different, overlapping circles of artistic activity. First, all the arts attracted amateur practitioners and developed new ways to involve art-lovers in them. Urbanization, technology, and belief in the importance of self-cultivation combined to make more art available to more people. The legal end to timeless copyright in 1867 brought about a boom in the publication of 'classics' by both writers and composers. Book and music stores were soon awash with the works of Goethe and Beethoven, Schiller and Mozart. Promoting and consuming these classics provided a satisfying way to express one's national identity. With the shift in piano manufacture from craft shop to factory by mid-century and the consequent development of standardized types, the production of pianos increased eightfold in Germany between 1870 and 1910, their cost was cut in half, and the piano came into its own as the centrepiece of middle-class cultivation. The genre of *Hausmusik*, or simple compositions for amateur players, became the profitable foundation of many music publishing houses. Such publishers oversaw an explosive increase in the sheer amount of available printed music up to a high point around 1910. Anthologies with titles like *German Music for the Home from Four Centuries* included easy instrumental and vocal pieces and piano reductions from both currently popular operas and symphonies of the great German masters. One can scarcely exaggerate the importance of the piano in the parlour for middle-class sociability, for the persistence of an idealist view of art's edifying effects, and for the growing certainty among ordinary Germans about Germany's special musical gifts.

The people who participated in the amateur artistic activities of Imperial Germany were also among the most avid students of the past—early and persistent consumers of the historical scholarship that assembled a genealogy of German artistry across the centuries. The repertoire of serious musical amateurism was historical in orientation, and associations of amateur musicians had been among the pioneers in the recovery of the German musical Baroque. But hand in hand with a nationally tinged reverence for the past went an openness to contemporary artists and composers, especially those who saw themselves as contributing to this tradition. Of these, Hamburg-born Brahms was uniquely able to combine profound musical language with accessibility to performance and understanding. Obsessed with his late entry into a musical tradition of near-unapproachable greatness (he famously spoke of hearing the footsteps of the giants who came before him), Brahms paid homage to that tradition with works that sought to extend the models from the musical past. A direct consequence of his historical interests was his continuing attention to such genres as the string quartet and the piano sonata. In an era that saw chamber music moving increasingly out of the salon and private drawing room and into the concert hall, Brahms composed a number of chamber works dedicated to the serious musical amateurs who were his friends and supporters. The piano—the instrument par excellence of the amateur musician—also stood, in Leon Botstein's words, 'at the very heart of his compositional genius'.[9]

Brahms composed hundreds of *Lieder*, or art songs—another musical genre central to serious music-making in the home and small gatherings. The genre of the *Lied* that Brahms carried forward was closely linked to German identity through its integration of the texts of Germany's poets with the music of its composers. Brahms and his younger Austrian contemporary Hugo Wolf helped to shape the culture of feeling and subjectivity that marked middle-class participation in the arts. Its characteristic milieu was not solitude but intimacy—intimacy between the keyboard and the vocal lines of music, between pianist and singer, between performers and their audience. The *Lied* expressed a German community constituted through close communication. Its ubiquity in the middle-class household created a commonality of experience as crucial to national consciousness as visits to large public monuments or participation in the popular historical parades.

The performance of a *Lied* formed the central subject of the most often-reproduced painting at the turn of the century. Titled the *Billet Outside Paris* and completed in 1894, its painter, Anton von Werner, was the director of the Royal Academic Institute for the Fine Arts in Berlin and celebrated for his depictions of the proclamation of the new German Empire at Versailles (also frequently reproduced in postcards and prints for the drawing room). 'Billet Outside Paris' illustrated a scene from the Franco-Prussian War, now some two decades past. Like all Werner's work, this painting had a cinematic realism to it, with Werner's characteristic attention to every detail of decor and uniform. Set in a rococo drawing room of an occupied French chateau, its focal figure was a Prussian officer, standing by a piano and singing a Schubert *Lied* to the accompaniment of another officer. The spontaneous house concert evoked the intimate culture of the German home. The soldiers' valour now combined cultivated domesticity with military tradition, elevating both to a national monument of German greatness and contrasting its ineffable substance to the material superficiality of French society in which it now resounded.

Amateurism also took more public forms. Hamburg's Alfred Lichtwark was exemplary in this regard. In 1886, Lichtwark became director of the Hamburg Art Museum and transformed it from a second-rate provincial art collection to the vehicle for a wide-ranging project of cultural renewal through aesthetic education. Lichtwark's plans, which he cannily laid out first in high-profile speeches, aimed to create a broader public for art through active involvement in its appreciation. A museum library with extensive hours, engravings framed so that they could be picked up and scrutinized, instruction in drawing and painting for schoolteachers and the interested public, lectures for working-class audiences, exhibitions of amateur art, and of course that staple of modern museum culture, the guided tour for squirming schoolchildren—Lichtwark used all these innovations to narrow the distance between the activity of art and the passivity of its reception.[10]

For music lovers, increasing numbers of choral societies, orchestras, and brass bands filled the schedules of performance halls and city bandstands to the bursting point. Dresden, the fourth largest city in Germany, boasted fifty male choirs, and even the new industrial city of Ludwigshafen had more than twenty amateur choral groups. Typical of all such groups was the Ludwigshafen Choral Society, whose director, the grammar-school teacher Jakob Gutwein, kept his singers on a steady diet of 'folk songs and the easier art songs', rehearsed 'to stand up to the most exacting criticism'.[11] In industrial areas, a distinctive culture of mine and factory bands and choruses developed. The Saarland's coal and steel industries generated nearly fifty such organizations, with links both to factory music associations elsewhere in Germany and to middle-class musicians in the Saarland's cities.[12] Max Bruch, a composer now largely forgotten, enjoyed tremendous success in Imperial Germany because of the many works he wrote for amateur choruses. His first great success, *Frithjof*, an un-Wagnerian oratorio based on a thirteenth-century Icelandic saga, was rapturously received by the public.[13] The oratorio, old and new, became an important form of religious expression in Imperial Germany. Not part of religious services, its performance represented a modernized piety, all the more pervasive for being freed from traditional sacred spaces. Bruch himself wrote fourteen sacred oratorios. Brahms's *German Requiem*, the texts for which he drew not from the Latin requiem mass but from Luther's translation of the Bible, offered contemplation of this world's sorrows and consolation to those who grieve. Its debut in Bremen in 1868 and its progress through the choral societies of not only Germany but Switzerland, England, and the Netherlands—all places with choral traditions that paralleled Germany's own—established Brahms's reputation as a major composer.

Serious art and the art establishment

Amateurs, as Goethe had long ago described them, merely followed the 'tendencies of the times', whereas the true artist 'commanded' them.[14] Amateur involvement in culture and the arts remained dependent—for repertoire, for instruction, for directors and conductors, for the prestige that amateurs hoped to absorb secondhand—on three other circles of artistic activity, all of which were shaped by professional artists and their creations. These circles might be characterized as the serious, the light, and the avantgarde. Of these three, the most commanding arena of artistic activity was the first, that of the serious artistic establishment. It consisted of art academies and city art unions; master classes, juried exhibitions, and museums; opera houses, orchestras, and music conservatories; royal or ducal or municipal theatres; and prestigious journals for literature, the visual arts, and music.

Disparaged by its critics for being little more than a system of rule enforcement, the artistic establishment of Imperial Germany was not as old and secure in its institutional power as it sometimes seemed. This was particularly true in the case of musical life, the institutions of which had hardly reached adolescence when they came under attack for being hidebound and conservative. The concert had early modern precedents, but its defining characteristics—the hall, the formal clothing, the silent audience, the performance of entire works—all reflected a new seriousness, not an old one. They also reflected a new process of canon formation and professionalization, led by a new breed of conductors who commanded their increasingly large forces like generals in a war on fashion and superficiality. The historical editions of Bach's and Handel's works only reached completion in the 1880s; the first full-fledged music conservatory in Germany, Felix Mendelssohn's Leipzig Conservatory, dated back just to 1843; the Berlin Philharmonic, soon the epitome of the serious music ensemble, was founded only in 1882.

Although the concert repertoire became overwhelmingly historical in the course of the nineteenth century, with the symphonies of Ludwig van Beethoven at its heart, serious orchestras did not close their lists to new compositions. The death of Beethoven in 1827 had led to a crisis in the composition of large-scale instrumental works, as composers faced the impossibility of either ignoring or imitating him. But after relatively little symphonic composition in the middle decades of the nineteenth century, Brahms's First Symphony, premiered in 1876, took the symphonic tradition (four movements, an old-fashioned array of instrumental forces) and made it once again the centrepiece of the established concert. Brahms's ability to fuse tradition with profound innovation suggests that the musical establishment of Imperial Germany was not an inert and backward-looking set of institutions incapable of encouraging new creative energies.

The institutional situation of the visual arts was somewhat different. The most prominent art academies could trace their origins to the seventeenth and eighteenth centuries. But as with music, the impression of age and conventionality that they exuded in the late decades of the nineteenth century derived in part from their determination to uphold a relatively new artistic ideal, that of the autonomy and moral purpose of art. For many an establishment figure, art was a serious matter and the pathway to true freedom. In Imperial Germany, it seemed threatened not by frivolous aristocrats but by the short attention span of the paying public; that is, by commerce and its works. This attitude towards the arts found its most fervent defender in Kaiser Wilhelm II. 'Art should contribute to the education of the people', Wilhelm informed his subjects; 'even the lower classes, after their toil and hard work, should be lifted up and inspired by ideal forces.'[15]

Anton von Werner, the quintessential establishment painter, was only thirty-two when he became director of the Berlin art academy in 1875. But this power base allowed him to exert and extend his influence well into the twentieth century. Although he could be tyrannical and intolerant, his artistic ethos was up-to-date and even liberal: in his 'meticulously executed paintings', in the 'reforms established at the art institute', and in his 'anti-elitist policies supporting the large number of average artists within the societies and associations', one saw the bourgeois age at its most confident.[16] The artists most celebrated within the artistic establishment—Werner himself, Franz Lenbach, Hans Makart, Adolph Menzel, Friedrich August von Kaulbach, Karl von Piloty—were also not so easily pigeonholed. Most did favour pictorial representations of historical and contemporary scenes, with recognizable figures in fully realized settings; but in their theatricality, allegory, monumentalism, and historically accurate detail, they differed substantially from one another. From Piloty's *Thusnelda at the Triumphal Entry of Germanicus into Rome* (1875) to Menzel's *Iron-Rolling Mill* (1875), the search for a national style in the artistic mainstream encouraged variety as well as conformity, whatever one might ultimately say about the quality of its results.

Most of the new buildings of the imperial period likewise reflected many historical styles, from the Gothic to Renaissance to Classical and Baroque, each dominant within a sphere deemed appropriate (German Renaissance for city halls, very often). Here, too, the search for a distinctively German architecture resurrected many imagined pasts in which religious and secular traditions became entangled. The Kaiser Wilhelm Memorial Church in Berlin, built in 1891–94 to honour Wilhelm I by his grandson Wilhelm II, took a neo-Romanesque style, rich in reference to Germanic medieval empires. Wilhelm I, the 'white beard on the red beard's throne', became the reincarnation of Friedrich Barbarossa, and his memorial served as church, museum, and monument, incorporating a pre-Reformation Catholic past within the frame of a Protestant church/dynasty. But the placement of the memorial church in the Augusta-Victoria square in central Berlin, also rebuilt in neo-Romanesque style under Wilhelm II's direction, pointed forward as well as back—an urban space, with apartment buildings and restaurants, and even, soon, a thriving artists' community centred on the neo-Romanesque Romanisches Café.[17]

Art for entertainment

The idealism inherent in both the concert repertory and the art academy annual exhibition, however hidebound they came to seem, contrasted with what was perhaps the largest arena of artistic production and consumption in Imperial Germany, that of art for popular entertainment, marked by its commodity status and unaccompanied by claims to moral edification. 'Light music of quality', as one music historian has dubbed it, had its spiritual home in the Vienna of the waltz kings, Johann Strauss the father and Johann Strauss the son, and in the Paris of Jacques Offenbach's operettas.[18] It was performed by professional musicians in venues consistent with its easy-going premise: in restaurants and parks, at spas, in ballrooms and theatres, in popular concert series that provided an alternative to the Beethoven-based repertoire of the symphony concert. The ubiquitous military bands of the nineteenth century were not commercial, but they also performed essentially 'light music of quality' and were a much-loved feature of Sunday afternoons in the public gardens. Much of the opera repertoire fell into this category as well. Even Wagner's music dramas—the whole point of which was to elevate dramatic music beyond an evening's diversion and into the higher realm of the symphonic—became a paradoxical kind of high-brow entertainment for the paying public, especially in regional opera houses with their countless performances of *Lohengrin* and *Tannhäuser*. The bridal chorus from *Lohengrin* began to redefine the bourgeois wedding ceremony, and it was a rare brass band, whether made up of miners or middle-class civil servants, that did not perform some simplified version of Siegfried's Rhine Journey.

Despite their patina of seriousness, most of the monuments that sprang up all over Germany, in epidemic numbers after 1871, could also be included in this category, not just because of the banality and sheer bad taste of their design but because of their place in a physical ensemble with strongly recreational overtones.

People took hikes to the Bismarck towers scattered across the hilltops of Germany, and they dined practically in the shadow of Germania on the Rhine. Then there were the panoramas, the high-tech rotundas that 'popped up like mushrooms' across Europe in the last three decades of the century. These circular landscape paintings, usually depicting battle scenes, were designed and executed by professional artists and interior decorators and were celebrated as a 'new art form for the common people'. In Germany, about 10 million visitors viewed them in cities from Stettin to Karlsruhe. The panoramas were big business, organized by joint-stock companies (many of them Belgian) and attracting attention in serious art journals as well as the penny press.[19] The 'staple of the bourgeois market', however, and the bulk of what lay behind the rapid growth of the art market in the last decades before the war, was not so much large battle scenes as small landscapes and genre paintings. This art was 'cabinet-sized', studio-finished, and 'calculated to evoke a mood of wistful nature romanticism in an increasingly urban public'.[20]

A comparable realization of the commercial potential for straightforward yet artful renderings of history, travel, nature, and modern life came in the field of what we might call 'light literature of quality'. The expansion of literacy, the institution of the commercial lending library, and the growing number of publishing houses, journals, and newspapers all underlay an outpouring of fiction for the German middle classes. From former opera singer Eugenie Marlitt (a pseudonym), whose serialized novels were said to have been responsible for the quadrupling of the circulation of the family journal *Die Gartenlaube*, to Karl May and his adventure stories about Old Shatterhand, Winnetou, and Hadschi Alef Omar ibn Hadschi Abu Abbas ibn Hadschi Dawud al Gosarah, the decently educated German reader had plenty of reading matter that demanded little of him or her except the expenditure of time.

German Modernism and the avant-garde

The fourth circle of artistic activity in the German Empire was that of the avant-garde. It was the most self-conscious and self-defining group of cultural producers: too elitist for the everyday artists of amateurism, at once too iconoclastic, too market-oriented, and too separatist for the establishment, and too philosophically and artistically demanding for the consumer of art as entertainment. Its self-consciousness explains its ability to generate names for its activities (Naturalism, Expressionism, neo-Realism, *Jugendstil*), which in turn created movements out of small numbers of people and disparate, even incoherent, stylistic innovations. That Imperial Germany could even claim to have had an avant-garde has been disputed. Its secessionist artists have sometimes seemed unoriginal, its composers conflicted (or Viennese, and hence not to be counted), its architects provincial, its writers uninspired. But however their work is ultimately regarded, there can be no doubting the sheer variety of ways that artists found to escape the confines of established institutions and to combat the idiocies of commercialized modern life.

The avant-garde in Imperial Germany also took shape as a form of opposition to—but also under the constraint of—government censorship. Such censorship usually involved *ex post facto* prosecutions of art or literature for breaking laws concerning blasphemy, obscenity, and other forms of disrespect for authority and heads of state. Censorship, as it evolved over the course of the imperial era, became itself a moving target for those trying—sometimes in equal measures—to evade it and to provoke it. Initially a matter to be decided by hereditary rulers and their civil servants alone, questions of censorship soon involved elected representatives and the public itself. Both were just as likely to call for more public support for artistic innovation as they were to clamour for a crackdown on artists who offended 'feelings of modesty and morality'.[21] The set-piece of censorship in this period became the debate over the 'Lex Heinze', a bill introduced in the Reichstag in 1892 that sought to expand existing laws against obscenity by explicit reference to theatre and art. The parliamentary debate split the political parties into opposing camps, which was hardly surprising. But the public controversy mobilized in opposition a powerful cross-section of cultural leaders in all fields of artistic endeavour, which *was* surprising. It suggested that the lines dividing established artists and avant-garde ones, the conventional and the innovative, were to some extent artificial and certainly a matter of context and perception.

Nevertheless, if avant-gardism included many artists with full establishment credentials, it operated in different ways and venues. The most public of the declarations of independence from accepted artistic practices were the various 'secessions' from the annual salon exhibitions organized by the artists' equivalents of trade associations. The salon exhibitions were probably the single most important venue for sales of art works, but the conditions under which art was displayed were crowded and inadequate. This situation itself testified to the growing number of artists in Imperial Germany and the growing market for their works. The first secessionists, in Munich in 1892, were not so much rejected as disgruntled artists, eager to get away from the cluttered exhibition halls and establish freer conditions for the production and appreciation of art. The Munich secessionists received plenty of publicity and favourable reviews, and their example was soon followed in other cities—Berlin most prominently, in 1898. The twenty-five or so years before the outbreak of war in 1914 were marked by waves of secession from whatever group of artists had most recently established itself as the dominant force in the art community; secession itself generated publicity and with it sales. All secessionists retained a sense of rejecting the aesthetic tyranny of the art academies. But at the same time, all retained a close relationship to the art markets, working with gallery owners and museum directors.

Art historians have often regarded the works of the German secessionists and avant-garde artists in general as tame forms of rebellion. Yet they did arouse controversy. Initially their notoriety came from their choice of subject matter, which abandoned great men and ancient gods in favour of the ordinary and sometimes the bizarre. The latter was the specialty of the eccentric Arnold Böcklin and the dream-haunted Max Klinger, both of whom deployed all the symbolic paraphernalia of the sublime (stormy seas, mysterious figures, lyres, and hunting horns) to achieve a kind of avant-garde kitsch. Max Liebermann, the leading representative of Naturalism in Germany, had been attracting criticism since the 1870s for his portrayal of what were considered miserable, depressing subjects: a painting of tired, grim-looking women plucking geese seemed to its establishment critics an image unlikely, paraphrasing Wilhelm II, to lift up the toiling classes. When in 1879 the Jewish Liebermann dared to paint a young, almost stereotypically Jewish-looking Jesus with the elders in the temple in Jerusalem, the storm of criticism became explicitly antisemitic and hysterically defensive of Christian Germany.[22] In the decade of the 1880s, the Christian painter Fritz von Uhde aroused both criticism and praise (also tinged with antisemitism) for a series of paintings of Jesus, his apostles, and his early followers, all with the faces and clothes of German peasants and situated in the plain settings of German countryside and village. In this case, the mainstream art critics proved far more ready to embrace this naturalistic image of a German Jesus than were the Protestant or Catholic church establishments. The latter remained suspicious of the socialist sympathies implicit in all forms of Naturalism.

By the time von Uhde joined the Munich Secession in 1892 and Liebermann led the Berlin Secession in 1898, both had, in a sense, left their most controversial days behind them. What came to be called Expressionism claimed the status of the new avant-garde, experimenting with a style that would express the intensity of interior emotion rather than try to reproduce the outward visual impression of things. The two main groups of Expressionist artists, The Bridge (*Die Brücke*) formed in Dresden in 1905 and The Blue Rider (*Der Blaue Reiter*) formed in Munich in 1911, moved toward abstract representation in their use of vivid colour and violent, often primitive imagery. In the heyday of Expressionism, the whole notion of a modernist avant-garde in conflict with the establishment had become almost a cliché of art criticism and consumption—a phenomenon that subtly detracted from their capacity to shock the audience into new consciousness.

Other kinds of secession marked the theatrical, musical, and literary communities. Richard Wagner, for instance, can be seen as Imperial Germany's first and most important avant-garde artist, breaking all rules, musical, social, and otherwise—a veritable one-man secession movement. After all, he cut himself loose from existing musical and theatrical institutions and built his own centre at Bayreuth, which he organized according to all his own rules of tonality, architectural design of theatres, social conduct at performances, and professional expectations of performers. Yet even while his music dramas continued to enact a radical challenge to existing politics, society, and religion, he became (or at the very least allowed himself to become) the cultural focus of a radically antisemitic and racialist movement, which sought to exclude and to shut down much that was vibrant in Imperial Germany's cultural and artistic life. The musical avant-garde after Wagner thus found little to inspire or sustain them in the Bayreuth ruled over by Wagner's widow Cosima. Wagner's influence, enduringly important in purely musical terms, lost its revolutionizing potential to the suffocating cult of one man's genius.

In the world of non-operatic theatre, the difficulties of staging Naturalist plays under existing commercial and political conditions led to the creation of new, essentially private theatrical societies, the model for which was Berlin's Free Stage. Here the premiere of *The Weavers*, Gerhart Hauptmann's controversial dramatization of the 1844 revolt of the Silesian weavers, created a sensation. In order to extend the moral uplift of theatre to the working classes, socialist activist Bruno Wille founded the Free People's Stage in 1890, an organization with radical egalitarian goals but conventional, even conservative, tastes in drama. Secession from popular entertainment led to the growth of cabaret culture after 1900 in the major urban centres. Satirical, humorous, at times blasphemous and grotesque, the German cabaret movement developed a distinctive kind of urban entertainment that was both intimate and challenging, aspiring neither to high cultural seriousness nor to broad acclaim or commercial success.[23] Satirical journals, such as the aging *Kladderadatsch* in Berlin (founded in 1848) and the newer *Simplicissimus* in Munich (launched in 1896), developed large circulations with their irreverent content and high-quality cartoons and illustrations. Many of these images had strong affinities with modernist art's drive to simplification, exaggeration, and abstraction. Shortly before war broke out in 1914, *Simplicissimus* published the first chapters of novelist Heinrich Mann's biting critique of German arrogance and servility, *The Loyal Subject*.[24] While far from serving as political gathering points, cabarets, open theatres, and satirical journals did provide venues for artists to dissent from the Straussian 'rejoicing' in German achievements that Nietzsche had warned at the outset of the empire would be the death of German culture.

Finally, secession was also the watchword for a colourful array of life reform movements that proliferated in the 1890s and beyond. Many of these appropriated Nietzsche as their spiritual mentor, glorifying the author of *Thus Spoke Zarathustra* (the first complete edition of which appeared in 1892, three years after Nietzsche's final mental breakdown), with its endless calls for self-overcoming, life-affirming, and faithfulness to the earth. Whether carrying Nietzsche in their back pockets or not, life reformers sought to make clothing more comfortable, bodies more beautiful, houses more restful, foods more digestible, and diets more vegetable. Striving for any, let alone all, of these things in the modern cities of Imperial Germany usually involved abandoning them. Thus the turn of the century, in Germany as elsewhere, saw a new enthusiasm for the countryside, seaside, and mountainside, all of which provided vistas of a new kind of cultural progress for a new kind of human being. The artists' colony at Worpswede was the most famous of these retreats from the city. Founded in 1889, when the painters Fritz Mackensen and Otto Modersohn left their art academies for a peat-bog in Lower Saxony, Worpswede soon gathered a group of like-minded artists and poets and, in the way of such things, founded an official association in 1894 (called, unimaginatively, the Worpswede Artists' Association). Worpswede was only geographically isolated; its artists participated in, and provided a distinctive German contribution to, a number of broader international movements. National romanticism, a Scandinavian movement to recover vernacular styles and building materials like brick and wood for the regeneration of architecture and interior design, had important German participants, in Worpswede and elsewhere. So too did the closely linked arts and crafts movement, the main exponents of which were the *Jugendstil* artists and designers in Munich and in Darmstadt, the latter at the Mathildenhöhe colony established in 1899 by Grand Duke Ernst Ludwig.

Yet each of these movements had tendencies not only to secession and retreat but also to urbanism and commerce. This is well illustrated in the career of Peter Behrens, a founding member of Munich's United Workshops for Art in Handicraft. Behrens was inspired by the idea of small communities of artists and craftsmen, integrating style and practicality to achieve social and cultural reform. In 1899, he left Munich to join the ducal community at Mathildenhöhe, there designing a house that was part curving *Jugendstil*, part vernacular brickwork in the spirit of national romanticism, with interior designs inspired by Nietzsche's *Zarathustra*. In 1907, with designer Hermann Muthesius, he helped to found the German Crafts League (*Deutscher Werkbund*), still recognizably part of the arts and crafts movement but increasingly focused on industrial design and the possibilities of mass consumption. In the same year, Behrens became the artistic consultant to the electrical mega-corporation AEG (General Electric Company), for whom he created the first corporate identity, in the form of a logo, publicity materials, and the basis of the modern steel-and-glass aesthetic that came to full maturity in the Bauhaus movement closely associated with Behrens's younger colleague Walter Gropius.

By the post-war Weimar years, the culture of Imperial Germany had come to seem, in Thomas Mann's retrospective description, 'equivocal' and 'laughable' in its attachment to 'liberal ideas of reason and progress', 'crass' in its materialism, and absurd in its 'wilful love of mere largeness' and its 'taste for the monumental and standard, the copious and grandiose'.[25] This was a weighty critique, especially coming from a writer whose first novel, *Buddenbrooks* (1901), represented a finely honed portrait of nineteenth-century culture in one German family. Yet with all due respect to Mann and to the critical spirit he sought to uphold and encourage, a great deal of art that did endure and that did prove influential over the long term came out of the workshops, studios, rehearsal halls, and drafting rooms of Imperial Germany. This was culture that did not merely seduce the Germans who appreciated it into believing themselves the most cultured nation on the earth.[26] It also provided an illumination of its world and revealed the sorrows as well as the joys of a German modernity.

---

[1] Friedrich Nietzsche, *Untimely Meditations*, ed. Daniel Breazeale, trans. R. J. Hollindale (New York, 1997), 10.

[2] Ibid. 17–18; David Friedrich Strauss, *The Old Faith and the New: A Confession*, trans. Mathilde Blind (New York, 1873), 3.

[3] Nietzsche, *Untimely Meditations*, 3–6.

[4] Richard Wagner, 'What is German', *Richard Wagner's Prose Works*, 8 vols, iv. *Art and Politics*, trans. William Ashton Ellis (New York, 1966), 155.

[5] Sabine Baring-Gould, *Germany: Present and Past* (London, 1879), 328. Whereas the familiar German term *Kleinstaaterei* can be loosely translated as 'the fetish of small statehood', this author chose to refer not to states (*Staaten*) but to cities (*Städte*).

[6] Beth Irwin Lewis, *Art for All: The Collision of Modern Art and the Public in Late-Nineteenth-Century Germany* (Princeton, 2003), 11–12.

[7] Hannu Salmi, *Imagined Germany: Richard Wagner's National Utopia* (New York, 1999), 163–5.

[8] George Bernard Shaw, *The Perfect Wagnerite* (Mineola, NY, 1967), 127.

[9] Leon Botstein (ed.), *The Compleat Brahms: A Guide to the Musical Works of Johannes Brahms* (New York, 1999), 89, 151.

[10] Jennifer Jenkins, *Provincial Modernity: Local Culture and Liberal Politics in Fin-de-Siècle Hamburg* (Ithaca, NY, 2003), 61–6.

[11] Wilhelm Jakob Jung, *Musikgeschichte der Stadt Ludwigshafen am Rhein vom Jahre 1850 bis 1918*, ed. Siegfried Fauck (Ludwigshafen am Rhein, 1968), 84.

[12] Christoph-Hellmuth Mahling, 'Werkschöre und Werkskapellen im Saarländischen Industriegebiet', in Monica Steegman (ed.), *Musik und Industrie. Beiträge zur Entwicklung der Werkschöre und Werksorchester* (Regensburg, 1978), 107–12.

[13] Cited in Christopher Fifield, *Max Bruch: His Life and Works* (Woodbridge, UK, 2005), 54.

[14] Cited in Gerhard Baumann, 'Goethe: Über den Dilettantismus', *Euphorion: Zeitschrift für Literaturgeschichte*, 46 (1952), 350.

[15] Cited in Matthew Jefferies, *Imperial Culture in Germany, 1871–1918* (New York, 2003), 185.

[16] Lewis, *Art for All*, 31.

[17] Barbara Miller Lane, 'Memory, Myth, and Ideas of Community in modern German and Scandinavian Architecture', http://www.brynmawr.edu/emeritus/gather/Lane/lane.html. See also her *National Romanticism and Modern Architecture in Germany and the Scandinavian Countries* (Cambridge and New York, 2000).

[18] Jim Samson, 'Music and Society', in Samson (ed.), *The Late Romantic Era, from the Mid-19th Century to World War I* (Englewood Cliffs, NJ, 1991), 15.

[19] Lewis, *Art for All*, 32–8.

[20] Robin Lenman, 'From "Brown Sauce" to "Plein Air": Taste and the Art Market in Germany, 1889–1910', in Françoise Forster-Hahn (ed.), *Imagining Modern German Culture, 1889–1910* (Washington, DC, 1996), 55.

[21] Robin Lenman, 'Art, Society, and the Law in Wilhelmine Germany: The Lex Heinze', *Oxford German Studies*, 8 (1973–74), 93.

[22] Cited in Lewis, *Art for All*, 47.

[23] Peter Jelavich, *Berlin Cabaret* (Cambridge, MA, 1993), 1–7.

[24] This serialization of *Der Untertan* was broken off when war began in August 1914. It was published in full, however, within weeks of the war's end in November 1918.

[25] Thomas Mann, 'Sufferings and Greatness of Richard Wagner', in Mann, *Essays of Three Decades*, trans. H. T. Lowe-Porter (New York, 1947), 307.

[26] A leading German intellectual has recently suggested that the encouragement of a wilfully anti-political belief in culture is the regrettable legacy of the nineteenth century; see Wolf Lepenies, *The Seduction of Culture in German History* (Princeton, 2006).

Gendered Germany

Angelika Schaser

On 18 August 1896—more than a quarter century after Imperial Germany was formally unified—the Reichstag finally legislated its first Civil Code (*Bürgerliches Gesetzbuch*). The code, which took effect in 1900, left little doubt that the gender order in twentieth-century Germany was based not just on a distinction but on a hierarchy between the sexes. While this hierarchy was endorsed in the political, economic, and legal arenas, the Civil Code's paragraphs on marriage law were particularly revealing:

§1354. The husband is responsible for decisions in all matters affecting joint married life; in particular, he determines where the family is to reside.

The wife is not obliged to follow her husband's decision if it represents an abuse of his rights.

§1355. The wife assumes her husband's family name.

§1356. The stipulations of §1354 notwithstanding, the wife has the right and duty to manage the common household.

The wife is obliged to perform tasks in the household and the husband's business to the extent that such activities are customary in the circumstances in which the spouses live.

§1357. The wife is authorized to take care of the husband's business affairs and to represent him within her domestic sphere of activity. Legal transactions that she undertakes within this sphere of activity will be considered as undertaken in her husband's name unless circumstances demand otherwise.

The husband can restrict or exclude his wife from exercising these rights. If the restriction or exclusion represents an abuse of the man's rights, it can be lifted upon the wife's petition to the guardianship court.

Final passage of the German Civil Code in 1896 concluded more than two decades of lively public debate, which included the vigorous protests and agitation of the German women's movement. Legal codification cemented the husband's authority to make all important decisions within marriage.[1] While it was perfectly legal within this framework for spouses to choose to make joint decisions about their lives together, women had no right to equality within marriage. On this point the law was clear.

This document must be seen in its proper European and temporal contexts. In the wake of the French Revolution of 1789, a European-wide discussion had begun about the proper social order, which continued as industrialization transformed Germany. After 1871, the idea of the nation took centre stage as the unifying element of the newly created empire; more and more Germans also reflected on the future role of their nation state in international affairs. When we say that these twin discourses—on the construction of society and the construction of the nation—addressed and engaged 'Germans', one gains the impression that the term referred to the entire population. On closer scrutiny, however, women and men were assigned different roles and functions and differing significance. Men did not always appear in this debate as 'men', but often as essentially sexless human beings; by contrast, women were perceived primarily in terms of their gender. The equation of human beings with 'men' meant that women were declared a subordinate 'second sex'.[2] Political, economic, and legal reforms that had swept Europe since the Enlightenment seemed to have bypassed German gender relations.

Of course 'women' or even 'Woman' no more existed in Imperial Germany than 'men' or 'Man'. Like men, women were members of a family and of distinctive social, regional, and religious groups. They belonged to different age cohorts, they sympathized with a particular political milieu (or had no interest in politics), they practised various occupations. They were single, married, widowed, or divorced. Alongside gender, all of these aspects constituted part of the concept of the 'person'. No matter how diverse their individual identities and experiences, however, women in Imperial Germany had one thing in common: their legal, economic, and political disadvantages in comparison to men. Those disadvantages restricted their opportunities and agency in determining the course of their own lives. Whether one's name was entered into a church or civil register under the rubric 'male' or 'female' was an all-important distinguishing characteristic for every inhabitant of the German Empire. From cradle to grave, this single characteristic divided the population into two distinct groups.

This chapter explores how gender distinctions were maintained or challenged in Imperial Germany and their ramifications. It does so by exploring the demographic changes affecting German families and women's roles within them; women's experience of childhood, schooling, work, leisure, and politics; organized efforts to expand women's rights; and the varieties of anti-feminism that those efforts elicited. This analysis will demonstrate that gender distinctions inflected aspects of Imperial Germany discussed in every other chapter of this volume: the economy, class relations, religion, culture, bourgeois reform, political culture, militarism, radical nationalism, Germany's place in the world, and the experience of 'total war' after 1914.

The gendered distribution of life's opportunities

Industrialization, together with advances in medical care and hygiene, produced rapid demographic changes in Imperial Germany. Among those changes with a gender-specific quality, rising life expectancies merit attention. After centuries of female 'excess mortality'—frequently caused by death in childbirth but also by hard work and poor nutrition, from which women suffered more than men—women now enjoyed a far greater life expectancy. While the average life expectancy of men born between 1871 and 1880 was only 35.6 years, principally because of high infant mortality, men born between 1901 and 1910 could already hope, on average, to reach the age of 44.8 years. In those same periods, the average life expectancy for women was 38.5 and 48.3, respectively.[3] The life experiences of women and men were also affected by number of children, age at marriage, household income, increases or decreases in consumption, and the possibility of amassing savings. Among the business-oriented middle class (*Wirtschaftsbürgertum*) the average number of children per married couple fell from 4.1 to 2.8 children between 1875 and 1914. By the First World War, among the educated middle class (*Bildungsbürgertum*) the average number of children had dropped further, to 2.1.[4]

In the second half of the nineteenth century, Germans largely agreed that the 'Women's Question' had demographic roots. The spectre of 'surplus women' and the 'spinster emergency' exercised the minds of middle-class fathers, who found it increasingly difficult to find suitable husbands for their daughters.[5] Population data and marriage quotas, however, offer no clear evidence for the widespread feeling in this class of the population, which persisted into the twentieth century, that it was becoming increasingly difficult to marry. In this case statistics are not particularly helpful, because the alleged undersupply of husbands was not a purely demographic problem. Lily Braun, a leader of the women's movement at the turn of the century, understood clearly that the 'surplus daughters of the bourgeoisie' could not be expected to look for their future husbands among the 'equally surplus sons of the proletariat'.[6] The emphasis middle-class fathers placed on the 'surplus' of females and on the diminishing matrimonial chances of their daughters was 'a clear indicator of the mood of crisis' among this group—a mood that was not without some basis in reality.[7] Indeed, in nineteenth-century Germany, certain segments of the educated middle classes, above all civil servants, had seen their incomes and living conditions decline sharply relative to those of other social classes. A significant gap had opened up between the reality and the image of middle-class comfort, which included demonstrative leisure by middle-class women in particular.

Childhood and youth

Whereas children living in the countryside and among the urban lower classes were integrated into the everyday life and work routines of adults according to their strength and abilities, among the urban middle classes, childhood became a distinct and privileged stage of life. Children were distinguished sharply from adults and provided with their own nurseries in the home. The emotional relationship between parents and children was cultivated with particular care. Thus the childhood and youth of boys and girls, considered together, varied greatly according to class. However, the increasing polarity and hierarchy of the genders shaped the 'life-world' (*Lebenswelt*), and thus also childhood and youth, in all strata of society. In general, fathers expected to make the important decisions concerning child-rearing, whereas mothers—together with nursemaids and governesses in well-to-do families—looked after the children's everyday needs. Girls were prepared for their future role as housewives and mothers, whereas boys were raised with an eye to their future role as a provider (often a professional) and head of their own household. Women were not only expected to manage an orderly household and perform or supervise all the necessary tasks and child-rearing; increasingly they were also held responsible for the family's emotional well being and social contacts. In order to support the social aspirations of their husbands, especially in the educated middle classes, wives were increasingly expected to have a well-rounded education, artistic talent, and conversational abilities. The curricula of girls' secondary schools were gradually adapted to meet these demands.

The polarized gender model still offered plenty of room for differentness and ambivalence. Thus, upon closer scrutiny, we can see that nineteenth-century men who wished to fulfil their role in an exemplary fashion faced a wide range of expectations that were difficult to meet. They were supposed to exhibit such typically 'manly' qualities as ambition and decisiveness; but at the same time they were also expected to be well educated, cultivated, sensitive, passionate, elegant, and charming. At the turn of the century, with middle-class society's fixation on hard work and efficient time management, the challenge of being a 'whole man' grew enormously. Educated men in particular were criticized for their tendency to become social bores because they spent all their time pursuing business careers.[8] In short, gender relations and definitions of femininity and masculinity were negotiated in middle-class circles in complex ways—yet not so complex that gendered models of 'proper' middle-class behaviour could not be adopted by both the nobility and the lower classes.

Education and training

Population increase in Imperial Germany was accompanied by an expansion of primary and secondary education. Although the state sought to limit church influence in education during the *Kulturkampf*, primary schools generally remained denominational. 'Simultaneous schools' (*Simultanschulen*), in which children of different religions were taught together, remained the exception until the First World War. By and large, compulsory schooling was successfully enforced. In both town and country, boys and girls alike first attended primary school at the age of six and continued thereafter for six to eight years. Especially well-to-do Germans would have liked to enforce gender separation in the primary schools, but schools often had to provide instruction to boys and girls together for reasons of cost and space. For most boys and girls, formal schooling, whether in a state or primary school or (in wealthy families) at home with private tutors, ended at age fourteen, when they were confirmed.

Higher education was reserved for a small male elite. After 1900, some 90 per cent of pupils never went beyond primary school. Of secondary school pupils, even after 1900, 66 per cent attended a so-called humanist *Gymnasium*, with an emphasis on the Classics. After 1900, the secondary-school leaving certificate (*Abitur*) that gave pupils access to university studies could also be obtained from the other secondary schools, the *Oberrealschulen* and the *Realgymnasien*. Yet classical languages, which as a rule were not taught at girls' secondary schools, were still considered a special mark of cultivation.[9] Further education for girls was available only at the 'schools for young ladies' (*höhere Töchterschulen*) reserved for the offspring of well-to-do families. Because these schools had neither uniform curricula nor textbooks and offered no final examinations, it is difficult to make broad statements about them. Surviving curricula show, however, that the focus was on religion, German, French and English conversation, music, drawing, and needlework. That was the pinnacle of schooling for girls. If no suitable husband could be found after this 'higher education', which offered no formal qualification certificate, even intelligent young women full of intellectual curiosity found themselves suspended in 'temporary retirement'.

There had always been critics who lamented these limited educational opportunities for girls. In the second half of the nineteenth century, the number of men and women calling for a reform of female education rose. Numerous private initiatives, particularly women's educational associations, demanded improved girls' education. In Prussia, until 1908 girls' secondary education was administered, tellingly, by the department of *elementary* education. That far more private than public secondary girls' schools existed in Germany at the *fin de siècle* shows how little priority the state accorded girls' education. In 1901, for example, there were 213 state and 656 private secondary schools for girls in Prussia. The public girls' schools were also overwhelmingly run by men. In 1893, roughly 92 per cent of public girls' secondary schools in Prussia had headmasters, while roughly 88 per cent of the private schools had headmistresses.

Important milestones in the reform of girls' education included the 'Yellow Brochure' on girls' school reform published by Helene Lange in 1887, the academic secondary school courses for girls she set up in Berlin in 1893, and the girls' *Gymnasium* that Hedwig Kettler established that same year in Kassel. In a petition of 1887 to the Prussian ministry of education and the Prussian Landtag, Lange called for academic training for female teachers and more influence for them in the public girls' secondary schools. She used gender difference as an argument, claiming that only women were in a position to train growing girls in 'true femininity'.[10] In May 1894 a ministerial decree established the first curriculum for girls' secondary schools and introduced academic examinations for female teachers. A further breakthrough came when a ministerial commission on the reform of girls' secondary education convened in 1906. It established a ten-year school for girls, known as a *Lyzeum*. By contrast, the women's movement's call for female teachers for girls was only partially heeded. As girls' schools increasingly resembled boys' schools, posts in these schools became more attractive for male teachers. The (male) teachers' associations successfully lobbied Prussian administrators to ensure that both private and state schools for girls had to hire nearly as many men as women.

Meanwhile, a series of reforms provided women with access to German universities in all states of the empire, from 1899/1900 (in

Baden) to 1909 (in Mecklenburg-Schwerin). Women's university studies developed quickly: in 1908/9, 1,132 women were enrolled in German universities, rising to 4,128, or 6 per cent of students, in 1914. This first generation of women students were generally older than their male counterparts. Most came from educated homes. And 87 per cent studied in the philosophical faculties—mainly because after 1909 women in Prussia could enrol in a philosophical faculty after successfully completing a teacher-training course and two years of work experience at a girls' secondary school but without the *Abitur*. After six semesters of study they could then take the state teachers examination.[11] This so-called fourth path to university offered young women an opportunity to study that could be viewed as a wise investment for future wives and mothers, even if they taught only for a short time. Because families with limited financial resources preferred to invest in the training of sons, they often rejected their daughters' desire to study with the argument that it was a poor investment: women were expected to marry, not earn an income. Any ambitions women might have had to complete their *Habilitation*—a sort of second doctoral dissertation required to become a university professor—were nipped in the bud. Applications from female candidates were simply refused. Many professional examinations, such as the state examination for judges, were also closed to women until after 1918.

Overall, the expansion of Germany's educational system was based on ambivalent motives and produced ambiguous results. Women were incorporated into the system of secondary and academic education, which offered them certain career opportunities. Yet they were accorded a separate role. In the long term the male-orientated system of academic disciplines cemented discrimination against women.

Employment

Women's paid employment rose rapidly in Imperial Germany. However, in 1895 only 6.5 million women were employed, compared to 15.5 million men; thus women made up about 25 per cent of the workforce. Contemporary economists explained this great difference between male and female employment by arguing that women's occupations did not mean as much to them, since a woman's 'true calling' in life remained her role as 'wife, mother, and housewife'. Yet the occupational censuses of 1895 and 1907 left one form of work invisible: women's household and family work. The most basic reality of life for nearly all women, whatever their age, was work. But those who did not earn money were not considered to be working, and census takers used highly restrictive criteria for including women in the rubric 'helping family members'. For that reason, the tasks of maidservants, cooks, laundresses, and governesses were not considered work if they were performed by an unpaid wife, daughter, sister, or other female family member. This practice existed despite the fact that in the final pre-war years some 44 per cent of family income in the countryside was earned by those working within the household economy. Even if this figure does not reflect the exact proportion of housewives' income, it shows that these 'non-employed' women contributed substantially to supporting the family.[12] This disregard for household and family work had crucial ramifications for the way women's roles within the family and marriage were assessed. Women's economic inferiority was cemented with the 'discovery' and subsequent devaluation of housework, for which payment was rarely demanded because it was 'priceless'.[13]

Women worked not just in private households, but in all sectors of the economy: in agriculture, industry, and services. Although the importance of German agriculture steadily waned after 1875, Imperial Germany continued to exhibit the traits of an agrarian state. Female employment in agriculture fell between 1882 and 1907 from 61.4 to 49.8 per cent.[14] One thing remained constant: with few exceptions, women always earned less than men. The gap between male and female wages was widened by urbanization. Whereas the male-to-female ratio of average local daily wages in the countryside was 1.53, in the large cities it was 1.60.[15]

Urban society proved to be a trendsetter in the gender-specific development of the labour market. Many young, unmarried rural women moved to the cities to work as domestic servants, where they performed the household tasks necessary to uphold the middle-class family ideal that relieved the housewife of everyday chores. Domestic servants worked under a wide variety of conditions but usually without fixed working hours, for low wages, and sometimes under the threat of sexual exploitation.[16] Understandably, jobs in factories, commercial offices, and retail stores became far more attractive to women. The rate of female employment in domestic service fell between 1882 and 1907 from 18 to 16.1 per cent, whereas it rose during the same period from 12.8 to 19.5 per cent in the industry and trade sector and from 7.7 to 14.6 per cent in the tertiary sector.[17]

Among the working classes, women and children generally performed the same work in the factories as they did in cottage industries and in manufacturing. Even in these new workplaces a gender-specific division of labour was established. This division varied greatly by region and size of locality, but it assigned women and children subordinate and poorly paid jobs. Female factory workers were viewed with particular suspicion by their middle-class contemporaries, who saw the gender order threatened by women working together with men outside the home. Male workers also resented women's 'dirty competition' because factory owners deliberately made use of female and child labour to depress wages.[18] White-collar employment became an attractive occupational field for women. One official gazette registered a total of 312,924 female salaried employees in Germany in 1907. Women were increasingly employed in offices, retail shops, department stores, and telegraph and telephone services. There they operated new machines while male salaried employees secured managerial and supervisory posts. As soon as they were taken over by women, previously highly valued jobs at the till or adding machines were devalued as 'mechanical tasks'. Women were often accused by their male colleagues of seeking employment merely to escape domestic boredom.

For women of the educated middle classes, 'socially suitable' occupations developed slowly. 'Typically' female professions that resembled women's traditional tasks within the family were the first to gain acceptance. The male teachers' lobby was able to enforce the formalization and professionalization of teaching careers, and in 1907 achieved a parity of rank with judges and higher civil servants for secondary school masters; yet schoolmistresses, though they had gained in qualifications since the mid-nineteenth century, found that their education was still deemed inferior to that of men. To become a schoolmistress primarily meant to be an assistant to a male teacher.[19] Here, too, women earned less than their male colleagues and taught in the elementary schools and the overwhelmingly private girls' schools. In the few state or municipal schools for young ladies, they taught almost exclusively in the lower forms and were not permitted to teach as many hours as male teachers. In Prussia, they were not offered permanent employment in the civil service until 1863. If they married, they were dismissed and lost their claim to a pension. A key difference between male and female work on all levels was the generally held view that women's paid employment could only be a temporary solution on the way to marriage—the goal of any successful female career. Because this attitude influenced the upbringing and education of girls and boys, employment generally played a subordinate role in women's identity. In contrast to men, women apparently had no problem adjusting their performance at work to the needs of their family and their specific life phase.[20]

Ways of life

The nuclear family was the accepted norm in Imperial Germany, the 'natural' objective of a successful life. Middle-class men married late, on average at the age of thirty, because of their long period of education and training, whereas women tended to marry by their mid-twenties.[21] Although financial considerations and family connections continued to influence matrimonial behaviour, love matches became increasingly important. All men and women faced strong pressures to find a suitable spouse. But not all of them could or wished to choose marriage as a way of life. While women usually felt deficient if they could not follow their 'natural calling' as wives and mothers, unmarried men could at least still fulfil part of the role assigned them in their professional lives.[22]

Where one resided and for how long; the size and furnishings and number of occupants of one's home; how much rent one paid—all these factors presented Germans with widely varying opportunities for comfort, happiness, health, and a better future for their children. In the cities most people lived in rented accommodation. Working-class families generally had only one or two rooms: in 1905 such flats represented more than half of all dwellings in the large cities. These small flats were often dark and unhygienic. Sinking incomes, rising rents, and the necessity of reaching work-places and schools by public transport meant that poor families had to move house often.[23]

Even in well-to-do circles, few people in German society lived alone. The unmarried tended to live with their relations, and women frequently kept house for their unmarried brothers or fathers. Many employed women lived with their sisters, aunts, or female friends. Well-off, politically active middle-class wom-en could live an alternative lifestyle largely independent of their families of origin. Among those who adopted same-sex life and work partnerships were Helene Lange and Gertrud Bäumer, Anita Augspurg and Lida Gustava Heymann, and Ika Freudenberg and Sophie Goudstikker. The middle-class lifestyle and the accompany-ing notions of sexual morality were so dominant that any serious deviations frequently attracted the attention of the authorities. Many working-class families not only had several children, but also took in lodgers. These were mainly younger workers who had not yet settled down, and some 25 per cent of them were female. They rented beds from families, often only for certain hours of the day if they worked shifts. Under such living conditions, flats offered no privacy. Whereas men could flee to the pub, women had to do the housework in their crowded homes. In order to play, children took refuge in stairwells, courtyards, and the street.

The degree to which the middle classes sought to impose their own values on the working classes is evident in the number and variety of solutions proposed to relieve the distress of alcoholics, widows, orphans, infants, 'idlers', and those cohabiting in over-crowded dwellings. Although the German Criminal Code of 1871 contained no penalties for cohabitation between a man and a wom-an in a domestic relationship similar to marriage, the pressure for people living together to legalize their situation was immense. The individual states declared cohabitation to be punishable if it caused a 'public nuisance', offering ample opportunities for denunciation. Local clergymen, neighbours, children, parents who feared for their inheritance, or vengeful abandoned spouses only had to report the couple in order to show that they constituted a public nuisance. The authorities reacted with large fines and prison sentences for cohabiting couples.

Old age and death

The way Germans experienced the final phase of life also varied according to gender, marital status, occupation, and income.[24] The gender-specific dimensions of inequality became sharper in old age. Women in Imperial Germany not only had a higher life expectancy, but they were also incomparably more likely than men to live in poverty.[25] Although the chances of remarriage rose overall, widowers had far better prospects because they were usually in a more stable financial position. Particularly when the father had died young and left behind several children, drawing the severely reduced widow's pension usually meant a dramatic worsening of what might already have been a precarious financial situation. For widows who did not inherit money or remarry quickly, the death of a husband usually meant reduced circumstances and, frequently, social isolation or decline.[26] The situation of widows made it abundantly clear that even a good marriage did not necessarily provide women with adequate security.

Death and dying were further privatized and enwrapped within the family in Imperial Germany. Ideally, one would die at home, surrounded by one's family.[27] That men and women were unequal even in death is evident not least from an imperial regulation on cremation. Before cremation, women's corpses had to be checked to see whether they were virgins. The state sought to control women's bodies and morality even in death. Only in 1912, after fierce protests from the women's movement, did the Prussian ministry of the interior dispense with this practice.[28]

The women's movement and anti-feminism

After 1871 some Germans yearned for the 'good old days' of recognized authorities and apparent certainties; others were dazzled by the possibilities of change and acquired an unlimited faith in progress. These attitudes towards change affected women and men differently. For example, men of all classes over the age of twenty-five benefited from the Reichstag's direct, secret, equal, and 'universal' suffrage—unless they received poor relief. Women, however, were entirely excluded from this 'universal' suffrage. In many areas of the empire, it was not until 1908 that women could join the (male) political parties that offered access to 'high politics'. Until that point, women's options for participation were mainly in self-help organizations, auxiliary work for the parties, and local charitable and church associations. That women were interested in party work soon became evident. For example, whereas overall membership in the Social Democratic Party rose from 633,309 to 1,085,905 between 1908 and 1914, the increase in the number of female SPD members was even more explosive, rising from 29,458 to 174,754 during the same period.[29]

In Imperial Germany, the mainstream women's movement defined itself largely as a women's *education* movement.[30] In so doing, it distanced itself both from the women active in the labour movement and from a wing within its own ranks that had grown stronger since the turn of the century, which placed greater emphasis on employment and political equality than on expanding women's education. Women activists in the labour movement had frequently gained their training in the educational projects of the 'moderate' women's movement, and afterwards they tried to develop educational concepts for women workers. They generally focused their efforts on the working women's educational associations; from the outset they sought to help women cope with the 'double burden' of family and workplace.

Members of the women's movement sought evolutionary rather than revolutionary social change. The foundation in 1865 of the General German Women's Association by Louise Otto-Peters and Auguste Schmidt marked the inception of the organized women's movement. This was the German women's movement's first supraregional organization. In Otto-Peters's estimate it already had close to 12,000 women members by 1877. It described its aims as 'increasing the education of the female sex and freeing women's work of all the obstacles that hinder its development'. Louise Otto-Peters had championed the democratic movement and political equality as an author of social critical prose and a journalist before and during the Revolution of 1848–49. She felt a special commitment to the working class, particularly women workers, throughout her life. Yet efforts to integrate women workers into the movement as active agents of change, rather than mere targets of relief programmes and other charitable activities, proved difficult. When German women founded an umbrella organization, the League of German Women's Associations, in 1894, they did not invite the Social Democratic women's associations to join. Mutual recriminations arose in the wake of this decision, but they obscured the fact that middle-class women concentrated mainly on their own problems, while politically interested working-class women expected more support from Social Democracy. The league was somewhat inflexible because its programme stipulated that it would promote only aims that enjoyed the support of all member associations; it nevertheless conveyed a sense of collective consciousness and solidarity to its activists through national conferences, publications, and committee work.

At first scarcely noticed by the media, by 1900 the lobbying efforts and activities of these women's associations met with a positive response, especially among the liberal press. The membership of the league rose from 70,000 in 1900 to some 200,000 in 1908. By 1918 the official figure had grown to 328,000. The growth of this umbrella organization could not obscure the fact that the upswing was dominated by professional and welfare organizations. Meanwhile, such 'general' associations were forced onto the defensive by larger professional and trade associations that had more clearly defined goals and did not feel bound by political neutrality.

The growth of the women's organizations also intensified their differences. After the turn of the century, new divisions appeared within the League of German Women's Associations and its affiliates. Under Gertrud Bäumer as chairwoman (1910–19) the League clung to the unity of the women's movement and invoked the dogma of impartiality, but it also tried to accommodate conservatives opposed in principle to women's emancipation. In so doing, Bäumer supported a trend that had begun in 1908 with the admission to the league of the German Protestant Women's League. The latter league's founding can be viewed to a certain extent as a conservative reaction to the separate organization of 'radical' women that same year (1899) in the Federation of Progressive Women's Associations. The German Protestant Women's League, which openly lobbied against women's suffrage, was accorded special conditions, including a large number of votes in the general meetings of the League of German Women's Associations. This initially considerably strengthened the position of the 'moderates'.[31] May 1915 saw the establishment of the Federation of German Housewives' Associations, later known as the Imperial Federation of German Housewives' Associations. This founding increased the reservoir of members with no interest in women's emancipation but a deep dedication to traditional gender roles. The entry of the housewives' associations into the League of German Women's Associations developed a dynamic of its own, including resistance to women's suffrage, which the league's leadership proved powerless to halt. Thus Bäumer's idea that housewives could be won over to the cause of women's emancipation proved illusory.

The League of German Women's Associations saw itself as an interdenominational organization. Regarding the religious affiliation of its members as a private matter, it was extremely sceptical of separate confessional women's organizations. Nevertheless, after Protestant women had shown the way, in 1903 the Catholic Women's Association of Germany was established, followed in 1904 by the Jewish Women's Association.[32] These two confessional women's associations also sought to develop their ideas about women's proper position in society and marriage by taking into account religious doctrine. The Jewish Women's Association reportedly enrolled about one-quarter of all Jewish women over thirty years of age. It was particularly active in lobbying organizations within the Jewish community to endorse female suffrage.

As these women's organizations grew in size after the turn of the century, as they sponsored more events, and as they published more printed material to sway public opinion, their opponents also found it necessary to organize. The German League to Combat Women's Emancipation was founded in 1912. This organization aimed to secure male dominance on all levels. It rejected women's suffrage, wanted women to work only in typical female occupations, and opposed equal educational opportunities for women (not to mention co-educational programmes). Its members were recruited largely from aristocratic and upper-middle-class circles, including the new class of salaried employees and teachers. Female members—only about one-quarter of all members—were generally already organized in German nationalist, antisemitic, and *völkisch* associations. They were already filling traditional roles as wives and mothers and had little interest in changing this situation: raising their daughters to be future wives and mothers, and finding them suitable marriage partners, attracted most of their energy.

There was nonetheless one common denominator in the programmes and activities of both groups: explicit reference to the nation and women's national duties. The advocates of emancipation deployed nationalism as an emancipatory strategy with such success that the anti-feminists regarded this apparently 'moderate' wing of the women's movement as their main adversary. Because they were more socially acceptable, these women represented a far greater challenge to the opponents of women's emancipation than the 'radicals' did. The anti-feminists stirred up the fears of Germans who placed little trust in women's new opportunities and who expected that higher education or sport would make girls unfeminine, ruining their chances of marriage. Educated women were often ridiculed and denigrated as 'bluestockings' and 'old maids' who had missed their 'natural calling in life'. The anti-feminist defamation campaigns frequently adopted arguments used against socialists. For example, they referred to advocates of emancipation as the 'enemy within' and stressed their international connections (thus implying that they lacked national commitment).

Nationalism, 'high politics', and war

As German nationalism grew more strident, questions of citizenship rights and masculinity became closely intertwined. For example, women's advocates noted that early in the nineteenth century, during the Wars of Liberation against Napoleon, the 'second half of the nation' had joined with 'men at arms' to defend the nation. Other occasions were cited when German women had participated in military conflicts, revolutions, and violent uprisings. Yet these visible eruptions of 'female nationalism' were not unique to one sex: they were part of German society's larger process of national self-discovery. It was natural that women's place in the nation should be contested as nationalism changed its form and function after 1871 and gripped wider circles of society.

Recent research has addressed the themes of nationalism and regional identity, but it has (at best) treated gender issues only in passing.[33] This exclusion of women is closely related to a definition of politics that equates it with the activities of governments, parliaments, and parties. These arenas of 'high politics' were exclusively reserved for men. Only the Reich Association Law of 19 April 1908 established uniform national regulations that superseded various existing state laws and allowed women to join (men's) political parties and participate in political meetings. Before 1908, Germany's political parties—with the notable exception of the SPD—had not seriously addressed women's political equality. But historians have downplayed the fact that, from the 1860s onwards, mainly middle-class women had founded separate organizations, parallel to the male associations and parties, which presented the parliaments and parties with numerous petitions and educational material. Over time these activities and publications contributed directly to nationalist discourse. After 1900 the League of German Women's Associations and its affiliated groups supported plans to build a battle fleet and the acquisition of colonies. Other women's auxiliary organizations included the German Women's Association for the Eastern Marches (founded in 1895); the Naval League of German Women (1905); and the Women's League of the German Colonial Society (1907). These women activists were determined to make their own specifically female contribution to the nationalist cause.[34]

For both women and men, the fascination of nationalism as a concept seems to have been its openness to different possible futures for Germany. Even the 'purely charitable activities' allocated to women, such as nursing the sick and wounded, were regarded as the counterpart to male military service; again, proponents of such activities cast their gaze back to the Wars of Liberation around 1813. While some women sought to define or cement the traditional division of labour with their 'genuinely feminine activities', others used nationalism as an emancipatory ideology, hoping that it would bring women better educational opportunities, wider choice among professional and other occupations, and real political influence—even, for some, full political equality. Such equality lay far in the distance, however, when the 'Jubilee Year 1913' was celebrated with national pathos and a mingling of masculine-military tropes. When the First World War broke out soon thereafter, the League of German Women's Associations regarded it as the great test of the German people in general and of women in particular. The initial euphoria at the outbreak of war appears to have been equally strong among women and men. Like Germany's male cultural elites, middle- and upper-class German women hoped the war would revitalize German culture.

In order to concentrate and organize all female energies on the home front, even before mobilization the League of German Women's Associations proposed to the Prussian ministry of the interior that the National Women's Service should be established. In contrast to the Red Cross, which was responsible for nursing in the field, the National Women's Service sought to gather all available women for educational work, organizing the food supply, war relief, and job placement. Although it was not organized along the same lines everywhere—some sixty local initiatives can be counted—and although tensions arose among different factions, this service was successfully launched on a national basis. A network of aid offices, staffed by well-trained women, supplemented the work of public relief agencies and were integrated with institutions of public administration.

Despite women's strong commitment to the war effort, they were not 'conscripted' by the Auxiliary Service Law of 6 December 1916. This law was intended by the Army Supreme Command to mobilize and concentrate all forces behind the war as part of the Hindenburg Programme. Women's efforts remained voluntary. Nevertheless, in December 1916, a women's employment office was attached to the government department charged with enforcing the Auxiliary Service Law. In the autumn of 1917, when reformers inside and outside parliament proposed new ways of 'drawing upon all the energies of the entire people to participate joyfully in the state', the League of German Women's Associations called for women's inclusion in these plans. Despite the hardships of war, in November 1917 the League unequivocally demanded women's suffrage, which the Council of People's Commissars then introduced immediately after the revolution of 9 November 1918.

Historians continue to debate what ultimately led to the intro- duction of women's suffrage at that time. The Council of People's

Commissars may have been influenced by the general expectation that the female vote would particularly benefit the two leftist parties. But precisely this outcome was deeply feared by many others both within government and outside it. The historian Ute Rosenbusch has pointed out that, even at this point, German society was temperamentally unprepared for women's suffrage. For many Germans it represented such a great threat to public order that they were unwilling to endorse it for municipal elections, let alone in the national arena. In Rosenbusch's view, even women's work on behalf of the war effort had not changed public opinion on this point.[35] Historians such as Gisela Bock, by contrast, postulate that the activities of the women's movement *had* paved the way for the granting of women's suffrage.[36] Women's suffrage revolutionized neither society nor the gender order, as would soon become evident. It did, however, provide a foundation for women to gain equal rights in society and promised them opportunities for influence in the Weimar Republic's new parliamentary institutions.

Conclusion

Imperial German society was marked by numerous forms of inclusion and exclusion. Like ethnic minorities, women had the legal and economic status of social outsiders. At the same time, women could not possibly have enjoyed greater 'insider' status among family, class, and confessional groups. How women should and could be integrated as a group defined by their common gender, and how they could also be granted political and legal equality as individuals, remained controversial in all segments of society. Certainly, gender norms were prescriptive: they did not always conform to the everyday experience of men and women. They were also porous: under certain conditions, women could overstep the boundaries imposed on them. Emphasizing gender difference, the women's movement successfully fought for women's right to personal growth and individual autonomy.[37] But it was an uphill battle. Despite the diversity of women's actual circumstances and scope of action in Imperial Germany, they were constantly reminded that their chief purpose in life was to be a (house-)wife and mother.

Such reminders took literal form in lithographs that depicted the so-called 'life staircase' (*Lebenstreppe*) that women and men were expected to ascend over their lifetimes. These prints, immensely popular and widely distributed, wholly reduced a woman to her role within the family. They suggested that she would reach the pinnacle of her life, its turning point, at the age of thirty when she became a mother. The 'life staircase' for a man, by contrast, de-emphasized his family role; in these prints he was surrounded instead by the symbols of his professional career. The man reached the high point of his life ten years later than the woman; indeed, most versions showed him at his peak at age fifty. These depictions were of course schematic and oversimplified. However, their popular appeal suggests how deeply gender roles were inscribed on Imperial Germany's girls, boys, women, and men.[38]

[1] *Bürgerliches Gesetzbuch für das Deutsche Reich vom 18. August 1896*, ed. Werner Brandis (Leipzig, 1896), 302–3.

[2] Elisabeth Gnauck-Kühne, *Die Deutsche Frau um die Jahrhundertwende. Statistische Studie zur Frauenfrage*, 2nd edn (Berlin, 1907), 5.

[3] Peter Marschalk, *Bevölkerungsgeschichte Deutschlands im 19. und 20. Jahrhundert* (Frankfurt a.M., 1984), 166.

[4] Heidi Rosenbaum, *Formen der Familie. Untersuchungen zum Zusammenhang von Familienverhältnissen, Sozialstruktur und sozialem Wandel in der deutschen Gesellschaft des 19. Jahrhundert* (Frankfurt a.M., 1982), 352–3.

[5] Herrad-Ulrike Bussemer, 'Bürgerliche Frauenbewegung und männliches Bildungsbürgertum 1860–1880', in Ute Frevert (ed.), *Bürgerinnen und Bürger. Geschlechterverhältnisse im 19. Jahrhundert* (Göttingen, 1988), 190–205, esp. 196.

[6] Lily Braun, *Die Frauenfrage. Ihre geschichtliche Entwicklung und ihre wirtschaftliche Seite* (orig. 1901) (Berlin and Bonn, 1979), 156–70, esp. 159.

[7] Herrad-Ulrike Bussemer, *Frauenemanzipation und Bildungsbürgertum. Sozialgeschichte der Frauenbewegung in der Reichsgründerzeit* (Weinheim and Basel, 1985), 28.

[8] Martina Kessel, 'The "Whole Man". The Longing for a Masculine World in Nineteenth-Century Germany', *Gender & History*, 15 (2003), 1–31.

[9] Hans-Ulrich Wehler, *Deutsche Gesellschaftsgeschichte*, 4 vols to date, vol. 3, *Von der 'Deutschen Doppelrevolution' bis zum Beginn des Ersten Weltkrieges 1849–1914* (Munich, 1995), 1203.

[10] James C. Albisetti, 'Could Separate Be Equal? Helene Lange and Women's Education in Imperial Germany', *History of Education Quarterly*, 22 (1982), 301–17.

[11] Claudia Huerkamp, 'Frauen, Universitäten und Bildungsbürgertum. Zur Lage studierender Frauen 1900–1930', in Hannes Siegrist (ed.), *Bürgerliche Berufe. Zur Sozialgeschichte der freien und akademischen Berufe im internationalen Vergleich* (Göttingen, 1988), 200–22.

[12] Oliver Grant, *Migration and Inequality in Germany, 1870–1913* (Oxford, 2005), 281.

[13] Karin Hausen, 'Wirtschaften mit der Geschlechterordnung', in Hausen (ed.), *Geschlechterhierarchie und Arbeitsteilung. Zur Geschichte ungleicher Erwerbschancen von Männern und Frauen* (Göttingen, 1993), 40–67.

[14] Volker R. Berghahn, *Imperial Germany, 1871–1914*, 2nd edn (Oxford, 1994), 308, Table 29.

[15] Grant, *Migration*, 282.

[16] Martina Kessel (ed.), *Zwischen Abwasch und Verlangen. Zeiterfahrungen von Frauen im 19. und 20. Jahrhundert* (Munich, 1995), 63–4.

[17] Berghahn, *Imperial Germany*, 308, Table 29.

[18] On the feminization of factory work, see Kathleen Canning, *Languages of Labor and Gender. Female Factory Work in Germany, 1850–1914* (Ithaca, NY, and London, 1996), and Karin Zachmann, 'Männer arbeiten, Frauen helfen. Geschlechtsspezifische Arbeitsteilung und Maschinisierung in der Textilindustrie des 19. Jahrhunderts', in Hausen (ed.), *Geschlechterhierarchie*, 71–96.

[19] Marion Klewitz, 'Lehrerinnen in Berlin. Zur Geschichte eines segregierten Arbeitsmarktes', in Benno Schmoldt (ed.), *Schule in Berlin. Gestern und Heute* (Berlin, 1989), 141–62, esp. 145.

[20] Martina Kessel, 'Individuum/Familie/Gesellschaft—Neuzeit', in Peter Dinzelbacher (ed.), *Europäische Mentalitätsgeschichte. Hauptthemen in Einzeldarstellungen* (Stuttgart, 1993), 38–53, esp. 42.

[21] Rosenbaum, *Formen*, 330–4.

[22] Bärbel Kuhn, *Familienstand ledig. Ehelose Frauen und Männer im Bürgertum (1850–1914)* (Cologne, Weimar, and Vienna, 2000).

[23] Thomas Nipperdey, *Deutsche Geschichte 1866–1918*, 2 vols, vol. 2, *Machtstaat vor der Demokratie* (Munich, 1990), 137–43.

[24] Christoph Conrad, *Vom Greis zum Rentner. Der Strukturwandel des Alters in Deutschland zwischen 1830 und 1930* (Göttingen, 1992), 95.

[25] Helene Lange, *Die Frauenbewegung in ihren modernen Problemen* (Leipzig, 1908), 5–8.

[26] Bussemer, *Frauenemanzipation*, 25–7.

[27] Kessel, 'Individuum', 266.

[28] 'Virginität und Feuerbestattung', *Die Frau*, 19 (1911/12), 310–11.

[29] Gerd Fesser, 'Zur Reformpolitik im deutschen Kaiserreich 1890–1914', in Helmut Bleiber (ed.), *Revolution und Reform in Deutschland im 19. und 20. Jahrhundert* (Berlin, 2005), 181–91, esp. 186.

[30] See also Angelika Schaser, *Die Frauenbewegung in Deutschland 1848–1933* (Darmstadt, 2006).

[31] Ursula Baumann, *Protestantismus und Frauenemanzipation in Deutschland 1850 bis 1920* (Frankfurt a.M. and New York, 1992).

[32] Gisela Breuer, *Frauenbewegung im Katholizismus. Der katholische Frauenbund 1903–1918* (Frankfurt a.M. and New York, 1998); Marion A. Kaplan, *The Jewish Feminist Movement in Germany. The Campaigns of the Jüdischer Frauenbund, 1904–1938* (Westport, CT, 1979).

[33] Ute Planert (ed.), *Nation, Politik und Geschlecht. Frauenbewegungen und Nationalismus in der Moderne* (Frankfurt a.M. and New York, 2000).

[34] Angelika Schaser, 'Women in a Nation of Men: The Politics of the League of German Women's Associations (BDF) in Imperial Germany, 1894–1914', in Ida Blom, Karen Hagemann, and Catherine Hall (eds), *Gendered Nations: Nationalism and Gender Order in the Long Nineteenth Century* (Oxford and New York, 2000), 249–68.

[35] Ute Rosenbusch, *Der Weg zum Frauenwahlrecht in Deutschland* (Baden-Baden, 1998), 500.

[36] Gisela Bock, 'Frauenwahlrecht—Deutschland um 1900 in vergleichender Perspektive', in Michael Grüttner, Rüdiger Hachtmann, and Heinz-Gerhard Haupt (eds),

Geschichte und Emanzipation. Festschrift für Reinhard Rürup (Frankfurt a.M. and New York, 1999), 95–123, esp. 123; Karen Hagemann, 'Feindliche Schwestern? Bürgerliche und proletarische Frauenbewegung im Kaiserreich', in Inge Stephan and Hans-Gerd Winter (eds), *'Heil über dir, Hammonia'. Hamburg im 19. Jahrhundert* (Hamburg, 1992), 345–68, esp. 361–3; Ute Planert, 'Nation und Nationalismus in der deutschen Geschichte', *Aus Politik und Zeitgeschichte*, 39 (2004), 11–18, esp. 18.

[37] Ann Taylor Allen, *Feminism and Motherhood in Germany, 1800–1914* (New Brunswick, NJ, 1991).

[38] Cornelia Will, ' "Was ist des Lebens Sinn?"—Lebensalterdarstellungen im 19. Jahrhundert', in Peter Joerissen and Cornelia Will (eds), *Die Lebenstreppe. Bilder des menschlichen Lebensalter* (Cologne and Bonn, 1983), 73–91, illustrations 146–8.

The bourgeoisie and reform

Edward Ross Dickinson

In 1891 Wilhelm Baur, an important figure in the Inner Mission (the German national organization of the Protestant charities), used that organization's journal to issue a troubling warning to his colleagues. The feverish pace of some conservative Christians' charitable activities—what Baur called the 'instrumentalization of Christian personalities for the common good'—threatened to undermine 'the intimacy and warmth of family life' in their own homes, and thereby to become self-defeating in the long term. 'Running around in the city while forgetting to sweep before one's own door,' he reflected, and 'an associational life that deprived the house of mother or father in undue measure, would turn reason into nonsense and good deeds into a plague. In any case . . . this much is clear: just as the problems of the whole people can largely be traced back to domestic problems, so healing them depends on the cultivation of domestic life'—including, or perhaps starting, in middle-class Christian homes.[1] Baur may have been speaking from personal experience: he himself was active in any number of different Inner Mission initiatives, with a particular focus on the 'rescue' of 'fallen' women (single mothers and women working in the sex trade); and his wife Meta was for almost two decades the head of the Association of Female Friends of Young Women, which did preventative work with morally 'endangered' girls (such as those who migrated to Germany's large cities in search of work).

Baur's warning spoke to a profound tension within German bourgeois culture more broadly. On the one hand, middle-class identity was defined in large part in terms of values and patterns of living that were fundamentally private, domestic, and apolitical. A respectable middle-class existence was built first and foremost around a successful marriage and a stable family. Bourgeois men and women demonstrated their moral character and their social substance—their capacity for hard work, self-sacrifice, and self-discipline, their usefulness as citizens and people—by living out the domestic ideal. The family was also believed to be the essential school of the bourgeois virtues, the one place in an otherwise competitive, dog-eat-dog social order where individuals experienced the necessity and the benefits of honesty, self-denial, altruism, and responsibility. On the other hand, bourgeois Germans also had a powerful sense of *civic* responsibility, of their obligation—precisely as people of character and substance—to participate in the government of their communities, to help maintain order, humanity, and stability, and to foster moral and material progress in society more broadly. In fact, the bourgeois conception of private domesticity was profoundly politicized, in that the respectable bourgeoisie were convinced that those who did not meet the domestic ideal were politically unqualified. Without the experience and training only an orderly family life could provide, the individual could not develop the personal qualities that made one a good citizen—including, particularly, the capacity to see beyond one's own desires and needs to those of the community. Baur confronted this essential tension in bourgeois culture at the precise moment when it was becoming most acute.

Identity, politics, values

In the last decades of the nineteenth century a growing number of middle-class Germans were able to adopt in practice the bourgeois family ideal, according to which the father worked outside the home while the mother presided over a household of children and servants. At the same time, in the late 1880s and early 1890s the accelerating expansion of bourgeois associational life, which had its origins in the first half of the century, kicked into high gear. Across Germany and indeed across Europe, this period saw an outpouring of organizational energies in response to the problems, opportunities, and threats people faced in the emergent industrial social order. In Germany the social transformation of industrialization and urbanization was particularly rapid, and the organizational response—the expansion of the institutional structure of civil society—appears to have been correspondingly massive. Germans organized themselves at a furious and accelerating pace: in professional organizations (such as those of farmers, teachers, doctors, or engineers), economic interest groups (labour unions, employers' associations, producers' and consumers' cooperatives), scientific societies (of physicists, sociologists, anthropologists, engineers), recreational groups (cycling clubs, soccer clubs, swimming clubs, choral societies), cultural groups (museum societies, music societies, local history associations), social groups (women's organizations, youth groups, ethnic associations), religious or philosophical organizations (such as Bible-study, missionary, Christian parents', free-thought, or occultist organizations), imperialist and militarist groups (veterans' organizations, the Navy League, the Colonial Society)—in every area of social life, these organizing activities unfolded from the middle of the 1880s to the outbreak of the First World War. Baur himself was part of one of the most active sectors of this organizational efflorescence: charitable and social-reform organizations.

Not all such organizations, of course, aimed at the 'reform' of German society: many were purely concerned with developing recreational opportunities, for example, or with securing important professional or economic advantages for their members. Neither were they all organizations of the bourgeoisie; in fact some of the largest—the trade unions (both socialist and Christian)—were self-consciously working-class organizations. Not surprisingly given their resources and opportunities, however, members of the bourgeoisie—the urban elite of educated, affluent professionals, businessmen, and civil servants—played a crucial if not dominant role in this process. The educated bourgeoisie of professionals and civil servants (the *Bildungsbürgertum*, as opposed to the business class or *Wirtschaftsbürgertum*) in particular was very heavily over-represented in a large proportion of such associations. And a striking number of these bourgeois organizations were conceived of and acted specifically as reform organizations: they aimed to improve their society in myriad ways, by deploying the superior expertise, the organizational and managerial talents, and the deeper insight of the 'best' people to make society more rational, more efficient, more just, more stable. As the historian Thomas Nipperdey remarked in an early study of the political potentials of this organizational boom, 'Wilhelmine society was a society of reform movements and of reforms'.[2]

For many bourgeois Germans, reform activity in private associations seems to have been an alternative form of political engagement—a means of shaping and governing their society independent of the formal political process. There were two reasons such an approach to political action might have appealed to this particular social group. First, the central value around which the respectable bourgeois concept of citizenship was built was that of independence, or autonomy (*Selbständigkeit*, in German, literally the ability to stand on one's own). Bourgeois politics was of course built around the ideal of the financially independent citizen, whose vote could not be bought. For this reason most polities (cities and states) in the German Empire imposed some sort of property qualifications for voting, or weighted votes according to how much the voter paid in taxes, or at least restricted office-holding to those who met certain financial qualifications. But independence was also understood as a personal quality, a habit or capacity of mind—the ability to exercise independent and dispassionate judgement, free either of intellectual dependence on others or of the undue influence of one's own passions and desires. The political parties, however, were increasingly seen both as the representatives of particular social groups' material interests and as the organizational embodiment of particular ideological systems. In both respects, party politics appeared suspect in bourgeois eyes: because the parties were believed to pursue selfish interests, and because they were believed to seek to impose particular dogmas. Moreover, because national elections were conducted under a free and equal adult male suffrage, at this political level the parties were increasingly seen to be appealing to the interests and competing for the votes of precisely those people who were *not* financially independent—and who in fact might not even be heads of households at all. Finally, as the political parties became more institutionalized from the 1890s onward, formal structures, party platforms, and party discipline left less scope for the kind of politics of individual conscience that appealed to prominent bourgeois citizens. Participation in private reform associations thus provided a way for bourgeois Germans to be involved in politics without endangering their identity and values. The importance of independence in the bourgeois canon of values, in other words, militated against the acceptance of mass politics and bureaucratic party discipline.

As many social reformers at the time rather crudely put it, they represented 'neither capitalism nor communism'—neither the interests of workers nor the interests of 'plutocrats', but the common good.[3] This formulation appealed to a long rhetorical tradition in which the bourgeoisie distinguished itself, as the embodiment of the common good and rationality, from both the dissolute and anarchic poor and the dissolute and selfish aristocracy. Within reform culture in the imperial period, this claim to objectivity, to represent the common weal rather than particular interests, was often founded on an appeal specifically to scientific expertise. This is a subject to which we will return later in this chapter. For now it suffices to say that whereas many bourgeois reformers viewed politics as a realm of dogmas and utopias as well as of the selfish pursuit of material interests and unprincipled 'horse-trading', reform was, by contrast, a matter of study, insight, and sober realism.

A second reason reform appealed to bourgeois Germans was that they were squeezed, politically, between a rather rigid conservative state and the most powerful revolutionary socialist movement in Europe. Unlike France, Great Britain, and a number of the smaller states of Western Europe, the German Empire was not a fully parliamentary system: government ministers were chosen not by the parties that held a majority in parliament, but by the monarch. This was true of the national government and of the government of the largest state, Prussia; it was also true of a number of the middle-sized states that made up the federal empire. In practice this meant that the upper reaches of the national and of most state government structures were to a large degree the preserve of a conservative (and often aristocratic) elite not answerable to the political parties. At the same time, bourgeois political leaders faced intense competition for votes—and for the political initiative—from an extremely effective and popular Social Democratic movement. Therefore the degree of popular leverage they could exert on that conservative government was narrowly circumscribed. In this context, the prospects for reshaping German society through legislative action were limited; extra-parliamentary, non-political action to interpret and reshape the social environment through study and informational campaigns, institutional innovation, and the influence of neutral expertise was an attractive alternative.

Bourgeois Germans, then, were highly motivated to attempt to use non-political means to exercise what they saw as their natural right and obligation to play a leading role in shaping their society, and particularly in shaping their society's response to the challenges and opportunities of modernity. The result was, again, a massive outpouring of organizational energies. By 1910 Germany was home to a vast spectrum of reform organizations or of organizations (such as professional associations) that saw the support and implementation of reforms in their areas of expertise as a major part of their mission. It is impossible to give an accounting of the full range of such reform organizations; but it may be helpful to list a few of the major varieties.

The range and diversity of reform

Social reform and charity were particularly active fields of organizational activity. Among the more academically oriented organizations we find the Central Association for the Welfare of the Working Classes (founded in 1844); the Public Health Association (1869); the Association for Social Policy (1872); the National Association of Welfare and Charities (1880); the semi-official Prussian Centre for Institutions for Workers' Welfare (1890); and the Society for Social Reform (1901). By 1900 these shared the stage with Christian groups such as the Protestant Social Congress (1890), the Independent Church Social Conference (1896), and the People's Association for Catholic Germany (1890). Major charity organizations included the Protestant Inner Mission (1848), the German Caritas Association (of Catholic charities, formed 1897), the Catholic Welfare Association for Women, Girls, and Children (1899), the Protestant Women's Auxiliary (1899), and the Patriotic Women's Leagues, which had already formed in the

1860s but grew rapidly in the 1890s. In child welfare, a national General Conference of Correctional Education—effectively a coalition of private reformatories—emerged in 1906; a (private) National Centre for Child Welfare was formed in 1907; a semi-private National Association for the Protection of Infants devoted to reducing infant mortality was formed in 1909; a National Conference of Juvenile Courts (which included both civil servants and charity activists working as volunteer social workers) began meeting that same year; and a National Society for Child Protection, committed to preventing child abuse, was founded in 1913. Organizations for young people, organized by adults as part of the effort to 'reform' the socialization of youth more broadly, flourished as well: whereas there were some 50,000 young people in such groups in 1875, there were at least 750,000 by the turn of the century.[4]

In the women's movement the General German Women's Association had been founded in 1865. But the really massive expansion of women's activism came in the two decades around the turn of the century, with the formation, for example, of the League of German Women's Associations (1894), the German Women Teachers' Association (1890), the German Protestant Women's League (1899), the Catholic Women's Association of Germany (1903), the Jewish Women's Association (1904), the Progressive Women's Association (1899), and the national Women's Suffrage Association (1902).

'Life reform' was another particularly fertile field, including vegetarianism, anti-vivisectionism, physical culture, dress reform, holistic health, and so forth. Germany's four major nudist associations were formed between 1906 and 1909. Less controversial were the countless recreational groups that claimed to foster not only good fun but also healthy living. For example, the German and Austrian Alpine Association, which was formed in 1873 and had over 100,000 members by 1910, declared that hiking fostered physical health and built manly character in its members. Similar claims were made by countless local and regional *Heimat* associations, which celebrated local landscapes, architectural traditions, dialects, and history, and often shaded over into conservationist activity. A national Association for *Heimat* Protection was formed in 1904.

The field of moral reform was equally active. Germany's major temperance organization was formed in 1883; a national association of Protestant men's morality organizations was formed in 1889, and a female equivalent in 1892; Catholic men followed suit beginning in Cologne in 1898, and formed a national association in 1907. A national conference on trashy and suggestive popular literature in Cologne in 1904 helped spark the formation of a Popular Alliance against Smut and Trash in that year. Such conservative Christian groups were opposed by the German Branch of the International Abolitionist Federation, formed in 1904 as the voice of more liberal women interested in the problem of public morality and particularly of police-regulated prostitution (which they sought to abolish—hence the name). And both groupings struggled to come to terms with the German Society for Combating Venereal Disease, an association of doctors (most of whom supported regulation) formed in 1902. Still worse, from the Christian point of view, were the National Society for Race Hygiene (1905); the League for the Protection of Mothers (also 1905), which agitated for a radically permissive new code of sexual ethics; and the Scientific-Humanitarian Committee (1897), which advocated the decriminalization of homosexual acts between men. The Medical Society for Sex Reform, formed in 1913, adopted a more academic posture.

This listing is merely suggestive of the scope and scale of German reform culture in this period. Indeed, in almost every case the national associations listed here rested atop a much more massive expansion of local and regional organizations and chapters. Such chapters were built up either before or after the formation of national umbrella organizations; in some cases their number reached into the hundreds of organizations at the local level. Nevertheless, it should be clear that one striking feature of German reform culture was its extreme diversity. Germans often complained in this period of the 'fragmentation' of reform efforts, both at the national level and, more importantly, at the local, municipal level. In many fields of activity—sports, health, charity, welfare, youth, women's rights, education, and so on—there were multiple and sometimes dozens of associations and organizations at work in any city of even moderate size. Coordinating their efforts, and developing a fruitful relationship between private reform associations and city governments (which often supported and relied on, for example, private youth groups, charities, or educational associations), had become a knotty problem by the 1890s. In some cases it was partially resolved by the formation of semi-official coordinating 'centres' (*Zentralen*) or clearing-houses—as for example in the case of child welfare, where such municipal centres were formed in growing numbers after about 1905 in order to coordinate the work of municipal agencies and volunteer social workers from multiple private organizations. Yet cooperation was not always easy to achieve, particularly where 'fragmentation' was the product of religious or ideological diversity. In response to the national Child Labour Act of 1903, for example, the Social Democratic Party organized a large number of Child Protection Associations; but it was almost impossible to secure cooperation between these socialist groups and the Christian charities, though often they did similar work. Catholics and Protestants also sometimes found it difficult to cooperate. These two communities organized parallel associational structures, rather than collaborating in creating interconfessional groups, in almost every field of reform endeavour. There were similar organizational divisions between Christian and Jewish groups, between liberal and conservative Protestant groups, and between 'neutral' social scientists and explicitly Christian organizations.

These divisions should make it clear that reform culture was anything but apolitical, despite the posture of personal independence and objectivity in the self-consciousness of many German reformers. A large proportion of reform associations in this period had close ties to the political parties. Unlike the two-party systems of the Anglo-American world, the more fragmented German party system tended to institutionalize and politicize cultural divisions: the political parties grew out of and drew on cultural communities, forming one facet of an increasingly dense organizational structure built up around shared values and interests. And those communities and organizational networks—which historians have labelled socio-cultural 'milieux'—cut right across the German bourgeoisie.

Thus Catholic reform organizations had close ties to the Centre Party which, while formally interconfessional, was very much dominated by Catholics. The conservative Protestant milieu had close ties to the conservative political parties. The general secretary of the (Protestant) National Conference of German Morality Associations, for example, was a member of parliament for the Conservatives; and the chairman of the People's Association for Catholic Germany (who also had close ties to the Catholic men's morality movement) was a member for the Centre Party. Once women could vote and hold office after 1919, the two long-time leaders of the German Protestant Women's League and the Catholic Welfare Association for Women, Girls, and Children would both become members of the national parliament—for the German National People's Party (successor to the conservatives) and the Centre Party, respectively. By contrast, a large number of educational reformers, municipal welfare advocates, the leadership of the non-confessional women's organizations, many child welfare advocates, and many medical reformers had close ties to the National Liberal party or, more frequently, to the left-liberal parties that came together in 1910 to form the Progressive People's Party. The chair of the League of German Women's Associations (from 1910), Gertrud Bäumer, was a political associate of Friedrich Naumann, a leading theorist of left liberalism after 1900. Another of Naumann's associates was Christian Jasper Klumker, the most important theorist of modern welfare policy and the most influential intellectual father of the modern German child welfare system. Finally, a surprising number of medical and health reformers, were middle-class adherents of Social Democracy, or at least of some form of socialism. They included Alfred Blaschko, general secretary of the Society for Combating Venereal Diseases; Magnus Hirschfeld, chair of the Scientific-Humanitarian Committee; Helene Stöcker, leader of the League for the Protection of Mothers; and, in his younger years, Alfred Ploetz, chair of the Society for Race Hygiene. Other eugenicists were adherents of radical right-wing populist (*völkisch*) politics. But whether they were attracted to the extreme Left or the extreme Right, many Germans in the eugenics, public health, and life reform movements were members of a diffuse but influential *alternative* to the four dominant milieus (Catholic, conservative Protestant, liberal Protestant, and socialist): these were middle-class people attracted to a self-consciously scientific world-view. Often they were also attracted to the idea of 'monism'—the belief that body and soul are not separate but unitary. The monists, one need hardly add, did not remain unorganized: a German Monist League was formed in 1906.

Such ideological divisions were not the only source of diversity in the German reform community, however, for the German bourgeoisie was internally divided in other important ways. One very important source of conflict within the German reform community was the power and importance of the professions. German professionals were supported and regulated by the state to an extent uncommon in the rest of the European world. Partly as a consequence of this they were unusually well organized and self-conscious. Four groups, in particular, frequently found themselves at loggerheads in German reform movements: lawyers, doctors, educators, and the clergy. While members of all these groups belonged to the educated middle classes and shared a wide range of fundamental values, they also had their own very strong professional interests, and sometimes they championed quite divergent values and perceptions. This was true, for example, in the field of reformatory education. In 1910 one Christian reformatory director thanked psychiatrists attending the annual conference of the General Conference of Correctional Education for 'participating so eagerly in our work'; but he also warned that if they tried to do away with the concept of sin in favour of the influence of heredity or social environment, 'well then, gentlemen . . ., we must declare war on the psychiatrists'.[5] In the same period, volunteer social workers (many of whom were teachers) involved in casework with juvenile delinquents argued stridently for a reform that would make 'education, not punishment' the watchword of a new system of juvenile courts; but some lawyers accused them of displaying an 'anti-juristic spirit, hostile to the law'. That spirit, the lawyers argued, would merely encourage young offenders by undermining the 'sense of legality' among Germany's youth.[6]

Another important division within the bourgeoisie fell between all the educated professions and the business world—between the *Bildungsbürgertum* and the *Wirtschaftsbürgertum*. In fact, the business class was heavily under-represented in most German reform movements; reform was above all the project of the educated elite. This is not to say that businessmen did not play an important part. Businessmen and their dependents often did make up a significant minority of the membership of certain reform groups.

Many reform associations recruited influential local employers as members or officers. And the business class was an important source of funding for many charitable endeavours. In some cases, moreover, exceptionally wealthy businessmen played a key role in funding influential centres of innovation. Christian Jasper Klumker, for example, worked in his early career for the very important Institute for the Commonweal in Frankfurt am Main, which was funded by the industrialist Wilhelm Merton. Another entrepreneur, Karl Schmidt, funded the 'garden city' and art colony of Hellerau in Saxony—an important centre of innovation in the arts, dance, and design in the last years of the empire. Nevertheless, there were clearly attitudinal differences between the two groups. Thus it is probably no accident that the man hired to head Merton's Institute, Wilhelm Polligkeit, had worked for some years in banks before becoming Merton's private secretary and devoting himself to social reform; nor is it coincidental that he vaulted himself into a leadership position in the National Association for Poor Relief and Charities in large part by championing a social-scientific and pragmatic approach to the problem of poverty, as opposed to a moralizing and principled one. Unquestionably tensions between some businessmen and some reformers arose because many of the latter explicitly rejected the free market, questioning the morality and community spirit of those who did not. For example, a contributor to the *Berliner Börsenzeitung* (loosely translated, the 'Berlin Financial Times') complained in 1889 that Berlin had been described by participants at a Protestant morality conference that year in a manner that 'borders on libel'. In 1905 a representative of Berlin's Property-Owners' Association took umbrage at the opposition to brothels voiced by the women's and Christian morality movements. Since brothels were a lucrative use of property in major urban centres, he described them as necessary 'for the good of the community, for the good of the family, for the good of the Church and schools', and for 'the public health'.[7]

A still more important source of conflict within the reform community was the division between men and women. The dominant bourgeois model of relations between the sexes, developed in the early nineteenth century, held that men and women had radically different and complementary natures, and should inhabit quite separate social worlds. Men were aggressive, competitive, rational, and scientific, whereas women were cooperative, caring, emotional, and religious. Men should engage in the hard business of making money and policy, whereas women should busy themselves with the 'soft' (but no less important) business of raising respectable, God-fearing children and caring for the young, the weak, the sick. As women became more organized and active in the decades around the turn of the century, it became increasingly clear in public life that one consequence of bourgeois commitment to this radical gender dichotomy was that middle-class men and women often had rather different values and perspectives, which could lead to serious conflicts within and between reform movements. Thus the sex reform theorist Christian von Ehrenfels accused women in the League for the Protection of Mothers of being 'mired . . . up to the ears in the moonstruck romanticism of anaemic girls'. The leading sexologist Max Marcuse left the organization in a huff in 1908 after concluding that his female colleagues were too concerned with 'abstract philosophical and literary-aesthetic themes' and insufficiently interested in science.[8] At the other end of the reform spectrum, conservatives in the Protestant men's morality movement initiated the formation of the German Protestant Women's League in 1899. Because the Protestant morality movement argued for the criminalization of all prostitution, rather than a system of licensing, these conservatives saw their new League as a counterweight to the formation of the first German chapters of the international abolitionist movement, which favoured simple decriminalization. But by 1912 a majority of men in the Protestant morality movement had been convinced by their female protégés that decriminalization was the right approach after all. Helene Lange, the most influential leader of the moderate non-confessional women's movement, recalled in her autobiography that many of her male opponents had charged women with trying to make their 'childish moral yardstick the measure of all things', adding pointedly that 'Jesus of Nazareth, among others, had the childish idea of making the moral yardstick the measure of all things'.[9] This was an echo of the cultural clash between a bourgeois men's culture that favoured 'hard-headed' pragmatism and a bourgeois women's culture that privileged Christian moral principle.

Lastly, perhaps the single most important cause of the diversity and complexity of German reform culture in this period was its very pronounced localist orientation. Whereas the theories of reformers—social, moral, aesthetic, spiritual—were universalizing, their practice was strongly local. Therefore most reform cultures remained rooted in local traditions and conditions long after they had grown to the point that it made sense to establish national associations of the kind listed in this chapter. There was a very good political reason for this. Because the suffrage for German municipal elections was in general severely restricted (usually to less than 10 percent of the population), the cities were the heart of bourgeois political power in the empire. It was here that bourgeois reformers could make a difference, here that members of their social grouping had control of the government. At the same time, of course, it was in Germany's cities that both the problems and the potentials of industrial society were most clearly apparent. It is not coincidental that the density of reform organizations was usually highest in the most rapidly industrializing and urbanizing regions of Germany: Westphalia and the Rhineland in the west, Saxony in the east, and Berlin.

In this respect, the impact of individual careers and commitments was very important. In the early stages of experimentation and institution-building, any reform movement was likely to be highly local in perspective for the simple reason that the people who played leadership roles became involved in reform efforts in their own communities. They often did so as a result of experiences that awakened them to particular problems or dangers in a very immediate and personal way. Thus Agnes Neuhaus, the long-time head of the Catholic Welfare Association for Women, Girls, and Children, was shocked into action when she accepted the invitation of a local official and visited the venereal ward of a local hospital. Gertrud Bäumer became involved in the women's movement and social policy after getting a job teaching in a working-class district of Magdeburg and coming face to face, for the first time, with the realities of working-class life. As a rule, it was only after building experience (and institutions) at the local level that individual reformers built their national profile (and national institutions). Their perspective often continued to be shaped in decisive ways by their own formative experiences in local reform work and by the conditions they faced locally.

Most of the national organizations and movements that arose in the 1890s and 1900s were effectively federal in structure: coalitions of influential local reformers and reform organizations (a structure that also characterized the bourgeois political parties). Not infrequently, important regional and local differences of perspective persisted well after formally unitary national organizations had been created. Thus Klumker and his colleagues in Frankfurt, for example, were ambivalent about transforming their innovative, privately funded child welfare programmes into nationally mandated government agencies. Reformers in Hamburg, where innovation was pioneered by civil servants in the city government, were more enthusiastic. Within the Catholic charitable community, there was a clear distinction between the cosmopolitan and government-friendly Rhineland (or 'Cologne') leadership, which was accustomed to living with a rough-and-tumble style of urban politics, and the more conservative and cautious south German (Munich and Freiburg) branch, whose members were rooted in less urban and diverse local communities, who were more closely tied to the Church, and who were frequently suspicious of public agencies.

Often such differences of approach and outlook were identified with particular individuals. Within the women's 'abolitionist' movement, for example, there was a more liberal Dresden branch (Katharina Scheven), a more radical Hamburg branch (Anita Augspurg), and a moderate Berlin branch (Anna Pappritz). Agnes Neuhaus was the embodiment of Rhineland Catholic charity leadership, Lorenz Werthmann, head of the Caritas Association, of the more cautious Freiburg strain. The eugenics movement was divided between a more progressive Berlin branch associated with the socialist Alfred Grotjahn and a more reactionary (and often more racist) Munich branch associated with Max von Gruber or Ernst Rüdin. In the Protestant morality movement, the Mönchen-Gladbach wing under Ludwig Weber was more open to the influence of Protestant women and of the Protestant worker's associations; the Berlin branch, often associated with Weber's close political associate Adolf Stöcker and the theology professor Reinhold Seeberg, was usually more conservative.

The potentials and dynamics of bourgeois reform

This, then, was the world of German bourgeois reform before the First World War: diverse, vibrant, and creative, yet fragmented by ideology, by professional and social interests, and by local interests and perspectives. As the historian Kevin Repp has put it, reform culture was part of the 'rich, complex, protean landscape of Wilhelmine modernity', and 'pushed in many directions at once'.[10] Was there nevertheless an underlying logic to reform in Germany in this period—one or more unifying themes or potentials, a coherent dynamic to its development?

Historians have come to divergent conclusions on this matter. In the 1970s and 1980s many scholars argued that the world of reform was fundamentally one more product of the failure of the German bourgeoisie to come to grips with the democratic imperatives and potentials of modernity by reaching an accommodation with what was then seen as the one genuinely popular force working to transform German society and institutions—the Social Democratic labour movement. Pointing to the elitist and technocratic quality of much of reform culture, to the bitter anti-socialism of many or even most reformers, and to the anti-modern, anti-urban, anti-industrial cogitations of Germany's educated middle classes, they found that German reform culture was symptomatic of Germany's drift toward radical authoritarianism (and, by the 1930s, fascism)—or at least of its failure to generate a viable alternative.

In the 1980s and 1990s, influenced by the thinking of Michel Foucault and other postmodern critics of the Enlightenment project of rationalism, efficiency, and progress, a growing chorus of scholars instead saw in the proliferation of reform programmes and organizations in Germany a thoroughly modern but still profoundly pathological development. Geoff Eley argued, for example, that it was not the anti-modern and 'conservative' reformers who were most dangerous; instead it was 'precisely the most striking manifestations of modern scientific and technocratic ambition in the sphere of social policy that laid the way for Nazi excess'—the best examples being those self-consciously modern and scientific reformers who embraced, for example, eugenics.[11] And even social reformers who did not share such frightful ideas about the relative genetic or social value (or lack of it) of individual human beings were still, in the Foucauldian model, trying to gain mastery over their fellow citizens. Criminologists, demographers, public health officials, social workers, moral reformers, psychologists, nudists—they were all trying to study, analyze, manipulate, direct, guide, improve, cure, train, indoctrinate, and 'fix' people (including, in some cases, themselves). In the process they were creating a whole world of institutions, disciplines, and contexts intended to exercise control over the social sphere as a whole. In Detlev Peukert's classic formulation, social reform was a form of 'inner colonialism', a bourgeois attempt to impose a set of alien norms and values from without and 'above'; indeed, it was guided by a 'totalitarian claim to validity' for bourgeois social and behavioural norms.[12] It is obvious where this was all headed.

This is still probably the dominant interpretation of German reform culture in this period; but in recent years doubts have been expressed with increasing regularity. As awareness of the sheer breadth and diversity of German reform movements and organizations has deepened, a growing number of scholars have begun to argue that reform culture in the imperial period had not one but multiple potentials. Thus recent studies have spoken of the 'fervid innovation' of Wilhelmine reform, which requires us to develop a 'more nuanced view of the political, social, and scientific dynamics' of the period; or of the 'multiplicity of "meanings of reform"', of 'political valences of "reform"' that were 'contradictory and confused', of the 'heterogeneous meaning of "the modern"'; or even of the 'bewildering variety and diversity' of reform movements and of their 'contradictions and ambivalences'.[13] A number of scholars have taken issue, in particular, with the argument that bourgeois reform was anti-modern—without, however, arguing that it was pathologically modern, either. Re-examining movements as diverse as moral reform, temperance, land-reform and urban planning, conservationism, the *Heimat* protection movement, alternative health and nudism, and even occultism, they have argued that in many cases the reformers involved were neither irrational anti-modern mutterers nor utopian modernizers bent on total rationalization, but had genuine and justified concerns—for example, about the dangers of environmental damage, or the public health problems of large industrial cities. Far from being hopelessly backward-looking romantics or technocratic utopians, they were pragmatic progressives, grappling in good faith with the problems and opportunities of modernity, seeking a rational and reasonable compromise between untrammelled development and rational-ization on one hand and a concern for human scale and human values on the other.

More strikingly, a smaller number of scholars have begun to argue that the very diversity of German reform in this period created, effectively, a powerful democratic potential. As issues of public policy came to be debated in the broad and rapidly expanding universe of reform associations (for example in their publications, their conferences, their studies, their contributions to parliamentary debates), control of policy increasingly slipped out of the hands of the political elite. Regardless of the actual content of reformers' proposals, the very proliferation of voices produced a powerful democratic potential, as assumptions were questioned, drafts critiqued, and alternatives articulated. At the same time, those who participated in such organizations gained experience in public action, seeing themselves, as citizens, as contributors to decision-making processes. As one historian has written of the cooperative movement in Germany, in some cases the organizations of civil society created an 'emergent democratic framework' in which Germans practiced democracy.[14]

There is a good deal of truth in each of these contending interpretations. Some recent comparative studies have tended to confirm the older view of the German bourgeoisie—and partic-ularly of the educated bourgeoisie—that it was pessimistic about modernity, frightened of democracy, bitterly and sometimes bru-tally anti-socialist. Indeed, recent studies of more self-consciously conservative groups have found them to be generally antisemitic, misogynist, antidemocratic, homophobic, xenophobic, chauvin-istic, elitist, and anti-modernist. Members of such groups were terrified by the seemingly anarchic energies of modern mass soci-ety and determined to re-impose order and authority. As historians have excavated the prehistory of Nazi racial policy over the past two decades, they have also shown that if many self-consciously modernist and 'progressive' reformers were progressing at all, they were progressing towards totalitarian barbarism. Nevertheless, some more recent studies of the cultural worlds, ambitions, and practices of specific reform groups have shown us another face of bourgeois reform—confident and optimistic, not merely open to social and political democratization but actively pursuing its integrative potentials, and excited by the dynamism, energy, and creativity of modern urban industrial society, scientific culture, artistic modernism, and even mass culture. They sought not to suppress or restrain the development of modern social and cultural forms, but to guide, exploit, and even encourage it.

These contrasting interpretations in part reflect the profound cultural division within the German bourgeoisie between two groups: those whose values and livelihoods were embedded in older social and institutional structures, and those whose values and livelihoods were more directly linked to the vitality of the emerging social and institutional structures of modern, urban, industrial, commercial culture. Even among the bourgeoisie, of course, there were winners and losers in the process of social transformation.

Unity in diversity: assumptions, orientations, strategies

Despite this diversity of perspectives and programmes, however, one thing that has become increasingly clear in the scholarship of the past decade is that whatever the content of their members' ideas, the great majority of reform movements adopted very similar institutional forms and political strategies. Most obviously, the universal organizational form of German bourgeois reform in this period was the legally incorporated voluntary association—the *Verein*. Across the reform spectrum, moreover, these organizations adopted similar techniques for influencing public opinion and policy. For example, most published regular periodicals—often a 'scientific' journal and an informational newsletter.

Most held regular conferences, with formal opening ceremonies featuring local or regional dignitaries, closed sessions for discussion and debate among members, and open sessions or addresses for the general public; and many published their conference proceedings. Many maintained their own presses, and put out occasional studies or even regular publication series. Most sought to influence the political process in two ways: through formal structures, such as studies and reports, petitions to various agencies and authorities, or by drumming up support within the political parties; and through more informal contacts and personal relationships between prominent members and key figures in the local, regional, or national political structure.

A central part of the public relations and policy approach of a very large proportion of reform organizations, moreover, was an appeal to the authority of science. This was particularly true of those organizations most closely connected to Germany's academic social-science community (such as the Association for Social Policy or the Society for Social Reform), which regularly published massive statistical studies of labour market conditions, consumption patterns, demographic trends, and much more. But even very conservative or revolutionary organizations undertook 'scientific' surveys to try to underpin their demonstratively values-based agendas with statistical or at least anecdotal evidence. In 1895, for example, the Protestant morality associations published the results of a massive survey of rural pastors concerning the sexual morality of the population in the countryside; they thereby sparked a firestorm of controversy because some were highly critical of rural landlords and employers. Similarly, the Scientific-Humanitarian Committee landed in court for sending out a survey to male university students asking whether they had had ever engaged in homosexual acts—a question regarded by some as libellous, since it implicitly questioned the addressees' 'honour'. Bourgeois reform organizations of all stripes were convinced that the techniques of social science would permit them (as the conservative author of an essay titled 'Reform or Revolution!' put it in 1895) to 'see things and people as they really are'—and to govern their own and their society's actions accordingly.[15]

Whether their agendas were modernist or anti-modernist, in other words, almost all bourgeois reform movements adopted a particular modern institutional structure, and a modern strategy of agitation aimed at influencing public opinion. Through their voluntary associations reformers of all stripes certainly sought to impose their agendas by means of legislative initiative, by influencing public administration in their capacity as experts, by taking positions in the civil service or city governments themselves, or by acting in concert with public agencies (a pattern particularly important in the fields of social work and education). But they also aimed to inform, persuade, recruit, and mobilize the bourgeois public. In this sense, whether they liked democracy or not, most German reformers assumed that they had to operate in a political context—or at least in a civil society—that was at bottom democratic in structure. The public-relations strategy of the People's Association for Catholic Germany reflected such assumptions. Bitterly anti-socialist and socially conservative, the organization's founders nevertheless self-consciously and determinedly steered clear of more reactionary anti-modernism. They sought instead 'to win the driving energies of our modern times, boiling up everywhere like a force of nature, for the Christian world-view by enabling Catholics to master those forces with expertise and understanding'. Unable to move the conservative Catholic establishment as a whole in a more progressive and modernizing direction, the organization nevertheless very effectively pursued its own course. It encouraged the integration of Catholics into Imperial Germany's political system; it used the techniques and findings of social science; it operated a 'social correspondence' service that supplied newspapers with information on topics relevant to socially active Catholics; it held regular local and regional 'social conferences'; and by 1914 it published pamphlets and leaflets that were distributed to a membership of over 800,000.[16]

On one question of values, moreover, most bourgeois reform associations *did* agree: with some exceptions at the radical left fringe, all were nationalists. They formed a broad spectrum reaching from moderate and cosmopolitan patriotism (which was happy to recognize the virtues and contributions of other nationalities) through commonsense imperialism (which saw imperial expansion as the self-evident consequence of Germany's growing economic power) to radical nationalist and racist chauvinism. There was considerable disagreement among these positions as to what the nation was, what it meant, what it required. But there was near consensus that the nation was a good thing. In fact, a vast range of reform associations argued that the realization of their own agendas would contribute to national strength. Such associations ranged for example from conservative Christian groups opposed to the popular acceptance of contraception, through infant health advocates who argued in favour of the economic benefits of a moderate fertility rate, to radical sex-reform women who argued that free love would improve the 'race'.

If we set aside for a moment the radically divergent agendas and perspectives of Germany's massively diverse reform movements in this period, then, in the end we can discern something rather coherent after all. Bourgeois reform was voluntarist in principle without being apolitical in practice; it was almost exclusively nationalist; it was potentially democratizing (or at least participatory), in its forms if not always in its values; and it accepted that the language of science was the language of modernity, allowing most reformers to embrace both the natural and the social sciences as the cure for modern humanity's ills. There was, in other words, an underlying unity to the 'culture' of bourgeois reform in the German Empire. Thus bourgeois reform in this period accurately reflected its social foundations: internally divided by divergent religious, ideological, professional, regional, local, and gender identities, the German bourgeoisie was also fundamentally united by a basic set of cultural commitments.

Most fundamentally of all, German reformers in this period were united by one last shared conception: the idea that it is possible and necessary to make the world a better place. In a recent essay on personal autonomy as the 'Archimedean point of the bourgeois way of life', the historian Manfred Hettling argued that 'the quality of being bourgeois' (*Bürgerlichkeit*) was by its nature utopian, in that bourgeois identity was founded on the concept of continual self-improvement.[17] The sheer range and diversity of reform in Imperial Germany suggests that the same was true of the bourgeois conception of society. Some of the utopias German bourgeois reformers thought out for themselves in this period are frightful by today's standards; but it is useful to remember that even the most reactionary, anti-modernist, and pessimistic reformers in this period were at least optimists of the will.

¹ Wilhelm Baur, 'Was sollen wir thun?', *Fliegende Blätter*, 48 (1891), 1–11.
² Thomas Nipperdey, 'War die Wilhelminische Gesellschaft eine Untertanen-Gesellschaft?', in Nipperdey, *Nachdenken über die deutsche Geschichte* (Munich, 1986), 178.
³ See Rüdiger vom Bruch, '*Weder Kommunismus noch Kapitalismus*'. *Bürgerliche Sozialreform in Deutschland vom Vormärz bis zur Ära Adenauer* (Munich, 1985).
⁴ Hermann Giesecke, *Vom Wandervogel bis zur Hitlerjugend* (Munich, 1981), 60–1.
⁵ Pastor Siebold, cited in *Bericht über die Verhandlungen des Allgemeinen Fürsorge-Erziehungs-Tages am 23.–27. Juni 1910 zu Rostock* (Berlin, 1910), 117.
⁶ Adolf Grabowsky, 'Die Notwendigkeit des Jugendgerichts', *Zentralblatt für Jugendrecht und Jugendwohlfahrt*, 1 (1909), 159–60.
⁷ 'Aus dem Männerverein', *Korrespondenzblatt für die Bekämpfung der öffentlichen Sittenlosigkeit*, 3 (1889), 29, 35; ' "Öffentliche Häuser zum Wohle der Kirche und Schule"?!' *Neue Generation*, 1 (1905), 203.
⁸ Christian von Ehrenfels, 'Sexuale Reformvorschläge', *Politisch-Anthropologische Revue*, 4 (1905/06), 442; ' "Sexual-Probleme" ', *Sexual-Probleme*, 4 (1908), 3.
⁹ Helene Lange, *Lebenserinnerungen* (Berlin, 1927), 271.
¹⁰ Kevin Repp, *Reformers, Critics, and the Paths of German Modernity: Anti-Politics and the Search for Alternatives, 1890–1914* (Cambridge, MA, 2000), 11.
¹¹ Geoff Eley, 'Germany and the Contradictions of Modernity: The Bourgeoisie, the State, and the Mastery of Reform', in Eley (ed.), *Society, Culture, and the State in Germany, 1870–1930* (Ann Arbor, MI, 1996), 101.
¹² Detlev J. K. Peukert, *Grenzen der Sozialdisziplinierung. Aufstieg und Krise der deutschen Jugendfürsorge, 1878–1932* (Cologne, 1986), 311, 307.
¹³ Suzanne Marchand and David Lindenfeld, 'Germany at the Fin de Siècle', in Marchand and Lindenfeld (eds), *Germany at the Fin de Siècle: Culture, Politics, and Ideas* (Baton Rouge, LA, 2004), 19, 7; Geoff Eley and James Retallack, 'Introduction', in Eley and Retallack (eds), *Wilhelminism and Its Legacies: German Modernities, Imperialism, and the Meanings of Reform, 1890–1930* (Oxford and New York, 2003), 5, 6; Matthew Jefferies, '*Lebensreform*: A Middle-Class Antidote to Wilhelminism?', ibid. 93, 103.
¹⁴ Brett Fairbairn, 'Membership, Organization, and Wilhelmine Modernism: Constructing Economic Democracy through Cooperation', in Eley and Retallack (eds), *Wilhelminism*, 47.
¹⁵ Carl von Massow, *Reform oder Revolution!* (Berlin, 1895), pp. iv–v.
¹⁶ Cited in Winfried Loth, 'Die Deutschen Sozialkatholiken in der Krise des Fin de Siècle', in Jochen-Christoph Kaiser and Wilfried Loth (eds), *Soziale Reform im Kaiserreich. Protestantismus, Katholizismus und Sozialpolitik* (Stuttgart, 1997), 129.
¹⁷ Manfred Hettling, 'Die persönliche Selbständigkeit: Der archimedische Punkt bürgerlicher Lebensführung', in Manfred Hettling and Stefan-Ludwig Hoffmann (eds), *Der bürgerliche Wertehimmel. Innenansichten des 19. Jahrhunderts* (Göttingen, 2000), 57.

Political culture
and democratization

Thomas Kühne

In March 1908, political trouble was brewing in the suburbs of
Cologne.[1] Elections to the Prussian state parliament (Landtag)
were scheduled just three months hence, and the dominant party
in the electoral district of Sieg-Mülheim-Wipperfürth, the Catholic
Centre Party, faced the prospect of open rebellion in its ranks. This
district lay on the east side of the Rhine River and had been a secure
seat for the Centre since the mid-1870s, when the mobilization of
Catholic voters during the *Kulturkampf* made it a 'bomb-proof'
bastion of party support. (The district's population was over 85 per
cent Catholic.) Even though this district sent three representatives
to the lower house of the Prussian Landtag, and even though
its social profile was very heterogeneous, no other party stood
a realistic chance of winning even one of those three mandates.
Partly for this reason, in the spring of 1908 metal-workers in the
city of Mülheim felt they deserved to have 'one of their own' in
the Landtag—a true worker, not just a candidate who adhered to
the Centre's programme or promised to lobby for working-class
interests. In fact, local workers had been voicing this demand
for three years. How would the Centre's nomination committee
respond?

Decades earlier, local artisans (*Handwerker*) had expressed their
own desire for representation in the Landtag. Eventually a safe Centre seat in a neighbouring constituency was found for one of their
leaders. Then in the 1890s the area's Catholic farmers staked their
own claim, nominating an independent agrarian candidate for
the 1893 Landtag elections and for subsequent Reichstag elections.

This problem was temporarily solved in 1898 when Karl Becker was offered one of the district's three seats. However, although Becker was a farmer and executive member of the Rhenish Farmers' Association, his principal occupation was as a justice official in Siegburg, so he was not considered a 'real' agrarian. In 1903, when both Landtag and Reichstag elections were held, a 'true' farmer, Wilhelm Geyr, was offered the seat. But Geyr died in 1905 and a by-election was called. Local farmers insisted that Geyr be succeeded by another farmer (Hubert Schlick) who sprang from their ranks and understood their problems. But this insistence alienated Catholic workers, who now began their three-year campaign to secure their own nominee. They no longer wanted to be represented by someone drawn from those groups who dominated local party affairs—mainly priests, farmers, lawyers, teachers, and civil servants.

As new elections approached in March 1908, the problem seemed about to solve itself when Schlick decided not to stand for re-election: at last a safe seat was available for a worker. But the farmers again dug in their heels. Eventually an alternative solution was found: a judicial official who had held one of the three Landtag seats since 1893 and who also sat in the Reichstag, was persuaded to step down as Landtag deputy and devote himself entirely to his duties in Germany's national parliament. A railroad worker from Dortmund, locksmith Heinrich Beyer, was nominated in his place. Thus the Landtag district of Sieg-Mülheim-Wipperfürth was represented from 1908 until 1918 by three Centre Party deputies who reflected the district's three most important occupational groups: agrarians, workers, and the urban middle classes.

This successful strategy to balance the interests of competing social groups with a local variant of 'proportional' representation broke new ground: it allowed party leaders to put an end to internal dissention and pre-empt other threats to a safe seat. Yet the case of Sieg-Mülheim-Wipperfürth speaks to larger questions about the evolution of political culture in Imperial Germany, of which four will be highlighted in this chapter. It helps us understand, first, that Germany's political parties faced the challenge of mobilizing new recruits and balancing the interests of divergent social groups not only in national elections and not only in districts where opposing parties squared off in fierce competition. Although the Centre Party held unassailable seats in other German parliaments, the situation in Sieg-Mülheim-Wipperfürth reflected the complexities and inequities of the Prussian three-class suffrage. Whereas the longterm trend was towards ever-higher turnout rates for Reichstag elections, participation in Prussian elections stagnated at a much lower level. Hence it is necessary to explore the diversity of suffrage laws and parliamentary institutions in Germany's federal states to understand the dynamics of political modernization in the nation at large.

Second, the political manoeuvring in Sieg-Mülheim-Wipperfürth illustrates how social groups staked their claims for representation—and how party leaders accommodated or resisted such claims—within a network of party institutions that was only loosely and ambiguously hierarchical. Although party machines became more centralized over time—though at vastly differing rates—it was not always clear who held the authority to nominate candidates, conclude alliances with other parties, devise policy initiatives, or undertake other kinds of consensus building.

Third, parties were successful only when they demonstrated to their voters that they could address and alleviate their everyday problems. The 'fundamental politicization' of German society was unstoppable; but the contours and appeal of mass politics looked different depending where you lived. The traditional face-to-face style of politics might persist in one locality, whereas elsewhere voters might feel slighted as anonymous members of a voting herd. A candidate might promise to attend to local needs, but would he follow through once elected? These questions became urgent as an older, more patrician style of politics (*Honoratiorenpolitik*) eroded more quickly in some parts of Germany than in others. Moreover, grievances could become neuralgic at one tier of politics and find easy remedy at another. A stick might be wielded to enforce party discipline in one parliamentary forum while a carrot was offered in another.

Fourth and lastly, the parties' need to devise new strategies for success at the polls was predicated on an unrelenting increase in the political engagement of German voters and their wish to participate in elections that were fair and equitable. This was broad-gauged democratization, which should be understood as a mainly social and cultural phenomenon rather than as one leading to a specific constellation of political institutions. Few Germans aimed to abolish the monarchy or introduce parliamentary government on the British or French model. Therefore, to understand how contemporaries interpreted political change and to gauge its historical significance, the last section of this chapter will historicize the notions of 'democracy' and 'democratization'. What bears emphasizing at the outset is that the rituals of casting a ballot were consensual in one way but they underscored difference too. Some Germans trouped to the polls to affirm social solidarities, others to declare their commitment to an ideology, still others to protest the discriminatory policies of an authoritarian state. Sometimes marking a single ballot allowed them to do all these things at once. Yet conflict never disappeared as a central feature of politics. The Centre Party's delicate balancing act in Sieg-Mülheim-Wipperfürth provided one answer to the problem of conflict management; other parties in other regions explored different options. Either way, they were all tested in a political environment that was also being reshaped by changing relations of power between state and society.

The authoritarian state and its historians

Imperial Germany collapsed in November 1918 at the end of a war. Ironically, it had been born in the same way in January 1871. The founding of the empire took place at Versailles, outside Germany, and was dominated by the new Kaiser and his military entourage. Hence, in the view of left-wing contemporaries and later 'Whig' historians, Imperial Germany appeared to be an authoritarian and militarist structure, imposed on a German population that actually deserved a better state, a better constitution, a better government. Conservative scholars, by contrast, have tended to argue that Germany's future was not so clouded, especially if the First World War had not intervened. Both historiographical perspectives were reshaped by the historian Fritz Fischer, who emphasized lines of continuity between monarchism, militarism, and other aspects of authoritarian governance, on the one hand, and Germany's deep involvement in two world wars, Nazism, and genocide, on the other. Yet today scholars still ask, 'What could have been done to avoid these catastrophes?'[2]

Unlike the situation in the British House of Commons, in Imperial Germany neither the national Reichstag nor any Landtag of a federal state was charged with responsibility for forming the government. Werner Frauendienst in the 1950s and Manfred Rauh in the 1970s suggested that Germany nonetheless experienced a process of 'silent parliamentarization'. They argued that the Reichstag not only achieved substantial legislative success, but was also able to expand its constitutional right to discuss, amend, pass, and reject legislation.[3] In their view, German political culture was on the right path and would have continued to advance had the First World War not disrupted this auspicious development. The 'silent parliamentarization' thesis, however, has now largely been discredited. The Reichstag never assumed control over state policy, nor did the majority of its members even want to. To understand why parliamentarism was not pushed more vigorously, historians have shifted the focus of their attention from high politics to the politicization of society. One influential interpretation reflecting this new focus was advanced by the German émigré historian Hans Rosenberg. Analyzing how the Agrarian League mobilized rural society after its founding in 1893, Rosenberg concluded that the league reflected only the 'pseudo-democratization' of the noble landowning class in Prussia. In Rosenberg's view, the *Junkers* successfully manipulated the middle and lower classes in the countryside by means of a nationalist and antisemitic ideology. Imperial Germany's 'political mass market', as Rosenberg later described it, did not spread democratic but rather decisively anti-democratic values and habits.[4]

A different but equally influential interpretation was advanced in 1966 by the sociologist M. Rainer Lepsius. Taking a longterm perspective stretching from the beginning of the 1870s to around 1930, Lepsius argued that the social basis of the major German parties was astonishingly stable. Unlike Rosenberg, Lepsius did not see blockages to reform principally as the result of elite manipulation of popular forces. He took voters' social and religious belief systems seriously. His most pioneering conclusion was that the

German party system suffered from a socio-cultural 'pillarization'; that is, the division of the society into subcultures—which
he called 'socio-moral milieux'—that stood, like pillars, sepa-
rately and durably. Lepsius's scheme postulated the existence of
four such milieux, each with its own values, interests, and social
organizations. The Catholic milieu was represented by the German
Centre Party; the urban Protestant working-class milieu supported
the Social Democratic Party; the rural Protestant milieu supported the German Conservative and Free Conservative parties; and
the urban Protestant middle-class milieu was drawn to the left-
liberal and National Liberal parties. These four milieux provided
voters—and non-voters, too—with stable organizational and ideological frameworks. Members of any given milieu would not
usually leave the milieu into which they were born, except in
certain circumstances—for example, if they migrated from the
countryside to an industrial area. Lepsius's sophisticated model
was a great advance over previous theories in helping to explain
why constitutional reform did not move forward. Party leaders were usually born and raised in their distinctive milieu and
experienced powerful feelings of belonging: indeed, they were as
much prisoners as members of their milieu. This situation con-
strained their ability to transgress the ideological horizons that
demarcated their milieu's boundaries; hence they were usually
unwilling to compromise with competing party leaders in parliament. These constraints in turn made it very unlikely that the
milieu-based parties would ever mutate into socially integrative
parties—broad-based parties that could legitimately claim to represent all social groups. It was not until the late Weimar Republic
that a 'people's party' was able to draw support from all four
milieux.[5]

Lepsius first presented his thesis of socio-moral milieux in a
short essay based not on primary research but on analysis of
the secondary literature. Even though critics have never undermined his basic insight, they have correctly noted that his picture
was too static. The political scientist Karl Rohe in the early
1990s pointed out that 'closed' milieux comprising socialists and
Catholics were fundamentally different from the more 'open'
milieu of liberals and conservatives. In 1997, Jonathan Sperber
demonstrated that voters switched frequently between different

parties—or at least much more frequently than Lepsius's model could accommodate.[6] Margaret Lavinia Anderson has offered the most decisive challenge to any 'static' interpretation of Imperial Germany's political culture. Her book *Practicing Democracy* (2000) argues that universal manhood suffrage after 1867 enmeshed male adults 'in ever more procedures and practices' which contributed directly to 'the growth of an increasingly democratic culture in the decades before 1914'. Anderson's book can thus be seen as the culmination of more than twenty-five years of revisionist research, mainly by Anglo-American scholars, that emphasizes the dynamic and 'modern' contours of Imperial Germany's political culture.[7]

Remarkably few of these Anglophone scholars have paid much attention to the impact of regional diversity on German domestic politics. What happens when we take the spatial dimension of politics more seriously? For one thing, it challenges both the 'optimistic' and 'pessimistic' views of Imperial Germany's political development. By the 1860s, southern Germany in general, and the Grand Duchy of Baden in particular, had already tested the viability of closer cooperation between monarchical government and the state parliament. Even though formal parliamentarization was never achieved before the monarchies fell in 1918, statesmen and party leaders in Baden, Württemberg, and Bavaria were consciously testing new ways to advance Germany's political modernization. The Landtag suffrage in each of the southern German states had been significantly broadened—made more democratic—by 1910. These reforms often produced parliaments with actual or potential left-wing majorities, which state governments could not ignore. However, the Prussian Landtag remained a reactionary stronghold of right-wing parties, because all attempts to reform its plutocratic three-class suffrage failed (most notably in 1910). But Prussia was not alone: restricted or decisively undemocratic suffrages characterized other state parliaments, mainly in northern Germany (including Mecklenburg and Saxony). The deputies sitting in these parliaments were even less interested than members of the Reichstag in reforming the constitutional foundation of Imperial Germany, for two reasons. First, they were afraid of what democratization would mean for the fate of their own parties in individual Landtage. Second, they were well aware that the delicate

constitutional balance between federalist traditions and centralizing tendencies worked out in 1867–71 would be put at risk by
constitutional reform across the board and by parliamentarization
specifically. Neither of these reform trajectories overcame the
roadblock represented by the Prussian Landtag.[8]

Scholars continue to seek new ways to interpret the contradictory
traditions, developments, and options available to those who
wanted to entrench or reform the political system established at
the outset of the imperial period. To avoid emphasizing one
feature of German political culture in a one-sided way—to
'balance elements of reform and stasis, of progressivism and
traditionalism'[9]—historians have stressed the pluralistic aspects
of German political culture. Thomas Nipperdey's two-volume
study of Imperial Germany famously suggested that the empire
must be painted in innumerable shades of grey, because these
more accurately capture the reality of Imperial Germany than any
black-and-white portrait.[10] James Retallack has suggested abandoning the idea of 'one Germany' in order to discover 'many
Germanys'.[11] Dieter Langewiesche has argued that the first German nation state was too contradictory to allow historians to claim
that its politics culture was marked by any one coherent style.[12]
While this emphasis on ambiguity and diversity has obvious merits, we should not forget that politics continued to revolve around
questions about power and the articulation of power—questions
that to ordinary Germans were decidedly *unambiguous*. How, then,
were the various parts of Germany, the rival political styles, the
countless shades of grey actually configured, and how were they
interrelated?

Before attempting to answer these questions in the balance of
this chapter, it may be helpful to explain that by speaking of
political culture rather than just 'politics' historians have signalled
their interest in exploring the *subjective* dimension of politics: the
social-psychological ambiance of a system of rule, the subjective
relationship between the state and its citizens, and the system of
norms, values, beliefs, attitudes, and sentiments that seem self-
evident to groups and people involved in political activity. Those
norms and values condition people's appraisals of what is possible
in the political realm.

Nation building and social pillarization

In January 1871 the 'inner consolidation' of the nation was far from complete. Nation building had just begun. Bismarck hoped that the political parties he deemed to be 'friends of the empire' (*Reichsfreunde*) would form a steadfast 'national' coalition; but these hopes were dashed when unanticipated outcomes were generated by the anti-Catholic *Kulturkampf*, the campaign against Social Democracy, and the struggle of ethnic minorities to protect their rights. The definition of 'insiders' and 'outsiders' was in turn always tied up with the question of how Germany's representative bodies should be elected. Hence suffrage questions proved to be a persistent thorn in the side of Bismarck and others who believed that national consolidation depended on a pliant electorate.

The National Liberals and the Conservatives were most troubled by universal and equal male suffrage, which Bismarck had introduced in 1867 and was carried forward in the German Empire's constitution of 1871. To Bismarck, equal suffrage was a popular—and successful—means to undermine the kind of liberal opposition that had hampered his attempts to control the Prussian Landtag before 1866. Rooted in the paternalist rural culture of his upbringing, Bismarck could not imagine that the lower classes would vote for anyone other than conservative candidates. The liberals, by contrast, were deeply suspicious of the 'levelling' principle of 'one man, one vote'. In 1865 the liberal Leopold von Hoverbeck identified the danger that universal suffrage posed for liberal men of wealth and influence: 'We, who are working for the people's freedom, are not provided with a solid social basis.'[13]

Catholics had good reason to welcome the new, broader suffrage. Catholic voters generally followed the advice of their priests and favoured Centre candidates over those presented by the liberals or conservatives. As a reaction to the *Kulturkampf* laws in the early 1870s, Catholic leaders found that universal suffrage helped them organize mass demonstrations and convince members of the Catholic milieu to turn out to the polls to elect Centre Party or Polish candidates (the latter were overwhelmingly Catholic and, if elected to parliament, almost always allied with the Centre Party caucus). Thus a reciprocal relationship existed between the introduction of universal suffrage and milieu formation: the democratizing effect of the Reichstag vote allowed Catholics to resist attempts to stigmatize them as outsiders and 'enemies of the empire' (*Reichsfeinde*), while the experience of discrimination galvanized new cultural solidarities within the emergent milieu that could be expressed through the ballot box.

Such 'affirmative voting', as historian Stanley Suval has labelled it, transformed Imperial Germany's political culture.[14] In fact articulating protest and affirming group solidarities became more important than victory. 'Pragmatic' voting, by contrast, focused on actually winning the parliamentary seat. It might be seen as the appropriate behaviour under an electoral system where one candidate was expected to win a majority of votes in a given constituency. If a minority candidate had no chance of winning the local seat, why waste time with voting at all? This reasoning helps explain why majority systems usually produce low turnouts. Pragmatic voting made more sense under an unequal system such as the Prussian three-class suffrage, where it was more likely that a single candidate would win an outright majority. That is why liberal and conservative parties, which did well under unequal suffrages, endorsed pragmatic voting. Doing so gave them little incentive to reform inequitable voting systems or to develop efficient, centralized party organizations.

For Reichstag elections, more than two parties usually competed on the first, main ballot; since one candidate rarely won an absolute majority, a run-off ballot was frequently necessary to decide the winner. During the first ballot, however, even hopeless candidacies allowed minority parties to 'show the flag' locally. The SPD was the first party to field candidates in all 397 Reichstag constituencies, for exactly this purpose: to rally the troops and maximize the party's votes nationally. The Centre Party did the same in regions with a significant Catholic population, but it was the socialists who really perfected affirmative voting. This process started during the period of the Anti-Socialist Law, from 1878 to 1890, which both consolidated the urban Protestant working-class milieu and gave the Social Democratic Party an effective political organization. In the Reichstag elections of 1878, SPD candidates gained 8 per cent of the popular vote, and their party held 9 of 397 Reichstag seats. By the Reichstag elections of 1890, the SPD's share of the popular vote had risen to 20 per cent—more than any other party—which translated into 35 seats in the Reichstag.[15]

If the system of allocating Reichstag seats had been more fair, the SPD in 1890 would have won more than 35 seats. For example, the two Conservative parties together also won about 20 percent of the popular vote in 1890, while the Centre Party won almost 19 percent; but after the election 93 conservative deputies and 106 Centre deputies sat in the Reichstag. This discrepancy between a party's share of the popular vote and the number of seats it won in the Reichstag arose largely because the boundaries of Reichstag constituencies were never redrawn between 1871 and 1918, despite massive demographic shifts. In 1871 all constituencies had approximately 100,000 eligible voters, and each one elected a single Reichstag deputy. By 1912 a single working-class suburban district of Berlin had 338,000 eligible voters, yet it still elected exactly the same number of deputies—one—as the tiny rural district of Schaumburg-Lippe, which had only 10,700 eligible voters.[16] The non-socialist parties, which drew most of their support from the countryside, were happy to condone such passive gerrymandering. Another important factor was the two-ballot system. The second and final ballot often pitted a socialist against a non-socialist candidate. In such cases conservatives and liberals usually supported each other against the socialist. Third and lastly, the campaign strategy of the SPD contributed to the gap between votes won and seats won. Socialists nominated candidates even in districts where they had no chance of winning. This was a costly strategy in some ways, but it paid dividends in others. No other party employed this strategy as systematically as did the SPD.

For the disadvantaged groups in society, then, affirmative voting facilitated political emancipation. The two most strongly organized milieux—Catholic and socialist—began to challenge the political ascendancy of the liberal and conservative middle classes. Both of these milieux, often referred to as 'subcultures', provided their members with practical advantages in their everyday lives: their own sporting clubs, cultural associations, and cooperative societies, for example. At the same time, both milieux inculcated in their members an understanding of political participation that undermined the classic liberal model. Voting could now be seen as a demonstration of social power. This lesson was not lost on the Protestant educated middle classes.

Lecturing on the dangers of socialism in 1874, Heinrich von Treitschke, a professor of history at the University of Berlin, articulated what many middle-class Germans thought about 'socialism and its patrons'. Treitschke was not principally upset by the results of the most recent Reichstag elections, where the socialists had done well: 'at least they mirror quite well the prevailing mood of the nation', he commented acidly. What most roused his ire was the 'complete moral degradation of the crowd'. 'There can be no doubt whatsoever,' he told his listeners, that 'universal suffrage has promoted among the masses a fantastic overestimation of their own power and worth.' He continued:

The irreconcilable contradiction between the democratic equality of political voting rights and the necessarily aristocratic organization of society . . . turns him into a faithful follower of demagogues. . . . Universal suffrage amounts to organized licentiousness; to the recognized arrogance of superior foolishness; to the superciliousness of the soldier towards the officer, of the journeyman towards the master, and of the worker towards the entrepreneur.

Treitschke, though, was intelligent enough to realize that there was no way to turn back the clock. 'Abolishing the electoral law, once given, would only provoke the long-awakened wantonness of philistinism even more vehemently.'[17]

Not all of Treitschke's fellow-travellers in the National Liberal and Conservative parties were as willing to resign themselves to the unintended consequences of universal suffrage. Plans to revise, limit, or even abolish universal suffrage circulated in centre-right and right-wing circles for decades. German liberalism had always had a strong elitist component, and this made it easier to consider cooperating with Bismarck and the Conservatives when schemes were discussed to limit 'damage' caused by universal suffrage. In the 1880s the National Liberal Party avoided statements explicitly supporting the Reichstag suffrage: its 1884 platform supported the principle of the secret ballot, but it did not mention the universal or equal aspects of the Reichstag suffrage. It must be emphasized, however, that sympathizing with reactionary policies and executing them are different things. All liberals, even National Liberals, were well aware of the risk of trying to overturn 'the electoral law, once given'. So the National Liberals never initiated any explicitly anti-democratic legislation. Instead they and the Conservative parties supported government legislation that sought 'redress' on other fronts. The *Kulturkampf* and the Anti-Socialist Laws must be understood as part of this strategy, which also included new laws passed in the late 1880s extending both the Reichstag and the Prussian Landtag legislative periods from three to five years. This 'reform' was intended to diminish the speed and intensity of political mobilization. Whether it actually did so is less clear.

All these efforts to defend, roll back, or 'compensate' for universal suffrage took place in a political climate shaped by fear and hope. The brightest hope of all was for a new monarch who would succeed Kaiser Wilhelm I and enact some of the reforms advocated by left liberals. This hope died in 1888 when Kaiser Friedrich III reigned for only 99 days before succumbing to throat cancer. When Friedrich's son, Wilhelm II, ascended the throne, fear proved to be more durable than hope. Over the next ten years, one of the strongest fears was that Wilhelm and the other German princes would unleash a *coup d'état* (*Staatsstreich*) by dissolving the Reichstag, radically changing the constitution, and abolishing universal suffrage. But the *coup* never happened, nor was it ever seriously planned, for good reason. Like Treitschke, most responsible authorities in Germany were aware that such a move would result in civil war. Nor were Reichstag deputies willing to legislate themselves out of existence. It is therefore difficult to ascribe as much substance to this threat as historians have done in the past. Nevertheless, even the notion that such a move could be contemplated in high political circles made German politicians, both before and after Bismarck's departure from office, reluctant to demand further democratization or parliamentarization.

New departures at the *fin de siècle*

Kaiser Wilhelm II wanted political peace at home to open the way for an imperialist policy. As well as voicing his disdain for universal suffrage and party politics, in the mid-1890s he endorsed a range of reactionary projects. These included efforts to curtail the activities of the socialist movement and to restrict civil liberties. By the end of the decade, the practical results of all this bluster were meagre. But in 1898 German constitutional affairs stood at a crossroads. In the midst of a Reichstag election campaign that year, the Social Democrats and left-wing members of the Center Party spread rumours that the government planned to revise the Reichstag suffrage. The government was forced to make a public disclaimer that it had no reactionary intentions, but the damage was done, and the pro-government parties fared badly at the polls. Thus, after the turn of the century, the idea of withdrawing the democratic suffrage became obsolete.

We cannot understand the significance of this turning point by considering only Prussia and the Reichstag; we must also consider Germany's periphery. In 1896, reactionary groups in the Kingdom of Saxony succeeded in implementing the constitutional rollback that Wilhelm II was unable to accomplish in national politics. In the face of growing SPD victories in Saxon Landtag elections since 1890, National Liberals and Conservatives in the Saxon parliament took the offensive and replaced Saxony's relatively liberal suffrage with a three-class voting system similar to that in Prussia. This new suffrage drove more and more socialist deputies out of the Saxon Landtag with each election until none were left in 1901. This was a Pyrrhic victory, though. The SPD launched a resounding protest against this brazen act of disenfranchisement in Saxony, which led to a landslide victory in the Reichstag elections of 1903. Socialists won 22 of 23 Saxon Reichstag constituencies, whereas previously they had held only 11. This sensational breakthrough sent a double message: Reactionary constitutional policy could not be pushed through even at the level of the federal states—the danger of a backlash was not worth the risk. Moreover, once an overly reactionary course was off the table, those groups seeking further constitutional reform could go on the offensive. Three decades of constitutional stagnation were over.

From 1900 onwards, the dominant political discourse in Imperial Germany was no longer about how to roll back universal voting rights or retard political modernization, but how to expand such rights and accelerate democracy's progress. This secular change no longer concerned only men. It was around the turn of the century that the movement for female suffrage became popular in Germany. Nevertheless, the idea of democratizing suffrage laws for Germany's federal Landtage generated more publicity than female suffrage. Most German states experimented with suffrage reforms, even if they were still less democratic than the Reichstag model. Prussia became the most prominent exception.

Another important development that gained momentum around 1900 was the willingness of parties to challenge the right of the government to recommend the election of candidates belonging to the 'state-supporting' parties. These were the parties of the old Bismarckian 'cartel'—the German Conservatives, the Free Conservatives, and the National Liberals. During election campaigns, especially in Prussia, the government and its local administrators had regularly communicated their support for these parties, sometimes discretely, sometimes openly. For example, in Prussia, the county councillor (*Landrat*) might call together the local notables in any given constituency and urge them to form an election alliance in aid of the 'national' (that is, the cartel) candidate. Sometimes the *Landrat* did not hesitate to present himself as the perfect candidate to facilitate such an alliance. More often, his office served as a clearing house for negotiations, information, and encouragement to the state-supporting parties. For the pre-1898 period, the importance of this role can hardly be overestimated, because the 'nationalist' parties were still burdened by only rudimentary organization. Thus county councillors, not party functionaries, often took in hand the task of distributing leaflets and intimidating voters. Especially at the middle and higher ranks of the civil service—Bismarck himself did not hesitate to let his wishes be known—clear signals could tilt the balance in favour of the cartel candidate. This strategy was pursued successfully in the Reichstag election campaign of 1887, which resulted in a great victory for the cartel parties.

At the end of the 1890s, however, things changed. For the Reichstag elections of 1898, the Prussian government tried the same tactic that had worked so well in 1887, this time proclaiming that the state-supporting parties needed to rally voters on behalf of naval expansion. But the government and its allied parties failed miserably. It was not just liberals in urban areas who refused to follow governmental 'advice'. The Agrarian League openly contested the choice of county councillors as rural candidates. Other interest groups also supported the kinds of arguments raised in the Rhenish district of Sieg-Mülheim-Wipperfürth, demanding that 'one of their own' represent them in far-away Berlin. This trend became stronger with each passing election: in rural and urban areas alike, in small villages and big cities, local committees nominated candidates who shared their own roots, lifestyles, and traditions. Thus social groups, not state authorities, showed themselves capable of meeting the challenges of mass politics.

This development marked a decisive turn in what Margaret Lavinia Anderson has called the 'learning process' of 'practicing democracy'. This does not mean that political mobilization happened overnight. Recall that the Catholic milieu had been mobilized in the 1870s, the urban Protestant working-class milieu in the 1880s, and the rural Protestant milieu (though more gradually) in the 1890s. Moreover, the government continued to try to rally the nationalist parties, with some success in 1907. However, Reichstag elections in 1912 again produced socialist gains and a reversal of nationalist fortunes, displaying more clearly than ever that voters were not willing to support the government's preferred parties.

A key point in evaluating the significance of these various trends at the local, regional, and national levels is that they had a reciprocal effect. Locally, the fact that usually no party won an absolute majority on the first ballot meant that party alliances became de rigueur. But with increasing frequency all parties wanted to 'show the flag' throughout Germany, so alliances became more complicated and unpredictable. The same was true in Germany's national parliament. From 1879 to 1906, the Centre Party often participated in majorities supporting government legislation. But when Chancellor Bernhard von Bülow in 1907 attempted to tar the Centre with the same 'unpatriotic' brush he applied to the Social Democrats, the trick backfired, albeit two years later, when the Centre and the Conservatives teamed up to force his departure from office. From 1909 to 1914, Chancellor Theobald von Bethmann Hollweg pursued a 'policy of diagonals'. But just as his county councillors had lost decisive influence at the base of political society, Bethmann Hollweg could not draw on unequivocal support from any of the Reichstag parties.

The National Liberals played an important role in accelerating these changes. During the 1890s, the party had lost much of its rural base, and by the turn of the century its leaders were reconsidering the party's *raison d'être*. Should it try to recapture its rural following, or appeal to society's wealthiest and most privileged classes, or serve as advocates for big business? And where would it find the most dependable allies? Gradually, the leaders of the National Liberal Party came to the conclusion that their party must first and foremost defend Germany's *national* interests. After 1900 National Liberal fortunes rose because the development of Germany's new, mass-based associations was in the same direction. As nationalist pressure groups and economic interest groups rose in number and influence after 1900, they brought to German political culture new ideals and a new political style. The new ideals revolved around social 'fairness' and national 'community', while the new style helped to enliven National Liberal politics at the grass-roots level. One such association was the Society for Social Reform. Founded in 1901, this society sought to redress the failed integration of the socialist working class into the German nation, again on the premise that a solution was not going to come from 'on high'. As Baron Hans von Berlepsch—a former minister of commerce in Prussia—put it in 1901, 'The social development of our time requires fairness and not just favours.'[18] To advocate 'fairness' was not to endorse the Social Democratic Party, but it was not meant to marginalize it either. Hesitantly at first, and then with more confidence, liberals and socialists began to organize their electoral campaigning on the principles of cooperation and compromise. Progress was slow—slower in the National Liberal camp than among left liberals—but steps towards reconciliation were evident on the eve of the First World War.

As members of Germany's urban Protestant middle classes followed this trend, they reoriented their focus towards the 'politics of togetherness'. They found 'togetherness' in nationalist, militarist, and imperialist associations, and in gatherings and festivals that celebrated the empire. Among the most successful organizations to achieve a mass membership after the turn of the century was the German Navy League, which soon numbered more than one million members. The Pan-German League and the Colonial Society retained a more exclusive membership and style of politics, whereas the veterans' associations became even more popular than the Navy League: they included almost three million members on the eve of the First World War.

To be sure, these associations pursued different agendas. Nevertheless, they provided Germans with an 'equal opportunity' forum for cultivating feelings of national belonging. They did so at all levels of politics—at the local *Stammtisch* (the table reserved for 'regulars' at the local pub, where branches of the national societies would typically meet); during the celebration of Sedan Day or the Kaiser's birthday; and at nationwide festivals such as those in 1913. Blue-collar workers rarely found their way into these associations: they were often considered unworthy, and the SPD condemned national, military, and colonial chauvinism as a matter of principle. However, the social exclusivity of these associations is less significant than their ability to foster a utopian belief in the power of political togetherness and symbolic politics. When teachers, artisans, and shopkeepers gathered at the *Stammtisch* or in mass marches, they focused on the vision of a 'national community'. Sometimes this was rendered as a 'people's community'—an idea that gained popularity around 1900, long before the Nazis made the *Volksgemeinschaft* the centrepiece of their ideology. For Wilhelmine Germans, this 'national community' would overcome inner division, class conflict, and party wrangles. Instead of succumbing to these differences, the 'national community', they thought, would function as an organic, harmonious whole, just as communities and families did (or were meant to). It was a utopian solution that seemed in August 1914 suddenly to come within Germany's grasp.[19]

Paths towards democracy

As the historian Brett Fairbairn has suggested, to review the evolution of Imperial Germany's political culture means 'to historicize democracy', 'to unpack the historical processes of democracy', and to admit 'that by today's standard no country was democratic a century ago'.[20] Germans from 1871 to 1914 were working on three different and yet overlapping models of 'democratization', understood historically. The first is the increasing trend to go to the polls and vote; this model focuses on the actual usage of constitutionally guaranteed individual political rights. The second is a grass-roots political movement, which increasingly demanded and favoured parliamentary candidates who shared the local ties or social background of their voters. The third is the fascination with the politics of togetherness, and with symbolic participation instead of formal political participation. All three models of democratization broadened the social basis of political participation, and all turned on the question of how to translate the pressures resulting from rapid social change and segmentation into 'fair' political representation and successful political management. However, they all failed to overcome social pillarization in Imperial Germany, and none of them charted a path to parliamentary democracy.

Universal and equal suffrage defined one of those uncertain paths. Introduced to provide the new nation state with popular support, in the 1870s and 1880s the suffrage principally facilitated the political protests of socio-moral milieux whose members suffered discrimination at the hands of the state. Paradoxically, universal suffrage became a permanent integrative symbol of the nation state and yet drew a line between the two milieux (Catholic and working class) who profited most from it and the other two milieux (rural and urban middle class) who continued to regard the suffrage with disdain or antipathy. Many middle-class Protestants in both urban and rural Germany identified universal suffrage with the negative features of mass politics. Yet they followed the rules of the game and eventually mobilized new supporters. Although supportive of the authoritarian state in principle, the members of these Protestant middle-class milieux refused to abide by the attempts of state authorities to control and channel political participation.

The second model of democratization evolved out of the first. When occupational groups like those in Sieg-Mülheim-Wipperfürth demanded 'one of our own' to represent them, the 'language of us' continually gained ground. As backward and narrow as this perspective seems in one regard, it was progressive in others. When local party committees demanded parliamentary representatives in parliament who shared their social background

or local outlook, they blocked the professionalization of parliament, thereby ensuring that even deputies operating in the realm
of high politics remained attuned to grass-roots opinion. The need
to accommodate the demands for representation from different
occupational groups also routinized conflict management at the
local level. Nevertheless, politics based on the 'language of us' did
not set Germany on a one-way path towards a democratic constitution or parliamentary democracy. Both paths were blocked by social
pillarization. The culture of compromise generated at the local level
usually remained *within* the four socio-moral milieux, and rarely
proved conducive to strong, long-lasting alliances between them.
This made it less likely that the parties representing these milieux
would form alliances durable enough to challenge the authority
of the state. Hence it was democratization itself, based on and
accelerated by introduction of the universal suffrage, that blocked
Germany's transition to a parliamentary form of government.

The third path towards democratization, the idea that the nation
would be united on the basis of the 'politics of togetherness', could
not overcome these obstacles, though this outcome was not pre-
ordained. In countless club meetings, local gatherings, and festivals
across the land, Germans from diverse social backgrounds met on a
regular basis. Political participation no longer unfolded according
to formal rules or in defence of economic interests exclusively;
increasingly it became a matter of reflecting the experience of
togetherness in symbolic ways. The politics of 'us', of togetherness,
of harmony, of consensus always required an 'other' against which
it could define itself, and often this 'other' was constructed in
the context of imperialist aggression. But such emotionally rooted
feelings of national belonging were not found only in Germany. Nor
was the Nazi version of the 'people's community' the only form that
such desires for national belonging could have taken. The future
still lay open in 1914. On the eve of the First World War, Germans
were eagerly working on different, and even contradictory, ways
of democratizing their political culture. They could not know in
which direction these paths would lead.

[1] For the following, see Klaus Müller, *Politische Strömungen in den rechtsrheinischen
Kreisen (Sieg, Mülheim, Wipperfürth, Gummersbach und Waldbröl) des Regierungsbezirks
Köln von 1879 bis 1900* (Ph.D. diss., University of Cologne, 1963), 270–2, 350–65,
370–88; Anni Roth, *Politische Strömungen in den rechtsrheinischen Kreisen (Mülheim,*

Wipperfürth, Gummersbach, Waldbröl und Sieg) des Regierungsbezirks Köln 1900–1919 (Ph.D. diss., University of Cologne, 1968), 145–75; Thomas Kühne, *Handbuch der Wahlen zum Preussischen Abgeordnetenhaus 1867–1918* (Düsseldorf, 1994), 712–15; and Kühne, *Dreiklassenwahlrecht und Wahlkultur in Preussen 1867–1914. Landtagswahlen zwischen korporativer Tradition und politischem Massenmarkt* (Düsseldorf, 1994), 355–7.

² For a recent literature review, see Thomas Kühne, 'Demokratisierung und Parlamentarisierung', *Geschichte und Gesellschaft*, 31 (2005), 293–316. See also Kühne, 'Die Jahrhundertwende, die "lange" Bismarckzeit und die Demokratisierung der politischen Kultur', in Lothar Gall (ed.), *Otto von Bismarck und Wilhelm II. Repräsentanten eines Epochenwechsels?* (Paderborn, 2000), 85–118.

³ Werner Frauendienst, 'Demokratisierung des deutschen Konstitutionalismus in der Zeit Wilhelms II.', *Zeitschrift für die gesamte Staatswissenschaft*, 113 (1957), 721–46; Manfred Rauh, *Die Parlamentarisierung des Deutschen Reiches* (Düsseldorf, 1977).

⁴ Hans Rosenberg, 'The Pseudo-Democratization of the Junker Class' (orig. 1958), in Georg Iggers (ed.), *The Social History of Politics: Critical Perspectives in West German Historical Writing since 1945* (New York, 1985), 81–112.

⁵ M. Rainer Lepsius, 'Parteiensystem und Sozialstruktur', in Gerhard A. Ritter (ed.), *Deutsche Parteien vor 1918* (Cologne, 1973), 56–80. For my evaluation of recent criticisms (and misunderstandings) of Lepsius's model, see Kühne, 'Demokratisierung', 306 ff.

⁶ Karl Rohe, *Wahlen und Wählertraditionen in Deutschland. Kulturelle Grundlagen deutscher Parteien und Parteiensysteme im 19. und 20. Jahrhundert* (Frankfurt a.M., 1992); Jonathan Sperber, *The Kaiser's Voters: Electors and Elections in Imperial Germany* (Cambridge, 1997).

⁷ Margaret Lavinia Anderson, *Practicing Democracy: Elections and Political Culture in Imperial Germany* (Princeton, 2000); cf. Geoff Eley, *Reshaping the German Right: Radical Nationalism and Political Change after Bismarck* (orig. 1980), 2nd edn (Ann Arbor, MI, 1991); Roger Chickering, *We Men Who Feel Most German: A Cultural Study of the Pan-German League, 1886–1914* (Boston, 1984), 152–82.

⁸ Kühne, *Dreiklassenwahlrecht*.

⁹ James Retallack, *The German Right, 1860–1920: Political Limits of the Authoritarian Imagination* (Toronto, Buffalo, London, 2006), 129.

¹⁰ Thomas Nipperdey, *Deutsche Geschichte 1866–1918*, 2 vols, vol. 2, *Machtstaat vor der Demokratie* (Munich, 1992), 905.

¹¹ James Retallack, *Germany in the Age of Kaiser Wilhelm II* (Basingstoke, London, New York, 1996), 92.

¹² Dieter Langewiesche, *Politikstile im Kaiserreich. Zum Wandel von Politik und Öffentlichkeit im Zeitalter des 'politischen Massenmarktes'* (Friedrichsruh, 2002), 3–5.

¹³ In a letter to a friend, 30 July 1865, cited in Ludolf Parisius, *Leopold Freiherr von Hoverbeck*, 2 vols in 3 (Berlin, 1900), ii. pt. 2, 55.

¹⁴ Stanley Suval, *Electoral Politics in Wilhelmine Germany* (Chapel Hill, NC, 1985).

¹⁵ See Gerhard A. Ritter with Merith Niehuss, *Wahlgeschichtliches Arbeitsbuch. Materialien zur Statistik des Kaiserreich 1871–1918* (Munich, 1980).

¹⁶ Ibid. 28.

¹⁷ Heinrich von Treitschke, 'Der Sozialismus und seine Gönner' (orig. 1874), in Treitschke, *Zehn Jahre Deutscher Kämpfe*, 2nd edn (Berlin, 1879), 500–1. For a longer extract in both English and German see http://germanhistorydocs. ghi-dc.org/sub_document.cfm?document_id=590.

¹⁸ Cited in Rüdiger vom Bruch, 'Bürgerliche Sozialreform im deutschen Kaiserreich', in vom Bruch (ed.), *'Weder Kommunismus noch Kapitalismus'. Bürgerliche Sozialreform in Deutschland vom Vormärz bis zur Ära Adenauer* (Munich, 1985), 137, 131.

¹⁹ See Gunther Mai, '"Verteidigung" und "Volksgemeinschaft". Staatliche Selbstbehauptung, nationale Solidarität und soziale Befreiung in Deutschland in der Zeit des Ersten Weltkrieges (1900–1925)', in Wolfgang Michalka (ed.), *Der Erste*

Weltkrieg. Wirkung—Wahrnehmung—Analyse (Munich and Zurich, 1994), 583–602; Robert von Friedeburg, 'Klassen-, Geschlechter- oder Nationalidentität? Handwerker und Tagelöhner in den Kriegervereine der neupreußischen Provinz Hessen-Nassau 1890–1914', in Ute Frevert (ed.), *Militär und Gesellschaft im 19. und 20. Jahrhundert* (Stuttgart, 1997), 229–44.

[20] Brett Fairbairn, 'Membership, Organization, and Wilhelmine Modernism. Constructing Economic Democracy through Cooperation', in Geoff Eley and James Retallack (eds), *Wilhelminism and Its Legacies: German Modernities, Imperialism, and the Meanings of Reform, 1890–1930* (Oxford and New York, 2003), 35.

Militarism and radical nationalism

Roger Chickering

In October 1906 Wilhelm Voigt, a petty criminal who had recently been released from prison, visited several used-clothes stores in Berlin in order to piece together the uniform of a captain in the Prussian army. Attired in it, he commandeered a squad of soldiers off the street and led them into the town hall of Köpenick, a suburban district of the capital, where he placed the mayor under military arrest and ordered the cashier to hand over nearly 4,000 Marks. Then he fled with the loot. The incident created a worldwide sensation. It subsequently provided the material for a famous play—and a movie adaptation—from the pen of Carl Zuckmayer; and to this day, the adventures of this 'Captain of Köpenick' stand as a symbol of the slavish deference to the military uniform that reigned in Imperial Germany.[1] However, as recent scholarship has made clear, the story of Wilhelm Voigt was more complicated and its implications more ambiguous. Much of the German uproar was critical not only of slavish deference to the uniform, but also of the police chicanery that had made Voigt's plight desperate enough for him to pull the stunt. This chicanery figured large in the trial that followed his capture, and it led to a lenient sentence, as well as to a great deal of public sympathy for the defendant.[2]

The incident in Köpenick offers a good point to begin an analysis of both militarism and radical nationalism in Imperial Germany. Whatever else it revealed, Voigt's feat did dramatize the power of the uniform—the immense influence and prestige that the army commanded in German politics and society. But the incident revealed as well that military matters provided the occasion for loud criticism of public power in Germany. While the concept of militarism is central to the one dimension of the story, the growth of radical nationalism is inseparable from the other.

Soldiers and policy

The word 'militarism' is itself a product of the late nineteenth century. The foremost student of the problem, the historian Gerhard Ritter, offered a useful definition when he wrote of the 'exaggeration and overestimation' of the military in politics and society.[3] While Ritter's own scholarship traced the heavy influence of soldiers in political councils everywhere in Europe in the era before the First World War, he concluded that the problem was nowhere as pronounced as in Imperial Germany. What appeared elsewhere in Europe as a 'necessary evil', he wrote, represented in Germany 'the nation's highest source of pride'.[4]

The reasons for this state of affairs were many and complex. They involved questions of Germany's political institutions, patterns of socio-economic growth, and the sorts of attitudes and habits of mind suggested in the word 'culture'. In all events, the fact that the German Empire was born on the battlefields of France in 1870–71—as the issue of one of the most splendid military campaigns ever fought—was of signal importance. The Franco-Prussian War certified the army as the agent and symbol of Germany's national destiny, and it ensured that soldiers would enjoy elite status in the state that emerged out of the conflict.

The constitution of the new state made this point immediately clear. It shielded the army from control or supervision by the civilian parliamentarians in the Reichstag.[5] Matters of command, military planning, personnel, organization, training, and justice remained in practice the exclusive prerogatives of the army's commander-in-chief, the Prussian king (and German emperor). The powers of the Reichstag were limited to approving the military budget, which came to the attention of parliament every seven years (after 1893 every five years), and to interpollating the minister of war, a soldier empowered to provide only narrow answers. The powers of this minister, who was technically a member of the Prussian government but became effectively a national official, were carefully circumscribed by the constitution; then, in the early 1880s, they were further whittled away in intrigue. The beneficiaries of the war minister's weakness were the Prussian General Staff and Military Cabinet—the latter of which oversaw questions of personnel in the army. As long as he served as the head of the government, Otto von Bismarck provided a degree of civilian oversight to the political ambitions of the military leadership, but his departure in 1890 removed this check. The direction of military affairs fell now to the new commander-in-chief, Kaiser William II, who was less alive to the perils of soldiers in politics, and less inclined or able to provide coordination among the civilian and military agencies of his government.

The result was the growing prominence of military (and naval) officers in the determination of German policy. Several notorious episodes marked the worsening of this problem. One involved a growing network of naval attachés, who were placed in German embassies abroad but circumvented the Foreign Office in Berlin as they reported directly back to Admiral Alfred von Tirpitz, the chief of the Imperial Naval Office. During the delicate negotiations over an Anglo-German naval pact in 1912, which would have relieved the competition between the two countries to build large warships, Tirpitz used information supplied to him by the attaché in London to sabotage an agreement that the German civilian leadership was seeking. The most fateful instance of military policy-making occurred in connection with German planning for the war that eventually broke out in 1914. On the basis of strategic calculations alone, the chief of the General Staff, Alfred von Schlieffen, had determined that the German army should invade the Low Countries immediately upon the beginning of hostilities. This decision had far-reaching political implications, insofar as it would likely bring Great Britain into the war on the side of Germany's enemies. This likelihood did not perturb Schlieffen, in part because he had not bothered to consult the diplomats in the Foreign Office, who might have been more sensitive to the problem. In the event, these civilian officials registered no protest when they learned of the army's decision.

The militarization of culture

The fact that civilian leaders deferred in this way to the judgement of soldiers spoke to the broader, cultural dimensions of militarism in Imperial Germany. The political prominence of soldiers was due in large part to the fact that important segments of the civilian population agreed with the soldiers' view of the world. Militarism rested on a perception of international relations that emphasized the importance, desirability, or inevitability of violent conflict. This proposition ratified the elite roles of soldiers, who were the professional custodians of national security and technicians of violence—men who had been trained to recognize and defeat the threats that lurked in the international arena. The same proposition lent cultural weight to 'military virtues'—vigilance, discipline, obedience, and a salutary anxiety about the nation's many enemies. The circumstances of Imperial Germany's birth and the military traditions of its dominant state, Prussia, fed the power of this analysis of international affairs, as both factors underwrote the systematic militarization of national symbols in the new state. To the extent that there was a central national holiday in the German Empire, it was Sedan Day, the annual celebration on 2 September of the crushing German victory over the French army in the Battle of Sedan in 1870.[6]

The cultivation of the corresponding civic habits of mind took place in several institutional contexts. After unification, the educational systems remained within the jurisdiction of Prussia and Germany's other constituent states. Nevertheless, curricula and instruction—particularly in history, literature, geography, and civics (*Heimatkunde*)—quickly adjusted throughout the land to the lessons of unification. In schoolbooks in Saxony, Bavaria, and Baden, the performance of local troops in the war of 1870–71 became the regional mark of validation and belonging in the new imperial state.[7] In these and other textbooks, the reigns of monarchs constituted the stuff of history, and battlefield triumphs were the measure of success.[8] 'Is this a history book or a manual of war?' asked a critic upon reviewing a number of history texts in circulation in 1904.⁹ In these and other texts, German unification stood as the climactic moment in a historical narrative whose nadir lay in the humiliation of the Prussian army at the hands of Napoleon in 1806. Military motifs also shaped the early encounters of schoolchildren with their language. One popular *Primer for Urban Children*, which was introduced into the schools in 1910, offered instruction in the alphabet by linking individual letters to military motifs. When pupils came to the letters 'P' and 'K', the list of associated objects that they encountered included 'powder' (*Pulver*), 'bullet' (*Kugel*), 'cannon' (*Kanone*), 'cannonier' (*Kanonier*), 'king' (*König*), 'arrow' (*Pfeil*), 'pistol' (*Pistole*), and 'cuirassier' (*Kürassier*).¹⁰

Primers were only one element in the comprehensive military ambiance that prevailed in the public schools. The harsh discipline here could appeal to military practices, as it sanctioned the corporal punishment of children. Whether in connection with the curriculum or in school celebrations, such as those on Sedan Day, song and play were likewise geared to military themes. The goal of patriotic celebrations in the schools, as one Prussian official explained in 1888, was to cultivate in children a 'powerful stimulus to emulate their fathers', the veterans of the war of 1870–71, who had 'risked everything to ensure the highest earthly blessings for their descendents'.¹¹ The songs best designed to provoke sentiments like these, counselled a school director in 1912 on the basis of his own experience, were set to march-time and had 'fresh patriotic and enthusiastic military content'.¹²

Boys were the principal objects of this pedagogy. Girls did not face the military service towards which much of the public school system was oriented. In theory, every German male was subject to this service, although for budgetary and other reasons only about half of each year's eligible conscripts were in fact called to the colours. Those who were inducted, normally at the age of twenty, spent the next three (after 1893, two) years of their lives in active service; thereafter they moved through a system of reserve levies that kept them liable for periodic training, as well as call-up, until they were forty-five. At every stage in this process, the training that they received at the hands of officers had to do not only with tactics and weaponry; it was political, too, and it dwelt on the virtues of obedience, sacrifice, loyalty, and hierarchical authority. Even after the expiration of their formal military obligations, old soldiers were encouraged to join veterans' associations, which in 1913 comprised nearly three million members. The political attitudes of these veterans were of no less concern to the army than their continued camaraderie.[13]

In cities and towns throughout the land, the veterans' associations represented a central component in an organizational network that underpinned what one might call—because it so enjoyed official sanction—'statist' or 'official' militarism. These groups cultivated skills, activities, and attitudes that had immediate military relevance. Male glee clubs and societies of gymnasts and sharpshooters, all of whom boasted their collective discipline, joined veterans in this network.[14] So did an assortment of women's groups, such as the Women's Patriotic Societies of the Red Cross, who supported the training of nurses for duty in wartime.[15] A national system of paramilitary youth organizations, which the army collected during the final years of peace into the Young Germany League, made up still another component of the network.[16]

The militarized culture of patriotism found expression in local public festivities and at monuments like the *Hermannsdenkmal*, the shrine to the Germanic hero who in 9 AD had defeated the Roman legions in the Teutoburg Forest.[17] This culture blossomed on national holidays and during the army's many colourful acts of self-display, which ranged from the spectacular army manoeuvres held each autumn to the parades of local garrisons. The 'Kaiser parade' in Berlin brought the rituals to fulfilment. 'How much might they wish to march along!' exclaimed an observer of the young people who watched one such parade in 1908. 'Not only the boys, but the girls too. How a day like this educates! In a couple of hours their hearts breathe in more enthusiasm and patriotism than in a hundred weeks of school.'[18] Heinrich Mann's depiction of the same phenomenon in his novel, *The Loyal Subject*, suggested that the spectacle made a similar impression on adults like Diederich Hessling, the novel's protagonist. 'There on the horse rode Power', wrote Mann of Hessling's fictional encounter with the Kaiser in Berlin. 'The Power which transcends us and whose hoofs we kiss, the Power which is beyond the reach of hunger, spite and mockery! Against it we are impotent, for we all love it! We have it in our blood, for in our blood is submission. We are an atom of that Power, a diminutive molecule of something it has given out.'[19]

The appeal of these rituals was particularly strong among the Protestant middle classes; and the political colouration of organizations that anchored them was principally National Liberal. In these circles, the symbols of military power stood as bulwarks of social and political order in a young state, whose civic unity had not only been problematic from the start, but was quickly challenged by wrenching social and economic change during the 'second' industrial revolution at the end of the nineteenth century. The symbolic language of war provided orientation to urban social groups that felt most threatened in this era of socioeconomic flux.

War and the discourse of politics

To judge from Heinrich Mann's novel and many other sources, the use of this language and the embrace of military values also had important effects on the behaviour of these social groups. Diederich Hessling has stood as a crown witness for the 'feudalization of the German bourgeoisie'. This term suggests the uncritical adoption by the Protestant bourgeoisie of the values, social practices, and political attitudes of the military aristocracy—hence the abandonment of its own legitimate aspirations to social and political hegemony in Imperial Germany. Additional indicators of the same process could be found in the pursuit of reserve-officers' commissions and aristocratic wives by male members of the German middle class, their grateful acceptance of patents of nobility or honorific titles from the government, and the avid duelling in which university fraternities engaged. The result of the duelling, wrote Hans-Ulrich Wehler in 1973, was 'to commit the sons of the bourgeoisie to a neo-aristocratic code of honour and behaviour' and to bind them to 'the pre-industrial aristocratic ruling groups'.[20] However, as Wehler himself has in the meantime conceded, to write of the feudalization of the German bourgeoisie raises as many problems as it resolves. To the extent that the term implies an effective technique of social control, the submission by one class to the values of another, it oversimplifies the complex dynamics of militarism in Germany. In particular, it obscures the extent to which 'military values' and the spectre of violent struggle were pervasive features of political and social conflict within the German Empire.

The idea of 'feudalization' is most plausible as a description of political intent. It is difficult to deny that the army leadership hoped to inculcate military values generally, in the interests of social control and authoritarian rule. In this respect, the army served by design as the 'school of the nation'. The pupils who were thought to need this education the most were the sons of the German industrial working class, because they were increasingly tempted by ideological schooling of another kind.[21] The ideology of German socialism was Marxist; it was itself riveted to conflict, but not the sort that the army emphasized. In the eyes of Germany's civilian and military leaders, the spectre of conflict at home—class war and social revolution—justified expanding the definition of the 'enemy' to include members of the Social Democratic Party (SPD); and against them the army mobilized. Common soldiers who were caught carrying socialist literature or frequenting socialist meetings or taverns were prosecuted and expelled from the army. The civic training carried out under the army's auspices not only featured the dangers that lurked in international affairs; it also emphasized the threats to Germany's security posed by a range of domestic enemies, in which socialists played the lead. The same themes pervaded the activities of the veterans' associations, from which the military authorities also sought to purge the socialists.

The results of this attempt to invoke military values in the campaign against the socialists were ambiguous and full of paradox. Despite the Social Democrats' role as the loudest critics of Germany's official militarism, many committed socialist workers recalled their military service in a favourable light; with no evident feelings of divided loyalty, they continued to hold the associated national symbols, such as the Kaiser and the army itself, in high regard.[22] More remarkable, however, was Social Democracy's own militarization. As the growth of the socialist labour movement gained momentum after 1890 (when its legal banishment ended), leaders of the movement could pride themselves on the discipline, organization, and resolve in their ranks. They also propagated their own vision of conflict, now in the name of a more just and equitable society. The popularity of martial images in this 'army of workers' was hardly inadvertent. Military accents seeped into the activities of Social Democratic voluntary associations—the myriad educational societies and recreational clubs that underpinned the 'alternative culture' of the socialist labour movement. The 'Workers' *Marseillaises*', which was regularly sung at socialist meetings of many descriptions, invoked the images of war:

> It is a heavy fight [*Kampf*] that we are waging
> Countless are the troops of the enemy,
> Even if flames and danger
> May break loose over us,
> We do not count the number of enemies,
> Do not worry about danger,
> We follow the path of courage.[23]

Festivals and parades were standard rituals in this milieu, too. Both were designed to display the militant solidarity of the working class. One festival of workers' singing societies, which was held in Hamburg in 1905, offered a programme that was punctuated by cannon blasts and featured marches, 'The Two Grenadiers' (a ballad for baritone solo), a 'character piece' called 'Reveille', and a 'Quadrille in the Military Style'.[24] A 'mighty procession' followed another socialist festival, this one in Gera in 1913. The parade featured, an observer wrote, 'several hundred gymnasts, in matching uniforms', who 'marched briskly and carried a whole series of flags'.[25]

Decades before the Social Democratic labour movement became the most traumatic symbol of social conflict, the militarization of domestic tensions had turned dramatic in another arena. The confessional conflict known as the *Kulturkampf* might be loosely translated as a 'culture war', for participants on both sides understood it in just this light, as they employed military metaphors to describe both themselves and their opponents.[26] In fact, it is difficult not to describe this conflict in the same metaphors today, for it featured a bitter assault by Protestant public authorities on the fortresses of Catholic power and identity during the first decades of the new empire. Germany found itself, as one Protestant deputy in the Reichstag characterized the situation, 'in a state of war with the Jesuit order', because Jesuits posed 'the most urgent, the most burning, the most immediate danger to the German Empire'.[27] Catholics found themselves branded generally as enemies of the state. So they mobilized in their own defense, and they too found a ready supply of martial tropes to guide them. The 'embattled church'—wounded, bleeding, but disciplined under fire—became what Helmut Walser Smith has called the 'root metaphor' of German political Catholicism, in which motifs of war and martyrdom combined easily.[28] Although the *Kulturkampf* abated in the 1880s, confessional relations remained tense in Germany. Militant organizations on both sides, such as the Protestant League and the People's Association for Catholic Germany, continued to deploy military imagery in public campaigns that broadened, after 1890, to encompass Social Democracy, the self-proclaimed foe of both Christian confessions. 'We must build a well-trained, well-equipped *army* out of *Christian workers*', as one Catholic explained. 'Our clergy—the officers of the Catholic Church—must appear on the battleground, train the men for the struggle, and arm them!'[29]

No less than international rivalries, domestic tensions were thus moulded in martial language.[30] Well beyond the circles that nurtured 'official militarism', images of battles, armies, enemies, victories, and treachery populated German political discourse, to the point that the idea of 'militarism as political culture' does not seem like an exaggeration.[31] The popularity of social Darwinism both symptomized and fed this process, as existential struggle became a basic idiom for the proponents—and opponents—of causes across the political spectrum. Metaphors of military conflict pervaded discussions of confessional parity, class enmity, welfare legislation, free trade, agrarian resettlement, and land reclamation (which David Blackbourn has recently analyzed as the 'conquest of nature').[32] Antisemitism, whose politicization began in earnest during the 1870s, was another symptom of domestic tensions that traded in these images.[33]

The pervasiveness of military values in Imperial Germany thus symptomized more than the subjection of one class to the interests of another, or, to use the language once employed by East German historians, a 'class alliance of the Junkers and bourgeoisie'.[34] Military tropes governed the language of domestic politics broadly. Every political camp sought to deploy military values to its own advantage—to anchor what in German are called '*Herrschaftsansprüche*', or claims to authority and power. In the calculus of official militarism, the deployment of military tropes was in fact supposed to anchor the authoritarian features of the German constitutional system—the claims of the monarch and the military aristocracy to authority, power, and precedence. Outside military circles, however, the same language was used to contest these claims. Moreover, within each political camp, the same language had important implications for questions of authority, power, and precedence. The appeal to military values encouraged the concentration of executive power and bureaucratic order in political organizations of all kinds, in the name of discipline and collective solidarity. In this respect, the widely remarked bureaucratization of Social Democracy and the 'ultramontanization' of German Catholicism in the era of the *Kulturkampf* were dimensions of the same phenomenon. Finally, the currency of military values fortified patriarchal gender roles in every camp. Insofar as military tropes were coded male, they prescribed that authority in the public realm be vested in men. They fostered the exclusion of women from leadership roles and basic forms of political participation (such as voting).

Populist militarism

Thanks in no small part to the militarization of domestic conflict, the prospect of war took on growing urgency in the realm where it was most indigenous, in international affairs. The links between foreign and domestic policy were tight in Imperial Germany. Bismarck himself set the tone when, in 1875, he conjured up a war-scare with France as the German army's budget navigated its way through the Reichstag. Bismarck's decision in the 1880s to establish formal German protectorates in Africa and Asia reflected his calculation that colonial empire would provide an outlet for social and political tensions at home.[35] This project rested on the hope that the spectre of international conflict (in this case, struggle for empire among the great powers) would generate consensus at home, or at least isolate the 'enemies of the state' like the socialists, who opposed imperial conquest. Bismarck's successors followed the same logic with less caution. Bernhard von Bülow, who became foreign secretary in 1897 and chancellor three years later, was devoted to the principle that foreign policy could have agreeable effects on domestic politics. 'The national moment must always be placed at the forefront by means of [pursuing] national goals,' as he explained it, 'so obligations to the nation do not cease to motivate, bind, and divide the parties.'[36] Bülow's principal object in foreign policy was to enlarge Germany's colonial empire—its 'place in the sun'—and to this end he encouraged the militarization of international politics as he pushed for the construction of a German battle fleet, whose purpose was to challenge British hegemony on the seas.[37]

Germany's pursuit of 'national goals' significantly complicated the dynamics of domestic conflict at the end of the nineteenth century. It encouraged a new, aggressive species of patriotic society, which accepted the values and virtues signalled in official militarism, as well as the underlying belief in the inevitability or desirability of war. The new societies embraced these principles, however, with a fearless logic that bred a new, 'populist' variety of militarism and ultimately challenged Imperial Germany's authoritarian constitutional structure. These patriotic societies embraced a new, 'radical nationalism', the proposition that the font of political power and authority lay not in the emperor and his ministers but instead in the '*Volk*', the nation as a collective actor. The nationalists who congregated in these organizations invoked the symbols of the nation as they criticized public power and official policies, but they were not democrats; they did not believe that the genuine representatives of the nation were to be found in parliament.[38]

Radical nationalist organizations represented a response to two problems that increasingly marked international tensions at the turn of the century. One was Germany's growing involvement in imperial rivalries outside Europe. The German Colonial Society, which was born in 1887, and the German Navy League, which was founded eleven years later, mobilized popular support for

Germany's colonial empire, as well as for the warships that this empire appeared to require. In the meantime, several other patriotic societies had been founded to mobilize popular emotions in connection with another problem, which grew out of intensifying conflicts over language and culture on the European Continent.[39] These conflicts pitted communities of Germans against other ethnic groups throughout central and eastern Europe, particularly in the Habsburg monarchy. This order of conflict had an additional dimension, for ethnic tensions were rife within Imperial Germany too, particularly among Germans and the Polish, French, and Danish minorities that inhabited the peripheries of the country. The German School Association (which in 1908 became the Association for Germandom Abroad) was founded in 1881 in order to support German schools in Austria-Hungary, while the German Society for the Eastern Marches, which was established in 1894, promoted the settlement of Germans in eastern Prussia.[40]

The challenge these organizations posed to the structure of power in Germany was not immediately apparent. Most of the patriotic societies took shape with encouragement not only from commercial and industrial interest groups, but also from the German government. The German Navy League, to cite the most dramatic instance, expanded to over a million members on the strength of industrial subsidies and massive support from public officials around the country. The imperial government rewarded the German Colonial Society for its support with lucrative concessions and other financial inducements.[41] Because of the dependencies created in this way, a condominium emerged between the government and most of these organizations, whose mobilization of opinion in favour of official policies was calculated to bring popular pressure to bear whenever so-called 'national issues'—such as the navy, the colonies, or the rights of Poles to use their own language—came before the Reichstag. This practice has led some historians to write of 'manipulation' of national opinion from the top down, or the government's 'mobilization of plebiscitary approval' for its own policies.[42]

Many of these groups continued to provide the government with welcome support, so this view is plausible; but it is too easy. Both the programmes and the political activities of the patriotic societies contained the seeds of conflict with the government.

The aggressive nationalism that they espoused was different in fundamental respects from the state-centred nationalism (*Staatsnationalismus*) that Bismarck had cultivated in the early years of the empire. To advocate colonial empire and to provide succour to German communities elsewhere in Europe both implied the insufficiency of the Reich as it had been constituted in 1871. Support for the communities of ethnic Germans was particularly problematic, insofar as it rested on an expanded, ethnic or '*völkisch*' definition of the 'German nation', which included all people who spoke German—wherever in Europe (or the world) they lived. Finally, the mobilization of popular sentiment in support of 'national' policies presupposed that the will of 'the nation', however defined, could not be ignored in the formulation of these policies.

The founding of another patriotic society in 1891, the Pan-German League, laid bare all these problems.[43] This organization grew out of a rebellion among members of the Colonial Society, who were furious over the German government's signing away large tracts of east African territory to Great Britain in exchange for the island of Heligoland in the North Sea. Frustrations of several kinds thereupon found a home in the Pan-German League, whose broadranging programme called not only for a more expansive colonial policy, but also for 'the support of German ethnic [*deutschvölkisch*] aspirations in all countries in which members of our *Volk* have to fight for the affirmation of their distinctiveness'.[44] Over the next decade, as the League grew to over 20,000 members (many of them simultaneously members of other patriotic societies), it became the spearhead of a 'national opposition' to the German government. The militancy of its criticism bred a succession of clashes with Chancellor Bülow over colonial policy, ethnic struggle in Austria, the pace of naval building, and German support for the Boers in southern Africa (whom the Pan-Germans regarded as an integral part of German '*Volkstum*').

The activism of the Pan-German League has suggested another reading of the politics of radical nationalism in Imperial Germany. In this view, the mobilization of radical-nationalist opinion proceeded less from the top down than from the bottom up. It resulted, as Geoff Eley has argued, from the 'widespread self-motivation of the subordinate classes', a revolt of the petty-bourgeois 'outsiders' in a political system that had been dominated by men of property

and education.[45] Radical nationalism's challenge to the established structures of power was thus related generically to the mass
mobilization of Catholics and socialist workers.

This view is also too easy. The leaders and members of the
patriotic societies were not outsiders. They were Protestant men
of property and education. A majority of the leaders in all these
organizations had trained at Germany's universities. Of these
leaders, a remarkable proportion (76 per cent of the Colonial
Society, 75 per cent of the Eastern Marches Society, 72 per cent
of the Navy League, and 54 per cent of the Pan-German League)
were themselves publicly employed—in the secondary schools or
the higher reaches of local and state bureaucracies.[46] They were
notables (*Honoratioren*), who played leading roles in local politics.
Their position in local hierarchies of power and prestige was the
source of the images of peril and conflict that permeated their
programmes and ideologies. As an academically educated and
cultivated elite, these men held themselves to be custodians of
German *Kultur* and *Bildung* (self-cultivation); as public officials,
they held themselves to be custodians of German authority. They
were, as a consequence, sensitive barometers of threats to German
culture and authority wherever these threats arose, whether in
Germany itself, at the hands of Catholic Poles or atheistic socialists,
or in the broader world, at the hands of Czechs in Bohemia, black
Africans, or British imperialists. Radical nationalism represented
the ideological vehicle of their claims to power.

The patriotic societies quickly became pillars in the broader
nationalist milieu in cities and towns throughout the land, particularly in Protestant northern and central Germany—in places
like Netzig, the fictional setting for Heinrich Mann's novel. The
political geography of radical nationalism resembled that of the
National Liberal Party, whose local committees also populated
this milieu and were run by many of the same men who led
the patriotic societies.[47] At the same time, the nationalist milieu
expanded, drawing from an assortment of other Protestant middle-
class organizations, which were linked primarily by their belief in
the German *Volk* as a central reference point—an ethnic body that
transcended the political boundaries of the German Empire. In
one way or another, most of these groups regarded themselves as
'reformist'; but in many cases the reformist impulse was politically

ambivalent, as likely to be pacifist as nationalist, because it was directed in the main toward lifestyles. Conservationists, preservationists, eugenicists, naturopaths, Nordic enthusiasts, nudists, anti-vivisectionists, and vegetarians could be found in their ranks.[48] So, however, could arrant racists whose politics were not ambivalent. These men believed that the *Volk* was an organic entity whose health required both territorial expansion and the forcible elimination of foreign impurities, like Jews.

The translation of racism into radical nationalism, the synthesis of biological and martial motifs as a guide to political action, became increasingly marked after the turn of the twentieth century, as the Pan-German League became both its leading proponent and central vehicle. A book published in 1912 by the leader of this organization, Heinrich Class, carried the most chilling statement of its ideological tenets. It identified the Jews as the source of all Germany's domestic ills. For Class, Jews provided the bond among every subversive force in Imperial Germany, from socialism and Catholicism to Poles, Danes, and people who spoke French in Alsace. The book accordingly advocated depriving Jews of their civil rights and outlawing the Social Democrats. To rally national opinion, it called for an 'active' and 'aggressive' foreign policy, as well as 'national rallies' and 'patriotic festivals for the people'. It proposed the refashioning of Germany's suffrage laws in order to produce a 'parliament of the best', which would be dominated by just the kind of propertied and educated men who ran the Pan-German League and other patriotic societies.[49]

The national opposition and the military

Class's book was entitled *If I Were the Kaiser*. The title captured one of the most provocative features of radical nationalism. Its protagonists had begun to question the authority and capacity of the Kaiser and his government to defend the national interest; they now portrayed themselves as the true representatives of the *Volk*, the chosen custodians of the national symbols. Class's provocation formalized claims that had been more broadly staked since the turn of the century, as the 'national opposition' grew in

212 212 | ROGER CHICKERING

size and confidence. Of particular importance were two dramatic confrontations between patriotic societies and the government over military issues. The army and navy, the two central symbols of German militarism and nationalism, had now become the objects of conflict among their leading champions.

The first confrontation originated in the Navy League.[50] Admiral Tirpitz's plans for the phased building of the German battle fleet rested on careful political calculations, which aimed from 1897 onwards to secure a parliamentary majority at home and to minimize anxieties among the other naval powers abroad, particularly the British, as the German fleet took shape. These calculations governed the role that the Navy League's agitation was supposed to play, but after 1905 they encountered growing resistance among a group of radicals who had gained control of the organization's leadership and who began to argue that the darkening international situation mandated the more rapid construction of German warships. Accordingly, the charges that began to emerge from the Navy League insisted that Tirpitz's plans were inadequate to the military challenges that faced the country; they also implied that the country's naval leadership was not competent to judge these challenges. The crisis festered for several years, before Tirpitz persuaded the Kaiser and the chancellor that the position of the Navy League's leadership rested on untenable assumptions and posed a challenge to the government's authority in the most essential matters. Resolution of the crisis came in 1908 with the intervention of the Kaiser himself, who forced the resignation of the radical leaders in the Navy League by withdrawing his brother's protectorship over the organization—a dramatic gesture that threatened the removal of bureaucratic patronage from the organization.

Many of the Navy League's leaders then migrated to the Pan-German League, where they prepared an even more troubling challenge to the government's prerogatives. This one involved the army. It was triggered in the aftermath of the Second Moroccan Crisis, which had brought the European powers to the verge of war in the summer of 1911. In Germany the diplomatic crisis mobilized the Pan-German League and other patriotic societies, now in the name of expanding and modernizing the army in light of an imminent war. To achieve this end, leaders of the League oversaw the founding of still another patriotic organization, the German Army League. This group, which remained formally independent of the Pan-Germans, began its activity early in 1912, just as the spectacular victory of the Social Democrats in parliamentary elections brought an additional shock to nationalist opinion.[51] Within months, the Army League had grown to over 100,000 members—a figure that reflected the forging of alliances among existing patriotic societies in some 300 localities around the country.

The demands of this organization for expanding the army far exceeded what the War Ministry thought prudent. In this ministry, political calculations rested on the central social corollary of official militarism—the belief that the army not only fought wars, but also served as the prop of domestic order and authority. This vision of the army's role prescribed limitations on its size, lest commoners take over the officer corps and socialist workers inundate the ranks. Leaders of the Army League, by contrast, recognized only the technical imperatives of war, which, they argued, mandated the uncompromising build-up of the army to the limits of Germany's demographic and financial capacities. The wide ideological gulf thus opened between the two poles of what the historian Stig Förster has called Germany's 'double militarism'—the official one and its populist variant. As it had earlier during the conflict over the navy, the central question again had to do with where the authority to judge the country's military requirements ultimately resided.[52]

The leaders of the Army League, who included prominent retired generals, insisted that this authority lay in the popular will, which their organization embodied. 'The pressure of opinion', they insisted, had 'in the final analysis to compel even the parties and the government to do their duty'.[53] The immediate issue became an Army Bill that the government laid before the Reichstag in 1912. The Army League's popular campaign featured an assault on the insufficiency of this legislation, as well as on the judgement and competence of the chancellor and war minister who had framed it. Passage of the bill later in 1912 only fed demands for further increases in the army. The energy of the popular agitation gained force as the Army League grew to almost 300,000 members and acquired allies in high places. The most important of these allies were soldiers in the General Staff, who themselves now began to pressurize the chancellor and war minister into a much greater expansion of the army. In 1913 these soldiers and the Army League got their way, as the Reichstag passed a massive new Army Bill. However, its price tag laid bare the paradox of German militarism.[54] Expanding the German army now fed domestic strife. It required the introduction of direct federal taxes. These taxes were bitterly opposed by the Conservative representatives of the country's 'military class'—and endorsed by the socialist 'enemies of the state'.

Shortly thereafter, war broke out. It provided the scenario for a final confrontation between the government and the radical nationalists. For a brief time the experience of war appeared to reward all those who had long claimed that war would forge domestic unity in Germany. Within months, however, domestic accord had broken down, owing in no small part to a new debate over the government's competence and authority in basic matters of military security. This debate had to do with Germany's foreign-policy aims during the war and the question of who was entitled to determine them. Leaders of the Pan-German League and other patriotic societies were prominent figures in a variety of committees that submitted angry petitions to the government, insisting that German security required extravagant annexations in the territories of the country's enemies. In their agitation these nationalists also calculated that, as one of them observed, the 'distraction' offered by such aggrandizement would help 'avoid internal difficulties'.[55] Regardless of his personal views, which have been the subject of lively debate among historians, Chancellor Theobald von Bethmann Hollweg could not publicly embrace these goals lest he alienate the Social Democrats, whose continuing support for the war was vital. In 1917 the left-wing parties in the Reichstag (including the socialists) repudiated aggressive war aims and passed a resolution that called for a negotiated peace with no annexations. The so-called Peace Resolution called forth a final, furious reaction from the nationalists, who, again with the connivance of the General Staff, founded the German Fatherland Party in the autumn of 1917. Now the object of popular agitation was a 'victorious peace', by which the nationalists meant a programme of far-flung annexations. The Fatherland Party looked at its core much like the Army League, only much larger; it counted more than a million members. This organization comprised an alliance of the familiar players, and it signified at once the culmination and last gasp of the radical nationalism of the Wilhelmine era. The Fatherland Party represented, as its historian has written, an outgrowth of the 'classic politics of notables in the German Empire'.[56]

The outcome of the First World War sealed the fate of this kind of nationalist politics and its leaders. While the radical nationalists who came to prominence during the Weimar Republic also embraced military values in their assault on the country's constituted leadership, they represented a new breed, socially and politically. But the soil in which their ideas took root had been well tilled.

---

[1] Carl Zuckmayer, *Der Hauptmann von Köpenick. Ein deutsches Märchen in drei Akten* (Berlin, 1930); cf. Wilfried von Bredow, *Moderner Militarismus. Analyse und Kritik* (Stuttgart, 1983), 24–7.

[2] Benjamin Carter Hett, *Death in the Tiergarten: Murder and Criminal Justice in the Kaiser's Berlin* (Cambridge, MA, 2004), 182–91.

[3] Gerhard Ritter, *Staatskunst und Kriegshandwerk. Das Problem des 'Militarismus' in Deutschland*, 4 vols (Munich, 1956–68), i. 13; cf. Alfred Vagts, *A History of Militarism, Civilian and Military* (New York, 1959); Volker R. Berghahn, *Militarism: The History of an International Debate, 1861–1979* (Cambridge, 1981); Bredow, *Moderner Militarismus*, 9–22.

[4] Ritter, *Staatskunst*, ii. 117.

[5] See ibid. 148–70; Gordon A. Craig, *The Politics of the Prussian Army, 1640–1945* (New York and Oxford, 1956), 217–98.

[6] Alon Confino, *The Nation as a Local Metaphor: Württemberg, Imperial Germany, and National Memory, 1871–1918* (Chapel Hill, NC, 1997), 52–60.

[7] Siegfried Weichlein, *Nation und Region. Integrationsprozesse im Bismarckreich* (Düsseldorf, 2004), 332–3.

[8] See Horst Gies, 'Geschichtsunterricht und nationalen Identitätsbildung in der Volksschule des Wilhelminischen Kaiserreichs', *Geschichte in Wissenschaft und Unterricht*, 57 (2006), 492–509; Horst Schallenberger, *Untersuchungen zum Geschichtsbild der Wilhelminischen Ära und der Weimarer Zeit. Eine vergleichende Schulbuchanalyse deutscher Schulgeschichtsbücher aus der Zeit von 1888 bis 1933* (Ratingen, 1964); Marieluise Christadler, *Kriegserziehung im Jugendbuch. Literarische Mobilmachung in Deutschland und Frankreich vor 1914* (Frankfurt a.M., 1979).

[9] Roger Chickering, *Imperial Germany and a World without War: The Peace Movement and German Society, 1892–1914* (Princeton, 1975), 171.

[10] Heinz Lemmermann, *Kriegserziehung im Kaiserreich. Studien zur politischen Funktion von Schule und Schulmusik 1890–1918*, 2 vols (Liliental bei Bremen, 1984), ii. 671.

[11] Ibid. ii. 745.   [12] Ibid. ii. 797.

[13] Thomas Rohkrämer, *Der Militarismus der 'kleinen Leute'. Die Kriegervereine im deutschen Kaiserreich 1871–1914* (Munich, 1990).

[14] On this tradition see Dieter Düding, *Organisierter gesellschaftlicher Nationalismus in Deutschland (1808–1847)* (Munich, 1984).

[15] Jean H. Quataert, *Staging Philanthropy: Patriotic Women and the National Imagination in Dynastic Germany, 1813–1916* (Ann Arbor, MI, 2001).

[16] Derek Linton, *'Who Has the Youth, Has the Future': The Campaign to Save Young Workers in Imperial Germany* (Cambridge, 1991).

[17] Charlotte Tacke, *Denkmal im sozialen Raum. Nationale Symbole in Deutschland und Frankreich im 19. Jahrhundert* (Göttingen, 1995).

[18] Jakob Vogel, *Nationen im Gleichschritt. Der Kult der 'Nation in Waffen' in Deutschland und Frankreich, 1871–1914* (Göttingen, 1997), 77.

[19] Heinrich Mann, *The Loyal Subject* (London, 1998), 44. This is but one of several unhappy translations of the title of Mann's novel, *Der Untertan* (Berlin, 1918).

[20] Hans-Ulrich Wehler, *Das Deutsche Kaiserreich 1871–1918* (Göttingen, 1973), 137; cf. Kevin McAleer, *Dueling: The Cult of Honor in Fin-de-Siècle Germany* (Princeton, 1994); and the most relentless statement of this argument in Arno Mayer, *The Persistence of the Old Regime: Europe to the Great War* (New York, 1981).

[21] Reinhard Höhn, *Die Armee als Erziehungsschule der Nation* (Bad Harzburg, 1963).

[22] Nicholas Stargardt, *The German Idea of Militarism: Radical and Socialist Critics, 1866–1914* (Cambridge, 1994).

[23] Vernon Lidtke, *The Alternative Culture: Socialist Labor in Imperial Germany* (New York and Oxford, 1985), 113.

[24] Ibid. 214–19.   [25] Ibid. 90–1.

[26] Christopher Clark and Wolfram Kaiser (eds), *Culture Wars: Secular–Catholic Conflict in Nineteenth-Century Europe* (Cambridge, 2003).

[27] Margaret Lavinia Anderson, *Practicing Democracy: Elections and Political Culture in Imperial Germany* (Princeton, 2000), 98. See also Michael B. Gross, *The War against Catholicism: Liberalism and the Anti-Catholic Imagination in Nineteenth-Century Germany* (Ann Arbor, MI, 2004).

[28] Helmut Walser Smith, *German Nationalism and Religious Conflict: Culture, Ideology, Politics, 1870–1914* (Princeton, 1995), 46–7.

[29] Raymond Chien Sun, *Before the Enemy Is within Our Walls: Catholic Workers in Cologne, 1885–1912. A Social, Cultural and Political History* (Boston, 1999), 69 (italics in the original). See also Róisín Healy, *The Jesuit Specter in Imperial Germany* (Boston and Leiden, 2003).

[30] See Michael Jeissmann, *Das Vaterland der Feinde. Studien zum nationalen Feindbegriff und Selbstverständnis in Deutschland und Frankreich* (Stuttgart, 1992), 241–94.

[31] Bredow, *Militarismus*, 38–41. See also Benjamin Ziemann, 'Sozialmilitarismus und militärische Sozialisation im deutschen Kaiserreich 1870–1914. Desiderate und Perspektiven in der Revision eines Geschichtsbildes', *Geschichte in Wissenschaft und Unterricht*, 53 (2002), 148–64.

[32] David Blackbourn, *The Conquest of Nature: Water, Landscape, and the Making of Modern Germany* (New York and London, 2006). See also Martin Baumeister, *Parität und katholische Inferiorität. Untersuchungen zur Stellung des Katholizismus im Deutschen Kaiserreich* (Paderborn, 1987); Alfred Kelly, *The Descent of Darwin: The Popularization of Darwinism in Germany, 1860–1914* (Chapel Hill, NC, 1981); and (with care) Richard Weikart, *From Darwin to Hitler: Evolutionary Ethics, Eugenics, and Racism in Germany* (New York, 2004).

[33] See Shulamit Volkov, *Germans, Jews, and Antisemites: Trials in Emancipation* (Cambridge, 2006), esp. 67–158.

[34] Helmut Otto, 'Der imperialistische deutsche Militarismus am Anfang des 20. Jahrhunderts', in Karl Nuss *et al.* (eds), *Der deutsche Militarismus in Geschichte und Gegenwart. Studien—Probleme—Analysen* (Berlin-GDR, 1980), 103.

[35] Hans-Ulrich Wehler, *Bismarck und der Imperialismus* (Cologne and Berlin, 1969).

[36] Volker R. Berghahn, *Der Tirpitz-Plan. Genesis und Verfall einer innenpolitischen Krisenstrategie unter Wilhelm II.* (Düsseldorf, 1971), 148.

[37] Ibid.; cf. Michael Epkenhans, *Die wilhelminische Flottenrüstung, 1908–1914. Weltmachtstreben, industrieller Fortschritt, soziale Integration* (Munich, 1991); Rolf Hobson, *Imperialism at Sea: Naval Strategic Thought, the Ideology of Sea Power and the Tirpitz-Plan, 1875–1914* (Boston and Leiden, 2002). One product of Bülow's efforts was to draw the British increasingly into the camp of Germany's enemies and to lend growing plausibility in Germany to the metaphor of 'encirclement' (*Einkreisung*) as a guide to this country's diplomatic plight. The metaphor derived originally from hunting, but its military overtones were clear. See Ute Daniel, 'Einkreisung und Kaiserdämmerung. Ein Versuch, der Kulturgeschichte der Politik vor dem Ersten Welkrieg auf die Spur zu Kommen', in Barbara Stollberg-Rilinger (ed.), *Was heisst Kultwgeschichte des Politischen?* (Berlin, 2005), 279–329.

[38] See Lee McGowan, *The Radical Right in Germany: 1870 to the Present* (London, 2002), 16–42.

[39] Richard Victor Pierard, 'The German Colonial Society, 1882–1914' (Ph.D. diss., State University of Iowa, 1964); Geoff Eley, 'The German Navy League in German Politics, 1898–1914' (Ph.D. diss., University of Sussex, 1974).

[40] Gerhard Weidenfeller, *VDA. Verein für das Deutschtum im Ausland. Allgemeiner Deutscher Schulverein (1881–1914). Ein Beitrag zur Geschichte des deutschen Nationalismus und Imperialismus im Kaiserreich* (Berne and Frankfurt a.M., 1976); Adam Galos *et al.*, *Die Hakatisten. Der Deutsche Ostmarken-Verein (1893–1934). Ein Beitrag zur Geschichte der Ostpolitik des deutschen Imperialismus* (Berlin, 1966).

[41] Roger Chickering, 'Patriotic Societies and German Foreign Policy, 1890–1914', *International History Review*, 1 (1979), 470–89.

[42] Wehler, *Kaiserreich*, 92–3.

[43] The literature on this organization is large. See Rainer Hering, *Konstruirte Nation. Der Alldeutsche Verband 1890 bis 1939* (Hamburg, 2003); Michel Korinman, *Deutschland über alles. Le pangermanisme 1890–1945* (Paris, 1999); Michael Peters, *Der Alldeutsche Verband am Vorabend des Ersten Weltkrieges (1908–1914). Ein Beitrag zur Geschichte des völkischen Nationalismus im spätwilhelminischen Deutschland* (Frankfurt a.M., 1996); Roger Chickering, *We Men Who Feel Most German: A Cultural History of the Pan-German League, 1886–1914* (Boston and London, 1984).

[44] Chickering, *We Men*, 49.

[45] Geoff Eley, *Reshaping the German Right: Radical Nationalism and Political Change after Bismarck* (New Haven, CT, and London, 1980), 9.

[46] Chickering, *We Men*, 314.

[47] Anthony J. O'Donnell, 'National Liberalism and the Mass Politics of the German Right, 1890–1907' (Ph.D. diss., Princeton University, 1973).

[48] Uwe Puschner *et al.*, *Handbuch zur 'Völkischen Bewegung' 1871–1918* (Munich, 1996); Puschner, *Die völkische Bewegung im wilhelminischen Kaiserreich. Sprache— Rasse—Religion* (Darmstadt, 2001). See also Diethard Kerbs and Jürgen Reulecke (eds), *Handbuch der deutschen Reformbewegungen 1880–1933* (Wuppertal, 1998); Kevin Repp, *Reformers, Critics, and the Paths of Modernity: Anti-Politics and the Search for Alternatives, 1890–1914* (Cambridge, MA, 2000), esp. 215–327; Michael Hau, *The Cult of Health and Beauty in Germany: A Social History, 1890–1930* (Chicago and London, 2003); Matthew Jefferies, '*Lebensreform*: A Middle-Class Antidote to Wilhelminism?', in Geoff Eley and James Retallack (eds), *Wilhelminism and Its Legacies: German Modernities, Imperialism, and the Meanings of Reform, 1890–1930* (Oxford and New York, 2003), 91–106.

[49] Daniel Frymann [pseud. Heinrich Class], *Wenn ich der Kaiser wär'. Politische Wahrheiten und Notwendigkeiten* (Leipzig, 1912); Chickering, *We Men*, 285–6.

[50] Wilhelm Deist, *Flottenpolitik und Flottenpropaganda. Das Nachrichtenbüro des Reichsmarineamts 1897–1914* (Stuttgart, 1976), 147–247; Eley, 'Navy League', 179–253; Eley, *Reshaping*, 239–79.

[51] Marilyn Shevin Coetzee, *The German Army League: Popular Nationalism in Wilhelmine Germany* (New York and Oxford, 1990); Roger Chickering, 'Der "Deutsche Wehrverein" und die Reform der deutschen Armee 1912–14', *Militärgeschichtliche Mitteilungen*, 1 (1979), 7–33.

[52] Stig Förster, *Der doppelte Militarismus. Die deutsche Heeresrüstungspolitik zwischen Status-quo-Sicherung und Aggression 1890–1913* (Stuttgart, 1985).

[53] Chickering, *We Men*, 270.

[54] See Volker R. Berghahn, *Germany and the Approach of War in 1914* (New York, 1973).

[55] Gerald D. Feldman, *Army, Industry, and Labor in Germany, 1914–1918* (Princeton, 1966), 136.

[56] Heinz Hagenlücke, *Deutsche Vaterlandspartei. Die nationale Rechte am Ende des Kaiserreichs* (Düsseldorf, 1997), 18.

Transnational Germany

Sebastian Conrad

On a rainy November day in 1900, four graduates of the Tuskegee Normal and Industrial Institute in Alabama set sail from New York harbour on the *Graf Waldersee*. Their journey would take them, via Hamburg, to the German colony of Togo. They had been recruited by Baron Beno von Herman for the Colonial Economic Committee with the explicit purpose 'to teach the negroes there how to plant and harvest cotton in a rational and scientific way'.[1] Togo had been a German colony since 1884. After an initial phase of private initiatives and exploitation, around the turn of the century reform-minded colonial bureaucrats began to aim at more systematic and sustained interventions. This new, scientific approach acknowledged the central role of the native population in any attempt to modernize the colonies and turn them into profitable enterprises. Schooling, health care, and the all-important 'education of the negro to work' were therefore among the central concerns of the reformers.

The German interest in the Tuskegee graduates derived from the conviction that the racialized labour relations in the American New South could provide a model for Germany's African colonies. German bureaucrats and social scientists were especially interested in the Tuskegee institute, where Booker T. Washington inculcated his ideas of natural class hierarchies into the minds of young African American students. His conservative view on social and ethnic relations resonated with the imperialist outlook that rested on the principles of control and segregation. For Beno von Herman, therefore, the Tuskegee graduates seemed the ideal agents of a modernizing project that did not infringe upon the political and racial order in the colonies. Conversely, Washington supported Western imperialism on the grounds that Africa was backward and needed to be 'civilized'.

After arriving in Togo, the Tuskegee graduates, under the leadership of John W. Robinson, founded a cotton school that trained hundreds of students to grow cotton for the European market. For several years, the quality of cotton grown in Togo improved considerably, and the output increased by almost sixty-fold. But interventions were by no means limited to the economic sphere. They rested upon assumptions that concerned work discipline, the gender-specific separation of work spheres, the relationship between production and the market, and the concept of modern subjectivity. The reformist zeal reached down to the level of everyday life, prescribing changes in architecture and housing, food habits, and hygiene. These transformations elicited growing resistance and strategies of evasion among the Togolese population that could only be countered by use of brute force. As a result cotton production dropped after 1909. In the end, the attempt to create a 'German Alabama in Africa' was not successful; Germany never imported more than 0.5 per cent of the cotton she needed from her own colonies.

The Togo experiment sheds light on the structures of Imperial Germany's transnational entanglement. The project was part of Germany's colonial politics, in which economic expectations played a crucial part. Around 1900, the German cotton industry was the third largest in the world; whole regions such as Saxony and Alsace produced Germany's most important export goods. Though exaggerating somewhat, Bismarck himself declared that 'I have been engaged in colonial politics mainly for the opportunity of securing our own cotton production.'[2] Apart from issues of profitability and exploitation, the Togo experiment illustrates the civilizing mission ideology which informed the colonial project. The rhetoric of 'improvement' and development was ubiquitous, and work was considered one of the central means by which to elevate and civilize the natives. It is equally clear that the colonial concept of modernization rested on assumptions about a gendered and racialized order and about a specific form of subjectivity that connected the individual to the state and the market.

Beyond its colonial dimensions, the transfer of African-American expertise to Togo illustrates the broader transnational context of turn-of-the-century Germany. Part of this context was the fascination with work ethics and labour relations in the United States, one of Germany's chief economic and political rivals. At the same time, Germans harboured the expectation that the social order in the New South might offer solutions to the problem of ethnically differentiated agricultural relations, not only in the colonies but also in the Polish-speaking territories in eastern Prussia. The interrelation of the New South, the Polish provinces of Prussia, and colonial Togo suggests the global outlook of social science debates about labour, mobility, production, and nation, just as it also illustrates the repercussions colonial experiences could have in the European metropole.[3]

Finally, the Togo project was an integral part of the global restructuring of the production of raw materials after the virtual end of slave labour. The Civil War in the United States had demonstrated to European politicians and entrepreneurs the inherent danger of continued dependency upon one single supplier of this important resource. The ensuing transformation of the global cotton economy was characterized by nominally free labour and increasing state intervention that replaced the slave plantations and, at least partly, market mechanisms of distribution.[4]

Transnational historiography

To what degree was the German Empire shaped by outside forces, and to what extent was Germany a global player in the decades before the First World War? Historiography has been remarkably silent on these questions for many years, but this was not always the case. In the imperial era a number of intellectuals saw the nation transformed fundamentally by the new global structures. The historian Karl Lamprecht, for example, spoke of a 'national society that will no longer be confined to a territory'. Foreign relations, international forms of cooperation, transatlantic migration, the expansion of the world market, and cultural exchange all contributed to a re-territorialization of the nation, for which Lamprecht proposed the term 'tentacle state'.[5] Lamprecht's colleague at the University of Leipzig, Friedrich Ratzel, was likewise among those who framed their ideas of geopolitics under the impact of changing structures of global entanglement.

Within the mainstream of the profession, however, world-historical perspectives like Lamprecht's were soon relegated to the margins. National history remained the reigning paradigm of the discipline. Discussion of Germany's embeddedness in larger contexts was confined to the field of diplomatic history, which continued to be a principal concern of historians. This largely changed from the 1960s onward, when the rise of social history was accompanied by the methodological decision to privilege a country's internal structures over its foreign relations. Before 1945, the outbreak of the First World War had served as a telos for the historiography of Imperial Germany, and attention therefore was devoted to the international balance of power and its disruptions. However, under the aegis of the *Sonderweg* thesis—the notion that German adopted a 'special path' to modernity—after the 1960s the interest of historians shifted to internal explanations of the authoritarian turn in German history. Seeking to explain 1933 and the Holocaust, historiography turned inwards and tended to interpret Imperial Germany as part of the pre-history of Nazism.

This is not to say that all issues transcending the nation state were consistently sidestepped. Apart from diplomatic history, scholars of economic history and the history of migration have continued to contribute to an understanding of Germany's role in the larger world. These fields remained, however, somewhat neglected subfields of the discipline; such was also the case with colonial history, which experienced a short boom in the wake of decolonization and the turmoil of 1968. Moreover, the central concern of most analyses was not with transnational connections or the colonial periphery, but with their effects on German society. In Hans-Ulrich Wehler's reading, where the colonial experience is rendered as 'social imperialism', this is particularly evident. For Wehler, the colonial endeavour was intended not only to grant access to the necessary resources to fuel the German economy, but also to provide Bismarck's rule with new appeal. The collective

project of overseas expansion was supposed to supply oppositional groups—above all the discontented working classes—with
a national purpose and divert their attention away from urgent
material concerns. By thus exporting internal problems abroad,
the 'counter utopia' of imperial glory furthered social integration
and the pacification of the lower strata of German society. Wehler's
main concern was not with the colonies but with class conflicts
and structural problems in the metropole.[6]

A number of developments in recent years have prepared historians for the current interest in questions of transnationalism
and its impact—an interest that has been spurred by European
integration and the effects of globalization since the 1990s. Among
scholars, the rise of comparative history since the 1980s helped
pave the way for perspectives that transcended the nation-state
point of view.[7] At the same time, calls for the Europeanization of
German history resulted in a number of book series comprehensively dealing with the European past. More recently, the impact of
post-colonial studies has spawned a renewed interest in Germany's
colonial history—one that is sensitive to the issue of repercussions
and effects on German society.[8] Finally, as global history and the
history of globalization have come into vogue, they have begun to
influence studies of German history.[9]

Since roughly the year 2000, then, one can observe a growing
tendency among historians of Imperial Germany, first, to take
larger, transnational contexts into account and, second, to make
them their objects of study. In most cases, a broad understanding
of 'transnational' is employed in pragmatic ways that are neither
limited theoretically nor confined to a specific level of analysis. Very
generally, these studies look for interactions and constellations that
transcend the borders of the nation state. They tend to jettison the
stark dichotomy of domestic and foreign policy so characteristic of
earlier programmatic debates. And they make a virtue of the fact
that, geographically, the term transnational is flexible. It is clear
that the closest relationships connected Germany to her European
neighbours. However, there is a tendency in most recent studies
to go beyond Europe and look for Germany in the world—and
for the ways in which the world reached deep into German
society.

Actors, media, public spheres

Germany's colonial and global engagements increased during the imperial era. This had to do with larger transformations. The early 1880s mark the beginning of the epoch of high imperialism and are conventionally seen as the moment when the dynamics of the globalization process accelerated. The expansive mood of Wilhelmine Germany was in many ways connected to these developments. The formation and coalition of interest groups supporting Germany's move beyond her borders reacted to internal competition and conflicts such as the antagonism between new industrial elites in the Rhine-Ruhr region and the landed aristocracy in the Prussian east. At the same time, these interests were themselves connected to and products of the opportunities and dangers that the integration of the world seemed to entail.

The most vociferous proponents of a more active German role in the world were the propagandists of 'world politics' (*Weltpolitik*) such as Chancellor Bernhard von Bülow, Admiral Alfred von Tirpitz, and the representatives of the numerous nationalist associations. Their impact was based on the support of large groups of the educated bourgeoisie. These groups included social scientists and other academics who increasingly became involved in international networks. Bourgeois women played an active role, for example in the colonial movement.[10] 'World politics' included a commitment to secure access to world markets, and therefore it found the support of industrialists and entrepreneurs.[11] The churches, too, were invested in the world through the missionary project; they helped to transmit the desire for tangible and spiritual acquisitions in exotic regions to social classes that might otherwise not have found it in their interest to support the colonial endeavours. Agrarian circles, by contrast, were much more sceptical in their assessments of the world market and its benefits. The agrarians' entrepreneurial activities, however, were increasingly dominated by global agricultural transactions. Peasants felt the pressure of Russian and American grain imports, and in large numbers they left their fields and homes to migrate to the industrial centres—and across the

Atlantic. Apparently least affected by intensifying global exchange were the lower middle classes and the working classes. Workers nevertheless increasingly felt dependent upon global demand structures, and the trade unions experienced highly emotional debates about the internationalization of the labour market.

It is important to take these different actors and interests into account. Engagement with the world was always of a contested nature; some Germans benefited from late nineteenth-century globalization, while others clearly did not. Moreover, while much attention has been devoted to questions of perception and representations of alterity (that is, of differentness or 'otherness'), the real people depicted in these representations have too often been neglected. In order not to invoke globalization and colonialism as natural phenomena, it remains crucial to ask questions about agency, institutions, and place. When we interrogate the historical record in these ways we find that representations and discursive patterns played a central role in permitting large groups of people to assimilate complex issues of the globalizing world and to relate global structures to local problems. The integration of the world was accompanied by, and accessible through, an emergent global consciousness.

In the Wilhelmine period, the rhetoric of 'world' became almost ubiquitous: world politics, world economy, world powers, world empires were catchwords of the day. For example, the internationalization of economic flows was reflected in the founding of the 'Institute for the World Economy' in Kiel in 1911. This proliferation of terms was an expression of the emergence of what can safely be called a global consciousness. Social and political actors increasingly made reference to similar developments outside of Germany. Not only were other countries used as a yardstick or model; Germans grew aware that what happened elsewhere no longer left their own society unaffected. Thus political and cultural processes were increasingly understood as embedded within a European context: rhetoric and ideologies travelled across borders, and the press turned local events into transnational media events. The focus of the debate about migration was even broader. For example, proponents of strict immigration controls referred not only to the British Alien Act but also to the United States and Australia. And of course technical innovation was closely bound up with these developments. The wide scope of public debate was one result of the communications revolution of the late nineteenth century: steamships, railways, and above all the telegraph contributed to a global flow of information, which was further increased by wireless telegraphy after 1901.

'World politics', world markets, mobility

In order to assess the relevance of Germany's transnational entanglement, it is helpful to differentiate between different spheres of activity. The new global outlook of Imperial Germany found its most palpable expression in the 'world politics' of Chancellor Bülow. It was based on the conviction that the system of interstate equilibrium had shifted from the European to the global stage. Spheres of influence, resources, and markets seemed indispensable in order to become one of the few world empires (*Weltreiche*) of the twentieth century—apart from Great Britain, the United States, and Russia. At the same time, Bülow's quest for a 'place in the sun', partly directed against British hegemony, always had a strong European dimension to it. The most important outcome of the globalized German–British rivalry was the naval politics that after 1897 increasingly preoccupied the German Foreign Office and the wider public. A whole generation of German youths began to wear sailor's uniforms on birthdays and Sundays. After the turn of the century, the focal points of foreign-policy attention moved to distant places like the Taku forts, Venezuela, Agadir, Samoa. This topography referred to conflicts that had local origins but were also indicative of the global aspirations of Germany's foreign policy. But nearly always the competition among the European powers remained a central point of reference. This was even true, to some extent, for colonial expansion, although it is clear that many different motives were behind Germany's colonial acquisitions from 1884 onwards. While Europe continued to structure Germany's colonial agenda, colonialism began to inform politics on the Continent. Recent research has argued that the most important field of German colonial projections and interventions lay not in Africa, but in the European east. 'The true German counterpart to India or Algeria', David Blackbourn has written, 'was not Cameroon: it was *Mitteleuropa*.'[12]

Economically, the overseas colonies never lived up to the high expectations for them entertained in government and industrial circles. German exports to Romania in 1913 were three times greater than exports to all the German colonies combined. If investments were made in the colonial world, they tended to flow into British possessions rather than into 'New Germany' in Africa and the Pacific. The marginal contribution of the colonies, however, did not impede Imperial Germany's advance as one of the central agents of economic globalization (in many sectors second only to Great Britain). Since the mid-nineteenth century, the Atlantic-centred world economy had expanded to integrate most other regional trade circuits. It was only now that a truly global economy emerged, driven by the Industrial Revolution, British free trade imperialism, and guaranteed by the gold standard that Germany adopted in 1871. Foreign trade rose to unprecedented proportions, reaching 34 per cent of the gross national product in 1914—a figure not surpassed before the 1960s. This had palpable consequences on the structure of industrial production within Germany. Chemical industries were primarily geared towards foreign markets that absorbed 35 per cent of her products (mainly transported on British ships). Electronics, metals and machines, and finished products in general found a growing demand beyond the borders of the German Empire. The rise in economic exchange was accompanied by a gradual convergence of market prices and wages: relative to production, the volume of global trade rose tenfold between 1850 and 1914.

Conversely, it was one of the consequences of the transformation of Germany into an industrial state that imports of raw materials grew in importance. The effects on agricultural production were considerable. Whereas the new industries produced for the world market, the landowners and peasants in the agrarian regions of eastern Prussia came to see themselves as the victims of global economic integration. Wool was imported from Australia and South Africa; the wheat used for bread was grown on the US prairies but also in Russia, Canada, and Argentina. Sinking transatlantic transportation costs made it possible for grain from Chicago to arrive at inland port cities like Mannheim at a cheaper rate than grain from domestic Prussian competitors that travelled via Berlin. This changed the geography of the world economy, and it radically transformed the structure of agriculture in Prussia's eastern provinces. The crisis of the grain market was countered, very successfully, with the expansion of highly profitable sugar beet cultivation; in 1880, the value of sugar exports had already surpassed that of machinery or chemical products.[13] Yet labour-intensive beet cultivation led to the recruitment of cheap Polish workers from the neighbouring provinces in Russia and Galicia on a mass scale. The indirect effects of these structural adjustments illustrate the degree to which local, regional, and transnational processes were always interlinked.

The emergence of the world market should not lead us to forget, however, that German goods continued to find their markets primarily in Europe, where 75 per cent of her exports ended up. Smaller export markets such as Argentina, Egypt, Morocco, China, and Japan grew in importance, but they did not reach the privileged status of Great Britain or the United States. Capital was mainly invested in Germany, but also in France and the Habsburg Empire, while projects like the Baghdad railway were more prestigious than economically significant. The German preference for investing in nearby countries contrasts strongly with the British case. The City of London had more than 18 billion dollars in foreign investments in 1914 (when the German figure stood at 5.6 billion dollars), but only 5 per cent of that was invested in Europe. Great Britain remained crucial for the economic performance of the German Empire—not only as a privileged market for industrial products, but also as the core of the world market and capital accumulation that would have not been possible without British free trade, her high import rates, and the integration of colonial economies.

Part cause and part consequence of economic interaction, migration was one of the forms through which large segments of the population experienced the global entanglement first hand. Mobility continued to be the privilege of individual 'globetrotters' (a neologism of the times) like Heinrich Schliemann, who not only famously discovered ancient Troy in the 1870s but also travelled extensively to St Petersburg, San Francisco, Peking (today's Beijing), and Edo (Tokyo). At the same time, it was a mass phenomenon that transformed whole cities and regions. For a long time, scholarship has treated the three waves of German migration in the nineteenth century as chapters of a continuing process. However, the third wave of transatlantic migration between 1880 and 1883, which sent more than two million people abroad (mainly to the United States), was not just the sequel to earlier movements. It was the result of very specific circumstances, related to the effects of industrialization, to the long economic slump of what was once called the 'Great Depression', and to the pressures of the world market. As a result, migration emerged as a central field of public debate. The alleged 'loss of national energies' was pitted against the advantages of migration as a 'safety valve' that ridded Imperial Germany of 'revolutionary elements'. Among the explicit goals of the early colonial movement, therefore, was the redirection of population flows to the colonies—so that Germans would remain Germans, albeit overseas, and not deteriorate into what was called 'fertilizer of the peoples' (*Völkerdünger*) in contemporary parlance, a comment on the allegedly too-rapid assimilation of Germans in the United States. Before 1914, however, there were never more than 20,000 Germans living in the colonies—fewer than inhabited the tiny German principality of Schwarzburg-Sondershausen.[14]

Paradoxical as it might seem, preoccupation with questions of mobility produced fears that Germany had both not enough people and too many: it faced a loss of 'national power' (*Volkskraft*) and overpopulation. This apparent contradiction is indicative of the anxieties that accompanied rapid social change and interactions on a global scale. Central tropes of German political culture were created around this time, including the belief that the German people (*Volk*) had to seek more 'living space' (*Lebensraum*)—a term coined by the geographer Friedrich Ratzel. While the idea of *Lebensraum* was taken up by fringe groups on the nationalist Right, most Germans failed to take note that after 1893 German emigration fell off sharply. At the same time, immigration figures soared. New arrivals came mainly from Russia and Austrian Galicia, but also from Italy and the Netherlands. From the mid-1890s, Germany in fact turned into a country importing cheap labour on a scale second only to the United States. Migrants from eastern Europe continued to travel through Germany on their way across the Atlantic: more than five million people embarked on their journey from Hamburg and Bremerhaven. Their sojourn through Germany had repercussions on many different levels. For example, just west of Berlin a new train station in Ruhleben was built in 1890 for the sole purpose of channelling incoming labourers to the outbound sea ports. On the national level, the high proportion of Jewish migrants aroused public suspicion in a climate increasingly dominated by antisemitism. Although only 78,000 of the more than two million Jewish migrants eventually settled in Germany, they provoked a heated debate in the nationalist press. Frequently, immigration laws in Australia and the United States were suggested as models to be adopted on Germany's eastern borders. The reference to anti-Chinese measures, in particular, evoked commonalities between the two marginalized groups (Chinese and Jews), allowing German nationalists to consider local issues and larger global trends within the same mental frame.[15]

Politics of the nation

The increasing interaction with the world propelled German people and goods outward, but it also had important repercussions at home. The debate about protectionism in the late 1870s is a case in point. The passage of protective tariffs can be seen as a response to agrarian and conservative demands that Germany's own liberal economic policies must end. There was also an anti-British dimension to these measures: free traders were frequently discredited as 'pioneers of English interests'. But the protective tariffs passed in 1879 were also a reaction to the pressures of the world market. They should not be seen, therefore, solely as a retreat from globalization, as has frequently been argued.[16] Instead, protectionism was one of a number of possible responses to the challenges of global entanglement, with lasting effects on German domestic politics as well. The end of the 'liberal era', the Conservative parties' ability to recruit a mass following, and the Reich establishment's successful deflection of attempts to reform and further democratize the country—all these developments can be understood at least in part as a consequence of global structures.[17] The protectionism debate that continued throughout the Wilhelmine period was only one of a number of conflicts in which the impacts of global integration were negotiated. Others included naval construction after 1897, the so-called 'Hottentot elections' of 1907, and the extended controversy about whether Germany should remain an agrarian country or should refashion itself into an industrial state. In each case Germany's actual or potential dependencies on the world market had to be taken into account.[18] For these reasons, the development of German society from the 1880s onwards, like the historical debates about it, must be considered—not exclusively, but increasingly—within the frameworks and dynamics of globalization.

The impact of transnational connections can also be observed in cases that have been analyzed primarily within the bounds of the nation state. Nationalism is a good example here. The radicalization of German nationalism in the 1890s has drawn the attention of historians since the 1960s. That radicalization is conventionally interpreted as part of the authoritarian turn of German politics—in effect, part of the pre-history of Nazism. The standard historical narrative charts the new importance of biology as a component of antisemitism, Germany's aggressive and increasingly expansionist foreign policy, its imperialist aspirations, and the discourse of racism and eugenics supported by contemporary scholars and other members of the bourgeoisie who had invested in 'world politics'. Internal conflicts certainly played a key role in shaping these forces; yet they should also be seen as effects of increasing global interaction. As a result of cross-border exchanges, for example, Germany strengthened its immigration controls, mainly on its eastern borders: authorities devised ways to enforce control over the mobility of people, introducing passports and other biometrical devices. Moreover, debates about mobility contributed to the ethnicization of notions of national belonging, even though ethnic and racial arguments had a longer prehistory. The colonial context, in particular, fed into practices of marginalization along ethnic lines. Migration was always an important factor shaping the way Germans tried to situate their nation in an international system and a global context.[19]

An important aspect of this larger transformation of the concept of the nation was the Citizenship Law of 1913. In the heated debates that preceded it, colonial issues such as the prohibition of ethnically mixed marriages and 'racial' conditions for citizenship played a large role, even if they in the end did not enter the legal provisions. A crucial shift occurred in 1913, however, which was clearly a consequence of the changing dynamics of German mobility. Whereas the law of 1870 had stipulated that citizenship ended ten years after a person left the country, after 1913 citizenship could not expire, and was even transferred to descendants. In the face of political support for the colonial project, it seemed essential to permit Germans to settle in the colonies without risking their legal status as citizens. The modification of the durability of citizenship thus was a direct outcome of the colonial experience. It is instructive to note that the effects of this legal adaptation survived the end of empire. When in the 1990s large groups of descendants of former emigrants 'returned', as they said, from the Soviet Union, they still benefited from this redefinition of 'Germanness' under colonial conditions.[20]

Subjectivities, representations, knowledge

The global context not only affected collective identities, but reached down to the level of the individual. It would be rewarding to explore further the thesis that bourgeois subjectivities in the German Empire were refashioned under the auspices of colonial globality. In the early nineteenth century, bourgeois identities were largely defined by championing the naturalness of bourgeois conduct against the artificial culture of the aristocracy. Over the course of the century, and parallel with the expansion of territory and imagination, the concept of bourgeois individuality was increasingly seen as something distinctly separate from 'nature'. The 'quality of being bourgeois' (*Bürgerlichkeit*) was now seen in terms of its *distance* from the primitive, savage, 'uncivilized' peoples of the world—no matter whether they were found on the colonial periphery or in working-class neighbourhoods of German cities.[21]

On the level of popular consciousness, the impacts of globalization were hard to deny. This is apparent in the ways that technological change and border-crossing interactions fundamentally changed how people experienced time and space. David

Harvey introduced the term 'time–space compression' to describe a process by which the world was integrated by a virtual anni-hilation of distance through new technologies. The effect was a widely shared impression of synchronicity, of coevalness.[22] In the imagination, the shrinking of the globe was further accelerated and resulted in utopias that soon were detached from social real-ity. 'A trip around the world', the influential *Meyer Encyclopedia* declared as early as 1890 in words that sounded more prophetic than descriptive, 'has become quite an ordinary event.'[23]

The transformation of space and time, also described eloquently by Stephen Kern, took many forms.[24] On the global level, the introduction of world time was both a symbol of global integration and an important tool of economic calculation. In Germany, Gen-eral Helmuth von Moltke was influential in lobbying parliament to adopt world time in 1893 in order to facilitate military planning. On an everyday level, the standardization of time translated into the spread of public clocks and pocket watches, the discourse of punctuality, and the gradual extension of the Gregorian calendar around the world. Steamships, railways, and the telegraph evoked the image of a revolution of velocity and made 'acceleration' one of the leading categories of social life. The seeming acceleration of social practices in turn produced resistance, and even pathologies. The discovery of neurasthenia in the 1890s was one of the symbols of, and reactions to, this age of speed. It was accompanied in the bourgeois imagination by the notion of a shrinking globe. One of the symbols of this time–space compression was the trip 'Around the World in 80 Days' that Jules Verne described in 1873. Instantly translated and distributed in several editions in Germany, Verne's book was an immediate success. When American jour-nalist Nellie Bly re-enacted the famous trip of Phileas Fogg in the real world—she needed only 72 days in 1889, one of them spent with Jules Verne along the way—a broad audience followed this transnational media event in the international press.

It was in the sphere of popular culture that the repercussions of colonial expansion were most clearly visible. The large colonial exhibition in Berlin-Treptow in 1896, which attracted more than four million visitors, was only the largest of a series of exhibitions bringing the empire to neighbourhoods across Germany (they frequently brought colonial subjects as objects of anthropological shows). Such exhibitions fostered the impression of 'natural' hierarchies between peoples and races, but they made the existing social order in Germany seem 'natural' too. Consumer products from the overseas territories—advertised by exotic images, colonial board games, and popular fiction such as Karl May's stories of the 'Wild West'—brought the colonial world into the homes and minds of ordinary Germans.[25]

The ways in which various forms of global consciousness seeded German high culture have not been systematically explored. In 1898 the novelist Theodor Fontane famously described the effects of distant events on an isolated lake, Lake Stechlin, in rural Brandenburg: 'Everything is silence here. Yet from time to time at this very spot things do get lively. That happens when far off in the outside world, perhaps on Iceland or in Java, a rumbling and thundering begins, or when the ash rain of the Hawaiian volcanoes is driven far out over the southern seas. Then things start to heaving at this spot too, and a waterspout erupts and then sinks down once more into the depths.'[26] This rather eruptive appearance of the global in the local found its equivalent in Japanese art that burst on the European scene in the 1870s. Different from the mass production of Orientalist imagery and from earlier fads like Rococo chinoiserie, the influence of late-nineteenth-century *Japonisme* was not restricted to decorative aspects; it offered solutions to problems of method and perspective with which the European avant-garde had been grappling. As was the case with the discovery of so-called 'primitive' art, which marked one of the origins of high modernity in European cultural production, German high culture must be seen as an integral part of a larger European appropriation of the world around 1900.

The broadening of cultural horizons found its institutional form in the academic disciplines that produced languages to 'objectively' come to terms with the global context. As has become increasingly clear since publication of Edward Said's book *Orientalism* in 1978, knowledge and power were intimately related; hence the attempts of contemporary German scholars to explore their world by means of academic study cannot be removed from the context of the imperialist world order. This did not preclude genuine interest in, and even attempts to overcome, Eurocentric forms of knowledge. A case in point is the anthropologist Leo Frobenius, who was not a principled critic of colonialism but whose concept of 'negroeness' (*Negerheit*) was to be influential for Leopold Senghor and his anti-colonial notion of 'negritude'.[27] In general, the emerging discipline of anthropology was most closely related to the colonial project. But the field of geography, too, experienced a marked boom as a result of colonial aspirations. and here scholarly motivation and territorial appropriation also frequently overlapped. This became clear, for example, when the geographer Hans Meyer, as the first European to climb Mount Kilimanjaro, subsequently claimed it as a 'German mountain'. Revealingly, Meyer took the summit stone with him and, after his return, presented it to the German Kaiser. 'The highest German mountain top', Meyer later wrote, 'now rests on the desk of the person who himself stands on top of Germany,' thus fusing natural and social hierarchies.[28] Similar articulations of scholarship and colonial desire can be observed in other disciplines as well. Among these, the most prominent and those with the most momentous implications were the racial sciences and eugenics.

Germany in the world

While thus being shaped by outside forces, Germany at the same time was projected into the world. The influence of German institutions and concepts is usually interpreted as part of a German *Kulturpolitik* that peaceably accompanied the nation's industrial exports and colonial interventions. Scholars typically refer to the many countries in which German models were adopted and German texts translated. It was mainly in the realm of academic learning that the German Empire became a central node in a global network of intellectual transfers and exchanges—in terms of organization and institutional structures, certainly, but also in terms of methodologies and research agendas in diverse academic disciplines. Most conspicuously, the model of the Humboldtian university spread within Europe over the course of the nineteenth century; it also reached the United States and Japan, albeit not without modifications. Among the academic disciplines that travelled easily across borders we also find German medicine, Orientalism, religious studies, the different philological disciplines, physics, psychology, history, and the new discipline of sociology, the latter led by such notable scholars as Ferdinand Tönnies, Georg Simmel, and Max Weber. Such exports were by no means limited to the academic realm. To move to a less esoteric field, numerous military advisors were dispatched to far-flung regions of the world after Prussia's victory over France in 1870–71. The best known example is Otto Liman von Sanders's deployment in the Ottoman Empire, where he played an important role in the diplomatic build-up to the First World War. Other experts were sent to Chile, China, and Japan; Jacob Meckel helped prepare the Japanese Imperial army for its victory over China in 1895.

It is important to note that the concept of cultural diffusion only partially captures the meaning of this dimension of globalization in the imperial era. 'Germany' for many intellectuals and political commentators outside of Europe denoted the geographical origin of cultural achievements, but it also inferred a model of social development distinct from other trajectories of modernization followed by France, Great Britain, and the United States. As a result, in the eyes of non-Western elites Germany frequently appeared more unified than it might have looked to a contemporary observer living in Munich or Karlsruhe—and more homogenous, certainly, than it appeared to Jews and Social Democrats. The general appeal of the German version of modernization resulted in a vogue of political and cultural borrowing that involved particular forms of knowledge and, in a more general sense, 'Germany's' cultural capital. The case of the German constitution is illustrative here. Interpreted as the institutional expression of a 'third way' between absolutism and democratization, it served as a model for other countries such as Meiji Japan in 1889. In late-comer societies—including Japan in the 1880s and Turkey after 1908—'Germany' was invoked as a blueprint for modernization, constituting a form of development that promised to reconcile modernity with indigenous cultural traditions. The notion of the German *Sonderweg* between East and West, so influential during the First World War and among scholars even today, was clearly given resonance in the way Imperial Germany was appropriated globally.

Did the catastrophe of 1914–18 bring an end to the crossborder exchanges and enthusiasm for the 'world' that was so typical of Wilhelmine Germany? Most contemporaries certainly thought so, and many historians have followed their lead. The novelist Stefan Zweig, for example, retrospectively described the interwar period as the end of all cosmopolitan visions: the 'outrageous downfall . . . into which the world has been thrown after the First World War'. Whereas 'before 1914 the earth had belonged to all people', declared Zweig, it was 'only after the war that xenophobia or at least the fear of foreigners set in'.[29] Economic historians have drawn similar conclusions. To them, the world before 1914 appears as a utopia of peaceful interaction and cultural entanglement, only interrupted by the 'original sin' of the First World War (and one of its consequences, the Great Depression of 1929). Jeffrey Williamson, for example, refers to the world before 1914 as the 'belle époque'; to the 'dark middle ages' brought about by the war; and finally to a 'renaissance' of globalization since the late twentieth century.[30]

From the point of view of economic and diplomatic history, the diagnosis of a phase of de-globalization after 1914 certainly has its merits. The mobility of people, too, was rigidly checked, while border controls and migration quotas became characteristic of the post-war period. But one should be careful not to jump to conclusions. The high noon of political internationalism was certainly not reached before 1914. The League of Nations signalled the beginning of an era of political cooperation during the interwar period. The First World War, in other words, seems to have been a turning point in some respects while not inhibiting transfers and interactions in others. But more importantly, it is necessary to recognize that integration is only one aspect of globalization, always accompanied by forms of differentiation and fragmentation. Protectionism, migration control, and a 'politics of difference' therefore should not be equated with an end to globalization, but rather with its transformation.

To reinforce this point it may be instructive to ask what interacting with the 'world' really meant to Germans before and after the war. As part of the broader European experience, German conceptions of the 'world' before 1914 were dominated by notions of transnational exchange that would eventually lead to a homogenized world. Among the 'civilized' peoples, the rise of international organizations and the concomitant trend towards standardization promised a unified world where national particularities would be overcome. Across cultures, too, interaction was seen as a means to spread progress and social development. Shaped by social Darwinism, this vision was not necessarily a peaceful one. But it typically envisioned the effects of global exchange as modernization writ large, albeit under conditions of asymmetric power relations. This view found its most prominent expression in the concept of Europe's civilizing mission, which became hegemonic after the 1880s. Colonial rule was believed to serve the interests of the colonized, who would be 'improved' through the benevolent hand of the enlightened master.

This blatantly Eurocentric world view began to be challenged in the wake of the war. Four years of European (self-)destruction led many people to question the notion of the inherent superiority of Western civilization. This questioning was not entirely new. Cultural pessimism had thrived since the 1890s, and several reform movements in the German Empire had been informed by doubts about the West's technological modernity. Yet many of these reformers now turned to Asia for inspiration: the rise of theosophy and the warmly received writings of Rabindranath Tagore, who received the Nobel Prize for Literature in 1913, were examples of this movement. After 1918, such critiques of Europe's civilizing mission resonated among even larger circles of intellectuals. As for Germany, it is hardly accidental that Oswald Spengler's classic expression of the imminent 'Decline of the West', like the acknowledgement that other civilizations should follow their own cultural trajectories, was formulated in a country that had just forfeited its colonial empire in the war.[31]

Taking stock

Imperial Germany was part of a globalizing world, as this synopsis has suggested; but at the same time the world reached deep into Germany. The German Empire was hardly less involved in late-nineteenth-century globalization than were France and the United States; only Britain was in a league of its own. German industry exported its goods to Europe and far beyond. Migration from, through, and into Germany increased over time. And global relations left their traces in the realm of both popular and high culture. Colonial empire was less important to Germany than it was to France, the Netherlands, and even Japan—not to mention Britain. But repercussions arising from colonial encounters were more important than historians once believed. Thus colonialism and globalization cannot be meaningfully separated. The global integration of the world around 1900 was inconceivable apart from the colonial structures that permeated economic and political exchange, migration, and cultural interactions. The experience of the world was one of colonial globality.

To be sure, not everything in Imperial Germany was globally entangled: domestic issues retained their priority for members of many social milieux. Moreover, even though transnational relations increased, they connected Germany to Britain, Austria, France, and Russia more closely than to Chile, Egypt, and Siam. For Germans before 1914 Western Europe remained the privileged point of reference. It is clear, however, that a neat separation of the 'domestic' from the 'European' and 'global' spheres is a blunt analytical tool that cannot help dissect the multiple overlaps and interdependencies in social practice. Germany's place in Europe and its relations with other Western nations were themselves embedded in larger contexts and networks: Polish immigration resulted in part from transatlantic migration that depopulated the Prussian countryside, and the impact of Cubism went beyond transfers between Munich, Berlin, and Paris. Because Europe itself was changed in the course of these developments, it is not helpful to discuss European history detached from the processes of global integration within which it unfolded. Finally, we should recognize that the apex of Wilhelmine Germany's global and colonial entanglements coincided with a fundamental transformation of German society and the formation of European high modernity. Around the turn of the century, new structures and conflicts emerged in social, political, economic, and cultural relations that were to characterize Western industrial societies well into the twentieth century. For this reason, the effects and repercussions of colonial–global interactions in this period deserve special attention and further study.[32]

¹ Cited in Andrew Zimmerman, 'A German Alabama in Africa. The Tuskegee Expedition to German Togo and the Transnational Origins of West African Cotton Growers', *American Historical Review*, 110 (2005), 1380. For the following, see also Sven Beckert, 'Von Tuskegee nach Togo. Das Problem der Freiheit im Reich der Baumwolle', *Geschichte und Gesellschaft*, 31 (2005), 505–45; Louis R. Harlan, 'Booker T. Washington and the White Man's Burden', *American Historical Review*, 71 (1966), 441–67.

² Quoted in Beckert, 'Von Tuskegee nach Togo', 516.

³ This is suggested by Zimmerman, 'German Alabama', 1372–6, 1393–4.

⁴ Beckert, 'Von Tuskegee nach Togo', 545.

⁵ Karl Lamprecht, *Zur jüngsten deutschen Vergangenheit* (orig. 1903) (Berlin, 1921), ii. 592.

⁶ Hans-Ulrich Wehler, *Bismarck und der Imperialismus* (Cologne, 1969).

⁷ Heinz-Gerhard Haupt and Jürgen Kocka (eds), *Geschichte und Vergleich. Ansätze und Ergebnisse international vergleichender Geschichtsschreibung* (Frankfurt a.M., 1996).

⁸ Sebastian Conrad and Shalini Randeria (eds), *Jenseits des Eurozentrismus. Postkoloniale Perspektiven in den Geschichts- und Kulturwissenschaften* (Frankfurt a.M., 2002); Birthe Kundrus (ed.), *Phantasiereiche. Zur Kulturgeschichte des deutschen Kolonialismus* (Frankfurt a.M., 2003).

⁹ Jürgen Osterhammel and Niels P. Petersson, *Geschichte der Globalisierung. Dimensionen, Prozesse, Epochen* (Munich, 2003).

¹⁰ See, for example, Rüdiger vom Bruch, *Weltpolitik als Kulturmission. Auswärtige Kulturpolitik und Bildungsbürgertum in Deutschland am Vorabend des Ersten Weltkrieges* (Paderborn, 1982); Lora Wildenthal, *German Women for Empire, 1884–1945* (Durham, NC, 2001).

¹¹ Woodruff D. Smith, *The Ideological Origins of Nazi Imperialism* (New York, 1986).

¹² David Blackbourn, 'Das Kaiserreich transnational. Eine Skizze', in Sebastian Conrad and Jürgen Osterhammel (eds), *Das Kaiserreich transnational. Deutschland in der Welt 1871–1914* (Göttingen, 2004), 322. See also Philipp Ther, 'Deutsche Geschichte als imperiale Geschichte. Polen, slawophone Minderheiten und das Kaiserreich als kontinentales Empire', ibid. 129–48.

¹³ Wolfram Fischer, *Expansion, Integration, Globalisierung. Studien zur Geschichte der Weltwirtschaft* (Göttingen, 1998), 101–22.

¹⁴ Klaus Bade, *Europa in Bewegung. Migration vom späten 18. Jahrhundert bis zur Gegenwart* (Munich, 2000).

¹⁵ Sebastian Conrad and Klaus Mühlhahn, 'Global Mobility and Nationalism: Chinese Migration and the Re-Territorialization of Belonging, 1880–1910', in Conrad and Dominic Sachsenmaier (eds), *Conceptions of World Order: Global Moments and Movements, 1880s–1930s* (New York, 2006), 181–212.

¹⁶ For this argument, see, for example, Osterhammel and Petersson, *Geschichte*, 69–70; Harold James, *The End of Globalization: Lessons from the Great Depression* (Cambridge, MA, 2001).

¹⁷ Rita Aldenhoff-Hübinger, *Agrarpolitik und Protektionismus. Deutschland und Frankreich im Vergleich, 1879–1914* (Göttingen, 2002).

¹⁸ Kenneth D. Barkin, *The Controversy over German Industrialization, 1890–1902* (Chicago, 1970).

¹⁹ Sebastian Conrad, *Globalisierung und Nation im Deutschen Kaiserreich* (Munich, 2006).

²⁰ Pascal Grosse, *Kolonialismus, Eugenik und bürgerliche Gesellschaft in Deutschland 1850–1918* (Frankfurt a.M., 2000); Dieter Gosewinkel, *Einbürgern und Ausschließen. Die Nationalisierung der Staatsangehörigkeit vom Deutschen Bund bis zur Bundesrepublik Deutschland* (Göttingen, 2001).

²¹ Andreas Reckwitz, *Das hybride Subjekt. Eine Theorie der Subjektkulturen von der bürgerlichen Moderne zur Postmoderne* (Göttingen, 2006).

22 David Harvey, *The Condition of Postmodernity: An Enquiry into the Origins of Cultural Change* (Oxford, 1989).

23 Cited in Hermann Bausinger (ed.), *Reisekultur* (Munich, 1991), 343.

24 Stephen Kern, *The Culture of Time and Space, 1880–1918* (Cambridge, MA, 1983); for the following, see also Wolfgang Kaschuba, *Die Überwindung der Distanz. Zeit und Raum in der europäischen Moderne* (Frankfurt a.M., 2004); Joachim Radkau, *Das Zeitalter der Nervosität. Deutschland zwischen Bismarck und Hitler* (Munich, 1998), 190–214.

25 Sara Friedrichsmeyer, Sara Lennox, and Susanne Zantop (eds), *The Imperialist Imagination: German Colonialism and its Legacy* (Ann Arbor, MI, 1998); Kundrus (ed.), *Phantasiereiche*; Alexander Honold and Klaus R. Scherpe (eds), *Mit Deutschland um die Welt. Eine Kulturgeschichte des Fremden in der Kolonialzeit* (Stuttgart, 2004).

26 Theodor Fontane, *The Stechlin* (orig. 1898), trans. and intro. William L. Zwiebel (Columbia, SC, 1995), 1.

27 Suzanne Marchand, 'Leo Frobenius and the Revolt against the West', *Journal of Contemporary History*, 32 (1997), 153–70.

28 Hans Meyer, *Ostafrikanische Gletscherfahrten. Forschungsreise im Kilimandscharo-Gebiet* (Leipzig, 1890), 255–6.

29 Stefan Zweig, *Die Welt von Gestern. Erinnerungen eines Europäers* (Frankfurt a.M., 1970), 465.

30 Jeffrey Williamson, 'Globalization and Inequality, Past and Present', *The World Bank Research Observer*, 12 (1997), 118.

31 Oswald Spengler, *Der Untergang des Abendlandes* (orig. 1918–22) (Munich, 1998).

32 Paul Nolte, '1900: Das Ende des 19. und der Beginn des 20. Jahrhunderts in sozialgeschichtlicher Perspektive', *Geschichte in Wissenschaft und Unterricht*, 47 (1996), 281–300; August Nitschke (ed.), *Jahrhundertwende. Der Aufbruch in die Moderne 1880–1930*, 2 vols (Reinbek, 1990); Geoffrey Barraclough, *An Introduction to Contemporary History* (Harmondsworth, 1967), 9–42.

War and revolution

Jeffrey Verhey

It is a war of such power and tension as the world has never seen. All our physical and intellectual powers have fused together in this war, are heightened to their limits. Natural powers have become weapons of defence and destruction. The war is not just being fought in the field. The press, trade, the complete economic and intellectual life is fighting; everything has become attack and defence. In the nations involved, all aspects of life are at war. War has become the total meaning and the only purpose . . . We are no longer the same people we were at the beginning of the war, and we can no longer return to those we were, we must move forward. The outbreak of the war hit us like an earthquake, shook our very foundations and, as if by a flood, we are being carried away to new shores. We have no connection any more with who we were, with how we lived.[1]

Johannes Müller, a Protestant pastor, wrote these lines in late 1914 in his capacity as editor of *Die Grünen Blätter* (*The Green Leaves*)—a religious magazine that sought to counsel church-goers in their daily lives. Before the war, Müller had often commented, sometimes quite whimsically, on the dangers to civilization posed by modernity. In 1914, like many of his contemporaries, Müller embraced the war as a fascinating experience, as a great, historic epoch: life for all Germans would never be the same. Müller did not state—as most contemporaries did not—how people had changed, or what the future would bring. Indeed, in 1914 almost no one predicted what was to come or that they were witnessing the death of Imperial Germany at war.

The spirit of 1914: public opinion in July and August

Ironically, the war that contemporaries so correctly interpreted as 'modernizing' Germany began as the last war of the 'long nineteenth century'. In August 1914, 'Germany' did not decide on war. The decision to go to war—or, more accurately, the decision to accept the risk of becoming involved in a European war by supporting the Austrian government in its campaign against Serbia with the infamous 'blank cheque'—was made by a small cadre of decision-makers, all of whom had been personally appointed by Kaiser Wilhelm II. These men had no democratic legitimacy and were not in any way representative of German society. The Kaiser himself has been aptly described by the historian John Röhl as a vain, unpredictable man.[2] Wilhelm's civilian statesmen deferred to military advice whenever questions of German security were being considered. Accordingly, in the July crisis of 1914 the most important decisions were made by the military with an almost complete disregard for political considerations.

Yet as Johannes Müller had noted, the First World War at the time was called a 'people's war', and most Germans were aware of this from the very beginning. When on 23 July newspapers reported that Austria had issued Serbia an ultimatum, due to expire on Saturday, 25 July, at 6:00 p.m., the German people did not need to be reminded that, because Germany was allied with Austria and because Russia traditionally supported Serbia, Germany could become involved in a wider European conflagration. In the late afternoon of 25 July, vast crowds of curious, nervous, excited people gathered in the larger German cities at the sites where they expected the news of the Serbian response first to be distributed—in city squares, in front of newspaper buildings, in downtown cafes. People gathered there because in 1914 special newspaper supplements ('extras') were the media that first informed them of their fate.

After learning that Serbia had rejected the ultimatum, in Berlin and a few other large cities 'parades' of enthusiastic youths marched through the streets, singing patriotic songs. On 1 August, when 'extras' proclaimed that Germany was at war, many in the curious crowds who had been waiting tensely responded with hurrahs and patriotic songs. Yet most people went quietly home. In the first two weeks of the war, as the troops moved out and Germans said goodbye to their loved ones, public opinion remained tense. Only toward the end of August, as the news of German military successes led many to believe that the war would soon be won, did public opinion change significantly to resemble a nationwide patriotic festival.

Many contemporaries characterized these crowds as evidence of a Germany united in war enthusiasm. But there were significant regional and class differences in how Germans responded to the outbreak of the war. The largest enthusiastic crowds were found in the major cities, such as Berlin, Hamburg, and Munich. They were composed mainly of youths, especially university students. In the working-class districts of these cities—as, indeed, was also the case outside the larger cities and university towns—there was little evidence of enthusiasm, and none at all in rural areas. This was no nationwide 'war enthusiasm'. There did nevertheless arise a kind of national unity, which transcended class and regional differences, insofar as most Germans embraced a sense of national duty to preserve their fatherland in a war of defence. This sense was heightened by the realization that Germany stood a chance to win this war—a people's war—only if everybody stuck together. This shared recognition of a common fate, in which one's own wellbeing depended on the efforts of all other Germans, was in itself a profound change in political outlook. It is not surprising that many contemporaries hoped that this recognition would contribute to overcoming the deep internal divisions between the workers and the bourgeoisie, the city and the countryside, and the different religions—divisions that had characterized German political culture before the war. Some even hoped that in this 'spirit of 1914' German 'society' would become a German 'community'.

National unity in a defensive war found its most poignant expression in the German Social Democratic Party's decision to support the war. Before 1914 the SPD had been international, pacifist, and revolutionary (at least in its party programmes). In parliament the SPD had never voted for military appropriations; indeed, it had followed a policy of almost complete opposition to government policy on armaments, imperialism, and many other issues. In the last week of July, the SPD had staged massive anti-war demonstrations throughout Germany, which were larger than any of the enthusiastic crowds. Yet on 4 August 1914, in the sitting of the Reichstag convened to approve war expenditures, the Social Democratic Party voted in favour of the military appropriations. This day's sitting had been opened by the Kaiser with the phrase, 'I no longer acknowledge any parties, I recognize only Germans.'

Many contemporaries described the SPD's approval of war credits as the most amazing, unexpected result of the 'spirit of 1914'. This national unity became known as the *Burgfrieden*, or civic truce (literally, peace within the fortress). Yet the vote was less a break with the past than it was a public acknowledgement of longterm developments. Social Democrats did not want Germany to lose the war: they feared the Russians, but they also hoped that what they called the 'politics of 4 August' was more than just a policy for the common defence of the fatherland. By rejecting internationalism, the socialists believed they could refute the government's and the other parties' charge that their party was nationally 'unreliable', which in turn would inspire the government to undertake a programme of internal reforms. In the words of one trade union official, the goal of the 'politics of 4 August' was

for the working classes to have the same access and the same right to work in government as all other Germans. We expect the end of all discrimination. We expect the recognition of the worker's independent associations as the given representative of the working class in all aspects of economic and social life. And we expect the state to continue to build up and complete our social welfare legislation.[3]

Most of these goals would be realized.

Military developments

The military history of the war can be quickly told. The German military plan in 1914, a modification of the so-called Schlieffen

Plan, was a bold gamble to avoid a two-front war by defeating the French in the west before the Russians could deploy in large numbers in the east. The war plan was an example of a dangerous German tendency to make decisions purely on the basis of military considerations. The Schlieffen Plan required that the German troops march through Belgium, thus invading a neutral country and ensuring that Germany was viewed as a brutal aggressor. The military simply brushed these issues aside.

At first, the plan went quite well. The German army rolled through Belgium, threatened Paris, and the French government fled to Bordeaux. However, when in the first half of September the French army turned back the Germans at the first Battle of the Marne, the Germans had the two-front war they had gambled so much to avoid. At the end of September 1914 the armies in the west had settled down into trenches. From the Flemish coast to the Swiss border, there was a continuous front of some 450 miles with up to 8 million soldiers engaged on both sides at any one time. The Western Front was essentially large-scale siege warfare—a grinding conflict of attrition with industrialized killing fields where the machine gun and reinforced trenches had made the defence immeasurably stronger than the offence. In a war of attrition, given the vast numerical, material, and economic superiority of the enemy, the German army would have to be very lucky not to lose.

Part of the reason German strategists and the German population failed to recognize their difficult situation after the Battle of the Marne was because the war in the east went well. In August and September 1914, at the battles of the Masurian Lakes and Tannenberg, the Germans destroyed one of the Russian armies. Germany's army would continue to do well in the east for the duration of the war, although it was often required to come to the aid of its ally, Austria-Hungary. But the German Army Supreme Command's main focus lay elsewhere, on the western front. Trained in the tradition of Karl von Clausewitz, who had taught that the destruction of the enemy's army was the main goal in war, the Supreme Command sought the decisive battle in the west: in 1916 against France with the attack on Verdun, and in early 1917 against England with unrestricted submarine warfare. What is perhaps remarkable about these two campaigns is that although the tactics were military—the application of force—the strategy was psychological. The Supreme Command did not actually believe Germany could annihilate the enemy's army; it hoped to weaken the enemy's morale such that the people would sue for peace. At Verdun Germany attacked France at a point the French could not afford to lose, forcing the French to enlist all their resources. The aim of General Erich von Falkenhayn, the head of the German Supreme Command, was to open 'the eyes of [the French] people to the fact that in a military sense they have nothing more to hope for'.[4] His plan failed. German losses were as high as the French—together there were about 700,000 casualties—and only a few square miles of territory changed hands. When the German Supreme Command resumed unrestricted submarine warfare in February 1917, they were gambling that the English people and the English economy could be starved into submission. But the German Navy did not have enough submarines to achieve this goal. The failure of this gamble meant that the United States, with its vast resources in men and material, joined Germany's enemies. By July 1918 the United States had one million men in Europe, with hundreds of thousands more arriving each month.

The failure at Verdun cost Falkenhayn his job. He was replaced in late 1916 with Erich Ludendorff and Paul von Hindenburg, the two leaders responsible for the victory of Tannenberg. Yet although the battles in the west in 1916 had shown that the Allies could out-produce the Germans in munitions, machinery, food, and men, Ludendorff and Hindenburg still believed that Germany could win. They therefore opposed all feelers for a negotiated peace. Like Falkenhayn, they did not really believe that the enemy's armies could be annihilated. But also like him they convinced themselves that the enemy would quit when he came to accept that the German army could not be defeated in the field and that the German home front would hold out.

The home front

The German home front was never really isolated from the fighting. German strategists concentrated on the domestic mobilization of material, including human material, and on the mobilization of what in Germany was known as 'nerves' or morale. The two, of course, were closely intertwined. Morale was a function not only of how well the war was going but also of the moral economy at home. The perception that German society was fair, that all hardships were equitably shared, that the community of war created in the 'spirit of 1914' was not being exploited by any influential individual or group—all this was an essential precondition for fighting this war. Accordingly, from the very beginning of the war, censors included 'harming the *Burgfrieden*' among the list of things to be censored: such 'negativism' allegedly endangered national security.

The degree of genuine social cohesion implied by the 'spirit of 1914' was tested immediately by the mobilization of the industrial and agricultural resources needed to supply a huge army of several million men. No one had expected a war of this scale, and stockpiles were quickly exhausted. Already in August 1914 Walther Rathenau, a future foreign minister in the Weimar Republic who was then president of the German General Electric Company (AEG), was able to persuade the government to establish a War Raw Materials Office within the War Ministry, under his direction. The agency intervened in the economy in order to steer adequate supplies of raw materials to the companies involved in war work. As the war continued, ever more agencies were created, and government expenditure, which before the war had never been over 10 per cent of gross domestic product, had risen by 1918 to over 50 per cent of GDP. In a moment of need, market mechanisms were replaced with planning: the capitalistic economic order was set aside. Indeed, many contemporaries spoke of 'war socialism', although the German economy remained far from a command economy in the later Soviet style. German armies did not run out of munitions during the war. Yet the bureaucracy created was inefficient and inadequate. Thus Germany was not able to transcend the very real limits to its own resources—in either material or manpower.

These limits became clear in the Hindenburg Programme, an ambitious scheme proposed by the military in 1916. This programme aimed to double the production of munitions by forcing every possible member of the adult population to join the active workforce. Central planning would coordinate not only issues of supplies and investment of capital but also manpower. Because the trade unions opposed this infringement of workers' rights, the government was forced to make a number of compromises in its effort to get the Hindenburg Programme passed by the Reichstag. In the Auxiliary Service Law of December 1916, all male workers between 17 and 60 years of age were required to take up employment; they were severely restricted in their ability to quit work or to seek a different job. But the law also established 'local workers' committees and councils' (*Betriebsräte*) in factories. These were joint committees of labour and management in which the two sides could settle disputes over wages and conditions of employment.

The goals of the Hindenburg Programme were not met: there was simply too little additional labour or raw materials available to be mobilized. The law, however, provides an example of the broad modernization of Germany's political and economic institutions during the course of the war, furthering the development of a corporatist model of state and society. As the state expanded its role in the economy, new government ministries and powers were created and new laws were enacted. Many of these innovations, all designed to bolster the war effort, persist to this day (for example, in local workers' committees and councils). The war also brought a broad expansion of the welfare state, from family aid schemes to the paying of unemployment benefits. Yet the most important element in the modernization of Germany's economic and social structures was recognition of the right of the working classes to genuine representation. During the war, the government acknowledged the SPD and the trade unions as legitimate partners in order to be better able to manage labour. The working-class movement was able to realize its goal of establishing local workers' committees; it won the right to organize in war industries; and for the first time collective bargaining agreements became legally binding.

The idea that peace between the classes could be achieved in wartime Germany lay at the heart of the *Burgfrieden*. Yet changes in political and economic institutions were greater than in social attitudes. Middle-class citizens were still seldom seen in working-class pubs. Nor were workers invited to mix with executives at social events. True, the war did break down some of the economic foundations of class consciousness. A rise of over 200 per cent in the cost-of-living index between 1914 and 1918 hurt those whose wages did not keep up with inflation, including civil servants and workers not employed in a war industry. Inflation also lessened the value of the savings of the middle and upper classes—a trend that would continue and accelerate after the war. Nevertheless, class anxiety did not disappear. Quite the contrary. Those who previously had felt themselves to be stable members of the middle class, such as schoolteachers, saw their objective economic position erode and become more precarious; subjectively they perceived these developments as patently unfair.

The war reshuffled social relations in many other ways as well. A 'people's war' spawned an unprecedented level of volunteerism in support of the troops. Middle-class women engaged in campaigns of nursing, welfare work, and social aid; in the process, many found their religious faith reinvigorated. Some middle-class women joined working-class women in the factories. (It is one of the myths of the war that the war forced all women to work. Instead, the war prompted women to be redeployed into war industries who had previously worked in other sectors, and only some middle-class women worked.) Gender roles were called into question by women working as streetcar conductors, postal workers, or factory hands. Yet it is unclear how much attitudes actually changed. The effects of the war on women, especially on their self-perception, are difficult to assess: those effects may have been more psychological than social. After the war, when the German army was demobilized, women who had been working in factories gave the returning men their jobs back, almost without opposition.

These were difficult strains, yet what tore most at the fabric of German society was the lack of food. Germany had been a net importer of food before 1914 (approximately 25 per cent of its consumption). The British blockade effectively cut Germany off from its imports. Added to this difficulty was a decline in the number of horses available on German farms (they had been taken by the military), and the loss of many able men. Accordingly, production decreased by as much as 30 per cent. As food became scare, prices went up. Crop failures, such as the one that struck potato production in 1916, were calamitous. The government was in an impossible situation. As State Secretary of the Interior Clemens von Delbrück told a meeting of the Prussian state ministry on 25 October 1915, the government accepted responsibility for 'providing the population with sufficient foodstuffs at reasonable prices'.[5] To achieve this, the government set price controls. When the price controls led to irregularities in the market, the government realized the whole process would have to be controlled, and turned to rationing. Bread rationing began in March 1915; in October 1916 meat rationing was introduced. By the end of the war, virtually all foodstuffs were being rationed. The trouble was that, as the war progressed, rations inevitably declined. In peacetime, Germans had consumed a per capita average of about 380 grams of flour per day. Already in January 1915 the flour ration was down to 225 grams per day. In March 1917 the government decreased the ration to 170 grams (it would go up again when the harvest came in). Although the rations were miserable, often people were lucky to receive even these small amounts. Not only food was rationed; coal was, too. In the long and dismal German winters—and the winter of 1916–17 was especially hard on both counts—the lack of heating fuel turned misery to calamity for innumerable Germans. Although no Germans actually starved to death during the war, many were desperately hungry.

Such hardships could be sustained as long as a sense of justice prevailed. A sense of humour also helped. Postcards and humorists made fun of the term 'substitute' (Ersatz), which was used with increasing frequency to document the shrinking proportion of genuine nutrition and flavour to be found in German food and drink. Yet Germans lost their sense of humour when they began to recognize that society's moral economy was no longer functioning properly. The presumption that all Germans were sharing the national burden equally was not being borne out by reality. When farmers held back their goods in order to sell them on the black market, and then when the state intervened to try to force them to bring their goods to market, tension increased between farmers, city dwellers, and government officials. When the state demonstrated its incapacity to control the black market—by the end of the war Germans were purchasing one-third of all food there—confidence in the government eroded. This loss of confidence was especially marked among lower-class families, who spent a large proportion of their income on food. As early as 1915 general dissatisfaction found expression in spontaneous food riots, often set off by working-class women who had been standing in line for hours on end. As the war continued, these spontaneous 'demonstrations' increased in size and number.

Underlying all the dissatisfaction, of course, was the war itself and the harsh reality of death. One of the most common experiences in family life during these years was bereavement. Even if they survived, enlisted troops had to put up with the arrogance of officers. Although there can be no doubt that in the thick of the fighting there arose a strong sense of solidarity which momentarily lowered social taboos, soldiers who had been schooled in the lessons of Social Democracy had their pre-war views of Wilhelmine society broadly confirmed in their personal relations with the officer class. Those interactions were often filled with tension and animosity, and the soldiers shared these experiences with their relatives. Thus the battlefront and the home front were intertwined: how could it be otherwise when about one-half of the German soldiers were married and when there was a constant traffic of soldiers embarking on or returning from furlough? Some soldiers even wrote home to ask their friends and relatives not to subscribe to war loans because this would only extend the war. In November 1917 about 10 per cent of the German troops transported from the eastern front to the west used the opportunity to desert. This has led the historian Wilhelm Deist to speak of a 'covert military strike' in 1918, estimating that in the last months of the war between 750,000 and one million soldiers avoided battle by faking illness.[6] Nevertheless, despite the horror of war, the army remained largely reliable. Until the last two weeks of the war, there was no open mutiny as there had been, for example, in the French army. The physical reality of unparalleled death and destruction had a numbing effect, but it did not lead to open revolt.

Most contemporaries believed that a greater threat faced the German army: the danger of the home front collapsing. Although genuine pacifists were few and far between—there was little public opposition to the war—by 1916 discontent with the war was deep and widespread. If this discontent, and the sense of social injustice upon which it fed, could find a voice, if a new political grouping were to emerge to channel it, the situation could become very dangerous. By 1917 there were signs that things were moving in this direction. In April 1917 the Social Democratic Party split into two parties, one of which advocated continued support for the 'politics of 4 August', while the other offered complete, principled opposition to the war. In April 1917 the announcement of a reduction of the bread ration led to a strike in which 300,000 Berliners were involved. Massive anti-war strikes erupted throughout Germany in January 1918. Yet the antiwar Independent Social Democratic Party (USPD) was unable to gain the upper hand. The leaders of the Majority Social Democrats (MSPD) successfully found a way to portray themselves as the representative of the strikers, thus calming the situation. But if the discontent continued to grow, if the war continued much longer, the MSPD realized that it could be forced to give voice to the people's dissatisfaction with the existing order; in that case it would have to take on what it regarded as the unwelcome role of an oppositional, even 'revolutionary' party.

Given the importance of home-front morale, it is not surprising that already by late 1915 there were innumerable discussions within the government and among politically active citizens on how to improve it. One possible answer was put forward by a self-proclaimed 'war aims movement'. Members of radical nationalist organizations believed that vast territorial acquisitions were good for Germany; indeed, they believed that proclaiming the 'necessity' of vast territorial acquisitions would in itself improve morale. 'Establishing high goals', wrote the Pan-German publicist Manfred Kloss, 'awakens powers and makes a people capable of great accomplishments.'[7] In September 1914, when Germany still seemed to be doing well, Chancellor Theobald von Bethmann Hollweg privately agreed to a 'September Programme' of annexations in both western and eastern Europe. However, in November 1914 Bethmann's government forbade any public discussion of war aims: he was worried that the Left would respond to the Pan-German challenge and that this debate would prove divisive. In the autumn of 1916, as morale declined and the Right clamoured for the government to provide a rallying cry for the nation, the government ended its ban on the discussion of war aims. The Right initiated a vast political campaign, even going so far as to found a new political party in September 1917. This was the German

Fatherland Party, whose sole programme—or so its members claimed—was to ensure public support for Germany's territorial expansion. The Fatherland Party was founded in response to the Peace Resolution passed by the Reichstag in July 1917, which stated: 'The Reichstag strives for a peace of understanding and the permanent reconciliation of the peoples. With such a peace, forced acquisitions of territory and political, economic, or financial oppression are inconsistent.' The government had been correct: the topic was hotly debated. Members of the extreme Right had a very compelling argument on their side: the war could only be won with a superhuman effort by all Germans and (although they failed to mention this) with a great deal of luck. Yet the Right's interest in war aims was also a means to deflect the public's attention away from internal politics. The Fatherland Party and groups affiliated with it argued vehemently against any attempt to reform authoritarian principles or practice, to revise the constitution, or to diminish the military's privileged role in German society.

The other suggestion put forward by many on the Right was to establish a military dictatorship on a new, mass basis. After Ludendorff and Hindenburg assumed the leadership of the Supreme Command, there was a growing tendency on the part of the military leadership to dominate the formulation of civilian policy. Some historians have termed this a 'silent dictatorship'.[8] Ludendorff and Hindenburg did remove officials and stop policies they disliked, especially political and social reforms. Yet Ludendorff could never quite bring himself to assume full political responsibility: he recognized that a military dictatorship was the end of the monarchical idea. Perhaps Ludendorff also recognized that, in a people's war, a dictatorship would have to be genuinely popular if the state were to operate effectively, and that the Right would be unable to achieve this.

The Left, by contrast, argued that morale on the home front could best be sustained through political and constitutional reforms. It is thus a mistake to say—as Allied propaganda did at the time—that this was a war to make the world safe for democracy. The processes of democratization had already made important advances in Germany long before 1914. Germany was a constitutional monarchy; members of its national parliament were elected according to a suffrage law which was as progressive as any in the world (more so than in England, for example); and the Reichstag had the right and the duty to approve taxes, expenditures, and laws. Yet there is also a good deal of truth in the assertion that specific aspects of Germany's political system, and German political culture in general, were undemocratic. Germany was aptly characterized during the war by Hugo Preuss and Max Weber as an authoritarian state (*Obrigkeitsstaat*): a state in which a rational, intelligent bureaucracy governs, unencumbered by the whims of an irrational, mass public opinion. If Germany was to become a stronger state, one that had a better chance of sustaining morale and thus of winning the war, then—still according to Preuss, Weber, and others—Germany *must* undertake meaningful constitutional reform: only a parliamentary regime could provide the necessary foundation and legitimacy to the idea of a people's war. In the words of a contributor to one of Munich's leading newspapers, 'the German people can no longer be ruled according to the system set up fifty years ago; the people's patriotism, tested in a time of need, demands a different system, one which upholds a closer community between the governing and the governed'.[9]

   Chancellor Bethmann Hollweg tried to steer a course between retrenchment and reform with his 'policy of the diagonal'. To the political Right, Bethmann Hollweg offered the prospect of annexations; to the Left, he promised internal reforms, which he called a 'new orientation' of Prussian policy. In 1917, Bethmann Hollweg began to make more and more concessions to the Left in order to uphold internal unity. He did so most famously in the Easter Message of 1917, in which he had the Kaiser promise reform of Prussia's reviled three-class suffrage. Although the 'new orientation' was an attempt to reform an 'unpolitical' German state in ways that left most conservative privileges intact, many conservatives felt these reforms went too far. In 1917, intrigues led by Hindenburg and Ludendorff forced the Kaiser to replace Bethmann Hollweg as chancellor, first with Georg Michaelis and then with Georg von Hertling. Both of these men were weak politicians, and in the last year and a half of the war they were unable to put up much opposition to the military leadership. Although they were in charge of the civilian administration, they were scarcely in a position to challenge the military leaders when it came to the conduct of the war. As a result they were also unable to chart a political course premised on any more realistic assessment of Germany's predicament than the generals' stubborn insistence that total victory still lay within Germany's grasp.

Propaganda: giving meaning to the war

When wars are fought as bitterly over ideas as over territory, any account of the conflict cannot dismiss the importance of propaganda. After 1914, in all belligerent nations, few intellectuals remained 'above the fray' (to use Romain Rolland's famous phrase). In Germany, as in the other nations, intellectuals immediately put themselves at the service of their nation. As the historian Friedrich Meinecke noted in September 1914, 'from now on every one of us has to regard himself as only a part of the great apparatus of the state, and if a weapon is not pressed directly into his hand, he has only the choice of finding the spot where he can help most quickly and most effectively to strengthen the morale and physical power of the nation'.[10] Yet the 'ideas of 1914' were unimpressive. A war between peoples was widely interpreted as a war between cultures, even between civilizations. If the Russians were half-barbarians, if the French were superficial, nationalistic, atheistic, frivolous, and egotistical, if the English were individualistic, capitalistic, a 'land of shopkeepers', then Germans were heroes, whose spiritual values stood in opposition to the shallow commercialism of Western civilization. A few philosophers even went so far as to see in the ideas of 1914 the unfolding of a historical dialectic that stretched back to the ideas of 1789: finally, it was thought, German *Ordnung* would replace French liberty.

What was interesting and modern about German propaganda was not its content but its breadth. The years 1914–18 saw an explosion in the sheer amount of persuasion being doled out to the German public; some contemporaries even saw the war as the birth of propaganda. In the first months of the war, innumerable pamphlets were published, innumerable speeches were given; ministers preached the patriotic message from the pulpit every Sunday. The most important medium remained the newspaper. Most of the content was developed by private citizens, but because the state controlled and censored the news media, the state could put its own spin on the message. Schools were probably the most effective site for the dissemination of propaganda in the early years of the war. As one contemporary wrote, 'one reached the parents through the children—indeed, the children educated their parents. At no time have the schools had a greater influence at home then in the early period of the war. The children told others, very successfully, to do their patriotic duty.'[11]

In 1915 the German government created a War Press Office with an unlimited budget. Its staff hung posters in waiting rooms, in restrooms, and on advertising billboards. They distributed pamphlets, books, and brochures to children at school or when people picked up their ration cards. They even printed slogans on matchboxes and on the toilet paper used in government buildings. Nor was the War Press Office the only government agency engaged in persuading Germans. One contemporary estimated that over sixty different government agencies were engaged in propaganda. The Central Bank, for example, conducted a massive propaganda campaign on behalf of the war bonds programme. A new government-run film company, BUFA, was founded in 1917; by 1918 it supplied over 50 per cent of the movies shown in German cinemas. (BUFA later become UFA, the German film company that produced the most famous German films of the 1920s.) Then, in July 1917, besides these existing organizations, the military launched yet another propaganda initiative, the so-called 'patriotic instruction' programme, which largely duplicated existing efforts. These organizational attempts to mobilize German morale were so widespread that in 1916, when government ministers asked each other what else could be done, the Prussian minister of culture responded that he did not believe anything more was possible.[12] By the end of the war, almost every aspect of public and private life had been touched by this 'battle' to win the hearts and minds of ordinary Germans.

It is not clear that these propaganda efforts were very effective. The most important idea pushed by German propagandists was that Germany's determination to continue the struggle—the effort itself—would bring ultimate victory. Thus, if Germany could only 'hold out', it would win, and if it won it was sure to enjoy the fruits of its victory. By contrast, lack of will, failure to keep the faith, would bring immediate defeat, and defeat meant only ruin and destruction. Germany's propaganda machine continued to stay 'on message' until the end of the war: not a negotiated peace but a 'victorious peace' (*Siegfrieden*) would be the only acceptable outcome to the struggles and sacrifices already endured. The problem with this message was twofold. First, the claim that Germany was winning the war became more transparently false with each passing year. Second, the claim that whichever nation had more 'will' to win would in fact achieve victory was an insidious argument: it led people to believe that the power of faith alone would allow Germany to defeat the numerically and economically stronger enemy. Conversely, if Germany were to lose, its defeat would not be the consequence of any military or political inadequacy but could be ascribed instead to insufficiently patriotic elements at home.

Making peace, making revolution

In 1917, German newspapers reported nothing new on the western front. The war in the east was going much better. The first Russian Revolution in February 1917 raised hopes that Russia would soon pull out of the war. The second, Bolshevik revolution in October 1917 and the continuing disintegration of the Russian armies led to the Treaty of Brest-Litovsk in the spring of 1918, which moved German borders to the east. This in turn allowed the German Supreme Command to move troops from the eastern to the western front. The relative strength of the enemy in the west should have made the Supreme Command recognize that they would not be able to annihilate the enemy: the situation called for a negotiated peace. Yet the combination of military overconfidence and the public's unwillingness to recognize the true situation inspired the military leadership to attempt one last gamble. It was a big one: a great offensive in the west, designed to snatch victory from defeat before the Americans began to arrive in large numbers. In March 1918, Ludendorff's offensive (Operation Michael) began. As in August 1914, the offensive had initial success and, as in September

1914, it ultimately failed. On 15 July 1918, the Supreme Command called a halt to the offensive.

The Allies counterattacked three days later and never lost the initiative. On 8 August 1918 Allied armies broke through German lines. Although the German army was able to regroup, the military leadership, recognizing that the war was militarily lost, told the Kaiser in the night of 28–29 September 1918 that he must appeal to U.S. President Woodrow Wilson for peace, based on Wilson's famous Fourteen Points of January 1918. Falsely believing that this would lead to a better peace offer, the military also called for the creation of a parliamentary government. A decree to this effect was issued on 30 September and a new, 'democratic' government was formed on 3 October 1918 with Prince Max von Baden as chancellor. But the Allies refused to offer better terms. Hindenburg and Wilhelm Groener, who had replaced Ludendorff in the Supreme Command, therefore told the civilian leadership to accept unconditional surrender—the army could no longer fight. Finally, on 11 November 1918, at 11:00 a.m., it was truly all quiet on the western front. In later years, Ludendorff would claim that the home front had stabbed the army in the back. Notwithstanding the predictions of most strategists, the truth was that the war had been lost by the German army in the field. The home front, although greatly strained, had not cracked; it had held out for as long as there seemed to be a chance of victory.

There was, however, one last episode to be played out, an episode which allowed many post-war observers to lend credence to the stab-in-the-back myth. On 28 October, German naval officers, without the government's knowledge, ordered the High Seas Fleet to sail out and seek battle. These desperate officers were aware that the Allies had promised to destroy the German Navy; some of them sought a romantic end to their careers, and a few even suggested that Kaiser Wilhelm might appropriately share their fate. But the sailors under their command refused to go along. About a thousand naval mutineers were arrested at Wilhelmshaven. But other soldiers and sailors who were concerned for the fate of their comrades rallied and took charge of the ships. By 5 November a red flag flew atop every ship in Kiel. As news of the events in Kiel spread, so did the revolution—to Hamburg and Lübeck, to Hanover, Cologne, Magdeburg, Braunschweig, Leipzig, Dresden,

Munich, and finally, on 9 November, to Berlin. By this point, defeat on the battlefield convinced a war-weary and embittered civilian population that any further sacrifice was pointless. The military and police forces of Imperial Germany surrendered everywhere, virtually without resistance. In the late morning of 9 November, as masses of demonstrators marched through the streets of Berlin and as soldiers joined the movement, Max von Baden announced the Kaiser's abdication, although the Kaiser had not yet agreed to this. Prince Max also announced his own resignation and the appointment of the Social Democratic leader, Friedrich Ebert, as chancellor.

Germany's November Revolution was largely peaceful. It was not a planned campaign by revolutionaries, but an undertaking launched spontaneously by a population unwilling to press the deadly conflict a moment longer. Its legitimization came in the recognition that the old elites had proven themselves incapable of ruling. Theodor Wolff, editor of the liberal *Berliner Tageblatt*, wrote on 10 November that the authorities' admission of defeat fully surprised the German people: up to that point, they had believed overly optimistic official propaganda. When the people realized that they had been lied to, they did not just quit the war; their outrage at having been treated as unthinking subjects (*Untertanen*) of authoritarian, presumptuous leaders led them to reject a system that had failed to respect their basic dignity.[13]

But the revolution of 1918 was limited. Political institutions were transformed; yet social relations, the economy, and prevailing attitudes about national affairs were not genuinely revolutionized, at least not in the short run. There were no 'ideas of 1918'. Germany's November Revolution can therefore be best understood as the last act of a lost war rather than as a new beginning. The real irony was that the arguments for democracy that had been most often and most powerfully put forward during the war had been proven false by defeat in war. The writer Thomas Mann had declared in 1915 that 'those who today demand a democratic Germany . . . raise this demand not for doctrinaire, theoretical reasons, but for completely practical ones: first so that Germany can live, and second so that she can live powerfully and masterfully'.[14] But the war did not create popular support for the ideas of democracy and republicanism; what became the

Weimar Republic was chosen during the revolutionary excitement of November 1918 because it was the form of government that divided Germans least and because the Allies had promised to treat Germany better if it became a republic. Making the democratic idea genuinely popular was left up to the politicians who followed.

The legacy of the war

The legacy of the First World War hung heavy over the Weimar Republic. Germany had lost over 2 million killed and over 4.1 million wounded (out of a total population of about 65 million). Many soldiers who had been maimed became part of the street scene in every German city: disabled veterans to whom society had an obligation. Germany had spent the equivalent of approximately 40 billion dollars on the war, most of which had been borrowed from its own citizens. Almost all of these loans would never be repaid because the state went bankrupt in the hyper-inflation of 1923. In the Treaty of Versailles, grudgingly accepted by the German government in June 1919, Germany lost 13 per cent of its territory, including its colonies, and was required to pay 33 billion dollars as a war indemnity to the victors. These physical and monetary losses were enormous; but just as important were the psychological effects of the war. To many Germans, the war seemed to defy any attempt to specify its causes. It seemed to undo belief in a just and caring God. And it seemed to disprove the wisdom of bringing up a family responsibly, of saving for the future, indeed, of believing the future would be better than the present. A rationalist, optimistic, progressive philosophy, which had been so much a part of Imperial German society, lay in ruins.

The war had reshuffled the dominant norms and values of Germany's cultural and social traditions. It was a profound modernizer. The monarchical idea died a quiet death: it would not return with any strength during the Weimar Republic. The economic instabilities that afflicted Weimar Germany, the expanding role of the state, the new emotional investment in the nation rather than in one's home town—all this was a consequence of changes that began or accelerated during the war. Yet despite the war's modernizing effect, many Germans found it difficult to move forward. In the 1920s, the war haunted people's memories, though it did so in many divergent ways. 'Conservative revolutionaries' developed the idea of a *völkisch* dictatorship, and in doing so they looked back to (and kept alive) the stab-in-the-back legend. This had very dangerous implications, as the historian Michael Balfour has noted: 'by exaggerating the extent to which the German failure in 1918 had been due to a failure of will rather than to material inferiority, they encouraged the belief that greater will-power, derived from a more fervent conviction, would by itself be enough to produce a different result'.[15] But this was not the only attempt to rewrite history. Of course the hopes of August 1914 had been unrealistic. That did not make them less real—as hopes, as a political programme. Many middle-class Germans who had embraced the 'spirit of 1914' would later succumb to the hollow ideal of the 'people's community' (*Volksgemeinschaft*) propagated by the Nazis. Among such Germans was Pastor Johannes Müller, whose reflections in 1914 were cited at the outset of this chapter. For Müller and for millions of his countrymen, the turn to Nazism in 1933 was made possible not only by the war itself but also by their unsuccessful attempt to understand its meaning and accept its legacy.

[1] Johannes Müller, *Der Krieg als Schicksal und Erlebnis* (Munich, 1914), 1, 3.

[2] John C. G. Röhl, *The Kaiser and His Court: Wilhelm II and the Government of Germany* (Cambridge and New York, 1994).

[3] Quoted in Monitor, 'Die Sozialdemokratie und der Weltkrieg', *Preußische Jahrbücher*, 160 (April–June 1915), 52.

[4] Erich von Falkenhayn, *The German General Staff and Its Decisions, 1914–1916* (New York, 1920), 249.

[5] Geheimes Staatsarchiv Preußischer Kulturbesitz, Berlin-Dahlem, Rep. 90a Abt. B Tit. III 2b Nr. 6 Bd. 164, 249.

[6] Wilhelm Deist, 'Der militärische Zusammenbruch des Kaiserreichs. Zur Realität der "Dolchstoßlegende"', in Ursula Büttner (ed.), *Das Unrechtsregime. Internationale Forschung über den Nationalsozialismus*, 2 vols, vol. 1, *Ideologie—Herrschaftssystem—Wirkung in Europa* (Hamburg, 1986), 109 ff.

[7] Manfred Kloss, *Die Arbeit des Alldeutschen Verbandes im Kriege. Rede, gehalten auf der Tagung des Alldeutschen Verbandes zu Kassel, am 7. Oktober 1917* (Munich, 1917), 11.

[8] Walter Görlitz, *History of the German General Staff, 1657–1945* (New York, 1953), 179; Martin Kitchen, *The Silent Dictatorship: The Politics of the German High Command under Hindenburg and Ludendorff, 1916–1918* (London and New York, 1976).

[9] 'Der Kanzlerwechsel', *Münchner Neueste Nachrichten*, no. 352 (15 July 1917), 1.

[10] Friedrich Meinecke, 'Politik und Kultur', in *Süddeutsche Monatshefte*, 11 (Sept. 1914), 796.

[11] Günther Dehn, 'Volksjugend in der Heimat', in Wilhelm Müller (ed.), *Wie Deutschlands Jugend den Weltkrieg erlebt* (Berlin, 1918), 12.

[12] See the correspondence in Bundesarchiv Berlin-Lichterfelde, 15.01 Reichsministerium des Innern Nr. 12475.

[13] Theodor Wolff, untitled article in the *Berliner Tageblatt*, no. 534 (10 November 1918, morning edition), 1.

[14] Thomas Mann, *Reflections of a Nonpolitical Man* (orig. Berlin, 1918) (New York, 1983), 176.

[15] Michael Balfour, *Propaganda in War, 1939–1945: Organisations, Policies and Publics in Britain and Germany* (London, 1979), 10.

Looking forward

James Retallack

Less than 48 hours separated the collapse of the German Empire from the last shot fired in the First World War. Kaiser Wilhelm II's decision to flee to exile in Holland and the proclamation of the German Republic from the balcony of the Reichstag occurred not long after midday on 9 November 1918. The armistice that ended the conflict was invoked at 11 a.m. on 11 November.

Germans who experienced the cataclysm of the 'the war to end all wars'—together with those who looked back fondly to the years before 1914, before the empire had begun to sink under the weight of its own conflicts and contradictions—agreed that a historical threshold of immense significance had been crossed.

[Before it went under,] there was peace and the world had an even tenor to its ways. From time to time there were events—earthquakes, floods—which stirred the sleeping world, but not enough to keep it from resuming its slumber. It seems to me that this disaster not only made the world rub its eyes and awake, but wake with a start, keeping it moving at a rapidly accelerating pace ever since, with less peace and happiness.

The preceding lines were written by a survivor. But they were not written by a survivor of the carnage on the Western Front, nor by someone who lived through the trauma of defeat and revolution in 1918. They were not even written by a German. As we read in the concluding line of this reminiscence—'To my mind, the world of today awoke on 15 April 1912'—this observer, Jack Thayer, had survived the sinking of the luxury liner *Titanic* on her maiden voyage across the Atlantic.[1]

The loss of life in the 'unparalleled' disaster of 1912—of 1,320 passengers and 915 crew, 1,503 people drowned—was soon eclipsed by the slaughter of 1914–18, when an estimated 70 million soldiers were mobilized and over 10 million combatants and civilians were killed.[2] Still, the historical 'endpoint' of April 1912 provides food for thought for the historian of Imperial Germany. The *Titanic* took two hours and forty minutes to die, creaking and groaning before it finally cracked in two and sank. The death throes of the German Empire lasted much longer. Making a mockery of the 'women and children first' rule of ship-board evacuation, the death rate for children in third-class steerage was higher on the night of 14–15 April 1912 than for men in First Class. Class, gender, and generations in the empire often seemed topsy-turvy too.

The captain of the *Titanic* had wanted to set a speed record for crossing the Atlantic, though he was warned by a wireless dispatch from the French liner *La Touraine* on the afternoon of 12 April that a huge field of icebergs, with their tops visible slightly above the waterline, lay in its path. This message was acknowledged, with thanks, by the captain of the *Titanic*. Kaiser Wilhelm was as well informed by at least some of his advisors, who understood the economic consequences of building a German battle fleet and the diplomatic risks of *Weltpolitik*. It is perfectly legitimate to look to specific individuals and policy decisions to determine where Imperial Germany went off course. Yet a broader consideration of 'big structures, large processes, [and] huge comparisons'—as the historian Charles Tilly playfully put it—provides another way to get at what really matters in history.[3]

For passengers travelling in First Class, the evening meal on board the *Titanic* on 14 April included eleven courses. Nine wines were served. The menu included consommé Olga with sea scallops, poached salmon with mousseline sauce, and roasted squab on wilted cress. In Second Class, passengers made do with three courses. In Third Class, the main meal was served at noon.[4] German society seemed to be polarized between 'haves' and 'have-nots', but it was also becoming more finely layered. Historians cannot agree among themselves from which vantage point this social layering can best be assessed. While some scholars observe society and politics from the bridge of the ship of state, others claim that we can get down to the level of social reality only by prying open a window on lived experiences below decks. Cultural and intellectual contexts are also important. Theories of the elite, fear of rebellion amidships, conspicuous consumption, a fascination with speed and technology, a distinctively modern wish to make one's mark in the world—these led to both fear and hyperactivity, inducing Germans to take increasingly risky gambles.

According to London's *Observer* newspaper, between 1913 and 1955 not a single book was written about the *Titanic* until Walter Lord's study, *A Night to Remember*, sparked a 'Titanic frenzy'—the frenzy that culminated in the public reception of James Cameron's Oscar-winning film in 1997.[5] When they were willing to think about it at all, where did contemporary Germans believe their nation's social, economic, political, and cultural transformation since 1871 had brought them? Why have differences of opinion about the significance of that transformation contributed so often to a scholarly frenzy among historians?[6] The preceding chapters have proposed answers to these questions by suggesting how elements of continuity and rupture can be assessed from different perspectives.

In Imperial Germany change was not always sudden. It invariably resulted in transformations and adaptations that brought the old and the new together. Contemporary Germans liked to emphasize their sense of rupture when it symbolized progress and national achievement: hence the celebration of Bismarck's role in 'forging' the German Empire. Germany's rivalry with France was nothing new, as the trope of the 'eternal enemy' (*Erbfeind*) suggested; but the seizure of Alsace and Lorraine complicated matters, and Prussia's quasi-hegemony in central Europe was so startlingly new that Prime Minister Benjamin Disraeli told the British House of Commons in February 1871 that a German 'revolution' had just occurred.[7] These developments forced Germans (and others) to recast their expectations for German policy with a suddenness that was bound to be disquieting. The state had not previously refused intervention in society or the economy, but its claims and accomplishments in the imperial era broke all previous limits. The cultural ideals of classicism and romanticism were revived, with or without the 'neo-' prefix; but after 1890 the avant-garde was 'out there'—in front—further than ever before, creating its own backlash but unstoppable nonetheless. Faith in German philosophy, literature, rationalism, and idealism persisted, but it was now faith tinged with anxious appraisals of what values would stand the test of time.

Should we continue to look for turning points? There are too many candidates. In any case, in society, the economy, and cultural affairs, change occurs more slowly (generally), more quickly (sometimes), and less obviously (always) than a focus on political turning points can allow for. Examining political culture helps in this regard, accommodating the interpenetration of tradition and change. So does a reconsideration of Germany's international situation in transnational and global contexts.[8] Diplomacy can be seen in terms of crises and U-turns, caused by Bismarck's dismissal in 1890 or by ill-considered adventures that had to be reversed; but we must not lose sight of underlying fundamentals that guided German statesmanship throughout the imperial era. The same is true of the empire's constitutional system, which by and large was accepted after 1900. Localism never became irrelevant either: 'When contemporary Germans were forced to consider the ambiguities of place, they realized that a concern with the local . . . often created an expertise or a niche that had not existed before. Thus, they found that they could claim local memories as markers of erudition or as inspiration for commercial entrepreneurship, even as they also shared in national memories (or hopes) of grandeur.'[9] Only the diminishing upward mobility of the lower middle classes and the growing gap between the very rich and the very poor remind us not to prize the 'modern' distribution of opportunity too highly.

After 1900 the pace of change quickened. The period of slower economic growth (1873–96) was left behind and prosperity began to trickle down to the lower classes in the form of rising real wages, better health care, and education reforms. Cultural 'secessions' occurred more frequently, with each new artistic genre distinguishing itself from its predecessor in more radical ways. Social conflict was more dramatic than in the 1870s, although the bourgeoisie was busy building bulwarks of security above and below. Politically and diplomatically, it became difficult after 1905 to discern a way forward, although Germany drew back from the brink of war again and again. The head of state was mentally unstable, yet he seemed able to mirror many of the empire's most rational aspects. Prussia had been left in the dust, but not quite. Revolution and the workers' state were still visible on the horizon, but they were receding. The military was a source of pride or embarrassment, but it was neither irrelevant nor the guarantor of national security. In the war of the sexes and in the struggle to appropriate custodianship of the symbols of nationhood, it was growing more difficult with each passing year to be the 'whole man' or to embrace the 'whole nation'.

Was Imperial Germany headed for disaster from the moment of its birth in 1871? The question's premise is wrong: Germany's subsequent history held myriad possibilities, and even in 1918 the outcome of the Weimar Republic's many crises could not have been predicted. However, the sociologist Max Weber and others were not mistaken in 1917 when they identified patterns of German development since 1871 that pointed away from a democratic future, no matter whether Germany won or lost the war.[10] *Because* it lost, something close to a worst-case scenario unfolded.

We previously identified the pervasiveness of conflict in Imperial Germany as a recurrent theme in this volume. Keeping historical contingency in mind underscores the frequency with which conflict in Imperial Germany gave rise to dilemmas that had unforeseen and paradoxical consequences. A brief recap confirms that such dilemmas and paradoxes were addressed in each of this book's eleven chapters. Thus:

1. Bismarck claimed that Germany was a 'satiated nation' but he was forced always to grope his way towards new solutions to intractable problems: by 1890 the departure of the 'indispensable' founder was largely unlamented.
2. Wilhelmine Germany could seem powerful and parochial at the same time, allowing Germans to identify with their smaller homeland or with the larger nation, as the situation demanded; moreover, even the most conspicuous aspects of change were shaped by elements of order and tradition.
3. Industrialization changed almost everything and eliminated nearly nothing. It did not lead to the homogenization of workplace experiences, of economic sectors, or of regions, and it did not smooth relations among classes and ethnic groups; rather, it increased differentiation and conflict.

4. Secularization and religious revival were intertwined; the processes of milieu formation and political mobilization were dialectically interdependent; and confessional conflicts among Protestants, Catholics, and Jews fostered both bitterness and calls for tolerance.

5. Both conformity and variety characterized Germany's cultural scene: rebellious secession movements displayed impeccable establishment credentials even as the definition of Germany's cultural leaders grew more contentious.

6. Gender distinctions—monolithic yet ambiguous—were maintained and challenged at the same time: anxieties about gender roles grew as both sexes sought to fulfil their 'national duties'.

7. Local initiatives and voluntary associations gave members of Germany's broad reform movement an alternative to party politics; but both fragmentation and coordination helped integrate them into a formalized political realm where national priorities became paramount.

8. 'Pillarized' social groups and political parties survived as 'pluralization' gained ground; nevertheless, the proliferation of voices that demanded to be heard had its own destabilizing effect, and it remained unclear before the war whether the 'politics of togetherness' was likely to lead to a democratic or totalitarian future.

9. The Wilhelmine state's mobilization of public opinion behind an aggressive foreign policy created a backlash in which radical nationalists challenged the state's authority, despite official efforts to instil military values and propagate gender-coded military tropes.

10. As Germany's 'global entanglement' drove it 'out' into the world, the world also reached deep into Germany and helped shape bourgeois ideals of independence and a civilizing culture; thus the process of constituting the nation was a product of globalization, not its prerequisite.

11. During the First World War, the ideal of social cohesion was tested and found wanting; Germans' recognition that they shared a common fate could not invest the 'people's community' with meaning: the nation was more divided than ever when peace broke out in 1918.

What do all these historical paradoxes and ambiguities signify? One answer is that partisanship and polarization were not incompatible with the search for a transcendent national community. On the contrary: conflict fostered and accelerated that search. Germans' faith that the future would be better than the present was inspiring, but it was also chimerical. Bourgeois reformers, Imperial Germany's modernizers par excellence, epitomized the optimistic view, even though it was precisely within bourgeois ranks that crucial debates about the meanings of modernity were taking place. But against what international standards did bourgeois and other Germans measure the success of their state, and their society, in defending ideals that citizens of another nation termed 'life, liberty, and the pursuit of happiness'? Whether or not historians believe that most Germans were comfortable with the quality of life and the liberties they had won by 1914, and even if the mass of the population did not articulate this question because it was remote from their quotidian concerns, scholars have not yet probed very far into the psychology of the matter. Germans were worried about modernity because it had a homogenizing effect, but also because it led to clearer differentiation between the winners and losers of modernization. Fear of fragmentation troubled Germans when they considered the consequences of mass politics, but the perception that German society was becoming 'atomized' under the impact of industrialization and urbanization also had profound effects in the intellectual and cultural realms.

Another answer is that unresolved tensions not only led to conflict but also increased the likelihood that radical political ideas and practices would be proposed to overcome disunity and dissent within the national community. Here we are advancing into largely uncharted terrain. What level of violence existed in Imperial Germany, and in what circumstances was it condemned or condoned? We know a great deal about the state's campaigns against Catholics, Poles, and other minorities. We know rather less about the everyday forms of legal discrimination, workplace subordination, and physical intimidation experienced by German girls and women. We lack comprehensive studies of ordinary Germans' reactions to the use of violence by the army, the police, and political rowdies. And we know *much* less about Germans who ostracized, persecuted, silenced, harassed, beat, or murdered

Social Democrats and Jews. Until such issues are addressed more systematically and comprehensively by historians, we are unlikely to understand Germans' own estimation of the moral standing of their society, measured against what one historian has termed 'the decent opinion of mankind'.[11]

Much evidence in this volume suggests that that self-estimation was too high. This immediately raises the question of what moral yardsticks we can legitimately use to draw such comparisons, and *that* question has almost limitless ramifications. Nevertheless, historians should not be dissuaded from posing the question by the difficulties inherent in judging whether Imperial German society was more equitable than other societies.[12] Doing so could help us understand why the authoritarian state had not toppled before 1918, despite the tremors generated by social, economic, cultural, and political modernization. Both stories—the triumph of modernity and the long shadow cast by authoritarianism—are true. But when kept separate, their plot lines are too neatly drawn to depict an era when boundaries were fluid, beliefs were in flux, and conflict was the only constant. Rejoining these stories opens up possibilities for measuring Imperial German society against standards of human conduct that, while not timeless or universal, are being debated as vigorously in the twenty-first century as they were in the nineteenth.

What other research agendas might be explored by future students of Imperial Germany? A prime candidate is Germans' experience of 'total war'. A prodigious number of books on the German home front in 1914–18 have appeared over the past fifteen years, often drawing inspiration from similar studies done by historians of other combatant nations. Perhaps the war years will finally be properly integrated into histories of the imperial era. Moving in the opposite direction, over-concentration on the 1890s as the decade when mass politics was allegedly born and the political nation allegedly reconstituted suggests that budding PhD students should be encouraged to tackle the under-researched 1870s and 1880s. Nor has the promise of the history of everyday life (*Alltags-geschichte*) been realized for the German Empire, particularly when compared to similar work done on the early-modern and Nazi periods. Because the critics of *Alltagsgeschichte* partially succeeded in marginalizing it in the 1980s, we still lack basic studies of life in small-town, village, and rural Germany. The importance of understanding Prussia's role within the federation has been widely acknowledged for years; indeed, German scholars have recently offered pointed reminders, directed at critics of the *Sonderweg*, that the survival of Prussia constituted one of Imperial Germany's most important peculiarities.[13] A major study of Prussia has just appeared, authored by one of our contributors.[14] However, we have no reliable and comprehensive guide to the interplay of conflict and compromise among the other leading federal states or between them and Prussia. The Mecklenburg grand duchies in northern Germany, for example, have constituted a kind of 'no-fly zone' for historians. Full-length studies of the National Liberal and Christian Social parties constitute other lacunae. These topics are likely to loom large in future research on the prospects of democracy in pre-1918 Germany—as long as historians continue to address the question of exactly what they mean by democracy and democratization.

New sources will also drive future research, as they always do. The integration of literary sources is still relatively undeveloped in Imperial German historiography. Personal memoirs and political correspondence have long supported the writing of diplomatic history, but in other types of analysis they are less often used. The study of novels and poetry also has much to offer, as shown, for example, by a recent collection of essays on Germany's two unifications (1871 and 1990) by a team of historians, political scientists, and literary scholars.[15] Another neglected source is the reports of diplomatic envoys stationed in Berlin, Munich, Dresden, Stuttgart, Karlsruhe, and other federal capitals. These diplomats did not only represent foreign governments; the German states also exchanged envoys among themselves. The project to publish the reports of British envoys stationed in Germany now covers the period 1815–66; its continuation up to 1918 will provide a mother lode of new material.[16] But the situation reports and public opinion surveys written by their German counterparts make possible another kind of historical 'triangulation', even though the term does not convey the number of perspectives available.

Lastly, the expansion of the Internet as a research tool and the development of new classroom technologies will provide students unprecedented access to documentary and visual sources. In only the past five years the variety and sophistication of primary source materials available for researchers online has grown immensely.[17] URLs crop up in the footnotes of published works with increasing frequency; historical encyclopaedias on digital media are proliferating; and broadband connections make high-definition images, videos, and audio clips widely accessible at relatively low cost. The confluence of these developments is making even the 'traditional' political history of Imperial Germany come alive for a new generation of scholars, teachers, and the lay public—right before their eyes. Visual sources already allow us to reassess how the sinews of authoritarianism wove around and through German society. We can now count faces in the crowd, we can see whether they recoiled from brandished sabres and galloping horses, and we can even detect the slightest of bows as they dropped their ballot in the ballot box. By launching our browser we can embark for Versailles and peel back layers of meaning from Anton von Werner's three paintings of the *Kaiserproklamation* of 18 January 1871.[18] We can step across the virtual threshold of the Bavarian State Library and read every Reichstag speech delivered between 1867 and 1895.[19] And by wandering into the digital workshop of Heidelberg University we can parse the political subtext of every satirical cartoon published in *Kladderadatsch* between 1848 and 1944.[20] These examples only hint at the diversity of visual sources already available; but they demonstrate why culture in general and visual culture in particular properly belong in every historian's toolkit.[21]

By integrating older and newer approaches to the history of the German Empire, our authors have attempted to offer fresh insight into the broader sweep of modern German history. Collectively they have cast a distinctive, overarching argument that Germany could have been authoritarian and modern at the same time. They have posed difficult questions about individual liberty, public responsibility, and social fairness in new ways, meeting the historian's obligation to explain, assess, and judge history, not just chronicle it. The tracks on which German history was running between 1871 and 1918 were not leading directly towards Nazism and the Holocaust. Indeed, Germans would have registered genuine and legitimate astonishment if they had been told in 1871 that Auschwitz was even one of the endpoints awaiting them on their historical journey. The notion that the barbarity of the Third Reich was their *most likely* future would have strained their credulity to the breaking point. It should strain ours as well. That is why the chapters in this volume begin the process of emplotting the story of Imperial Germany differently. They view the imperial period as a transitional epoch when Germans were exploring how best to reconcile tradition and change, as an era when tensions and conflict had many possible outcomes, *and* as an object worthy of study in its own right.

[1] This passage and a number of following details are drawn from Michael Kesterton, 'Social Studies', *The Globe and Mail* (Toronto), 14 April 1997, sec. A.

[2] In addition, 20 million combatants were permanently disabled. The war cost an estimated US$208 billion. Stig Förster, 'Introduction', in Roger Chickering and Förster (eds), *Great War, Total War: Combat and Mobilization on the Western Front, 1914–1918* (Cambridge, 2000), 6.

[3] Charles Tilly, *Big Structures, Large Processes, Huge Comparisons* (New York, 1984).

[4] Rick Archbold and Dana McCauley, *Last Dinner on the Titanic* (New York, 1997).

[5] Walter Lord, *A Night to Remember* (New York, 1955). This book spawned revised and illustrated editions published in 1976, 1987, and 1998, as well as video recordings and multimedia CD-ROMs, before its success was eclipsed by Cameron's *Titanic*.

[6] The best guide is now Matthew Jefferies, *Contesting the German Empire, 1871–1918* (Oxford, 2007).

[7] Hansard, *Parliamentary Debates*, Ser. III, vol. cciv, February–March 1871, pp. 81–2, speech of 9 February 1871.

[8] Besides works listed under 'Further reading' for Chapter 10, see Gunilla Budde, Sebastian Conrad, and Oliver Janz, *Transnationale Geschichte. Themen, Tendenzen und Theorien* (Göttingen, 2006).

[9] David Blackbourn and James Retallack, 'Introduction', in Blackbourn and Retallack (eds), *Localism, Landscape, and the Ambiguities of Place: German-Speaking Central Europe, 1860–1930* (Toronto, Buffalo, London, 2007), 19. See also Michael B. Klein, *Zwischen Reich und Region. Identitätsstrukturen im Deutschen Kaiserreich (1871–1918)* (Stuttgart, 2005).

[10] Max Weber, 'Parliament and Government in Germany under a New Political Order' (orig. 1917), in Weber, *Political Writings*, ed. Peter Lassman and Ronald Speirs (Cambridge, 1994), 130–271, esp. 172.

[11] The term is used by Margaret Lavinia Anderson in *Practicing Democracy: Elections and Political Culture in Imperial Germany* (Princeton, 2000), 19.

[12] A provocative new assessment is offered in Helmut Walser Smith, *The Continuities of German History: Nation, Religion and Race across the Long Nineteenth Century* (Cambridge and New York, 2008).

[13] See inter alia Hartwin Spenkuch, 'Vergleichsweise besonders? Politisches System und Strukturen Preußens als Kern des "deutschen Sonderwegs"', *Geschichte und Gesellschaft*, 29 (2003), 262–93.

[14] Christopher Clark, *Iron Kingdom: The Rise and Downfall of Prussia, 1600–1947* (Cambridge, MA, 2006).

¹⁵ Ronald Speirs and John Breuilly (eds), *Germany's Two Unifications: Anticipations, Experiences, Responses* (Basingstoke and New York, 2005). See also Klaus Amann and Karl Wagner (eds), *Literatur und Nation. Die Gründung des Deutschen Reiches 1871 in der deutschsprachigen Literatur* (Cologne, Weimer, and Vienna, 1996).

¹⁶ Sabine Freitag et al. (eds), *British Envoys to Germany, 1815–1866*, 3 vols to date (Camden Fifth Series, vols 15, 21, 218) (Cambridge and New York, 2000–6). For a project résumé by the current editor, see Markus Mößlang, 'British Envoys to Germany—Britische Gesandtenberichte aus den Staaten des Deutschen Bundes (1816–1866). Ein Editionsprojekt des Deutschen Historischen Instituts London', *Jahrbuch der historischen Forschung in der Bundesrepublik Deutschland. Berichtsjahr 2002* (Munich, 2003), 28–33.

¹⁷ A large collection of primary sources in both German and English is now available online on the website of the German Historical Institute, Washington, DC. For volumes 4 and 5 of the collaborative project entitled 'German History in Documents and Images', see James Retallack (ed.), *Forging an Empire: Bismarckian Germany (1866–1890)* and Roger Chickering (ed.), *Wilhelmine Germany and the First World War (1890–1918)*, http://germanhistorydocs.ghi-dc.org/. Among many virtual museums—most of which require German language skills—one of the most extensive is hosted by the German Historical Museum in Berlin, http://www.dhm.de/lemo/html/kaiserreich/.

¹⁸ For the third, most famous version, http://germanhistorydocs.ghi-dc.org/sub_image.cfm?image_id=1403, with links to the other two.

¹⁹ http://mdz.bib-bvb.de/digbib/reichstag/.

²⁰ http://www.ub.uni-heidelberg.de/helios/digi/kladderadatsch.html.

²¹ For English and German introductions to the history of visual culture, see Deborah Cherry (ed.), *Art—History—Visual—Culture* (Malden, MA, 2005) and Gerhard Paul (ed.), *Visual History. Ein Studienbuch* (Göttingen, 2006).

Further Reading

General works

Synthetic works on Imperial Germany range from brief overviews to massive surveys. (Those that focus mainly on one period are listed under Chapters 1 and 2 below.) Relatively short works on the entire imperial period include Roderick McLean and Matthew S. Seligmann, *Germany from Reich to Republic, 1871–1918: Politics, Hierarchy and Elites* (London, 2000) and Lynn Abrams, *Bismarck and the German Empire, 1871–1918* (London and New York, 1995, 2nd rev. edn 2006). Somewhat longer surveys include Edgar Feuchtwanger, *Imperial Germany 1850–1918* (London and New York, 2001) and Volker R. Berghahn's *Imperial Germany 1871–1914: Economy, Society, Politics and Culture* (Oxford, 1994, 2nd rev. edn 2005). German readers may consult Volker Ulrich, *Die nervöse Großmacht 1871–1918. Aufstieg und Untergang des Kaiserreichs* (Frankfurt a.M., 1997), which has been abridged for the Fischer Kompakt series as Ulrich, *Deutsches Kaiserreich* (Frankfurt a.M., 2006); Hans-Peter Ullmann, *Das Deutsche Kaiserreich 1871–1918* (Frankfurt a.M., 1995); Wilfried Loth, *Das Kaiserreich. Obrigkeitsstaat und politische Mobilisierung* (Munich, 1996); and Dieter Hertz-Eichenrode's two volumes, *Deutsche Geschichte 1871–1890* and *Deutsche Geschichte 1890–1918* (Stuttgart, 1992–96).

Hans-Ulrich Wehler's *The German Empire 1871–1918* (Leamington Spa, 1985) first appeared in German in 1973 as *Das Deutsche Kaiserreich 1871–1918*. It is stimulating and suggestive, but its overarching thesis is now largely superseded. Thus it is treated mainly as the classic statement of the *Sonderweg* thesis and as representative of the 'Bielefeld school'. Twenty years of debate led Wehler to revise some but certainly not all of his conclusions when he included Imperial Germany in his massive five-volume societal history of Germany, *Deutsche Gesellschaftsgeschichte*, covering 1700 to 1990; volume 3 is entitled *Von der 'Deutschen Doppelrevolution' bis zum Beginn des Ersten Weltkrieges 1849–1914* (Munich, 1995). A countervailing argument to Wehler's, presenting a less authoritarian, more modern picture of the empire, is found in Thomas Nipperdey's equally monumental *Deutsche Geschichte 1866–1918* (Munich, 1990–92): vol. 1 (*Arbeitswelt und Bürgergeist*) focuses on social, economic, and cultural life, vol. 2 (*Machtstaat vor der Demokratie*) on politics. The third grand narrative published in the 1990s is Wolfgang J. Mommsen's two-volume account, *Das Ringen um den nationalen Staat. Die Gründung und der innere Ausbau des Deutschen Reiches unter Otto von Bismarck 1850 bis*

1890 and *Bürgerstolz und Weltmachtstreben. Deutschland unter Wilhelm II. 1890 bis 1918* (Berlin, 1993–95). Mommsen's collection of essays, *Imperial Germany 1867–1918: Politics, Culture and Society in an Authoritarian State*, trans. Richard Deveson (London, 1995) was first published in German in 1990; it is rich with insight but was not intended to serve as a general introduction to the period. Whereas many of Mommsen's essays bring domestic and foreign policy together, the latter is covered in Klaus Hildebrand, *Deutsche Außenpolitik 1871–1918*, 2nd edn (Munich, 1994). David Blackbourn's *History of Germany 1780–1918: The Long Nineteenth Century* (London, 1997, 2nd edn 2003) combines thematic and chronological approaches (roughly half the book is devoted to the German Empire); it is elegantly written, balanced, and up to date.

Students are well served by historiographical and interpretative surveys of the field. An outstanding guide has just been published by Matthew Jefferies, *Contesting the German Empire, 1871–1918* (Oxford, 2007). Still useful is Roger Chickering (ed.), *Imperial Germany: A Historiographical Companion* (Westport, CT, and London, 1996). See also the essays in Part 2 of John Breuilly (ed.), *Nineteenth-Century Germany: Politics, Culture and Society 1780–1918* (London, 2001). Two German books published in different series complement each other, combining brief narrative overviews with longer historiographical surveys: on the empire's political system see Hans-Peter Ullmann, *Politik im Deutschen Kaiserreich 1871–1918* (Munich, 1999), which appeared as vol. 52 of the *Enzyklopädie deutscher Geschichte*; more eclectic and thought-provoking is Ewald Frie, *Das Deutsche Kaiserreich* (Darmstadt, 2004), one of the *Kontroversen um die Geschichte* titles. An important *Festschrift* for Hans-Ulrich Wehler will include essays that take stock of research on Imperial Germany since the 1970s: Sven Oliver Müller and Cornelius Torp (eds), *Das Deutsche Kaiserreich in der Kontroverse. Probleme und Perspektiven* (forthcoming, 2008).

English readers seeking primary source materials in translation have long had to rely on slim collections such as Ian Porter and Ian D. Armour, *Imperial Germany 1890–1918* (London and New York, 1991), which often combine narrative overviews and a selection of documents, mainly on diplomacy and high politics. A much broader and more accessible collection of sources in both German and English translation is now available online on the website of the German Historical Institute, Washington, DC. For volumes 4 and 5 of a ten-volume project entitled 'German History in Documents and Images' (covering 1500 to the present), see James Retallack (ed.), *Forging an Empire: Bismarckian Germany (1866–1890)* and Roger Chickering (ed.), *Wilhelmine Germany and the First World War (1890–1918)*: the common gateway to these volumes is http://germanhistorydocs.ghi-dc.org/.

Among source collections in German, the following stress social relations and everyday life: Gerhard A. Ritter and Jürgen Kocka (eds), *Deutsche Sozialgeschichte 1870–1914* (Munich, 1982); Gerhard A. Ritter (ed.), *Das Deutsche Kaiserreich 1871–1914. Ein historisches Lesebuch*, 5th edn (Göttingen, 1992); Wolfgang Piereth (ed.), *Das 19. Jahrhundert. Ein Lesebuch zur deutschen Geschichte 1815–1918*, 2nd edn (Munich, 1997); Klaus Saul, Jens Flemming, Dirk Stegmann, and Peter-Christian Witt (eds), *Arbeiterfamilien im Kaiserreich. Materialien zur Sozialgeschichte in Deutschland 1871–1914* (Düsseldorf, 1982); and Jens Flemming, Klaus Saul, and Peter-Christian Witt (eds), *Quellen zur Alltagsgeschichte der Deutschen 1871–1914* (Darmstadt, 1977). Photographs of everyday life are featured in Günther Drommer, *Im Kaiserreich. Alltag unter den Hohenzollern 1871–1918* (Leipzig, 2003) and Michael Epkenhans and Andreas von Seggern, *Leben im Kaiserreich. Deutschland um 1900* (Stuttgart, 2007). Constitutional issues, foreign policy, and other political themes are more pronounced in volumes 2 and 3 of Ernst Rudolf Huber's *Dokumente zur deutschen Verfassungsgeschichte*, 5 vols. (Stuttgart, 1961, 3rd rev. edn 1978–86); Hans Fenske (ed.), *Im Bismarckschen Reich 1871–1890* (Darmstadt, 1978); Fenske (ed.), *Unter Wilhelm II. 1890–1918* (Darmstadt, 1982); Fenske (ed.), *Quellen zur deutschen Innenpolitik 1890–1914* (Darmstadt, 1991); and Rüdiger vom Bruch and Björn Hofmeister (eds), *Kaiserreich und Erster Weltkrieg 1871–1918*, 2nd edn (Stuttgart, 2002). Among the most important quantitative sources are Gerd Hohorst, Jürgen Kocka, and Gerhard A. Ritter, *Sozialgeschichtliches Arbeitsbuch II. Materialien zur Statistik des Kaiserreichs 1870–1914*, 2nd rev. edn (Munich, 1978), and Gerhard A. Ritter with Merith Niehuss, *Wahlgeschichtliches Arbeitsbuch. Materialien zur Statistik des Kaiserreichs 1871–1918* (Munich, 1980).

Chapter 1, Bismarckian Germany

In the surveys listed above, the Bismarckian period has often received less attention than the Wilhelmine period. Bismarck remains the defining personality of the pre–1890 era and he has been well served by recent biographers. The most comprehensive biography is the three-volume life and times by Otto Pflanze, *Bismarck and the Development of Modern Germany* (Princeton, 1990): vol. 2, *The Period of Consolidation, 1871–1880*, and vol. 3, *The Period of Fortification, 1880–1898*, contain many fresh insights. Lothar Gall, *Bismarck: The White Revolutionary*, trans. J. A. Underwood, 2 vols (London, 1986), was first published in German in 1980; it is an influential interpretation but a rather challenging read for students. The second volume of Ernst Engelberg's two-volume biography *Bismarck. Das Reich in der Mitte Europas* (Berlin, 1990) covers the period after 1871

FURTHER READING | 279

but has remained untranslated. The most up-to-date synthesis of recent scholarship on Bismarck and his era in a single volume is Katharine Anne Lerman, *Bismarck* (Harlow, 2004). Edgar Feuchtwanger has also written a short biography, *Bismarck* (London, 2002). Older interpretations, such as those by Erich Eyck, A. J. P. Taylor, and Edward Crankshaw, are now very dated. In German, Jost Dülffer and Hans Hübner (eds), *Otto von Bismarck. Person—Politik—Mythos* (Berlin, 1993) and Johannes Kunisch (ed.), *Bismarck und seine Zeit* (Berlin, 1992) are both useful collections of essays. Klaus Hildebrand, *Otto von Bismarck im Spiegel Europas* (Paderborn, 2006) and Lothar Gall, *Otto von Bismarck und Wilhelm II. Repräsentanten eines Epochenwechsels?* (Paderborn, 2000) offer different perspectives. See also Otto Pflanze with Elizabeth Müller-Luckner (eds), *Innenpolitische Probleme des Bismarckreiches* (Munich, 1983).

The key work on Bismarckian foreign policy is now Konrad Canis, *Bismarcks Außenpolitik 1870–1890. Aufstieg und Gefährdung* (Paderborn, 2004). This can be supplemented by Paul Kennedy, *The Rise of the Anglo-German Antagonism, 1860–1914* (London, 1980); Imanuel Geiss, *German Foreign Policy 1871–1914* (London, 1976); and Norman Rich, *Friedrich von Holstein: Politics and Diplomacy in the Age of Bismarck and Wilhelm II*, 2 vols (Cambridge, 1965). Gregor Schöllgen (ed.), *Escape into War? The Foreign Policy of Imperial Germany* (Oxford, 1990), discusses Bismarck's foreign policy in the context of the origins of the First World War. Other important recent works in German include Ulrich Lappenküper, *Die Mission Radowitz. Untersuchungen zur Rußlandpolitik Otto von Bismarcks (1871–1875)* (Göttingen, 1990); Axel T. Riehl, *Der Tanz um den Äquator. Bismarcks antienglischer Kolonialpolitik und die Erwartung des Thronwechsels in Deutschland 1883 bis 1885* (Berlin, 1993); Friedrich Scherer, *Adler und Halbmond. Bismarck und der Orient 1878–1890* (Paderborn, 2001); and Herbert Elzer, *Bismarcks Bündnispolitik von 1887. Erfolg und Grenzen einer europäischen Friedensordnung* (Frankfurt a.M., 1991).

On the army, Gordon Craig's *The Politics of the Prussian Army, 1640–1945* (Oxford, 1955) remains a classic study. On domestic politics, Lothar Gall (ed.), *Otto von Bismarck und die Parteien* (Paderborn, 2001), provides many insights into Bismarckian political culture. Important recent works in English include Ronald J. Ross, *The Failure of Bismarck's Kulturkampf: Catholicism and State Power in Imperial Germany, 1871–1887* (Washington, DC, 1998); Jonathan Sperber, *The Kaiser's Voters: Electors and Elections in Imperial Germany* (Cambridge, 1997); and Margaret Lavinia Anderson, *Practicing Democracy: Elections and Political Culture in Imperial Germany* (Princeton, 2000). Anderson's earlier biography of the Centre Party leader and Bismarck's adversary, *Windthorst. A Political*

Biography (Oxford, 1981), offers a welcome alternative perspective to that of Bismarck's biographers.

The implications of Kaiser Wilhelm II's accession to the throne are explored in J. Alden Nichols, *The Year of the Three Kaisers: Bismarck and the German Succession, 1887–88* (Chicago, 1987). John C. G. Röhl makes a compelling case for the significance of the imperial German monarchy in *The Kaiser and His Court: Wilhelm II and the Government of Germany* (Cambridge, 1995). The first two volumes of Röhl's biography of Kaiser Wilhelm II also contain much of relevance to Bismarckian Germany: *Young Wilhelm: The Kaiser's Early Life, 1859–1888* (Cambridge, 1998) and *Wilhelm II: The Kaiser's Personal Monarchy, 1888–1900* (Cambridge, 2004).

Chapter 2, Wilhelmine Germany

The classic introductions to the history of Wilhelmine Germany remain the complementary German studies by Thomas Nipperdey and Hans-Ulrich Wehler (see General works, above, and for other introductory and historiographical surveys). For the views of some participants in the fierce historiographical debates of the 1970s and 1980s see David Blackbourn and Geoff Eley, *The Peculiarities of German History: Bourgeois Society and Politics in Nineteenth-Century Germany* (Oxford, 1984); Geoff Eley, *From Unification to Nazism* (London, 1986); Richard J. Evans, *Rethinking German History* (London, 1987); and Jürgen Kocka, 'German History before Hitler: The Debate about the German *Sonderweg*', *Journal of Contemporary History*, 23 (1988), 3–16. Useful collections of essays that diverge from the *Sonderweg* perspective include Geoff Eley and James Retallack (eds), *Wilhelminism and Its Legacies: German Modernities, Imperialism, and the Meanings of Reform, 1890–1930* (Oxford and New York, 2003); Geoff Eley (ed.), *Society, Culture and the State in Germany, 1870–1930* (Ann Arbor, MI, 1996); and the earlier Jack R. Dukes and Joachim Remak (eds), *Another Germany: A Reconsideration of the Imperial Era* (Boulder, CO, 1988). A concise résumé of divergent interpretations is provided in James Retallack, *Germany in the Age of Kaiser Wilhelm II* (Basingstoke and New York, 1996).

Beyond the political, social, cultural, and diplomatic histories listed below, biographies constitute an important means of recapturing contemporaries' varying perspectives of the Wilhelmine era. On the politics of the imperial court one can turn to the volumes by John C. G. Röhl (see Ch. 1); Lamar Cecil, *Wilhelm II*, 2 vols (Chapel Hill, NC, 1989–96); Christopher Clark, *Kaiser Wilhelm II* (Harlow, 2000); Isabel V. Hull, *The Entourage of Kaiser Wilhelm II, 1888–1918* (Cambridge, 1982); and Annika Mombauer and Wilhelm Deist (eds), *The Kaiser: New Research on*

Wilhelm II's Role in Imperial Germany (Cambridge, 2003). On domestic politics in the 1890s, dated but still useful are J. Alden Nichols, *Germany After Bismarck: The Caprivi Era, 1890–1894* (Cambridge, MA, 1958) and John C. G. Röhl, *Germany without Bismarck: The Crisis of Government in the Second Reich, 1890–1900* (London, 1967). For government, state, and the military, see Katharine Lerman, *The Chancellor as Courtier: Bernhard von Bülow and the Governance of Germany, 1900–1909* (Cambridge, 1990); Konrad Jarausch, *The Enigmatic Chancellor: Bethmann Hollweg and the Hubris of Imperial Germany* (New Haven, CT, 1973); Norman Rich's biography of Friedrich von Holstein (see Ch. 1); Annika Mombauer, *Helmuth von Moltke and the Origins of the First World War* (Cambridge, 2001); and Jonathan Steinberg, *Yesterday's Deterrent: Tirpitz and the Birth of the German Battlefleet* (London, 1965). Finally, the following biographies of politicians, industrialists, bankers, journalists, and intellectuals are useful: Klaus Epstein, *Matthias Erzberger and the Dilemma of German Democracy* (Princeton, 1959); Gary Steenson, *Karl Kautsky, 1854–1938* (Pittsburgh, 1978); Richard Abraham, *Rosa Luxemburg* (Oxford, 1989); Peter Nettl, *Rosa Luxemburg*, 2 vols (Oxford, 1966); John G. Williamson, *Karl Helfferich, 1872–1924* (Princeton, 1971); Lamar Cecil, *Albert Ballin: Business and Politics in Imperial Germany, 1888–1918* (Princeton, 1967); Harry F. Young, *Maximilian Harden* (The Hague, 1959); Fritz Stern, *The Politics of Cultural Despair* (Berkeley, 1961); Wolfgang J. Mommsen, *Max Weber and German Politics, 1890–1920* (Chicago, 1980); James J. Sheehan, *The Career of Lujo Brentano* (Chicago, 1966); Arthur Mitzman, *Sociology and Estrangement: Three Sociologists of Imperial Germany* (New York, 1973); and Anthony Heilbut, *Thomas Mann: Eros and Literature* (London, 1996).

Chapter 3, Economic and social developments

Many surveys (see General works) provide excellent overviews of social and economic developments; especially important for quantitative study is the *Sozialgeschichtliches Arbeitsbuch II* by Hohorst *et al.* For a broad view of economic transformations in nineteenth-century Europe see the pioneering work of Karl Polanyi, *The Great Transformation* (Boston, 1957), or a textbook synthesis such as Tom Kemp, *Industrialization in Nineteenth-Century Europe*, 2nd edn (London, 1985). For Germany's place in nineteenth-century globalization the key work so far is Cornelius Torp, *Die Herausforderung der Globalisierung. Wirtschaft und Politik in Deutschland 1860–1914* (Göttingen, 2005). Toni Pierenkemper and Richard Tilly, *The German Economy during the Nineteenth Century* (New York, 2004), provides a synthesis from the perspective of economic historians; cf. Sheilagh Ogilvie and Richard Overy (eds), *Germany: A New*

Social and Economic History, vol. 3, *Since 1800* (London and New York, 2003). Older works that focused on Imperial Germany's early economic development include Helmut Böhme, *Deutschlands Weg zur Großmacht. Studien zum Verhaltnis von Wirtschaft und Staat während der Reichsgründungszeit 1848–1881* (Cologne and Berlin, 1966) and Hans Rosenberg, *Große Depression und Bismarckzeit. Wirtschaftsablauf, Gesellschaft und Politik in Mitteleuropa* (Berlin, 1967). One of the comparative research projects on the German bourgeoisie during the 1980s was centred in Bielefeld: see Jürgen Kocka with Ute Frevert (eds), *Bürgertum im 19. Jahrhundert. Deutschland im europäischen Vergleich*, 3 vols (Munich, 1988); this collection was distilled for English readers as Jürgen Kocka and Alan Mitchell (eds), *Bourgeois Society in Nineteenth-Century Europe* (Oxford and Providence, RI, 1993).

First-hand accounts of urban working-class conditions are found in *The German Worker: Working-Class Autobiographies from the Age of Industrialization*, ed. and trans. Alfred Kelly (Berkeley, 1987). For context see the survey by Gerhard A. Ritter and Klaus Tenfelde, *Arbeiter im Deutschen Kaiserreich 1871 bis 1914* (Bonn, 1992). On German agriculture, see Kenneth D. Barkin, *The Controversy over German Industrialization, 1890–1902* (Chicago, 1970) and J. A. Perkins, 'The Agricultural Revolution in Germany', *Journal of European Economic History*, 1 (1981), 71–118. Regional economic variations are an important topic: see the groundbreaking work by Frank B. Tipton, Jr, *Regional Variations in the Economic Development of Germany during the Nineteenth Century* (Middletown, CT, 1976) and the more recent and incisive Gary Herrigel, *Industrial Constructions: The Sources of German Industrial Power* (Cambridge, 1996). Herrigel's work builds on earlier work by Sidney Pollard, Hubert Kiesewetter, Klaus Megerle, and other scholars.

On social mobility, training, bureaucracy, and the middle classes, Klaus Bade, Jürgen Kocka, and Hartmut Kaelble have published numerous important works. See, for example, Klaus Bade (ed.), *Auswanderer—Wanderarbeiter—Gastarbeiter. Bevölkerung, Arbeitsmarkt und Wanderung in Deutschland seit der Mitte des 19. Jahrhunderts*, 2 vols (Ostfildern, 1984) and Bade (ed.), *Population, Labour, and Migration in 19th- and 20th-Century Germany* (Leamington Spa and New York, 1987); Jürgen Kocka, *Industrial Culture and Bourgeois Society: Business, Labor, and Bureaucracy in Modern Germany* (New York, 1999); and Hartmut Kaelble, *Soziale Mobilität und Chancengleichheit im 19. und 20. Jahrhundert. Deutschland im internationalen Vergleich* (Göttingen, 1983). Also emphasizing demographic mobility, see David Crew's *Town in the Ruhr: A Social History of Bochum, 1860–1914* (New York, 1979). Our knowledge of rural Germany is less developed, but see Ingeborg Weber-Kellermann, *Landleben im 19. Jahrhundert*, 2nd edn (Munich, 1988) and the older work by Frieda Wunderlich, *Farm Labor in Germany, 1810–1945* (Princeton, 1961). Gendered perspectives on the centrality of work are provided in Kathleen Canning, *Languages of Labor and Gender: Female Factory Work in Germany, 1850–1914* (Ithaca, NY, 1996) and Barbara Franzoi, *At the Very Least She Pays the Rent: Women and German Industrialization* (Westport, CT, 1985) (see also Ch. 6). A new survey of the history of social security from its roots in the imperial era is Hans-Walter Schmuhl, *Arbeitsmarktpolitik und Arbeitsverwaltung in Deutschland 1871–2002. Zwischen Fürsorge, Hoheit und Markt* (Nuremberg, 2003).

Chapter 4, Religion and confessional conflict

Since the 1980s, religion has been a major focus of interest in the historical literature on the German Empire. Important studies in English include Ellen Evans, *The German Center Party, 1870–1933* (Carbondale, IL, 1981); Jonathan Sperber, *Popular Catholicism in Nineteenth-Century Germany* (Princeton, 1984); and Margaret Lavinia Anderson's biography of Ludwig Windthorst (see Ch. 1). Anderson's *Practicing Democracy* and Jonathan Sperber's *The Kaiser's Voters* (see Ch. 1) also argue for the centrality of religious forces in German political culture after 1871: Anderson examines the place of religion in processes of partisan mass mobilization, showing that religion was deeply implicated in the transitions we associate with 'modernization'; Sperber argues that the most fundamental cleavages in the electorate were confessional in character. David Blackbourn's *Marpingen. Apparitions of the Virgin Mary in Nineteenth-Century Germany* (New York, 1993) uses the methods of micro-history and social history to explore the resonances of religious difference at every level of German society and highlights the importance of confessional antagonisms. Helmut Walser Smith's *German Nationalism and Religious Conflict. Culture, Ideology, Politics, 1870–1914* (Princeton, 1995) emphasizes confessional fault-lines in the associational landscape of German politics but also explores the links and affinities that transcended religious boundaries. Ronald J. Ross's study of Bismarck's *Kulturkampf* (see Ch. 1) focuses on the mismatch between the objectives formulated by Bismarck and the means available to sustain his campaign against the Catholics.

A number of recent studies in German have focused specifically on the Catholic experience in Imperial Germany. Norbert Busch, *Katholische Frömmigkeit und Moderne. Die Sozial- und Mentalitätsgeschichte des Herz-Jesu-Kultes in Deutschland zwischen Kulturkampf und Erstem Weltkrieg* (Gütersloh, 1997), examines the history of the cult of the Sacred Heart as a means of reconstructing the history of Catholic piety. Thomas Mergel,

Zwischen Klasse und Konfession. Katholisches Bürgertum im Rheinland 1794–1914 (Göttingen, 1994), analyses the tension between confessional and class identities among Rhenish middle-class Catholics, showing that after 1870 many found it difficult to reconcile their position within an urban bourgeois elite with the imperatives of confessional solidarity. Other important works include Werner K. Blessing's incisive overview of Bavarian Catholicism, *Staat und Kirche in der Gesellschaft. Institutionelle Autorität und mentaler Wandel in Bayern während des neunzehnten Jahrhunderts* (Göttingen, 1982); Otto Weiss's monumental study of a specific Catholic order, *Die Redemptoristen in Bayern (1790–1909). Ein Beitrag zur Geschichte des Ultramontanismus* (St Ottilien, 1983); and Wilfried Loth's *Katholiken im Kaiserreich. Der politische Katholizismus in der Krise des wilhelminischen Deutschlands* (Düsseldorf, 1984). Important studies of Protestant piety include Lucian Hölscher, *Geschichte der protestantischen Frömmigkeit in Deutschland* (Munich, 2005) and Friedrich Wilhelm Graf, *Die Wiederkehr der Götter* (Munich, 2004). On the Jews, antisemites, and continuing efforts to integrate Jewish history and German history, one might begin with Michael A. Meyer with Michael Brenner (eds), *German-Jewish History in Modern Times*, vol. 3, *Integration in Dispute, 1871–1918*, ed. Stephen M. Lowenstein *et al.* (New York, 1996); the survey provided in Massimo Ferrari Zumbini, *Die Wurzeln des Bösen. Gründerjahre des Antisemitismus* (Frankfurt a.M., 2003); and Helmut Walser Smith (ed.), *Protestants, Catholics and Jews in Germany, 1800–1914* (Oxford and New York, 2001). The best recent overview of confessional relations in the empire is Olaf Blaschke and Frank-Michael Kuhlemann (eds), *Religion im Kaiserreich. Milieus—Mentalitäten—Krisen* (Gütersloh, 1996).

Chapter 5, Culture and the arts

The superb recent study by Matthew Jefferies, *Imperial Culture in Germany, 1871–1918* (Basingstoke and New York, 2003), fills a long empty place in the historiography of the German Empire; it provides an overview of the artistic and cultural movements which played a crucial role in defining Germany in the decades after its founding. It supplants two helpful, brief, and provocative chapters on imperial culture which are still worth consulting: Wolfgang J. Mommsen, 'Culture and Politics in the German Empire', in Mommsen, *Imperial Germany* (see General works); and Robin Lenman, John Osborne, and Eda Sagarra, 'Imperial Germany: Towards the Commercialization of Culture', in Rob Burns (ed.), *German Cultural Studies: An Introduction* (New York, 1995).

A number of notable recent studies treat important intellectual trends and figures. Illuminating German academic culture is Suzanne

Marchand's *Down from Olympus: Archeology and Philhellenism in Germany, 1750–1970* (Princeton, 2003). George S. Williamson's *The Longing for Myth in Germany: Religion and Aesthetic Culture from Romanticism to Nietzsche* (Chicago, 2004) explores the cultural influence of intellectuals engaged with religion and myth in modern life. Stimulating explorations of the many aspects of intellectual, social, and cultural responses to modernity are to be found in Suzanne Marchand and David Lindenfeld (eds), *Germany at the Fin-de-Siècle: Culture, Politics, and Ideas* (Baton Rouge, LA, 2004). A welcome re-issue of R. J. Hollindale's trustworthy and comprehensive biography of Friedrich Nietzsche will help readers approach this enigmatic figure, by now the most widely read philosopher in the world and a key intellectual in the shaping and the critique of Imperial German culture: see his *Nietzsche: The Man and his Philosophy*, 2nd edn (New York, 2001). For the other towering figure of German intellectual culture in this period, the Anglo-American reader can hardly do better than consult Reinhard Bendix's *Max Weber: An Intellectual Biography* (Berkeley, 1978), which does justice to Weber's full range of thought while suggesting his place in his own times.

On musical life and composers, the irreplaceable work of Carl Dahlhaus can be read in overview in his *Nineteenth-Century Music*, trans. J. Bradford Robinson (Berkeley, 1989), which provides a powerful synthesis of aesthetic, social, cultural, and compositional aspects of European musical life in general. For Dahlhaus's interpretation of the most influential aesthetic idea in nineteenth-century German musical culture, see *The Idea of Absolute Music*, trans. Roger Lustig (Chicago, 1991). Walter Frisch's important recent study, *German Modernism: Music and the Arts* (Berkeley, 2005), integrates German composers such as Arnold Schoenberg into their broader cultural and artistic milieu. Jim Samson illuminates the social history of music in *The Late Romantic Era: From the Mid-19th Century to World War I* (Englewood Cliffs, NJ, 1991), while Jon Finson's *Nineteenth-Century Music: The Western Classical Tradition* (New York, 2001) provides a reliable overview of the canonical German composers in their European context. For three stimulating and contrasting approaches to Richard Wagner, his music, his thought, and his significance, see the monumental new biography by Joachim Köhler, *Richard Wagner: The Last of the Titans*, trans. Stewart Spencer (New Haven, CT, 2004); the intellectual biography by Bryan Magee, *The Tristan Chord: Wagner and Philosophy* (New York, 2002); and the provocative interpretation of his operas by Marc A. Weiner, *Richard Wagner and the Anti-Semitic Imagination* (New York, 1997). Jan Swafford's *Johannes Brahms: A Biography* (New York, 1999) reveals the man behind the beard, as well as providing rich accounts of Brahms's music and his cultural milieu.

German literature in the second half of the nineteenth century is best appreciated by reading it, but a guide to what to read can be found in volumes 9 and 10 of the reliable Camden House History of German Literature series: Clayton Koelb and Eric Downing (eds), *German Literature of the Nineteenth Century, 1832–1899* (Rochester, NY, 2005), and the first two chapters of Ingo R. Stoehr (ed.), *German Literature of the Twentieth Century: From Aestheticism to Postmodernism* (Rochester, NY, 2001). A number of studies of literature in context by historians of Imperial Germany are worth noting, starting with Gordon A. Craig's urbane and lively study, *Theodore Fontane: Literature and History in the Bismarck Reich* (New York, 1999). Katherine Roper has also examined Fontane as well as a number of other authors in her *German Encounters with Modernity: Novels of Imperial Berlin* (Atlantic Highlands, NJ, 1991). Kirsten Belgum studies the most widely read magazine of the period in her *Popularizing the Nation: Audience, Representation, and the Production of Identity in Die Gartenlaube, 1853–1900* (Lincoln, NE, 1998). Peter Jelavich illuminates the literature and culture of the dramatic arts in two books, *Munich and Theatrical Modernism: Politics, Playwriting, and Performance, 1890–1914* (Cambridge, MA, 1985) and *Berlin Cabaret* (Cambridge, MA, 1993).

German art of the imperial period, like German literature, needs to be experienced directly (in this case, seen not read) to be appreciated for its variety, richness, and illumination of its world. For readers interested in the context of art, one should begin with a superb new study by Beth Irwin Lewis, *Art for All? The Collision of Modern Art and the Public in Late-Nineteenth-Century Germany* (Princeton, 2003). Older but equally illuminating is Peter Paret, *Art as History: Episodes in the Culture and Politics of Nineteenth-Century Germany* (Princeton, 1988). See also Robin Lenman, *Artists and Society in Germany, 1850–1914* (Manchester, 1997). A more politically focused and local study of artistic culture is Jennifer Jenkins, *Provincial Modernity: Local Culture and Liberal Politics in Fin-de-Siècle Hamburg* (Ithaca, NY, 2003). An institutional study that illuminates both art and its public is James J. Sheehan's *Museums in the German Art World: From the End of the Old Regime to the Rise of Modernism* (New York, 2000). Architectural modernism finds a stimulating new treatment in Barbara Miller Lane, *National Romanticism and Modern Architecture in Germany and the Scandinavian Countries* (New York, 2000). At the opposite end of the aesthetic spectrum is the urge to historism, illuminated by Robert R. Taylor in *Castles of the Rhine: Recreating the Middle Ages in Modern Germany* (Waterloo, Ont., 1998). Studies of specific artists and artistic movements also abound. On Expressionism, Donald E. Gordon's *Expressionism: Art and Idea* (New Haven, CT, 1987) is helpful, as is Barry Herbert, *German Expressionism: Die Brücke and Der Blaue Reiter*

(New York, 1983). On Peter Behrens, see the definitive work of Tilmann Buddensieg *et al.*, *Industriekultur. Peter Behrens and the AEG, 1907–1914*, trans. Iain Boyd Whyte (Cambridge, MA, 1984). Important works on the secession movements include Maria Makela, *The Munich Secession: Art and Artists in Turn-of-the-Century Munich* (Princeton, 1990) and Peter Paret, *The Berlin Secession: Modernism and Its Enemies in Imperial Germany* (Cambridge, MA, 1980).

Chapter 6, Gendered Germany

Until now only certain aspects of the history of Imperial Germany have been studied from a gender perspective. On the place of gender history within German historiography, see the insightful remarks by a pioneer of German women's and gender history, Karin Hausen, 'Die Nicht-Einheit der Geschichte als historiographische Herausforderung. Zur historischen Relevanz und Anstößigkeit der Geschlechtergeschichte', in Hans Medick and Anne-Charlott Trepp (eds), *Geschlechtergeschichte und Allgemeine Geschichte. Herausforderungen und Perspektiven* (Göttingen, 1998), 17–55. Some initial reflections on the integration of gender history into the literature on Imperial Germany can be found in essays dealing with the contradictions of modernity in Eley (ed.), *Society* (see Ch. 2). See also the very recent collection edited by Karen Hagemann and Jean H. Quataert, *Gendering Modern German History: Theories—Debates—Revisions* (Oxford and New York, 2007).

The history of women in Wilhelmine Germany has been studied most intensively thus far. Recommended overviews are Ute Frevert, *Women in German History: From Bourgeois Emancipation to Sexual Liberation* (Oxford and Washington, DC, 1990) and Gisela Bock, who discusses the history of German women in a European context in her *Women in European History* (Oxford, 2002). In his *Imperial Germany* (see General works), Volker R. Berghahn swims against the tide of meta-narratives on the history of Wilhelmine Germany by drawing attention not just to minorities but also to gender-specific particularities and differences in the population. The two pioneering studies on the German women's movement are still worth reading: Richard J. Evans, *The Feminist Movement in Germany, 1894–1933* (London and Beverly Hills, CA, 1976) and Barbara Greven-Aschoff, *Die bürgerliche Frauenbewegung in Deutschland 1894–1933* (Göttingen, 1981). Apart from a number of monographs, most of them in German, new inspiration for the study of the women's movement is also offered by the path-breaking work of Ann Taylor Allen, *Feminism and Motherhood in Germany, 1800–1914* (New Brunswick, NJ, 1991). Allen compares the Wilhelmine women's movement with its Anglo-American counterparts and investigates the model of 'spiritual motherhood' as a phenomenon distinct from the Nazi view of women. Allen concludes that the German women's movement, with its emphasis on essential difference between the sexes, opened new paths to individual autonomy and new occupational fields for women, garnering them a good deal of attention in the social reform debates of Imperial Germany. See also Angelika Schaser, *Frauenbewegung in Deutschland 1848–1933* (Darmstadt, 2006).

One of the best-informed and most detailed accounts of girls' schooling is James C. Albisetti, *Schooling German Girls and Women* (Princeton, 1988). Individual aspects of girls' and women's education are presented in the essay collection edited by Elke Kleinau and Claudia Opitz, *Geschichte der Mädchen- und Frauenbildung*, vol. 2, *Vom Vormärz bis zur Gegenwart* (Frankfurt a.M., 1996). A number of monographs have been published on female students. Pioneering works on this subject include Edith Glaser, *Hindernisse—Umwege—Sackgassen. Die Anfänge des Frauenstudiums in Deutschland* (Pfaffenweiler, 1992) and Claudia Huerkamp, *Bildungsbürgerinnen. Frauen im Studium und in akademischen Berufen 1900–1945* (Göttingen, 1996). Harriet Pass Freidenreich's *Female, Jewish, and Educated: The Lives of Central European University Women* (Bloomington, IN, 2002) also examines German Jewish women.

For important works on labour from a gender history standpoint, see Karin Hausen (ed.), *Geschlechterhierarchie und Arbeitsteilung. Zur Geschichte ungleicher Erwerbschancen von Männern und Frauen* (Göttingen, 1993) and Kathleen Canning's *Languages of Labor* (see Ch. 3). These studies call into question the model of the apparently sexless working class common in older works of German social history. More recently, Canning has pointed out once again the new horizons that gender historical approaches can open up for the 'old labour history'. See her *Gender History in Practice: Historical Perspectives on Bodies, Class and Citizenship* (Ithaca, NY, 2006).

Some initial studies have now appeared in the fields of legal history, national history, and the history of masculinity. In legal history, gender studies have concentrated on marriage law and women's political rights. Ute Gerhard has opened up a new perspective with her stimulating edited collection, *Frauen in der Geschichte des Rechts. Von der frühen Neuzeit bis zur Gegenwart* (Munich, 1997). This book not only demonstrates how legal discrimination against women could be extremely obvious or very subtle, but also attempts to trace the effects of the legal situation on women's actual lives. One of the authors in this collection, Beatrix Geisel, has now published a very instructive monograph on the legal advice centres maintained by the women's and labour movements: *Klasse, Geschlecht und Recht. Vergleichende sozialhistorische Untersuchung der Rechtsberatungspraxis von Frauen- und Arbeiterbewegung (1894–1933)* (Baden-Baden, 1998). The topic of women and the nation in Imperial Germany is treated in three essay collections, each with a knowledgeable introduction by the editors. See Frauen & Geschichte Baden-Württemberg (eds), *Frauen und Nation* (Tübingen, 1996); Ute Planert (ed.) *Nation, Politik und Geschlecht. Frauenbewegungen und Nationalismus in der Moderne* (Frankfurt a.M. and New York, 2000); and Ida Blom, Karen Hagemann, and Catherine Hall (eds), *Gendered Nations: Nationalism and Gender Order in the Long Nineteenth Century* (Oxford and New York, 2000), which addresses the subject in a transnational framework. Jürgen Martschukat and Olaf Stieglitz trace the path from women's studies to the study of masculinity in their excellent introductory study, *Es ist ein Junge! Einführung in die Geschichte der Männlichkeiten in der Neuzeit* (Tübingen, 2005). Their book provides a wealth of inspiration, not just for the history of masculinity but for gender history more generally. The fragility and ambivalence of masculinity in the nineteenth century is emphasized in Martina Kessel, 'The "Whole Man". The Longing for a Masculine World in Nineteenth-Century Germany', *Gender & History*, 15 (2003), 1–31.

Chapter 7, The bourgeoisie and reform

A good place to begin reading on the bourgeoisie is Jonathan Sperber's 'Bürger, Bürgertum, Bürgerlichkeit, Bürgerliche Gesellschaft: Studies of the German (Upper) Middle Class and Its Sociocultural World', *Journal of Modern History*, 69 (1997), 271–97, which offers a critical discussion of most of the relevant literature published to that date. Among the works reviewed there, particularly useful are David Blackbourn and Richard J. Evans (eds), *The German Bourgeoisie* (London, 1991), with essays on various groups (e.g., lawyers, civil servants, the business elite, doctors) and relationships (with the state, the working class, liberalism), and Klaus Tenfeld and Hans-Ulrich Wehler (eds), *Wege zur Geschichte des Bürgertums* (Göttingen, 1994), with similar essays in German. Since the late 1990s historians have turned their attention increasingly to the culture of the bourgeoisie: good examples include the broad collection edited by Peter Lundgren, *Sozial- und Kulturgeschichte des Bürgertums* (Göttingen, 2000); Thomas Althaus (ed.), *Kleinbürger. Zur Kulturgeschichte des begrenzten Bewusstseins* (Tübingen, 2001), on the lower middle class; Jan Palmowski's *Urban Liberalism in Imperial Germany: Frankfurt am Main, 1866–1914* (Oxford, 1999); Simone Lässig's *Jüdische Wege ins Bürgertum. Kulturelles Kapital und sozialer Aufstieg im 19. Jahrhundert* (Göttingen, 2004), on the Jewish middle class; and Manfred Hettling and Stefan-Ludwig Hoffmann (eds),

Der bürgerliche Wertehimmel (Göttingen, 2000), on middle-class values more generally.

The notes to this chapter cite some of the most influential works on middle-class reform. Particularly useful is Kevin Repp's *Reformers, Critics, and the Paths of German Modernity: Anti-Politics and the Search for Alternatives, 1890–1914* (Cambridge, MA, 2000), an exemplary treatment of the interconnections and relationships that held one of the major reform milieux (the left-liberal milieu) together. There is a rich overview of reform movements in Diethart Kerbs and Jürgen Reulecke (eds), *Handbuch der deutschen Reformbewegungen 1880–1933* (Wuppertal, 1998). The classic grim assessment of the potentials of bourgeois reform is Detlev J. K. Peukert, 'The Genesis of the "Final Solution" from the Spirit of Science', in Thomas Childers and Jane Caplan (eds), *Reevaluating the Third Reich* (New York, 1993). Recent monographs seeking to revise that perspective include Andrew Lees's *Cities, Sin, and Social Reform in Imperial Germany* (Ann Arbor, MI, 2002), which examines the biographies of a number of liberal moral reformers and concludes that they were not confused anti-modernists; Corinna Treitel's *A Science for the Soul: Occultism and the Genesis of the German Modern* (Baltimore, 2004), which does something similar for occultism, as does Harry Oosterhuis, *Stepchildren of Nature: Krafft-Ebing, Psychiatry, and the Making of Sexual Identity* (Chicago, 2000) for sexology; and both William Rollins, *A Greener Vision of Home: Cultural Politics and Environmental Reform in the German Heimatschutz Movement, 1904–1918* (Ann Arbor, MI, 1997) and Thomas Lekan, *Imagining the Nation in Nature: Landscape Preservation and German Identity* (Cambridge, MA, 2004), which seek to rehabilitate German conservationism. Among the vast number of studies of eugenics, contrasting interpretations are found in Sheila Faith Weiss's 'The Race Hygiene Movement in Germany, 1904–1945', in Mark B. Adams (ed.), *The Wellborn Science: Eugenics in Germany, France, Britain and Russia* (New York, 1990) and Paul Weindling's *Health, Race, and German Politics between National Unification and Nazism, 1870–1945* (Cambridge, 1989). Ute Planert's 'Der dreifache Körper des Volkes: Sexualität, Biopolitik und die Wissenschaften vom Leben', *Geschichte und Gesellschaft*, 26 (2000), 539–76, provides a stimulating overview of body-focused, biologistic reform thought. The complexities of the 'life reform' movement are taken up in Kai Buchholz et al., *Die Lebensreform* (Darmstadt, 2001), a treasure trove of interesting essays. Michael Hau's *The Cult of Health and Beauty in Germany: A Social History, 1890–1930* (Chicago, 2003) is particularly stimulating in making connections among life reform, aesthetics, and medical discourse.

The literature on conservative reformers is less well developed. Ute Planert's *Antifeminismus im Kaiserreich. Diskurs, soziale Formation und politische Mentalität* (Göttingen, 1998) is a fascinating study of the intellectual world of right-wing reformers and anti-reformers, particularly those in the League Against Women's Emancipation. Conservative Christian moral reform is treated in Isabel Lisberg-Haag, *'Die Unzucht, das Grab der Völker'* (Hamburg, 2000); Edward Ross Dickinson, 'The Men's Christian Morality Movement in Germany, 1880–1914: Some Reflections on Sex, Politics, and Sexual Politics', *Journal of Modern History*, 75 (2003); and Andrew Lees, 'Deviant Sexuality and Other "Sins": The Views of Protestant Conservatives in Imperial Germany', *German Studies Review*, 23 (2000). At the other end of the spectrum of opinion on sexuality, Lutz Sauerteig has studied the Society for Combating Venereal Diseases; for a good introduction see his essay ' "The Fatherland is in Danger, Save the Fatherland!" ': Venereal Disease, Sexuality and Gender in Imperial and Weimar Germany', in Roger Davidson and Lesley A. Hall (eds), *Sex, Sin, and Suffering: Venereal Disease and European Society since 1870* (New York, 2001).

The literature on bourgeois women and reform is immense in its own right. For an English-language overview on the non-confessional women's movement (with references to much of the literature), see Angelika Schaser, 'Women in a Nation of Men: The Politics of the League of German Women's Associations (BDF) in Imperial Germany, 1894–1914', in Blom *et al.* (eds), *Gendered Nations* (see Ch. 6). On religious women's organizations, Ursula Baumann, the leading scholar on Protestant women, gives a good overview in 'Religion, Emancipation, and Politics in the Confessional Women's Movement in Germany, 1900–1933', in Billie Melman (ed.), *Borderlines: Gender and Identities in War and Peace, 1870–1930* (New York, 1998). Among works published since that essay, on Jewish women see particularly Christina Klausmann, *Politik und Kultur der Frauenbewegung im Kaiserreich. Das Beispiel Frankfurt am Main* (Frankfurt a.M., 1997); on Catholic women see Gisela Breuer, *Frauenbewegung und Katholizismus. Der Katholische Frauenbund 1903–1918* (Frankfurt a.M., 1998). An excellent recent study of women's charities is provided by Jean H. Quataert's *Staging Philanthropy: Patriotic Women and the National Imagination in Dynastic Germany, 1813–1916* (Ann Arbor, MI, 2001). On women and social reform more broadly, see Iris Schröder, *Arbeiten für eine bessere Welt. Frauenbewegung und Sozialreform 1890–1914* (Frankfurt a.M., 2001).

For a comparative perspective on the bourgeoisie, a good starting point can be found in Kocka and Mitchell (eds), *The Bourgeoisie* (see Ch. 3). On reform see Axel Schäfer's *American Progressives and German Social Reform, 1875–1920* (Stuttgart, 2000), and on the development of associational life across Europe, see Stefan-Ludwig Hoffmann, 'Democracy and

Associations in the Long Nineteenth Century', *Journal of Modern History*, 75 (2003), 269–99.

Chapter 8, Political culture and democratization

The most important study of German electoral culture in the imperial era is Anderson's *Practicing Democracy* (see Ch. 1). Its focus on national elections and its optimistic view of German democratization need to be counterbalanced by such regional studies as Andreas Gawatz, *Wahlkämpfe in Württemberg. Landtags- und Reichstagswahlen beim Übergang zum politischen Massenmarkt (1889–1912)* (Düsseldorf, 2001) and Thomas Kühne, *Dreiklassenwahlrecht und Wahlkultur in Preussen 1867–1914. Landtagswahlen zwischen korporativer Tradition und politischem Massenmarkt* (Düsseldorf, 1994). English readers can gain a flavour of regional peculiarities from James Retallack (ed.), *Saxony in German History: Culture, Society, and Politics, 1830–1933* (Ann Arbor, MI, 2000). Important local studies include Rudy Koshar, *Social Life, Local Politics, and Nazism: Marburg, 1880–1935* (Chapel Hill, NC, 1986) and Palmowski, *Urban Liberalism* (see Ch. 7). Wide-ranging appraisals of German political culture and its dynamics are found in Larry Eugene Jones and James Retallack (eds), *Elections, Mass Politics, and Social Change in Modern Germany: New Perspectives* (Cambridge and New York, 1992).

Many studies of changing political styles, with or without a regional emphasis, now take the Bismarckian period seriously. The following provide useful starting points: Lothar Gall (ed.), *Regierung, Parlament und Öffentlichkeit im Zeitalter Bismarcks. Politikstil im Wandel* (Paderborn, 2003); Lothar Gall and Dieter Langewiesche (eds), *Liberalismus und Region. Zur Geschichte des deutschen Liberalismus im 19. Jahrhundert* (Historische Zeitschrift, Beiheft 19) (Munich, 1995); Gerhard A. Ritter (ed.), *Wahlen und Wahlkämpfe in Deutschland* (Düsseldorf, 1997). On Bismarck and his parliamentary opponents, see Hans-Peter Goldberg, *Bismarck und seine Gegner. Die politische Rhetorik im kaiserlichen Reichstag* (Düsseldorf, 1998). A pioneering study of political parties is Thomas Nipperdey's *Die Organisation der deutschen Parteien vor 1918* (Düsseldorf, 1961). See also Karl Rohe, *Wahlen und Wählertraditionen in Deutschland. Kulturelle Grundlagen deutscher Parteien und Parteiensysteme im 19. und 20. Jahrhundert* (Frankfurt a.M., 1992), and Sperber, *The Kaiser's Voters* (see Ch. 1).

Students interested in the history of liberalism are well advised to consult Dieter Langewiesche, *Liberalism in Germany*, trans. Christiane Banerji (Princeton, 2000) and James J. Sheehan, *German Liberalism in the Nineteenth Century* (Chicago, 1978). On conservatives, see James Retallack, *Notables of the Right: The Conservative Party and Political*

Mobilization in Germany, 1876–1918 (Boston and London, 1988), and Retallack, The German Right, 1860–1920: Political Limits of the Authoritarian Imagination (Toronto, Buffalo, London, 2006). Sperber's Popular Catholicism (see Ch. 4) not only provides intriguing insights into the rise of the Catholic milieu but is also a path-breaking exploration of social milieux in general. Wilfried Loth's Katholiken im Kaiserreich (see Ch. 4) is a model study of how parties in parliament responded to social change. Thomas M. Bredohl, Class and Religious Identity: The Rhenish Center Party in Wilhelmine Germany (Milwaukee, 2000) offers a regional perspective. Those interested in Social Democracy will eventually have to consult the German literature, including Gerhard A. Ritter, 'Die Sozialdemokratie im Deutschen Kaiserreich in sozialgeschichtlicher Perspektive', Historische Zeitschrift, 249 (1989), 295–362; Gerhard A. Ritter with Elisabeth Müller-Luckner (eds), Der Aufstieg der deutschen Arbeiterbewegung. Sozialdemokratie und Freie Gewerkschaften im Parteiensystem und Sozialmilieu des Kaiserreichs (Munich, 1990); or the fine local study by Thomas Adam, Arbeitermilieu and Arbeiterbewegung in Leipzig 1871–1933 (Cologne, Weimar, and Vienna, 1999).

Connections between nationalism and the new political style that revolved around community and festivals are not yet well researched. Among the most innovative studies in exploring the rise of a new nationalism from below, see Geoff Eley, Reshaping the German Right: Radical Nationalism and Political Change after Bismarck (New Haven, CT, 1980, 2nd edn 1991), and Roger Chickering, We Men Who Feel Most German: A Cultural Study of the Pan-German League, 1886–1914 (Boston, 1984). See also Thomas Rohkrämer, Der Militarismus der 'kleinen Leute'. Die Kriegervereine im deutschen Kaiserreich 1871–1914 (Munich, 1990) and Ute Schneider, Politische Festkultur im 19. Jahrhundert. Die Rheinprovinz von der französischen Zeit bis zum Ende des Ersten Weltkrieges (1806–1918) (Essen, 1995). Future research can still profit from George L. Mosse, The Nationalization of the Masses: Political Symbolism and Mass Movements in Germany from the Napoleonic Wars through the Third Reich (New York, 1975).

Chapter 9, Militarism and radical nationalism

There are several good introductions to the problem of militarism in German history. They include Volker R. Berghahn, Militarism: The History of an International Debate, 1861–1979 (Cambridge, 1981) and the older study by Alfred Vagts, A History of Militarism, Civilian and Military (New York, 1959). The classic histories are Gerhard Ritter, Staatskunst und Kriegshandwerk. Das Problem des 'Militarismus' in Deutschland,

4 vols (Munich, 1956–68), which is available in English translation as *The Sword and the Scepter: The Problem of Militarism in German History*, 4 vols (Coral Gables, FL, 1969–88), and Gordon A. Craig's study of the Prussian army (see Ch. 1).

Most of the scholarship on the militarization of German society is in German, but several English-language studies provide an introduction, including Jean H. Quataert, *Staging Philanthropy* (see Ch. 7) and Derek Linton, *'Who Has the Youth, Has the Future': The Campaign to Save Young Workers in Imperial Germany* (Cambridge, 1991). On the confessional dimensions of the problem, see Christopher Clark and Wolfram Kaiser (eds), *Culture Wars: Secular-Catholic Conflict in Nineteenth-Century Europe* (Cambridge, 2003); Helmut Walser Smith, *German Nationalism* (see Ch. 4); and Michael B. Gross, *The War against Catholicism: Liberalism and the Anti-Catholic Imagination in Nineteenth-Century Germany* (Ann Arbor, MI, 2004). The literature on German antisemitism in the Wilhelmine era is immense. A good place to start is the essay by Shulamit Volkov on 'Anti-Semitism as a Cultural Code', which has now been published in an extended form in Volkov, *Germans, Jews, and Antisemites: Trials in Emancipation* (Cambridge, 2006), 67–158.

The historiography of radical nationalism has been marked by a number of controversies, some of which have had immediately to do with the polemics over the German *Sonderweg*. The opposing poles in one controversy can be found in Wehler, *German Empire* (see General works) and Eley, *Reshaping the German Right* (see Ch. 8). The poles in another controversy lie in Eley's book and Chickering, *We Men* (see Ch. 8). Aside from the latter book, which analyses the Pan-German League, and Eley's, which focuses on the Navy League, most of the literature on the individual radical nationalist organizations is in German. Marilyn Shevin Coetzee, *The German Army League: Popular Nationalism in Wilhelmine Germany* (New York and Oxford, 1990) is an exception. The major titles in German include Gerhard Weidenfeller, *VDA. Verein für das Deutschtum im Ausland. Allgemeiner Deutscher Schulverein (1881–1914). Ein Beitrag zur Geschichte des deutschen Nationalismus und Imperialismus im Kaiserreich* (Berne and Frankfurt a.M., 1976); Adam Galos et al., *Die Hakatisten. Der Deutsche Ostmarken-Verein (1893–1934). Ein Beitrag zur Geschichte der Ostpolitik des deutschen Imperialismus* (Berlin, 1966); Rainer Hering, *Konstruirte Nation. Der Alldeutsche Verband 1890 bis 1939* (Hamburg, 2003); and Heinz Hagenlücke, *Deutsche Vaterlandspartei. Die nationale Rechte am Ende des Kaiserreichs* (Düsseldorf, 1997).

Chapter 10, Transnational Germany

Transnational Germany is a fairly recent field of academic inquiry, and so far no comprehensive synthesis using this approach has appeared. A good beginning point is the collection *Das Kaiserreich transnational. Deutschland in der Welt 1871–1914* (Göttingen, 2004), edited by Sebastian Conrad and Jürgen Osterhammel. It is important to keep in mind, however, that some of the themes now revisited under a transnational agenda were raised in earlier scholarship on foreign policy, economics, migration, and colonialism—even if connections to German society were frequently not spelled out in the older literature.

Much of the current interest in questions of transnationality has been sparked by postcolonial approaches and cultural studies. Important works shaped by this concern with issues of representation include the pioneering volume by Sara Friedrichsmeyer, Sara Lennox, and Susanne Zantop (eds), *The Imperialist Imagination: German Colonialism and its Legacy* (Ann Arbor, MI, 1998) as well as Birthe Kundrus (ed.), *Phantasiereiche. Zur Kulturgeschichte des deutschen Kolonialismus* (Frankfurt a.M., 2003); Susanne Zantop, *Colonial Fantasies: Conquest, Family, and Nation in Pre-colonial Germany, 1770–1870* (Durham, NC, 1997); and Alexander Honold and Klaus R. Scherpe (eds), *Mit Deutschland um die Welt. Eine Kulturgeschichte des Fremden in der Kolonialzeit* (Stuttgart, 2004). In this context, the way the colonial encounter has shaped academic disciplines has been the subject of several richly documented studies, in particular Andrew Zimmerman, *Anthropology and Antihumanism in Imperial Germany* (Chicago, 2001) and H. Glenn Penny, *Objects of Culture: Ethnology and Ethnographic Museums in Imperial Germany* (Chapel Hill, NC, 2000).

A further field of scholarly activity is the gendered dimension of the colonial encounter, most importantly Lora Wildenthal, *German Women for Empire, 1884–1945* (Durham, NC, 2001). Birthe Kundrus, *Moderne Imperialisten. Das Kaiserreich im Spiegel seiner Kolonien* (Cologne, 2003) is also helpful. In the wake of the cultural turn, much transnational scholarship is concerned with questions of representing and appropriating the 'other'. Dirk van Laak's impressive study *Imperiale Infrastruktur. Deutsche Planungen für eine Erschließung Afrikas 1880 bis 1960* (Paderborn, 2004) follows colonial planning far beyond the official demise of the empire. By contrast, questions of colonial rule have scarcely been addressed: notable exceptions are the well-researched works by Michal Pesek, *Koloniale Herrschaft in Deutsch-Ostafrika. Expeditionen, Militär und Verwaltung seit 1880* (Frankfurt a.M., 2005) and George Steinmetz, *The Devil's Handwriting: Precoloniality and the German Colonial State in Qingdao, Samoa, and Southwest Africa* (Chicago, 2007).

Finally, the repercussions of the colonial experience have been examined with particular attention to connections between colonialism and the Holocaust. Jürgen Zimmerer has been most prominent here, provocatively probing the complex issue of continuities between the Herero war of 1904–8 and the genocide of the Jews in the 1940s—a debate with which historians and the larger public will continue to grapple. See Jürgen Zimmerer, *Von Windhuk nach Auschwitz. Beiträge zum Verhältnis von Kolonialismus und Holocaust* (Münster, 2007) and Jürgen Zimmerer and Joachim Zeller (eds), *Genocide in German South-West Africa: The Colonial War of 1904–1908 and its Aftermath* (London, 2007).

Whereas a rediscovered interest in Germany's colonial past has spawned and provided much of the dynamic behind research into German transnationalism, it is equally clear that Germany's shortlived colonial empire was only one among many possible points of reference in a world rapidly integrating globally. In light of current interest in the history of globalization, it is to be expected that the larger, global context of German history will receive increasing attention in the years to come. For two works explicitly addressing the issue of globalization, see Torp, *Herausforderung der Globalisierung* (see Ch. 3) and Sebastian Conrad, *Globalisierung und Nation im Deutschen Kaiserreich* (Munich, 2006).

Chapter 11, War and revolution

The two best recent general histories of Germany during the war are Roger Chickering's *Imperial Germany and the Great War, 1914–1918* (Cambridge, 1998, 2nd edn 2004) and Holger H. Herwig's *The First World War: Germany and Austria-Hungary, 1914–1918* (London, 1997). Those who read German can consult Gerhard Hirschfeld, Gerd Krumeich, and Irina Renz (eds), *Enzyklopädie Erster Weltkrieg* (Paderborn, 2003). Students interested in the vast historiography on the First World War should read Jay Winter's and Antoine Prost's *The Great War in History: Debates and Controversies, 1914 to the Present* (Cambridge, 2005). See also the online collection of documents and images on the war edited by Roger Chickering (listed in General works). A superb overview—both of the events themselves and of the vast debate on the outbreak of the war—can be found in Holger H. Herwig's chapter on 'Germany' in Richard F. Hamilton and Herwig (eds), *The Origins of World War I* (Cambridge, 2003), 150–87. John C. G. Röhl's *The Kaiser and His Court* (see Ch. 1) captures the peculiarities of Wilhelm II's personality and explores their significance for German history. On German public opinion at the outbreak of the war, see Jeffrey Verhey, *The Spirit of 1914: Militarism, Myth, and Mobilization in Germany* (Cambridge, 2000). The *Burgfrieden* and wartime developments within the German Social Democratic Party are well described in Wolfgang Kruse, *Krieg und nationale Integration. Eine Neuinterpretation des Sozialdemokratischen Burgfriedensschlusses 1914/1915* (Essen, 1993).

The military history of the war is also quite extensive. Hew Strachan's *The First World War: A New History* (London, 2003) is a good place to start. Bernd Ulrich, in his *Die Augenzeugen. Deutsche Feldpostbriefe im Krieg und Nachkriegszeit 1914–1933* (Essen, 1997) and in his collection of published documents (with Benjamin Ziemann), *Frontalltag im Ersten Weltkrieg. Wahn und Wirklichkeit* (Frankfurt a.M., 1994), has described the wartime experience of the common soldier. Gerald Feldman's early study *Army, Industry, and Labor in Germany, 1914–1918* (Princeton, 1966) remains unmatched in its account of the difficulties Germany experienced in developing wartime economic institutions. Fritz Fischer's *Germany's Aims in the First World War* (New York, 1967) is also still worth reading, especially for its description of the lobbying efforts of right-wing industrialists.

Attention has turned recently to everyday life and to women. Ute Daniel, in *The War from Within: German Working-Class Women in the First World War* (Oxford, 1997), persuasively argues that the war did not 'modernize' women's position in German society (and hence did not 'emancipate' them). Belinda J. Davis, in *Home Fires Burning: Food, Politics, and Everyday Life in World War I Berlin* (Chapel Hill, NC, 2000), notes that women were at the very least 'empowered' and analyses how they used this power on a local, everyday level. A number of local studies have added to our understanding of such issues. See especially Jay Winter and John-Louis Robert (eds), *Capital Cities at War: Paris, London, Berlin, 1914–1919* (Cambridge, 1997) (vol. 2, subtitled *A Cultural History*, was published in 2007); Benjamin Ziemann, *War Experiences in Rural Germany, 1914–1923*, trans. Alex Skinner (London, 2006); and Roger Chickering, *The Great War and Urban Life in Germany: Freiburg 1914–1918* (Cambridge, 2007). There is an excellent overview of German propaganda in the First World War in David Welch, *Germany, Propaganda and Total War, 1914–1918* (New Brunswick, NJ, 2000).

Wilhelm Deist's essay, 'The Military Collapse of the German Empire: The Reality behind the Stab-in-the-Back Myth,' *War in History*, 3 (1996), 186–207, is essential reading for those interested in understanding the morale of the German army in 1918. Wolfgang J. Mommsen, in *Max Weber* (see Ch. 2), uses Weber's perspective on German internal politics as the basis for his own broad, profound analysis. Of course Weber's writings themselves are still worth reading. The most important texts have been translated and appear in Max Weber, *Political Writings*, edited by Peter

Lassman and Ronald Speirs (Cambridge, 1994). A very interesting account of the result of these political developments, the revolution of 1918, can be found in Sebastian Haffner, *Failure of a Revolution: Germany 1918–1919* (La Salle, IL, 1973).

The legacy of the war is well described in George Mosse, *Fallen Soldiers: Reshaping the Memory of the World Wars* (New York, 1990); Robert Whalen, *Bitter Wounds: German Victims of the Great War, 1914–1919* (Ithaca, NY, 1984); and Deborah Cohen, *War Come Home: Disabled Veterans in Britain and Germany, 1914–1939* (Berkeley, 2001). More generally, see Jay Winter's *Sites of Memory, Sites of Mourning: The Great War in European Cultural History* (Cambridge, 1995).

Chronology

1871

King Wilhelm I of Prussia proclaimed German Kaiser in the Hall of Mirrors at Versailles; founding of the German Empire. Paris capitulates (Jan.). Provisional peace with France allows the annexation of Alsace and Lorraine (Feb.). First Reichstag elections of the German Empire held (Mar.). Constitution of the German Empire approved (Apr.). Treaty of Frankfurt ends the Franco-Prussian War (May). The *Kulturkampf* (cultural struggle) begins when the Roman Catholic section of the Prussian Ministry of Ecclesiastical Affairs is dissolved (Jul.). Intended as an attack on the Catholic Church, the Pulpit Law criminalizes discussion of politics by clerics (Dec.). August Rohling publishes *The Talmud Jew*. Archaeologist Heinrich Schliemann begins excavation of Mycenaean Troy.

1872

August Bebel and other leading Social Democrats tried for treason in Leipzig (Mar.) and sentenced to two years in prison. Catholic control of schools ended in Prussia with the School Inspection Law (Mar.). Jesuits expelled from the territory of the Reich (Jul.). Theologian David Friedrich Strauss publishes *The Old Faith and the New*.

1873

Onset of the 'Great Depression', lasting until 1896. The Prussian House of Deputies passes the 'May Laws' which subordinate the training and appointment of Catholic clergy to Prussian authorities. Berlin Victory Column (*Siegessäule*) unveiled (Sept.). Three Emperors' agreement between Germany, Russia, and Austria-Hungary signed (Oct.). Imperial Patent Law passed (Nov.). Friedrich Nietzsche writes his *Untimely Meditations* (1873–76).

1874

Reichstag elections bring success to the liberal parties (Jan.). Reichstag passes seven-year army budget (Apr.). Imperial Press Law passed (May). Law for the Administration of Vacant Bishoprics and Parishes further restricts the freedom of the Catholic Church in Germany.

1875

Obligatory civil marriage introduced (Feb.). Establishment of a central bank (*Reichsbank*) (Mar.). Breadbasket Law places additional constraints on German Catholics (Apr.). Pope Pius IX condemns Germany's repression of Catholics. 'War in Sight' crisis between Germany and France

(Apr.–May). The Gotha Congress unites the two wings of the Social Democratic movement to form the Socialist Workers' Party of Germany (May). The *Hermannsdenkmal* (Hermann Monument) is completed. Adolph Menzel completes his painting *The Iron Rolling Mill*.

1876
Protection of Motherhood Law passed (Jan.) The Mark established as the universal German currency. Central Association of German Industrialists founded to advance the interests of German industry. Prussian Landtag decrees that only German may be used in its mainly Polish provinces for public administration, in the courts, and in all official political activities. Berlin's National Gallery opens. Richard Wagner's *Ring* cycle performed in its entirety.

1877
Reichstag elections bring the Social Democrats 500,000 votes and 12 Reichstag seats (Jan.). Common court system established throughout the empire; Supreme Court established in Leipzig (Apr.). Otto von Bismarck begins to move away from his liberal supporters. Anton von Werner completes his first historical portrait of the proclamation of the German Empire. Friedrich Spielhagen publishes *Storm Surge*.

1878
Two assassination attempts against Kaiser Wilhelm I (May–Jun.). Reichstag rejects Bismarck's first Anti-Socialist Law and is dissolved (Jun.). Reichstag elections bring conservative gains and liberal losses; socialists win nine Reichstag seats (Jul.). German Africa Society establishes posts in East Africa. Congress of Berlin seeks to mediate between the great powers over the Balkan crisis; Bismarck plays role of 'honest broker' (Jun.–Jul.). Reichstag abolishes child labour except in domestic and agricultural work (Jul.). Anti-Socialist Law passed (Oct.). Antisemitic Court Preacher Adolf Stöcker forms the Christian Social Workers' Party (later the Christian Social Party). Death of Pope Pius IX allows subsequent easing of the *Kulturkampf*. Theodor Fontane publishes his first novel, *Before the Storm*.

1879
Publication of Wilhelm Marr's antisemitic tract *The Victory of Judaism over Germanism*. August Bebel publishes *Women under Socialism*. Bismarck abandons free-trade policy and introduces protective tariffs (Jul.). Subsequently, he loses the support of the National Liberal Party and seeks the favour of conservative political parties. Dual Alliance signed by Germany and Austria-Hungary (Oct.). The nationalist historian Heinrich von Treitschke fuels antisemitic sentiment with journal article declaring

'The Jews are our misfortune' (Nov.). First electric tram exhibited in Berlin.

1880

Antisemitism widens but evokes a countermovement among liberals and Jews (*Berliner Antisemitismusstreit*). Second seven-year army budget passed (May). First law ameliorating the *Kulturkampf* passed. Anton von Werner paints a second version of the proclamation of the German Empire (1880–82). After 580 years, work is completed on Cologne cathedral (Oct.).

1881

Bismarck fails to win approval for his first accident insurance law. At the urging of Prussia, Saxony invokes martial law ('minor state of siege') in Leipzig, permitting the banishment of Social Democratic leaders; similar measures have previously been invoked for Berlin and Hamburg. Three Emperors' League formed among Germany, Russia, and Austria-Hungary (Jun.). Left-liberal parties improve their standing in Reichstag elections and the Social Democrats withstand repression (Oct.). Kaiser Wilhelm I's royal decree (*Kaiserliche Botschaft*) announces a comprehensive programme of social welfare legislation intended to bind the working classes to the state (Nov.).

1882

Triple Alliance formed among Germany, Austria-Hungary, and Italy (May). First Anti-Jewish Congress takes place in Dresden (Sept.). Physician Robert Koch identifies the bacillus responsible for tuberculosis (and for cholera a year later), for which he later receives a Nobel Prize. Berlin Philharmonic founded.

1883

Trader Adolf Lüderitz acquires Angra Pequeña in South West Africa, inaugurating Germany's formal acquisition of colonies. Four-hundredth anniversary of Martin Luther's birth celebrated across Germany. Niederwald Monument of 'Germania' paid for by public and state funds. Reichstag passes medical insurance law for German workers (Jun.). Friedrich Nietzsche publishes *Thus Spake Zarathustra*.

1884

Several left-liberal groups unite in the German Radical Party (Mar.). Accident insurance law passed by Reichstag (Jul.). Reichstag elections focus on colonial issues (Oct.). The Berlin Africa Conference brings together 14 nations to work for the suppression of slavery, extension of free trade, and safeguarding of neutral territory in Africa (Nov.). The explorer Carl Peters concludes treaties with local leaders in eastern Africa.

1885
Kaiser Wilhelm I places 140,000 square kilometres of southern Africa under German protection (Feb.). Society for German Colonization founded (Mar.). Expulsions of Russian and Galician Poles, including many Jews, living in eastern Prussian territories.

1886
Prussian Landtag authorizes government funding for German land purchases in Prussia's Polish provinces, creating the Royal Prussian Colonization Commission. The Protestant League is founded, but the *Kulturkampf* gradually subsides. Gottfried Daimler produces his first gas-powered automobile.

1887
Reichstag dissolved over its refusal to endorse the government's military budget (Jan.). Reichstag elections produce a majority for the governmental ('cartel') parties of Conservatives, Free Conservatives, and National Liberals (Feb.). This majority approves Bismarck's military budget (Mar.). Secret Reinsurance Treaty with Russia signed (Jun.). War council discusses possible war with Russia. German Colonial Society founded (Dec.)

1888
'Year of the Three Kaisers'. Death of Wilhelm I, coronation of Friedrich III (Mar.) Death of Friedrich III, coronation of Wilhelm II (Jun.). Samoan groups revolt against German colonists. Abushiri revolt begins in German East Africa. Military agreement completed between Germany and Italy for Italian assistance in case of Franco-German conflict. Carl Peters marches across Africa to rescue Emin Pasha and extend German influence. Theodor Storm publishes his last and longest novella, *The White Horse Rider*.

1889
Mass strikes in mining industry in the Ruhr district spread to the Saar basin, Saxony, and Silesia (May). Disability and old age insurance laws passed by the Reichstag. Free Stage Association sponsors first performance of Gerhart Hauptmann's Naturalist drama *Before Daybreak* (Oct.).

1890
Anti-Socialist Law is not renewed (Jan.) and expires on 30 Sept. Kaiser Wilhelm II issues his 'social decree' on the workers' question. Reichstag elections bring defeat for Bismarck's 'cartel' parties; for the first time Social Democrats win more votes than any other party (Feb.). Bismarck's confrontation with Wilhelm II over social policy leads to his dismissal; Leo von Caprivi named new chancellor (Mar.). Caprivi's 'New Course' reflects Wilhelm II's wish to win over the working classes; Workers'

Protection Law passed. Protestant-Social Conference convenes in Berlin (May). Secret Reinsurance Treaty with Russia allowed to lapse. First School Conference in Prussia evaluates the social value of state system of education (May). Heligoland Treaty with England concluded (Jul.). Founding of the Free People's Stage Association. Publication of Julius Langbehn's *Rembrandt as Educator*, critical of historism in the arts and advocating cultural expression based on folk art. General German Female Teachers' Association founded.

1891

Electrification of Germany begins with the first successful transmission of electrical current over 175 kilometres. Sunday work abolished. Association for the Defence against Antisemitism founded. Founding of the General German League (Apr.), a precursor to the Pan-German League. Franco-Russian entente formed (Aug.). Trade treaties concluded with Austria-Hungary, Italy, Belgium, and Switzerland (Dec.). Progressive income tax introduced in Prussia following Saxony's example from 1877/78.

1892

Munich Secession. German Peace Society established. Karl May achieves popular success with his serialized accounts of a fictional Wild West. Antisemitic agitation rises. German Conservative Party adopts antisemitic plank in its 'Tivoli Programme' (Dec.).

1893

First private performance of Gerhart Hauptmann's *The Weavers* (Feb.), which after its public performance in 1894 (Sept.) prompts a sharp rebuke from Kaiser Wilhelm II and a police ban. Agrarian League founded to agitate for higher agricultural tariffs (Feb.). Caprivi's Army Bill is opposed by Reichstag deputies; parliament is dissolved. In Reichstag elections Social Democrats capture almost one-quarter of the popular vote; antisemitic candidates win 16 seats (Jun.). Army Bill passed (Aug.). Central Association of German Citizens of Jewish Faith established in Berlin.

1894

German Society for the Eastern Marches founded to promote German expansion in Poland. Trade agreement between Germany and Russia signed (Feb.). Efforts at détente between England and the Triple Alliance fail. League of German Women's Associations founded (Mar.). Pan-German League founded at mid-year. Chancellor Caprivi falls prey to high-level intrigue and Kaiser Wilhelm II's increasingly hard line against Social Democracy; he is replaced by Chlodwig zu Hohenlohe-Schillingsfürst (Oct.). New Reichstag building designed by Paul Wallot completed.

1895

Kaiser Wilhelm Canal opened, linking the North Sea and Baltic Sea and allowing future naval expansion (Jun.). Max Weber's 'Freiburg Address' favours Germany's 'world policy'. Kaiser Wilhelm Memorial Church completed in Berlin, commemorating Wilhelm II's grandfather. Theodor Fontane publishes *Effi Briest*. Government fails to pass Anti-Revolution Bill.

1896

First publication of the weekly periodical *Jugend* (*Youth*) and the beginning of the *Jugendstil* movement. Kruger Telegram incident takes place and tensions with Britain rise (Jan.). Satirical periodical *Simplicissimus* begins circulation (Apr.). German Civil Code (*Bürgerliches Gesetzbuch*) legislated by the Reichstag, taking effect in 1900. Left-liberal historian Ludwig Quidde imprisoned for *lèse majesté* after implicitly comparing Wilhelm II to the Roman emperor Caligula. Right-wing parties in the Saxon Landtag adopt a three-class voting system on the Prussian model, prompting socialist charges of 'suffrage robbery'.

1897

Kaiser Wilhelm II seeks to impose his 'personal regime'. Appointment of Alfred von Tirpitz to the Reich Naval Office (Jun.). The government's 'politics of rallying together' (*Sammlungspolitik*) attempts to bring industry and agriculture together on the basis of agrarian tariffs and construction of a German battle fleet. Germany gains possession of Kiao-chow concession in China after intervening against Chinese murders of German missionaries. Voices in favour of a Jewish homeland strengthen the Zionist movement. State Secretary of Foreign Affairs Bernhard von Bülow is appointed (Oct.) and announces that Germany will seek its 'place in the sun' (Dec.). Vienna Secession. Carl Peters's misdeeds in Africa inaugurate the 'Peters Scandal' and reveal wider abuses by German officials in the colonies. Wilhelm II refers to Social Democrats and other opponents as 'rogues without a fatherland'.

1898

First Navy Law begins expansion of a German battle fleet. German Navy League founded (Apr.). Reichstag elections reveal disarray among governmental parties and strong support for the Centre Party (Jun.). Beginning of Germany's foreign policy of the 'free hand'. Berlin Secession, led by Max Liebermann, challenges traditional genres and patronage in German art.

1899

Wilhelm II suggests an Anglo-German détente and is rebuffed. Germany gains Pacific colonies after the Spanish-American War; another conflict is narrowly averted over German Samoa. Talks begin over a proposed Berlin–Baghdad Railway. Government fails to pass Hard-Labour Bill. Houston Stewart Chamberlain publishes his racist tract *The Foundations of the Nineteenth Century*. Sigmund Freud in Vienna publishes *The Interpretation of Dreams*. Theodor Fontane publishes his last novel, *The Stechlin*.

1900

Second Navy Law intensifies antagonism with England (Jun.). In his 'Hun speech' Wilhelm II calls upon Germany's soldiers to behave with great savagery against their enemies (Jul.). Chancellor Hohenlohe resigns and Bernhard von Bülow becomes Germany's fourth chancellor (Oct.). Max Planck elaborates his quantum theory of physics. The journal *Heimat* (*Homeland*) begins publication and focuses upon traditional and rural German ideals. First flight of a Zeppelin airship takes place.

1901

The *Siegesallee* (Avenue of Victory) in Berlin is inaugurated by Wilhelm II but belittled by critics. Baden becomes the first German state to allow women to graduate from university. Thomas Mann's *Buddenbrooks* is published. The Naturism movement and Free Body Culture grow in Germany; publication of the naturist journal *Kraft und Schönheit* (*Strength and Beauty*). *Wandervogel* youth movement established in Berlin (Nov.).

1902

The Society for the Study of the Science of Judaism, the German Association for Women's Suffrage, and the German Garden City Association are established. New tariff law raises duties on agricultural products, contributing to rising prices for consumers (Dec.).

1903

Reichstag passes child protection law (Mar.). Reichstag elections bring dramatic gains for the Social Democrats (Jun.). Berlin–Baghdad Railway Crisis arises when Britain, France, and Russia oppose German influence in the Ottoman Empire. Crimmitschau textile workers' strike (1903–4) results in a partial victory for employers.

1904

War erupts in German South West Africa (Jan.), pitting the German military against the Herero and Nama peoples (1904–7). Diplomatic moves between Germany and Russia in hopes of an alliance are frustrated, but a commercial treaty is concluded. Environmental conservation movement expands. Max Weber's *The Protestant Ethic and the Spirit of Capitalism* published. Kaiser-Friedrich Museum (now Bode Museum) completed on Berlin's 'Museum Island'. Imperial League Against Social Democracy founded. Elections in Baden eventually lead to formation of the Grand Bloc.

1905
Wilhelm II visits Tangiers, angering France and causing the First Moroccan Crisis by supporting Moroccan independence (Mar.). Miners' strike in the Ruhr. Herero and Nama revolt suppressed through what will later be termed genocide. Expressionist artists found *Die Brücke* (The Bridge) in Dresden (Jun.). Albert Einstein advances his special theory of relativity in physics. The Schlieffen Plan is drafted to prepare for a possible two-front war, foreseeing the invasion of France through Belgium (Dec.). German Society for Racial Hygiene formed in Berlin.

1906
Extended Reichstag debates over the brutality of Germany's recent colonial wars take place, led by Centre Party critic Matthias Erzberger. Algeciras Conference sees a growing split between Germany and France (Apr.). Censorship of cinema begins in Germany. Third Navy Law passed in response to launch of the British warship *Dreadnought* (Jun.). Chancellor Bülow dissolves the Reichstag and calls new elections ('Hottentot elections') in the hope of undermining support for the Centre Party and Social Democracy (Dec.).

1907
Reichstag elections produce a setback for Social Democrats but support for the Centre remains steady (Jan.). 'Bülow Bloc' of conservative and liberal political parties formed. Triple Alliance renewed (Jul). German Crafts League (*Werkbund*) established in Munich to coordinate and reconcile the needs of industrial design, aesthetics, and mass production.

1908
Reich Association Law advances civil liberties and allows women's participation in political parties and assemblies (Apr.). Fourth Navy Law passed (Apr.). Casablanca Affair over European citizenship in Morocco further escalates Franco-German tensions (Sep.). Wilhelm II's ill-considered statements to a British newspaper lead to the *Daily Telegraph* Affair, involving public outcry and Reichstag debates (Oct.–Nov.). Austria-Hungary annexes Bosnia-Herzegovina and provokes the Bosnian Crisis and German displeasure (Oct.). Association for Germandom Abroad is founded. Architect Peter Behrens designs the AEG turbine factory in Berlin.

1909

Franco-German reconciliation over Morocco. German tensions with Russia grow. Bülow Bloc collapses over the finance reform issue when the Conservative parties and the Centre withdraw their support (Mar.) and defeat the government's proposed inheritance tax (Jun.). Chancellor Bülow resigns and is replaced by Theobald von Bethmann Hollweg (Jul.). Ernst-Ludwig Kirschner's Expressionist work *Bathers at Moritzburg* completed.

1910

Bethmann Hollweg's moderate attempt to reform the Prussian three-class voting system fails, despite mass demonstrations in support of reform. Germany and Russia come to agreement over Middle Eastern disputes.

1911

Second Moroccan Crisis; German warship 'Panther' arrives at Agadir (Jul.). The *Blaue Reiter* (Blue Rider) group founded in Munich under the guidance of Wassily Kandinsky and Franz Marc. A new constitution for Alsace-Lorraine includes universal manhood suffrage for the provincial assembly.

1912

Reichstag elections reverse the Social Democrats' setback of 1907; SPD now fields the largest caucus in the Reichstag, holding 110 of 397 seats. German Army League founded (Jan.). Haldane Mission attempts to reduce tensions between Britain and Germany (Feb.). Proposed naval and army bills published, escalating Anglo-German tensions (Mar.). Mixed marriages between Germans and colonial populations become illegal in Samoa, latest in a series of ordinances in other colonies. Army increases approved (Jun.). Wilhelm II holds a 'war council' to plan for a future conflict (Dec.). First publication of Martin Buber's periodical *Der Jude* (*The Jew*), which popularizes critical understanding of Judaism and Zionism. Over 2 million workers belong to the socialist trade unions; the SPD claims one million members. The Centre Party dominates the state government in Bavaria. Pan-German leader Heinrich Class publishes the pseudonymous pamphlet, *If I Were the Kaiser*. First and Second Balkan wars are fought (1912–13).

1913

Army Bill passed (Jul.). German general Liman von Sanders contributes to tension between Germany and the *Entente* powers by assisting Turkish war preparations. Work completed on the Battle of Nations Monument (*Völkerschlachtdenkmal*) commemorating the 1813 battle near Leipzig. Reich Citizenship Law comes into effect. A German officer assaults and insults Alsatian citizens, leading to the Zabern Affair and rising tensions between the military and civilian critics (Nov.).

1914

Anglo-German agreement over the Berlin–Baghdad Railway (Jun.). Assassination of Archduke Franz Ferdinand (heir to the Austrian throne) in Sarajevo, Serbia (Jun.). Germany gives Austria-Hungary a 'blank cheque', stating it will support any actions it should decide upon against Serbia; Austria-Hungary declares war on Serbia; Russia declares war on Austria-Hungary (Jul.); Russia mobilizes against Austria-Hungary; Germany mobilizes in support of Austria-Hungary; Germany declares war on France, which reciprocates. In line with the Schlieffen Plan the German army invades Belgium; Great Britain declares war on Germany. Kaiser Wilhelm II declares that he no longer recognizes political parties, 'only Germans'. All Reichstag parties vote for war credits and embrace the *Burgfrieden* (domestic truce). The German army commits atrocities as it moves through Belgium and into France. Russian army routed at the Battle of Tannenberg (Aug.). German forces reach the environs of Paris, but the First Battle of the Marne stops the German advance (mid-Sept.). The German government plans for postwar Europe with its 'September Programme'. Russian defeat at the Masurian Lakes. First Battle of Ypres. Paul von Hindenburg appointed commander-in-chief of the eastern front, with Erich Ludendorff as his Chief of Staff (Nov.). National Women's Service established to organize women's voluntary work. Agreement concluded between the government and the labour unions for the renunciation of strikes during the war. Alban Berg begins work on his Expressionist opera, *Wozzeck*.

1915

Germany launches unrestricted submarine warfare against Britain (Feb.). Bread rationing begins (Mar.). Germans first use poison gas against the Allies (Apr.). A German submarine sinks the British liner *Lusitania* (May). Unrestricted submarine warfare temporarily halted (Sept.). War Press Office set up to oversee German propaganda.

1916

Battle of Verdun begins (Feb.). Naval battle near Jutland between British and German fleets (May–Jun.). Russian 'Brusilov Offensive' pushes back the forces of the Central Powers (Jun.–Aug.). Battle of the Somme (Jul.–Nov.). Hindenburg and Ludendorff are appointed to head the German Supreme Command, replacing Erich von Falkenhayn (Aug.). Hindenburg Programme introduced to coordinate the home front and concentrate all efforts on the war. Supreme War Office established.

Rationing is extended to more sectors of the German economy; War Food Office created. War aims debate re-emerges. Auxiliary Service Law aims to organize civilian labour in support of the war effort (Dec.). 'Turnip winter' of 1916–17: widespread shortages of food contribute to severe malnutrition, suffering, and political protest.

1917
Germany resumes unrestricted submarine warfare (Feb.). With the Zimmermann Telegram Germany urges Mexico to take action against the United States (Feb.). The United States enters the war against Germany (Apr.). Kaiser Wilhelm's Easter Message ambiguously promises universal suffrage for elections in Prussia and constitutional reforms. Further reductions to bread rations cause 300,000 workers to strike. SPD divides into an Independent Social Democratic Party (USPD) and a Majority SPD (Apr.). The Reichstag Peace Resolution is passed by the Social Democratic, liberal, and Catholic Centre parties against the opposition of the Conservatives (Jul.). Chancellor Bethmann Hollweg forced from office by the Army Supreme Command and replaced by Georg Michaelis (Jul.). German Fatherland Party founded by Wolfgang Kapp and others to strengthen German resolve to hold out for a 'peace with victory' (Sept.). War Press Office intensifies its propaganda efforts with a 'Patriotic Instruction' programme. Celebration of the 400th anniversary of Luther's posting of his Ninety-Five Theses. Chancellor Michaelis is replaced by Georg von Hertling (Dec.).

1918
Industrial strikes and rioting in Berlin (Jan.). Germany and Russia sign the Treaty of Brest-Litovsk, which brings Germany vast annexations in the east (Mar.). Germany's offensive on the Western Front (Operation Michael) begins (Mar.) but fails to achieve its objectives. Second Battle of the Marne is fought (Jul.). 'Spanish Flu' epidemic begins, eventually killing between 50 and 100 million worldwide (Aug.). Allies break through at the Battle of Amiens (the 'black day of the German army'). Hindenburg and Ludendorff concede that the war cannot be won and advise Wilhelm II to seek an armistice based on President Wilson's 14 Points; by suggesting that the civilian government should sue for peace they lay the groundwork for the 'stab-in-the-back' legend (Sep.). Wilhelm II appoints Prince Max von Baden as chancellor. Major revisions to the imperial constitution make the government more dependent on the Reichstag (early Oct.). Sailors in Kiel and Wilhelmshaven mutiny and begin Germany's November Revolution (late Oct.–early Nov.). SPD deputy Philipp Scheidemann declares a 'German Republic' in Berlin. Wilhelm II abdicates and flees to exile in Holland. Other

German monarchs abdicate and the German Empire collapses. A Council of People's Commissars, led by Friedrich Ebert and other members of the two socialist parties, initially assumes control of republican Germany. German women gain the vote (Nov.). Heinrich Mann publishes *The Loyal Subject (Der Untertan)*, which satirizes German society and politics.

MAPS

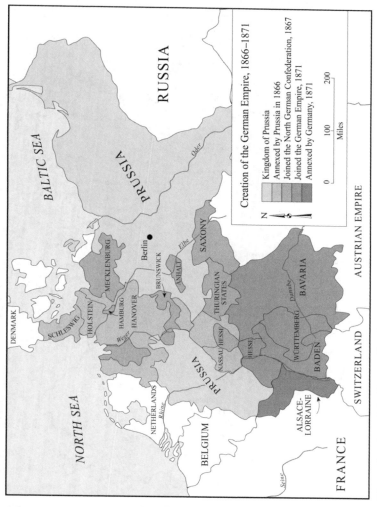

Map 1 Creation of the German Empire, 1866–1871

Map 2 The German Empire, 1871–1918

KINGDOMS
Prussia
Bavaria
Saxony
Württemberg

GRAND DUCHIES
Baden
Hessen
Mecklenburg-Schwerin
Mecklenburg-Strelitz
Saxe-Weimar*
Oldenburg

DUCHIES
Brunswick
Saxe-Meiningen*
Saxe-Altenburg*
Saxe-Coburg-Gotha*
Anhalt

PRINCIPALITIES
Schwarzburg-Sondershausen*
Schwarzburg-Rudolstadt*
Waldeck
Reuss, Older Line*
Reuss, Younger Line*
Schaumburg-Lippe
Lippe

HANSA CITIES
Lübeck
Bremen
Hamburg

IMPERIAL TERRITORY
Alsace-Lorraine

* Thuringian States

Map 3 Germany and Europe in the First World War

Index